Food Price Policy
in Asia

Food Price Policy in Asia

A Comparative Study

EDITED BY

Terry Sicular

CORNELL UNIVERSITY PRESS

Ithaca and London

First published 1989 by Cornell University Press.

International Standard Book Number (cloth) 0-8014-2213-2
International Standard Book Number (paper) 0-8014-9619-5
Library of Congress Catalog Card Number 88-43291
Printed in the United States of America
*Librarians: Library of Congress cataloging information
appears on the last page of the book.*

*The paper in this book is acid-free and meets the guidelines for
permanence and durability of the Committee on Production Guidelines
for Book Longevity of the Council on Library Resources.*

Contents

Preface

At the heart of most food policies is the question of pricing. In national programs designed to promote growth, improve the distribution of income, raise nutritional levels, and increase national food security, food pricing is both an explicit and an implicit actor. Pricing assumes this role because it links food production, consumption, marketing, and processing; agriculture, industry, and services; government and private sectors; and the domestic and international economies. For this reason a focus on food pricing provides a useful framework for assessing how countries address their food problems and rank various food-related policy objectives.

The aim of this book is to understand food pricing, and through it broader food policy choices in a variety of country settings. Chapters examine food price policy in six Asian countries—Indonesia, the People's Republic of China, the Philippines, Nepal, the Republic of Korea, and Thailand. Each is written by a scholar who has devoted substantial time to the study of that country's agricultural economy. Each chapter presents an informed analysis of food price policy and outcomes in a particular country. At the same time, the chapters have been written to a common outline and share a common perspective. As a group, then, they provide a broad comparative picture of the motivations behind and consequences of differing approaches to food policy.

The common perspective underlying the chapters of this book borrows heavily from the ideas Peter Timmer, Walter Falcon, and Scott Pearson expressed so lucidly in their book *Food Policy Analysis*. In particular, we follow their view that food policy includes not just measures narrowly aimed at the food system but also macroeconomic and trade policies whose impact can be as strong as, if not stronger than, more direct measures. Food price policy, therefore, is defined to include both explicit price interventions and macroeconomic, exchange-rate, and trade policies that significantly affect the structure of food prices.

This book is the product of a three-year project on Asian food price policy supported by the Rockefeller Brothers Fund. We owe gratitude to the Rockefeller Brothers Fund not only for its support of the research and writing of this volume but also for providing the resources that made possible an authors' workshop at Stanford University in March 1986 and a conference at the International Rice Research Institute in Los Baños in January 1987. These gatherings spurred our work and provided essential forums for feedback and discussion.

Two other institutions deserve special mention. The Food Research Institute at Stanford University supplied generous institutional support throughout this project. In addition, the International Rice Research Institute kindly provided logistical and financial support for the Los Baños conference.

We owe gratitude to the many individuals whose thoughtful reading and critical comments have added to the quality of this volume. Some of these individuals have aided authors in their work, and their names are mentioned in the separate chapters. Here I thank those whose help has been pervasive. The many participants in the Los Baños conference, too numerous to name individually, supplied insightful discussion and comments that are reflected throughout the volume. Graham Donaldson, Robert Herdt, Robert Bates, and Raymond Hopkins read through broad sections of the volume, joined in the authors' workshop, and provided critical perspective. Peter Timmer read and supplied thoughtful comments on several chapters. Anne Hoddinott's administrative and organizational contributions to the project aided immeasurably. To them I express my gratitude.

The following individuals, publishers, and institutions have kindly granted nonexclusive world rights to reprint tables or figures from copyrighted works as part of this book in all languages and for all editions: The Asian Development Bank and the Philippine Institute for Development Studies for figure 7 in chapter 2; Cornell University Press for figures 2, 4, 5, and 10 in chapter 2; Dr. Paul Dorosh for figures 1 and 3 in chapter 2; the Institute of Developing Economies (Tokyo) for table 4 in chapter 3; the *Journal of Rural Development* (Korea Rural Economics Institute) for table 14 in chapter 4; and the World Bank for tables 1, 2, 3, 5, 6, and 10, and figures 1 and 2 in chapter 3, and for table 10 in chapter 4.

Lastly, I express special thanks to Wally Falcon, who has so generously given time, counsel, and support to this endeavor.

TERRY SICULAR

Cambridge, Massachusetts

Contributors

Kym Anderson is Senior Lecturer in Economics at the University of Adelaide.

Cristina C. David is Agricultural Economist at the International Rice Research Institute.

Theodore Panayotou is Research Associate at the Harvard Institute for International Development and Lecturer in Economics at Harvard University.

Terry Sicular is Associate Professor of Economics at Harvard University.

C. Peter Timmer is Thomas D. Cabot Professor of Development Studies, At-Large, Harvard University.

Michael B. Wallace is Program Officer, Asia Division, Winrock International.

Food Price Policy
in Asia

1. Introduction: Food Price Policy in Asia

Terry Sicular

Microeconomic theory yields certain standard hypotheses about the relation between food pricing and key variables in economic development. Agricultural production, an important component of national product in most developing nations, should respond positively to high food prices. Policies that raise the prices of farm inputs relative to those of food products should reduce input use and slow growth in production. Overall economic growth, as opposed to that of the agricultural sector alone, is thought to be best served by a price structure that reflects underlying economic scarcities. From this perspective, then, optimal food prices are neither high nor low but those which are "right" in the sense that they reflect opportunity costs. Food pricing is also thought to affect living standards and income distribution: higher food prices reduce the absolute and relative incomes of consumers while benefiting producers.

Regardless of these conventional hypotheses, developing countries follow no predictable pattern of food pricing policies. Some countries maintain policies that raise food prices, whereas others have policies that lower them. Few countries intentionally or, for that matter, inadvertently implement policies to keep food prices in line with relative scarcities however defined. Furthermore, as the countries examined in this volume demonstrate, the effects of food pricing on economic variables do not conform closely to conventional expectations. Food and agricultural production have grown rapidly both in countries that overvalue and in countries that undervalue food. Similarly, rapid overall GNP growth and improved income distributions have occurred under a wide range of food price policies and food price structures.

The six country studies in this book illustrate clearly the diversity of food pricing policies and outcomes. These countries—China, Indonesia, Korea, Nepal, the Philippines, and Thailand—have all implemented policies that have directly or indirectly influenced the structure of food prices. Approaches vary from extensive direct intervention, as in China, to more limited measures in Nepal. Food price structures range from substantial

I thank Walter Falcon, Raymond Hopkins, and Peter Timmer for helpful suggestions on this chapter.

overvaluation of food in Korea to substantial undervaluation in Thailand. Economic performance, whether measured by sectoral growth rates, overall growth rates, or distributional outcomes, have also differed substantially and for the most part show little correlation with observed food price structures.

Food pricing policies and economic outcomes are diverse for several reasons. One reason is that the effects of pricing depend on the setting in which prices function. Relevant aspects of the setting include the country's natural endowment, level of development, economic structure, degree of market integration, and political situation. The influence of these factors, and also of other economic policies, frequently overshadows the effects of pricing. The importance of setting is a theme that recurs throughout this book.

In addition, pricing measures are designed in response to different constraints and objectives. Geography, government financial resources, and political considerations are among the factors that can limit the feasible range of food policy choices. The existence of such constraints has at times provided compelling reason to follow policies apparently at odds with economic reasoning. National objectives also influence food pricing policy. A country that places great weight on food self-sufficiency, for example, would choose different food price measures than one that emphasizes efficient growth. A fair analysis of national food pricing policy, then, must treat not only the ultimate effects but also the factors motivating a country's food pricing policies. These motivating factors are addressed explicitly in the chapters of this book.

Food Price Policy: A Definition

In this volume *food price policy* is defined broadly to encompass policies directly governing the farm and retail prices of food products as well as macroeconomic policies that influence exchange rates, land prices, interest rates, wages, and inflation rates, any of which can affect the relative prices of inputs to outputs for food producers and the price of food relative to incomes for consumers. Defined thus, food price policy includes programs whose primary intent may be to influence variables other than food prices, but wittingly or unwittingly also have a significant effect on food prices.

Food pricing is an integral part of national food policy. National food policy and its component food price policy usually emerge in response to multiple objectives. These objectives include (1) rapid overall economic growth, of which efficient growth in agriculture is one component; (2) distributional goals, which often encompass the desires to promote rural employment and welfare while at the same time maintaining the income status of politically influential, usually urban, groups; and (3) food security, that is, the provision of sufficient and stable food supplies. Any particular food policy initiative can promote some aspects of these objectives, while detracting from others. In the process of developing a coherent food policy, governments need to assess the tradeoffs among these various objectives, assign priorities, and search for policies that promote priority goals with acceptable compromise of nonpriority objectives.

Tradeoffs arise because of the numerous food policy linkages across economic sectors, groups, and governmental bodies. Measures aimed at one aspect of the food sector, say, food production, inevitably also influence other aspects—food consumption, marketing, and processing—as well as the balance of trade, government revenues, and government expenditures. Specific food programs carried out by a Food and Agricultural Ministry can therefore fail if not accompanied by complementary exchange rate, budgetary, and trade policies. Consequently, effective food programs entail coordination among the Ministry of Agriculture, the Central Bank, and the Ministries of Finance, Trade or Commerce, and Planning.[1]

Many such linkages operate through the pricing system. Trade policies that protect domestic industry, for example, affect agriculture because they raise the prices of manufactured inputs relative to the prices farmers receive for their products. An overvalued exchange rate can similarly depress relative food prices. Raising farm prices to increase rural incomes and provide incentives for long-run growth in food production can, by increasing retail food prices, have a devastating effect on poor consumers and cause dissatisfaction among politically influential groups. As a consequence of these and other price-related linkages, pricing decisions require careful weighing of the tradeoffs among national objectives.

The Countries

The countries examined in this volume—Nepal, the People's Republic of China, Indonesia, the Philippines, Thailand, and the Republic of Korea—are all in Asia. Although differences among countries in Asia are substantial, the extent of variation within Asia is considerably less than that among Asia, Africa, and the Americas. Most Asian countries, for example, are relatively land-scarce, have rice as a major food product, and have fairly similar farm size distributions and land tenure systems. These characteristics for the most part apply to the six countries examined here (table 1). The regional focus thus permits one to hold some of the many relevant variables constant in cross-country comparison.

Despite basic similarities, important differences exist among the six countries. Country size, whether measured by population, land area, or

1. See Timmer, Falcon, and Pearson (1983) for further discussion of these issues.

TABLE 1.   Comparative statistics on agricultural land, farm-size distribution, and the importance of rice

Country/region	Arable land per person, 1984[a] (hectares)	Average size of farm holding[b] (hectares)	Gini coefficient for farm-size distribution[c]	Harvested paddy area as a percent of total cereals harvested area, average 1983–85[d]	Percent of calories consumed in the form of rice, average 1979–81[e]
Nepal	.14	1.0	.700	54%	50%
China	.10			36%	35%
Indonesia	.13	1.1	.553	76%	58%
Philippines	.21	3.6	.507	50%	38%
Thailand	.39		.455	83%	64%
Korea	.05	0.9	.195	78%	49%
Asia	.17	2.2	.195–.665	42%	37%
Africa	.34	9.1	.399–.822	7%	6%
South America	.47	47.6	.868–.938	17%	11%

[a]Country population data are from World Bank (1986), *World Development Report*. Arable land includes permanent crop land and is from FAO, *Production Yearbook, 1985*.
[b]FAO (1981), *1970 World Census of Agriculture*, p. 32.
[c]Nepal gini coefficient from table 2 of Wallace chapter in this volume. Gini coefficients for other countries are from Berry and Cline (1979), pp. 38–39.
[d]FAO, *Production Yearbook, 1985*.
[e]Country data (except China) are from FAO (1984), *Food Balance Sheets: 1979–81 Average*; China data are from Piazza (1983), pp. 74–76. Regional data are for 1974 and are taken from FAO (1977), *Provisional Food Balance Sheets: 1972–74*.

gross national product (GNP), ranges from very large to very small (table 2). Some of these nations (for example, Thailand and Indonesia) have relatively generous endowments of natural resources such as arable land, minerals, and oil, whereas Nepal and Korea are poorly endowed.

Levels of development and economic structure also vary widely (tables 2 and 3). The GNP per capita ranges from $2,110 in Korea to only $160 in Nepal. The size of the agricultural sector as a proportion of GNP is inversely related to GNP per capita and declines from a high of 56 percent in Nepal to a low of 14 percent in Korea. The importance of trade also spans a wide range: in Korea merchandise trade is equal to 72 percent of gross domestic product (GDP), in China 18 percent of GDP. The importance of trade in Indonesia, Thailand, the Philippines, and Nepal falls in the middle of this range.

Finally, income distributions and political settings vary. Distributions of income appear to be most equal in China and Korea, and least equal in Nepal (table 4). Political settings range from stable to unstable, and the strength of national governments from strong to weak. The Indonesian government, for example, is relatively strong and stable. In contrast, current instability in the Philippines limits the government's ability to implement innovative policy measures. These variations in setting, whether natural, economic, or political, have influenced the nature and effects of national food price policy.

TABLE 2. Indicators of country size and endowment

	Population, mid-1984[a] (millions)	Total land area, 1984[b] (1000s hectares)	Arable land as a percent of total land area, 1984[b]	GDP 1984[a] (million U.S. dollars)	Merchandise trade as a percent of GDP, 1984[a]
Nepal	16.1	13,680	17%	2,290	24%
China	1,029.2	932,641	11%	281,250	18%
Indonesia	158.9	181,157	12%	80,590	44%
Philippines	53.4	29,817	38%	32,840	36%
Thailand	50.0	51,177	38%	41,960	43%
Korea	40.1	9,819	22%	83,220	72%

[a]World Bank (1986), *World Development Report*.
[b]FAO, *Production Yearbook, 1985*. Arable land includes permanent crop land.

TABLE 3. Indicators of economic structure and level of development

	GNP per capita, 1984[a] (U.S. dollars)	Agricultural output as a percent of GDP, 1984[a]	Percent of economically active population in agriculture, 1985[b]	Life expectancy at birth, 1983[a] Male	Life expectancy at birth, 1983[a] Female
Nepal	160	56%	93%	47	46
China	310	36%	72%	68	70
Indonesia	540	26%	52%	53	56
Philippines	660	25%	50%	61	65
Thailand	860	20%	66%	62	66
Korea	2,110	14%	31%	65	72

[a]World Bank (1986), *World Development Report*.
[b]FAO, *Production Yearbook, 1985*.

TABLE 4. Income distribution statistics

	Year	Lowest 20% of households (1)	Highest 5% of households (2)	Ratio of income shares (2)/(1)
Nepal	1976–77	4.6	35.3	7.7
China*	1978	6.8	12.5	1.8
Indonesia	1976	6.6	23.5	3.6
Philippines	1970	5.2	25.1	4.8
Thailand	1976	5.6	23.0	4.1
Korea	1976	5.7	16.1	2.8

SOURCE: World Bank (1983), *World Tables*, vol. 2.
*Distribution of people ranked by household per capita income.

The Design and Scope of Food Price Policies

Cross-country comparison brings to light similarities and differences in the design and scope of policies that affect food pricing. The design of such policies can range from direct control of prices (for example, state-set prices), to semidirect approaches (such as price ceilings and floors), to measures that work indirectly by influencing underlying market forces (for example, open-market operations or exchange-rate policies). Direct price setting has been surprisingly common in the countries examined here, although in recent years several of the countries have moved toward more indirect approaches. Usually direct and indirect measures are used concomitantly, sometimes complementing and sometimes offsetting each other.

Direct price interventions have been most common for retail sales of food. All the countries except one have at some time in the past twenty years directly set and controlled retail prices for one or more food staples. Such direct price control usually involves retail marketing by the state or parastatals combined with some form of rationing that limits sales to targeted groups, usually urban consumers. Indonesia, the exception, has not set retail prices, but has until recently announced retail price ceilings and maintained them through supply management. The stated intent of such retail price interventions has been to keep retail prices for key foodstuffs low and, secondarily, stable. Even targeted beneficiaries of such programs, however, do not always come out ahead. In Korea, for example, retail prices remain high by international standards, despite direct interventions to keep consumer prices low, because other policies keep the base against which the retail price is calculated, that is, the producer price, high.

Among the countries examined in this volume, direct interventions have been less common in producer pricing than in retail pricing for food. China's producer price policies have been the most direct: producers have been required to fulfill mandatory delivery quotas at low, state-determined prices. Thailand has used export taxes, the rice premium (essentially a fee for obtaining a rice export license), and a rice reserve requirement that stipulates some proportion of exported rice must be sold to the government at a low, fixed price. Nepal has set levies on rice exports and milling.

Interventions in Indonesia and South Korea have supported rather than reduced farm prices. Indonesia has used open market purchases to maintain a floor price for rice; South Korea has restricted food imports to keep producer prices high. Producer price policies, then, have been more diverse in intention and design than retail price programs.

In most of the countries studied, governments have intervened directly not only in the pricing of food products, but also in the pricing of inputs to agriculture. All but one of the countries examined in this volume have had some form of price or marketing subsidy for chemical fertilizers. Input subsidies often do not, however, reach farmers. In Thailand the fertilizer subsidy applies to only 13 percent of total fertilizer sales, and less than half of the subsidy reaches farmers. Similarly, despite price controls, tax-free importations, and direct subsidies to fertilizer companies, Philippine farmers continue to pay more than the world price for chemical fertilizers. In Korea input subsidies are offset by the indirect effects of trade policies: restrictions on fertilizer imports raise domestic fertilizer prices so that even with government subsidies the domestic price of nitrogen is 50 percent higher than the world price. Only in Indonesia do fertilizer subsidies effectively lower the nitrogen price paid by farmers below the world price. Direct and indirect price interventions for other inputs vary across the countries and are discussed in more depth in later chapters.

As the discussion to this point indicates, different pricing measures can offset each other. Korea's food marketing subsidies to some extent countervail the effect of high producer prices on consumers. In Thailand free water and low land prices partially compensate farmers for the underpricing of rice. Pricing measures can also be mutually reinforcing. In China, for example, farmers have faced both low farm prices and high input prices and thus have been squeezed on both ends. China's urban consumers, on the other hand, have enjoyed a double benefit, because marketing margin subsidies are applied to an already low producer price base.

The scope of a pricing policy is to some extent inversely related to how direct the intervention has been. Direct interventions of the sort just described usually affect only a few prices. Except for China, all the countries examined in this volume have used direct price interventions for, at most, one or two major foodgrains and one or two modern inputs. Rice and chemical fertilizer are common targets. Indirect interventions such as trade restrictions and foreign exchange policies influence broader categories of prices. Such macro-level policies can affect the rural-urban terms of trade and the relative prices of imports to exports.

Because their influence is so broad, macro-level policies can substantially alter the domestic food price structure. The Philippines provides an instructive example of such a situation. As David points out in chapter 5, the nominal rates of protection for rice (measured as the percentage difference between domestic and border prices, converted at the official exchange rate) has in recent years been slightly negative, suggesting that rice is slightly undervalued. Due to national currency policies, however, the exchange rate is overvalued by 30 percent or more. If the exchange rate bias is taken into account, the net effective rate of protection on rice becomes substantially negative. In other words, exchange rate overvaluation significantly increases the degree of price undervaluation for rice, as well as for numerous other food products in the Philippines. The anti-agriculture price bias has been further reinforced by industrial import substitution policies, which raise the domestic prices of industrial, relative to agricultural, products. Together, these two macro-level policies have biased the urban-rural terms of trade against agriculture, thus accelerating capital outflows from agriculture and worsening the urban-rural income distribution.

Food Price Structures

As the design and scope of food price policies have varied, so too has the observed structure of food prices. The countries differ in whether the prices received by producers are under- or overpriced by international standards, whether producer prices are high or low relative to the costs of modern inputs, and in how consumer retail prices compare to producer prices. Comparison of three price ratios—the ratio of the domestic producer paddy price to the international paddy or rice price, of the paddy price to the price of nitrogen, and of the farm paddy price to the retail rice price—provides a good picture of differences in price structure. More detailed examination of national food price structures appears in later chapters.

Table 5 gives by country the farm-level paddy price as a percentage of the world price. Five-year averages are used to smooth out year-to-year price variability.[2] As of the early eighties, the domestic price of paddy was lower than the international price for five of the six countries shown. Domestic paddy prices were low for a variety of reasons, ranging from direct price setting in China to taxation of rice exports in Thailand. The visible exception is Korea, where import restrictions maintain domestic prices well above the international levels.

A similar picture emerges in the comparison of paddy to nitrogen prices. The ratios given in table 6 indicate that in 1980–82 all but two of the countries overpriced chemical fertilizer nutrients relative to the paddy price. The two exceptions were Indonesia and, once again, Korea, both of whose nitrogen-to-paddy price ratios were lower than the world ratio. In general, then, food price structures in these countries do not favor rice producers.

The price ratios in table 6 reveal the sometimes complementary and sometimes contradictory design of food output and input price measures. As of 1980–82, three of the countries, China, the Philippines, and Thailand, kept the farm paddy price low and the fertilizer price high. Consequently, their nitrogen-to-paddy price ratios were higher than the world ratio. In Korea the output and input prices counterbalanced each other. Korean trade restrictions kept both paddy and nitrogen prices well above their world prices, but the domestic paddy price was so high that Korean farmers faced the lowest nitrogen-to-paddy ratio of the countries shown.

2. Domestic prices are converted into U.S. dollars using official exchange rates. According to Barker, Herdt, and Rose (1985), in 1979–80 the exchange rates of Korea, Indonesia, Thailand, and the Philippines were not significantly over- or undervalued (p. 197). At that time, however, the official exchange rates for China and Nepal were probably overvalued (see Wallace chapter in this volume, pp. 374–75, and Sicular chapter, p. 503). Consequently, the ratios given in table 5 for China and Nepal in the late 1970s overstate the true ratio. Note that China's official exchange rate was devalued considerably after 1979–80, possibly reducing overvaluation by the mid-1980s.

TABLE 5.   Farm price of paddy as a percentage of the world price, 1966–84

	1966–70	1971–75	1976–80	1981–84
Nepal[a]	129	100	74	85
				(1981–83)
China[b]	94–113	83–108	69–95	61–92
Indonesia	68	69	104	87
	(1967–70)			(1981–82)
Philippines[c]	96	94	75	73
				(1981–82)
Thailand[d]	51	64	67	66
				(1981)
Korea[e]	144	186	260	308
Adjusted world paddy price (U.S. $ per metric ton)	85	135	182	194

NOTE: Yearly domestic producer prices are converted into U.S. dollars at official exchange rates, then divided by adjusted world paddy prices. Figures shown are the multiyear averages of the resulting yearly price ratios. Adjusted world paddy prices are calculated from the total of world rice import plus export values divided by the sum of world rice import plus export quantities, multiplied by 0.80 to adjust for marketing margins between the border and farm gate, and then multiplied by 0.65 to convert to paddy equivalent prices. Domestic producer prices are from Rose (1985) except where noted below. Exchange rates are from IMF (1986), *International Financial Statistics Yearbook*, and world rice prices from various issues of FAO *Trade Yearbook*.

[a]Calculated using national unweighted average market prices (producer prices per se are unavailable), which, due to the large price differential between the plains and mountain areas, overstate the prices received in the major rice-producing regions (see Wallace chapter, this volume). To correct for this bias, I multiply these prices by 0.85. Domestic prices are from Nepal Department of Food and Agricultural Marketing Services, *Agricultural Statistics of Nepal* and *Agricultural Marketing Information Marketing Bulletin* (1985–86).

[b]Lower end of range is calculated using the quota procurement price, and upper end using the above-quota procurement price. Chinese prices are taken from the appendix tables of the Sicular chapter in this volume.

[c]Nineteen eighty-two domestic producer prices are from IRRI (1986), *World Rice Statistics, 1985*. All other years are from Rose (1985). These price ratios are lower than those given in table 1 of the David chapter in this volume, but they tell essentially the same story, i.e., that Philippines producer prices compared well to world prices in the 1960s and early 1970s but have fallen below world prices since then.

[d]Domestic producer prices are from the Thailand Ministry of Agriculture, Office of Agricultural Economics (quoted in World Bank, 1982, p. 221). These ratios are similar to those calculated using the Thai prices given in Rose (1985).

[e]Korean producer prices for polished rice are taken from the Anderson chapter in this volume, Table A. These are divided by the adjusted average world rice price divided by 0.93 to convert to a polished rice equivalent price. The resulting price ratios differ slightly from those given in the Anderson chapter because Anderson uses the Korean border price rather than an average world price for rice, and he also uses a marketing margin of 0.10 before 1970.

In order to cover the costs of milling and marketing, the retail price of rice would typically be about twice the farm paddy price (Barker, Herdt, and Rose, 1985, pp. 236–37). Table 6 suggests that in the early eighties retail-to-farm price ratios were more or less in line with marketing costs in Indonesia, the Philippines, Thailand, and perhaps Nepal. In China and Korea, the retail-to-farm price ratios were noticeably less than two, reflecting government subsidization of marketing costs. China's marketing subsidies in combination with a low farm price implies urban retail rice prices that are very low by international standards. For Korea, the marketing subsidy has partially offset the high farm price, but consumer prices are still unusually high.

TABLE 6.   Nitrogen-to-paddy and retail-to-farm price ratios,
1980–82

Country/region	Ratio of nitrogen to paddy price (producer prices)	Ratio of domestic nitrogen to world nitrogen price	Ratio of retail rice to farm paddy price
Nepal	2.9	1.33	1.5–1.9[a]
China	2.9–4.3[b]	1.36	0.9–1.32[b]
Indonesia	1.3	0.56	2.3
Philippines	3.8	1.33	2.2
Thailand	4.7[c]	2.13[c]	2.0
	(1979–81)		(1979–81)
Korea	0.9	1.49	1.1
			(1979–81)
World	2.1		

SOURCES: Paddy prices and exchange rates are the same as those in table 5. World fertilizer prices are from IRRI (1986), *World Rice Statistics, 1985*.
Nepal: Note that the "paddy" price is the national average market price for paddy, and the "retail rice" price is the national average market price for rice. Producer and retail prices per se are not available. All prices are from Nepal Department of Food and Agricultural Marketing Services, *Agricultural Statistics of Nepal* and *Agricultural Marketing Information Marketing Bulletin* (1985–86).
China: Urea price of 450 yuan per ton is taken from the Agricultural Technical Economics Handbook Editorial Group (1983). A national average state rice retail sales price of 293.4 yuan per ton was provided by the Chinese Academy of Social Sciences Institute of Finance and Trade.
Indonesia: The urea price is from the Timmer chapter in this volume, appendix table A. Retail rice prices are from Rose (1985).
Philippines: Urea and retail rice prices are from IRRI (1986), *World Rice Statistics, 1985*.
Thailand: The ammonium sulphate price is from O'Mara (1987), p. 82. The retail rice price is from Rose (1985).
Korea: Urea and retail prices from IRRI (1986), *World Rice Statistics, 1985*.
NOTE: Nitrogen prices are calculated using urea prices, except where noted otherwise.
[a]Lower ratio calculated using government rice distribution price; higher ratio uses market retail price.
[b]Lower ratio is calculated using the above-quota price and the upper ratio using the quota price.
[c]Urea is used very little in Thai rice production, so these ratios are calculated using domestic and world ammonium sulphate prices.

Explaining Differences in Food Price
Policies and Structures

The chapters in this volume indicate that food pricing policies and outcomes are to some extent endogenous. Consequently, an analysis of food pricing should not only judge food price policies on the basis of whether prices are low or high by international standards, but also should examine the factors that give rise to those policies.

The factors explaining differences in food price policies and structures are numerous and complex. In general, however, they fall into four broad, interdependent categories. The first is a country's natural or geographical endowment. In this category fall exogenous physical factors that cannot be altered by policy, at least in the short run. The second is the political context. Political factors include domestic and external political circumstances that limit or shape a government's ability to implement policy.

Third, the level of economic development can be influential. Finally, national objectives, through their effect on government policy, affect food pricing. National objectives are, of course, sensitive to a country's physical and political context, and to the level of development.

The geographical factor whose influence on food pricing is perhaps most obvious is the endowment of arable land. In the absence of foreign trade, a country with more, higher quality arable land per capita would, all else equal, tend to have lower food prices. Most countries, of course, participate in trade. Since trade barriers make imperfect the transmission of international prices to the domestic economy, however, national agricultural endowments continue to influence the domestic price structure.

Examination of the countries included in this study reveals an inverse relationship between arable land per capita and the level of the paddy price. Thailand, with the most arable land per capita, has over the past two decades consistently had the lowest domestic-to-world paddy price ratio. Korea, with the least arable land per capita, has dominated the higher end of the scale (tables 2 and 5). In both these countries trade policies have caused domestic prices to deviate from international prices. Consequently, their natural resource endowments are quite clearly reflected in their domestic price structures. The inverse relationship between arable land per capita and the level of paddy prices also holds for the remaining four countries, but the pattern is less clear because of differences in the extent to which world price trends are transmitted to the domestic economies.

The transmission of world price movements to the domestic economy can, in itself, be affected by geographical endowment. A country's geography influences accessibility to foreign trade, which in turn affects transfer costs and thus the relationship between world and domestic prices. Geography can also govern a nation's ability to control flows of commodities across its borders and so maintain prices that deviate from international prices. For Korea, Indonesia, the Philippines, and to a lesser extent, Thailand, in the absence of trade restrictions domestic and foreign prices for tradables would be nearly identical because most regions of these countries are close to a coast. At the same time, oceanic trade is sufficiently controllable that policy makers in these countries have been able to restrict imports and exports and so cause domestic and international prices to diverge. The larger the difference between domestic and international prices, however, the greater the costs of enforcing trade restrictions.

Although China has a long coastline and several major inland waterways, large areas of the interior are relatively inaccessible. If trade were unrestricted and if markets determined prices, then due to transfer costs, inland prices of imported commodities would be higher, and inland prices of exported commodities lower, than the world prices. Strict control of foreign trade in agricultural products and direct state intervention in

domestic food pricing has, however, obscured any correspondence between domestic and world prices. Nepal's inaccessible, landlocked location makes trade difficult except with India. Ironically, however, Nepal has
the least enforceable border. Nepal's boundary with India cuts through a
large plain. In the absence of any natural geographical barrier, Nepal has
difficulty maintaining a domestic price structure that deviates from that of
its large neighbor.

Natural endowment can influence pricing policy through its effect on
the government's fiscal status. Indonesia provides an illustration of this
point. During the 1970s and until the recent decline in petroleum prices,
Indonesia's oil resources provided an important source of government
revenue. Because of oil revenues, the Indonesian government could afford
to support a large fertilizer subsidy program and did not have to rely
heavily on agriculture as a source of revenue. Governments without such
resources face tighter fiscal budget constraints and thus more difficult
choices among different pricing objectives.

Natural endowment can also act upon the design of policy through its
impact on the consequences of policies. A country that has a large population and arable land area can generate agricultural import and export levels
that are sizable relative to the volume of trade on international markets.
Policy makers in such countries cannot assume that they face perfectly
elastic world supply or demand curves. Thus while Nepal and possibly
Korea can develop food policies with little regard to their impact on world
markets, China, Thailand, and Indonesia cannot do so. Thailand's rice
export policies provide an example of how a national food policy can be
motivated by the recognition of a downward sloping international demand
curve for rice. Assuming that curve to be inelastic, Thai policy makers have
used export restrictions on rice in an attempt to raise world prices and so
extract surplus from consumers abroad. The mixed results of this policy are
discussed in the Thailand chapter.

Similarly, a country's size and resources can determine the gains from
trade or, conversely, the costs associated with self-sufficiency. For Korea, a
country with limited land area and natural resources, the costs of self-
sufficiency policies are high. China, on the other hand, is large and diverse
enough to permit considerable internal diversification and trade. It is not
surprising, then, that the importance of trade relative to GDP declines as
country size increases (table 2).

A second set of factors that shape food pricing is political. Political factors
can be internal or external in origin. If a government's internal power base
is limited, a major consideration in its food policy program may simply be
to maintain the political support of key groups. Both Nepal and Indonesia,
for example, initially developed their state grain procurement and distribution systems in order to provide inexpensive staples to the military.

Later these systems were expanded to supply segments of the influential urban populations. Extension of these systems to assist rural producers has occurred only recently in Indonesia, and has not yet taken place in Nepal. Similar measures to protect urban consumers have been employed in Thailand and China. Usually food producers bear the costs of such programs, reflecting the fact that poorer, rural segments of the population are generally less influential.

External political factors can also weigh upon domestic food pricing. China's lack of attention to international prices and its efforts to be self-sufficient in food were in part the result of the West's foreign trade embargo on China during the fifties and sixties. For Korea and Nepal, the availability of foreign aid in the form of subsidized grain has, during certain periods, influenced domestic food pricing.

The overall level of economic development constitutes a third factor that shapes food pricing. Developed countries in general have price structures more favorable to agriculture than developing countries.[3] This pattern to some extent applies to the countries studies here. Data in tables 3 and 5 show that domestic-to-world paddy price ratios tend to rise with per capita GNP and other indicators of development, such as smaller shares of agriculture in GDP and the labor force.

The studies in this volume highlight several reasons why such a pattern occurs. First, during the development process potential sources of government revenue grow in number, so that it is possible to lighten the tax burden on agriculture. Since manufacturing sectors in lower-income countries are usually small, even with heavy taxation they could not provide substantial revenues. Consequently, lower-income countries by necessity rely on taxation of agriculture and trade to generate government revenue. The tendency to tax agriculture is often reinforced by the perception that taxation of incipient industry will hinder the development of a key sector.

In addition, the absence of enforcement and monitoring infrastructures often leaves governments in low-income countries with only a limited number of revenue-raising tools at their disposal. Implicit taxation through pricing and the extraction of levies on imports and exports are relatively easy instruments to implement and monitor, and so they are commonly used. With development, nonagricultural sectors grow and the selection of revenue-raising instruments broadens. Governments can successfully implement value-added, profit, and personal income taxes, and the bases to which such taxes apply expand (table 7). Thus the higher the level of development, the more feasible it is for countries to promote a price structure that favors agriculture.

As development proceeds, it also becomes politically safer to raise food

3. See, for example, Anderson and Hayami (1986), and World Bank (1986), pp. 11–13.

TABLE 7.   Government revenues and their selected components, 1983

	Central government revenues as a percent of GNP	Selected components of revenues as percent of total revenues	
		Taxes on income, profits, and capital gains	Taxes on international trade and transactions
Nepal	8.7	7.2	31.3
China	21.3[a]	85[b]	<0[d]
Indonesia	22.7	73.6[c]	4.3
Philippines	11.9	19.3	26.8
Thailand	15.2	19.6	21.4
Korea	19.5	22.9	15.8

SOURCES: World Bank (1986), *World Development Report*, pp. 224–25. China State Statistical Bureau (1986), *China Statistical Yearbook*, p. 597.
    [a]Calculated using revenue data from Sicular chapter in this volume and an official Chinese estimate for China's GNP of 549 billion yuan cited in Rock Creek Research (1986), *China Macroeconomic Newsletter*, p. 2. Chinese government revenue data include both central and local government revenues.
    [b]Estimated by author. Revenues from industrial profits plus industrial and commercial taxes alone exceed 80 percent of total revenues.
    [c]This number reflects revenues from taxes on oil extraction.
    [d]Chinese government revenues from international trade were negative in 1980–84.

prices. At higher levels of personal income, food, and especially staple foods, constitute a smaller proportion of household expenditures. The impact of an increase in the price of grain or other foods on consumers' real incomes is therefore reduced. Concurrently, with development rural interests begin to figure more prominently in national politics. As farmers become better organized and integrated in the national economy, their increased political clout creates pressures to protect and subsidize, rather than exploit, agriculture.[4]

These considerations suggest that low-income countries have compelling reasons for implementing policies that depress food prices. It is therefore not terribly constructive to propose that developing countries eliminate any antirural price biases. A more realistic approach would be to isolate the conditions that make feasible a more favorable pricing program, and to encourage correction of pricing biases as those conditions emerge.

Finally, national objectives can affect food pricing policies and structure. National objectives are, of course, formed within the context of a country's resource endowment, political environment, and level of development; moreover, food pricing may be used only to promote a subset of national goals, while other policies may be used to address the rest. Differing visions of countries' leaderships nevertheless account for some intercountry variation in food pricing.

Most developing countries place high priority on rapid economic growth, although the emphasis on industry as opposed to agriculture in the

4. See Anderson and Hayami (1986) for a discussion of the politico-economic reasons why agricultural protection increases with development.

development process has not been uniform. Several of the countries examined here have at one time emphasized rapid industrialization, for example, Korea in the 1950s and early 1960s, Thailand in the 1960s and 1970s, and China prior to the recent reform period, but especially in the 1950s. This emphasis on industry was translated into trade policies protecting domestic manufacturing and direct interventions to keep food prices low, both of which turned the terms of trade in favor of industry and against agriculture.

Several of these countries have since begun to place greater weight on the importance of agricultural growth in overall national development. Growth in agricultural production, especially of food, has also received greater attention as national leaders have increasingly placed priority on food self-sufficiency. Price regimes more favorable to agriculture have accompanied such shifts in priority, although nonprice measures, such as investment in new agricultural technologies and direct production planning (in China), have sometimes been used instead.

The agricultural sector began to receive greater attention in China in the early 1960s and in Korea during the late 1960s. Korea has, however, moved much further than China in implementing food price policies that benefit agriculture. Nepalese leaders have for many years acknowledged the need to promote agriculture, but successful policies have yet to be implemented. Indonesia provides a good example of favorable pricing to promote food production. In the early 1970s the Indonesian government introduced a paddy price support system, since which time rice production has grown to the point that Indonesia has shifted from a rice importer to exporter. Thailand, until recently able to rely on its land resources as a source of agricultural growth, has in the last few years begun to use price policies to promote food production.

Distributional objectives of one sort or another have also played a role in shaping the food pricing policies of most of these countries. Distributional measures, however, have often been motivated by political rather than equity considerations. As previously mentioned, most of these countries have taken steps to protect urban consumers from increases in and variability of staple food prices, usually at the expense of producers. Marketing margin subsidies have been used in China, Indonesia, and Korea to resolve the contradiction between urban consumer and rural producer welfare. Such subsidies have at times caused a substantial drain on the state budget, and when poorly designed can discourage food transport, processing, and storage activities.

Food Pricing and Economic Outcomes

Since food pricing is used to promote the various national objectives discussed above, one might ask whether, in fact, cross-country comparisons yield a discernible relationship between food price structure and economic outcomes. Interestingly, comparisons among the six countries studied in this volume show no clear correlation between food pricing structure and growth in food production, agriculture, or national product. The discussion in the next few pages mainly examines the paddy price level (relative to the world price) and its relationship to growth in rice production, agricultural value-added, and GNP. More comprehensive discussion of food price structures and outcomes can be found in later chapters.

The data presented in table 8 provides both a cross-sectional and longitudinal view of the pattern of pricing and outcomes. Neither cross-sectional nor longitudinal comparisons reveal a clearly positive relationship between the paddy price level and growth in rice production. During the late seventies and early eighties, for example, Korea had the highest paddy price ratios among the six countries, but growth in rice output over these years was slower than that in all but one of the other countries. In Thailand, whose paddy price ratios were considerably lower than those of the other nations, rice output grew 3.5–4.0 percent annually, a rate that falls in the middle of the range for the six countries. Nepal's rice production grew most slowly, even though its paddy price ratio was on average higher than Thailand's and the Philippines', and not significantly different from China's.

Longitudinal patterns similarly show no clear relationship between the paddy price and rice production. Historically China's paddy price ratio has slowly declined; however, the rate of growth in rice production has clearly accelerated since the late 1970s. Between 1965 and 1984 Indonesia's paddy price gradually rose to a level more or less in line with world prices. Since the early 1970s Indonesia's rice output has indeed grown at increasing rates. Nevertheless, this impressive growth in recent years has yet to surpass the 7 percent rates Indonesia achieved in the late 1960s.

Although the relationship between growth in rice output and the domestic-to-world paddy price ratio is weak, cross-country comparison shows a correlation between fertilizer price ratios and the levels of fertilizer use and yields. Data on fertilizer applications and yields per hectare (table 9) show that in Indonesia and Korea, the countries with the most favorable nitrogen-to-paddy price ratios, fertilizer applications are indeed higher than in Thailand, the Philippines, and Nepal. Paddy yields, and to some extent corn yields, are similarly in line with the level of fertilizer use. This pattern suggests that farmers in these countries are sensitive to the relative prices of inputs and outputs.

China deviates noticeably from the pattern: applications of fertilizer per hectare in China are extremely high despite an unfavorable nitrogen-to-paddy price ratio. The reasons for this are not completely clear but may have to do with the wide extension of irrigation, which raises the yield

TABLE 8. Domestic-to-world paddy price ratios and average annual rates of growth in rice output, agricultural value-added, and GNP[a]

	1965–70	1970–75	1975–80	1980–84
Nepal				
Price ratio	129	100	74	85 (1981–83)
Rice output	2.0	1.1	−1.5	3.9
Ag. value-added	2.8	1.6	−1.1	
GNP	2.6	1.8	1.3	
China				
Price ratio[b]	94–113	83–108	69–95	61–92
Rice output	2.9	2.2	4.6	4.7
Ag. value-added[c]	4.0	2.6	3.2	7.5
GNP[d]	8.3	5.5	6.0	7.4
Indonesia				
Price ratio	68 (1967–70)	69	104	87 (1981–82)
Rice output	7.1	4.4	5.5	6.0
Ag. value-added	4.3	4.1	4.0	
GNP	7.1	7.2	7.5	
Philippines				
Price ratio	96	94	75	73 (1981–82)
Rice output	5.2	3.2	4.7	1.4
Ag. value-added	3.7	4.3	5.4	
GNP	4.8	6.5	6.2	
Thailand				
Price ratio	51	64	67	66 (1981)
Rice output	2.2	1.5	3.6	3.8
Ag. value-added	6.2	5.2	3.2	
GNP	9.2	6.2	7.0	
Korea				
Price ratio	144	186	260	308
Rice output	1.3	3.6	0.3	3.6
Ag. value-added	3.0	4.3	1.6[e]	
GNP	10.4	9.0	7.2	

SOURCES: Price ratios are from table 5; Rice output is from *FAO Production Yearbook* (various issues); agricultural value-added and GNP are from World Bank (1983), *World Tables*, vol. 1, pp. 86, 87, 102, 103, 128, 129, 146, 147, 176, 177; China's agricultural value-added and national product data are from China State Statistical Bureau (1984, 1986), *China Statistical Yearbook*.

[a]Rice output growth rates are calculated using three-year averages for the base and endpoints to eliminate year-to-year variation. Agricultural value-added and GNP growth are calculated using constant prices.

[b]Lower end of range is calculated using the quota price, upper end using the above-quota price.

[c]Gross value of agricultural output (*nongye zong chanzhi*), excluding village industry.

[d]Net material product (*guomin shouru*).

[e]For 1975–81, because 1980 was an atypical year.

response to increased fertilizer applications, and perhaps also with a complicated planning structure that obscures the relationship between input prices and input use.

One might expect that growth in agriculture as a sector would be

TABLE 9.   Indicators of agricultural technology

	Nitrogen to paddy price ratio, 1980–82	Chemical fertilizer applications per hectare (ha), 1984 (kg nutrients/ha)	Paddy yields 1983–85 average (kg/ha)	Corn yields 1983–85 average (kg/ha)	Percent of arable land irrigated, 1984
Nepal	2.9	19.8	2,011	1,465	28%
China	2.9–4.3	180.6	5,300	3,709	45%
Indonesia	1.3	74.6	3,937	1,767	26%
Philippines	3.8	31.9	2,494	1,025	13%
Thailand	4.7	25.0	2,046	2,425	18%
Korea	0.9	331.1	6,339	4,392	55%

SOURCES: FAO *Fertilizer Yearbook, 1985*. FAO *Production Yearbook, 1985*.

positively correlated with farm prices for major foods. The statistics on table 8 suggest that this relationship is also weak. Those countries with the higher domestic-to-world paddy price ratios do not necessarily have the fastest growth in agricultural value-added. Countries with historically rising paddy price ratios, that is, Indonesia, Thailand, and Korea, have experienced slowing or, at best, constant growth in agricultural value-added. Those with deteriorating paddy price ratios have shown both slowing of growth in agricultural value-added (Nepal) and improvement (China), as well as fluctuation (Philippines).

The absence of a noticeably positive correlation between rice production or agricultural value-added and relative paddy prices could have several explanations. Production may be more responsive to the domestic price's increase relative to past domestic prices rather than relative to the world price. Changes in domestic prices over time are reflected only indirectly in the price data given in tables 5 and 8. Thus, for example, the recent decline in China's paddy price ratio is due largely to currency devaluation; the domestic paddy price index rose in 1979. Lack of a clear relationship between the price indicators and agricultural growth could also reflect simultaneity in the price-production relationship. Higher prices induce output growth, but output growth in turn causes prices to fall. Conversely, slow growth in output can drive prices up, either through market forces or because governments respond by raising prices.

In several of the countries, overall trends in agricultural growth have been largely due to growth in nongrain products such as livestock or cash crops. Such has been true in recent years for China and Korea. In these countries the relationship between paddy-based price indicators and overall agricultural growth may be weak because price interventions for selected food crops do not affect directly those products driving overall agricultural growth. Finally, price structure is only one of many factors that can influence agricultural production. Other factors—technological advances, demand trends, or changes in managerial organization—frequently obscure the price-production link. It is often these other factors that determine long-term rates of growth for rice and the agricultural sector.

Food prices are thought to influence not only agricultural production, but also the performance of other sectors and growth in national product. Views about what sort of price structure is most favorable to overall development differ: some suggest that overvaluation or undervaluation of agriculture can be beneficial, and others believe that prices that reflect opportunity costs are most consistent with rapid growth. Data for recent years (table 8) does not appear to favor one view over another. Growth of GNP has been rapid in Korea, which overvalues rice, in Thailand, which undervalues rice, and in Indonesia, where rice prices are more or less in line with world prices; GNP growth similarly does not seem to be correlated over time with the level of the paddy price.

Food pricing is often used to pursue objectives other than rapid growth, for example, distributional objectives. Unfortunately, changes over time in national income distributions are not available. Data on the proportion of total personal income received by the lowest 20 percent and highest 5 percent of households for the six countries for selected years (table 4) indicate that inequality is greatest in Nepal and smallest in China and Korea. Indonesia, the Philippines, and Thailand fall more or less in the middle of the range. Excluding China, the degree of equality appears to be greater in countries that have higher food prices. This pattern is consistent with the conclusion that efforts to keep rice retail prices low do not promote greater equity, possibly because the target groups of such policies are rarely the poorest segments of the population.

The inverse relationship between paddy prices and inequality suggests that food price increases can help promote equity. Price increases have been used explicitly to raise rural incomes in Korea and also in China. Although raising food prices can improve urban-rural equity, however, it does not necessarily improve the intra-rural income distribution. Rural residents consume as well as produce food, and higher food prices yield net benefits only to those segments of the rural population that produce more food than they consume (Hayami and Herdt, 1977).

Conclusion

The countries examined in this volume show considerable variation in food price policies and food price structures. As discussed in the following chapters, food price policies in these countries have been motivated not only by growth objectives, but also by distributional goals, the desire to generate government revenues, and food security. Furthermore, food pricing choices have been influenced by the presence or lack of natural endowments, the level of development, and the political setting. For these reasons, most of these countries have at some time maintained food pricing policies at odds with the usual policy prescriptions.

This is not to say that such policies have been costless. Indeed, as the chapters point out, in some cases significant short- and long-term efficiency losses can be attributed to national food price policies. Despite these costs, however, food price policy often does not lead to predictable outcomes. Economic progress, as well as economic stagnation, can occur under a variety of price regimes.

References

Agricultural Technical Economics Handbook Editorial Group. 1983. *Nongye Jishu Jingji Shouce* (Agricultural technical economics handbook). Beijing: Agricultural Publishing House.

Anderson, Kym, and Yujiro Hayami. 1986. *The Political Economy of Agricultural Protection: East Asia in International Perspective.* London: Allen & Unwin.

Barker, Randolph, Robert W. Herdt, and Beth Rose. 1985. *The Rice Economy of Asia.* Washington, D.C.: Resources for the Future.

Berry, R. Albert, and William R. Cline. 1979. *Agrarian Structure and Productivity in Developing Countries.* Baltimore: Johns Hopkins University Press.

Food and Agriculture Organization of the United Nations (FAO). (Various issues.) *Production Yearbook.* Rome.

———. (Various issues.) *Trade Yearbook.* Rome.

———. 1977. *Provisional Food Balance Sheets, 1972–74 Average.* Rome.

———. 1981. *1970 World Census of Agriculture: Analysis and International Comparison of the Results.* Rome.

———. 1984. *Food Balance Sheets, 1979–81 Average.* Rome.

———. 1985. *Fertilizer Yearbook,* Vol. 34. Rome.

Hayami, Yujiro, and Robert W. Herdt. 1977. "Market Price Effects of Technological Change on Income Distribution in Semisubsistence Agriculture." *American Journal of Agricultural Economics* 59(2):245–56.

International Monetary Fund. 1986. *International Financial Statistics Yearbook.* Washington, D.C.

International Rice Research Institute. 1986. *World Rice Statistics, 1985.* Manila.

Nepal Department of Food and Agricultural Marketing Services. *Agricultural Statistics of Nepal.*

———. 1985–86. *Agricultural Marketing Information Marketing Bulletin.* Special issue 2042.

O'Mara, Gerald. 1987. "Pricing and Marketing Policy to Intensify Rice Agriculture: The Example of Thailand." In Dieter Elz, ed., *Agricultural Marketing Strategy and Pricing Policy,* 76–91. Washington, D.C.: World Bank.

Piazza, Alan. 1983. *Trends in Food and Nutrient Availability in China, 1950–81.* World Bank Staff Working Paper no. 607. Washington, D.C.

Rock Creek Research. 1986. *China Macroeconomic Newsletter* 2(10):2.

Rose, Beth. 1985. *Appendix to "The Rice Economy of Asia."* Washington, D.C.: Resources for the Future.

State Statistical Bureau [of China]. 1984. *Zhongguo Tongji Nianjian, 1984* (China statistical yearbook, 1984). Beijing: China Statistical Publishing House.

——. 1986. *Zhongguo Tongji Nianjian, 1986 (China statistical yearbook, 1986).* Beijing: China Statistical Publishing House.

Timmer, C. Peter, Walter P. Falcon, and Scott R. Pearson. 1983. *Food Policy Analysis.* Baltimore: Johns Hopkins University Press.

World Bank. 1982. *Thailand: Program and Policy Priorities for an Agricultural Economy in Transition, Volume V.* World Bank Report No. 3705a-TH. Washington, D.C.

——. 1983. *World Tables*, vols. 1 and 2 (3rd ed.). Baltimore: Johns Hopkins University Press.

——. 1986. *World Development Report, 1986.* New York: Oxford University Press.

2. Indonesia: Transition from Food Importer to Exporter

C. Peter Timmer

As countries move along the path of economic development, the objectives of their price policies tend to become broader. One major text (Gillis et al., 1983) includes food prices as one of the key macro prices available to policy makers as they attempt to induce an economy down the path of economic development. The World Bank, the International Monetary Fund (IMF), and the United States Agency for International Development (USAID) have identified "distorted" agricultural prices as a major bottleneck to agricultural development and have begun to emphasize "getting prices right," in addition to project selection, as a way to improve agricultural sector performance. Strong links between the agricultural sector and the rest of the economy can mean that slow rural growth impedes the entire growth process. As a consequence, a country's agricultural price environment is a sensitive indicator of whether a country can make rapid progress in increasing output of goods and services in the whole economy (Timmer, 1986b, 1988).

This emphasis on keeping a broad perspective when viewing the objectives of food price policy grows out of experience over two decades in Indonesia, which has used its food price policy to pursue a wide range of objectives that include key macroeconomic goals, such as price stability and rates of economic growth, as well as narrower microeconomic targets for production and consumption.[1] With its extensive micro-macro links, price policy for rice provides the clearest example of such broad impact,

This chapter draws on sixteen years of work on food policy in Indonesia and is broadly interpretive rather than specifically empirical. The references provide a guide to what is now a rich and varied empirical treatment of the topics treated here. Help and guidance over the years from many people need to be acknowledged, especially from my guru on Indonesian food policy, Leon A. Mears. My colleagues at Stanford, Walter P. Falcon, and Scott R. Pearson, have collaborated with me on policy research for many years. My Indonesian mentors, particularly Professor Saleh Afiff and Generals Bustanil Arifin and Sukriya Atmaja, have patiently explained why academic models were often "too theoretical." And lastly, my wife Carol has patiently explained why the clever way I *wanted* to say something just wouldn't do at all. To her, as always, I owe the readability of this chapter.

1. No single paper can treat all of these topics. This chapter is primarily interpretive and integrative and relies heavily on a sequence of my own and other's research. See Afiff and Timmer (1971); Timmer (1975); BULOG (1971); Afiff, Falcon, and Timmer (1980); Mears (1959, 1981); Falcon et al. (1984); Timmer (1985, 1986a, 1987a).

but price policies for wheat, corn, sugar, soybeans, livestock products (i.e., eggs, milk, poultry, and beef), and vegetable oils have been used to influence not only production and consumption but also the government budget and the consumer price index.[2]

Anderson and Hayami (1986) have noted in the East Asian context how quickly agricultural price policy tends to shift from a narrow objective of keeping urban wages low and consumers happy to broader objectives of providing price incentives well above world market levels in an effort to raise agricultural output and improve rural incomes relative to rapidly rising urban incomes. In the mid-1960s, Indonesia's objectives were narrowly focused. Partly as a legacy from the Dutch and Sukarno eras, and partly because of real concern for the welfare of poor consumers in both urban and rural areas, the New Order government kept domestic rice prices for producers and consumers well below the trend of world prices and insulated domestic prices from the sharp instability in world markets. These actions revealed two clear objectives: a concern for consumer welfare, especially as reflected in the price of rice in urban retail markets, and a separate concern for stability. In the early years of the New Order government, it indeed built much of its political legitimacy on the economic stabilization efforts before and during the first five-year development plan (Repelita I).

Although much of the credit for the decline in the annual inflation rate from over 1,000 percent in 1965 to under 4 percent in 1971 must go to tight monetary policy and a constitutionally mandated balanced budget, the effort had a strong focus on commodities as well, and the supply-demand balances of important foodstuffs were controlled closely. A newly reorganized food logistics agency, BULOG (Badan Urusan Logistik), was given specific terms of reference to maintain retail price stability for rice and other basic commodities, and the head of the agency reported directly to President Suharto. The deputy and then chairman of BULOG, General Bustanil Arifin, was a close confidant of the president, and he also communicated easily and often with the inner circle of economists in the cabinet responsible for the stabilization and development plan. From 1968 to 1972, rice price stabilization was seen by the government and outside observers as one of the pillars of Indonesia's concerted efforts to rebuild an economy badly fragmented by hyperinflation and political upheavals.

A desirable objective for rice price policy in the early 1970s would have been to stimulate farm incomes and production. However, this goal con-

---

2. It should also be noted that price policy for rice has been used to fine-tune trends in production relative to domestic consumption and has been implemented primarily through varying subsidies on fertilizer. The fertilizer subsidy also affects the profitability of other crops, but fine-tuning of the domestic balance between production and consumption using price policy has been reserved for rice.

flicted directly with the objective of maintaining low and stable consumer prices if price incentives to farmers were to be a significant part of the production package. Because of the pressing budgetary constraint, extremely limited bureaucratic expertise, and a serious lack of understanding of how the rural economy functioned, there was relatively little opportunity to operate a dual price system of the type common on the Indian subcontinent. Although the desirability of maintaining both high farm prices and low urban prices was well understood, these constraints forced decision makers not to subsidize the marketing margin very much. Consequently, it was necessary to incorporate marketing costs in the private sector into the calculations in connecting floor and ceiling price policy for rice. These marketing costs could be squeezed by narrowing the margin between BULOG's procurement and distribution prices, but the objective of generating higher farm incomes and rice production via price incentives was constrained by several realities: tight budgetary resources, relatively low rice prices in international markets, and BULOG's limited capacity to procure a sizable proportion of rice from farmers in defense of higher prices.

These realities changed in the mid-1970s. Previous but unrealized objectives became more feasible and more important. Budget revenues soared because of higher oil prices, BULOG significantly improved its logistical capacity and managerial procedures, but the costs of defending low internal rice prices with imports rose after the world food crisis in 1973–74. The shortage of rice in world markets in 1973 and 1974 provided a shock to Indonesian policy makers, which has been indelibly etched into their thinking. Despite abundant foreign exchange from oil revenues, Indonesia was unable to purchase enough rice from either traditional or nontraditional suppliers to maintain internal price stability. Thailand, traditionally one of Indonesia's main suppliers, banned exports of rice for several months to protect its own consumers. Although self-sufficiency in rice had been a long-held objective of most post-Independence development plans, the scare in 1973–74 put new energy into the search for mechanisms to achieve it. Indonesia resolved that domestic food security meant rice self-sufficiency. Despite continued concern for consumer welfare, new producer price incentives were forthcoming by 1975.

From 1976 to 1978, outbreaks of the brown planthopper reinforced the sense of Indonesia's vulnerability to forces beyond the planners' control. In the second half of the 1970s, Indonesia was routinely the world's largest importer of rice, often taking one-fifth of supplies traded internationally, and significantly more in years of poor domestic production. Because of Indonesia's size in the world rice market, the objective of food security was intimately linked to the degree of rice self-sufficiency, even though the potential role of other staples in a diversified food economy was beginning to be recognized.

In all economic systems the objectives for price policy inevitably conflict with each other, at least in the short run. Domestic price stability can impede efficient reallocation of resources as relative scarcities in world markets shift. Low prices for consumers dampen incentives for farmers to expand output, and lower farm incomes are likely to contribute to a relatively stagnant rural economy. The slower growth in output can in turn jeopardize the goal of food security, especially for a large country such as Indonesia. Without growth in food production and a healthy rural economy, a society's productivity base might not expand rapidly enough to meet the needs of a larger population, thus threatening the very consumer welfare that the price policy sought to protect in the first place. Indonesia has grappled directly with this particular vicious circle, using a variety of price and nonprice policies. Its success is a model for other countries. While many important lessons about price policy are transferable in principle from the Indonesian experience to other poor countries, it is necessary first to make clear the particular circumstances of the evolution of Indonesian food price policy and the mechanisms of its implementation and impact.

Price Policy Instruments

In a mixed economy such as Indonesia's, food prices are formed in markets and reflect a combination of government interventions and basic market forces. Which is more important at any given time—government intervention or market forces—depends on the commodity and the degree of government effort to control its price. In Indonesia, rice prices have nearly always been heavily influenced by direct policy interventions, corn prices to a lesser extent, and prices of gaplek—the dried form of cassava that is traded internationally—only occasionally.

The government can also affect the basic market forces that influence commodity price information. Price policy for production inputs directly affects the profitability of growing crops, and hence the supplies available in the market. Indonesia has used a wide array of input subsidies—for fertilizer, irrigation water, pesticides, and the credit program designed to enable farmers to purchase the package of inputs available as part of the rice intensification program (BIMAS). These subsidies serve to speed the adoption of new technology. They also allow relatively lower farm prices and consumer prices for rice for a given level of domestic production. This cushions the direct food price dilemma—how to maintain price incentives for farmers and cheap food for consumers—at the expense of budget subsidies. The fertilizer subsidy in particular has been the focus of considerable analysis and debate because it claims such a large share of the budget for agricultural development. In 1984–85 the fertilizer subsidy was U.S. $680 million, or about 60 percent of the entire budget for agriculture and irrigation development.

Even apart from policies for agriculture, government policies in the trade and macro arenas can have direct influence on food price formation. The level of industrial protection affects the costs of manufactured inputs and consumer items farmers buy, as well as the equilibrium exchange rate in the "managed float" system that Indonesia has used since the devaluation in November 1978. Exchange rate policy itself obviously has a major impact on how domestic prices compare with border prices for potentially tradable commodities such as rice, corn, and gaplek. The impact of oil prices in particular on exchange rate formation and thus on commodity price formation is a key part of the food price story in Indonesia from 1974 to the present.

Commodity Price Policy for the Three Basic Foodstuffs

Government intervention has influenced price formation for rice, corn, and cassava in direct proportion to the role of the commodity in the food system, either directly, as for rice, or indirectly, as for corn in its role as livestock feed. For all three commodities, government price interventions relied almost entirely on control over imports and exports implemented by BULOG, complemented in the case of rice by an extensive direct marketing role in procurement and distribution. Even for rice, however, BULOG's procurement was never greater than 12 percent of total production and perhaps twice that for total marketings, nor were distributions more than 15 percent of total consumption. Consequently, the structure, conduct, and performance of the private food marketing sector is a crucial factor in the design and implementation of price policy in Indonesia. This accounts for the relatively large emphasis on this sector in the following review of price policy instruments.

Figures 1, 2, and 3, taken from Dorosh (1986, 1987), show how the wholesale domestic prices in rupiahs of rice, corn, and gaplek, respectively, have compared with their border prices from 1974 to 1984. For rice and corn, the figures also show how these prices have compared with the official floor price supported by BULOG through purchases from the village cooperatives (KUDs). The relative importance of direct price policy for these three commodities is obvious from the figures. The floor price for rice, which was in effect throughout this period, seems to have provided an actual floor to wholesale rice prices in East Java, the nation's leading producer of surplus rice. The floor price for corn, by contrast, was not introduced until 1978 and has been tested only rarely. In yet greater

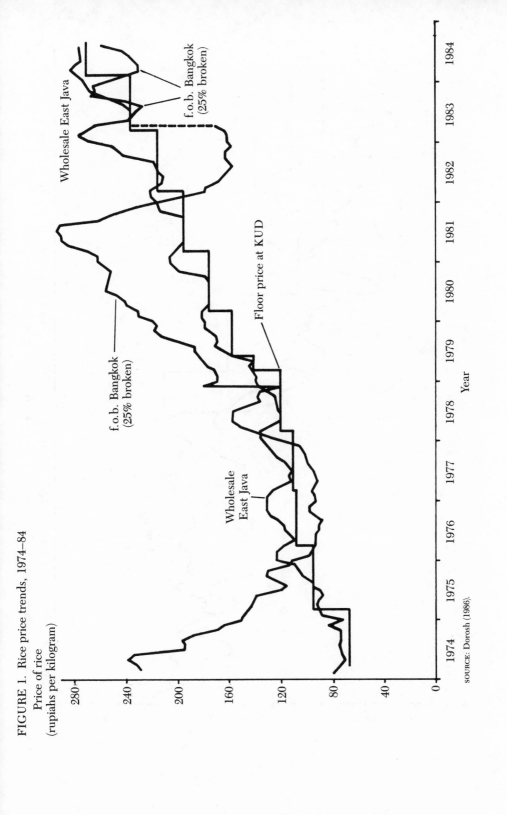

FIGURE 1. Rice price trends, 1974–84

Price of rice
(rupiahs per kilogram)

Wholesale East Java

f.o.b. Bangkok
(25% broken)

f.o.b. Bangkok
(25% broken)

Floor price at KUD

Wholesale
East Java

280
240
200
160
120
80
40
0

1974   1975   1976   1977   1978   1979   1980   1981   1982   1983   1984

Year

SOURCE: Dorosh (1986).

FIGURE 2. Corn price trends, 1974–84

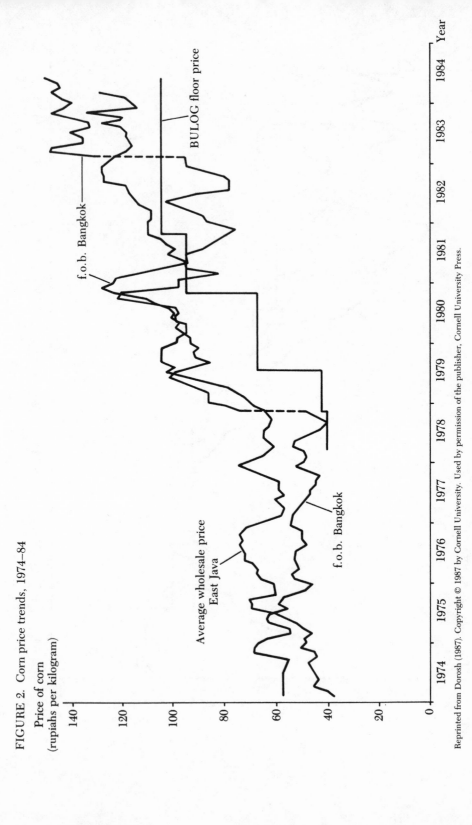

FIGURE 3. Gaplek price trends, 1974–84

Price of gaplek
(rupiah per kilogram)

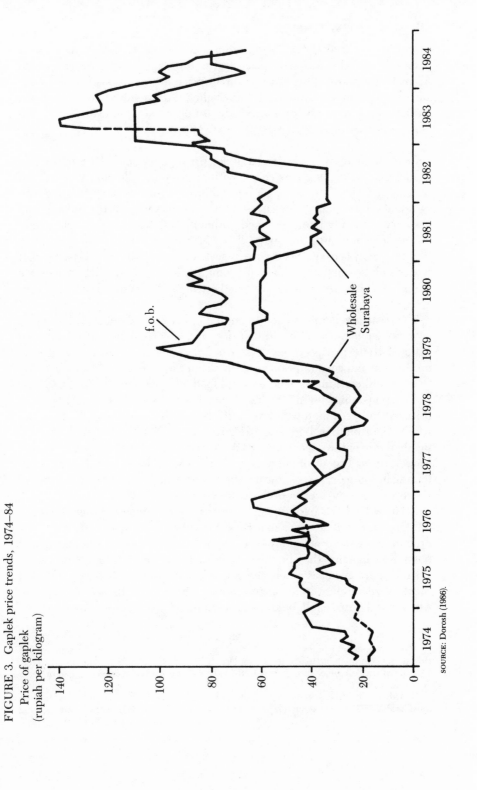

SOURCE: Dorosh (1986).

contrast, no direct price interventions on behalf of gaplek have been initiated, and the domestic price tracks the export price quite closely. Accordingly, most of the story of direct price interventions is about rice, and there is only a limited, yet revealing, experience with corn. Price formation for cassava is primarily a matter of private domestic supply and demand forces relative to exchange rate formation.

Rice. In many ways, Indonesia's rice price policy since 1968 provides a good example of long-run vision with respect to following world price trends, and short-run concern for stability and consumer welfare.[3] The systematic bias against rice farmers that was pervasive in the Sukarno era has very gradually been reversed, although full parity with world prices was not reached until the early 1980s.[4] Stabilizing prices around long-run trends in world rice prices is no easy task, of course; the world rice market trades only a small share of rice produced, and consequently prices are highly unstable (see Falcon and Monke, 1979–80; Siamwalla and Haykin, 1983).[5]

The basic mechanisms used to implement rice price policy in Indonesia have been a floor price, a ceiling price, and government-controlled international trade in rice to serve as the balance wheel between domestic production and consumption resulting from the respective prices faced by farmers and consumers. The national food logistics agency, BULOG, has had responsibility for procuring as much rice as necessary to hold rice prices at the preannounced level, effective at the village cooperative, the KUD. Coordination between BULOG and the KUDs was facilitated by the dual role of the chairman of BULOG who served also as the minister of cooperatives. Procurement was primarily in the form of milled rice, although in some provinces, most notably East Java, substantial quantities of rough rice (paddy) were purchased for storage.

Because BULOG had originally served a quartermaster function for the military and civil service, many local employees with responsibility for procurement were accustomed to buying fixed quantities as cheaply as possible. Changing the objectives of the organization to supporting a fixed price by purchasing as much rice as necessary was extremely difficult, and there were numerous instances from 1968 through the early 1970s in which local prices fell below the announced floor price. An intensive

3. See Timmer, Falcon, and Pearson (1983) for discussion of such a model.
4. Figure 1 shows wholesale prices in East Java above the Bangkok price from the end of 1975 to the beginning of 1978, but this was largely because the rupiah became progressively overvalued after oil prices rose sharply in 1974. This macro impact on domestic food prices is discussed in a later section of this chapter.
5. Although it is always possible to draw some trend through historical price data, there is considerable evidence that such trends cannot be used with confidence for future pricing decisions (see Schwartz, 1986).

training program in BULOG coupled with significantly improved financial procedures for arranging the credit necessary for procurement resulted in nearly a decade of successful defense of the floor price. Accordingly, the widespread failure to defend the floor price in 1985 came as a significant shock to farmers and government policy makers, including the senior leadership at BULOG. The problems in handling the large rice surplus that emerged in 1985 were significantly different from those in coping with continuing deficits, even when they were of variable size.

In the early days of the New Order government, considerably more attention was devoted to maintaining a ceiling price for rice in urban markets than in vigorous defense of the floor price. This concern was understandable, reflecting as it did an inherited view of rice as a political commodity on whose urban price numerous cabinets had fallen. Control of rice prices by the new government was essential to its short-term survival and its medium-term legitimacy in the eyes of the politically vocal urban workers and students. Longer-term legitimacy, of course, required that the entire economy be rejuvenated, and for this, price incentives and significant growth in rice production were essential. But from 1966 to 1972, controlling consumer prices for rice was the highest priority.[6]

This control was accomplished by carefully programmed supply management, as BULOG combined rice available from domestic procurement with imports in order to have adequate supplies to inject into urban markets. Until the late 1970s, a single urban ceiling price was announced and enforced on Java as well as the Outer Islands. In the early 1980s a new policy was quietly introduced: a ceiling price was no longer announced. Retail prices in the major cities on the Outer Islands began to be significantly higher than those on Java (except in surplus areas). The wider price margins between surplus and deficit regions were designed to provide greater incentives to private traders to transport rice within the vast archipelago, thus reducing the burden on BULOG's physical logistical capacity and its finances.

From the very beginning of the price policy in the late 1960s, the band between the floor price and urban retail prices within a province was supposed to be wide enough to permit extensive involvement of the private rice marketing sector in storage and distribution, but in fact this margin was often squeezed in a deliberate effort to keep urban prices low and still provide adequate farm incentives. The consequences of this squeeze were often not fully appreciated, and significant and unexpected budgetary subsidies were required. Figure 4 provides a simple graphical framework for understanding why the subsidies needed to enforce a narrower margin between floor and ceiling prices were underestimated. With

6. The experience with price stabilization and the relatively low priority given to price incentives for farmers during this period are discussed at length in Timmer (1975).

FIGURE 4. Impact of price policy on role of private marketing sector and size of government subsidies

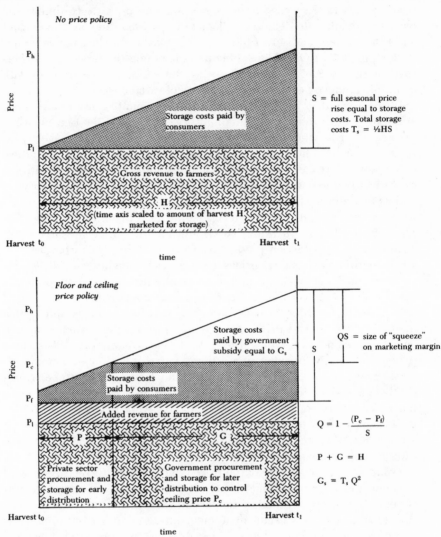

no price policy, the figure shows that rice prices rise from the harvest to the preharvest period, indicating competitive costs of storage. All storage costs are paid by consumers (top part of figure 4). When a floor and ceiling price is established, the government must pay some of the storage costs if the margin between the two policy-determined prices is not large enough to cover the full private costs of storage.

The bottom panel of the figure shows the seasonal price rise starting from a higher level than that before the price policy, and the price rise is truncated when the ceiling price becomes operative. The private trade can carry rice only during this short period of rising prices, after which the government becomes the primary supplier. Storage costs on the rice supplied by the government must be paid by direct or indirect subsidy, since BULOG is unlikely to have lower real storage costs than private traders.[7] The extent of subsidy required depends on the *square* of the squeeze on the marketing margin. This exponential relationship sometimes surprised officials in BULOG and the Ministry of Finance, who tended to set floor and ceiling prices independently of discussions of BULOG's financial requirements.[8]

Until the surpluses of the mid-1980s, BULOG used variable quantities of imports to provide enough supplies, after incorporating domestically procured rice, to enforce targets for urban retail prices. The highly variable prices in world markets made financial planning of these logistical operations difficult, but supplies were generally obtainable at good terms relative to announced export prices, at least after control was reestablished over domestic rice markets in 1975. But the memory of rice supplies being virtually nonexistent in the world market in 1973 and 1974, and of the high prices paid from 1979 to 1981, caused an understandable sense of vulnerability to external forces among key Indonesian leaders, including President Suharto. Since 1978, when dependency on imports seemed likely to threaten a decade of gains in economic performance, this sense of vulnerability was translated into sharply higher price incentives for rice production, even at the expense of rising urban prices. In what might be an important test of linkages between food prices and rural development, the period from 1978 to 1985 was also one of great dynamism in the entire rural economy. Rural-oriented macroeconomic policy contributed significantly to this dynamism, but it is likely that a major factor was price policy per se, a policy that involved input prices as well as floor and ceiling prices for rice.

Corn. Corn is primarily an upland crop in Indonesia, grown under rain-fed or marginally irrigated conditions. The heterogeneity and seasonal variations in these conditions cause corn production to fluctuate widely

7. The primary mechanisms used to cover BULOG's storage costs have been subsidized credit, low-cost warehouses, and opportunities to distribute at full book value to civil servants rice whose quality has deteriorated in storage.

8. It is clear that Q is larger than Q^2 when $0 < Q < 1$, but the issue is whether Q^2 grows larger exponentially as Q goes from near zero to near one, because the size of the subsidy depends on Q^2 and not on Q.

from month to month and year to year.[9] When farm households consumed corn primarily from own production, such fluctuations caused few problems for the economy.[10] When a modern livestock industry began to need regular supplies each month, however, fluctuating supplies led to fluctuating prices, which were worrisome to a government committed to maintaining retail price stability for important foodstuffs. Although corn has never been seen as an important foodstuff directly—virtually no dry corn grain is consumed as food by households in urban areas—the emergence of a modern poultry industry raised the importance of corn in policy makers' minds.

Since 1978 efforts have been made to stimulate the production of corn through the BIMAS *palawija* program (for nonrice food staples and secondary crops), research on new seed technology, and a guaranteed floor price for yellow corn (white corn remains the variety preferred for consumption by humans in several areas, but yellow corn is preferred by poultry feeders [Monteverde and Mink, 1987]). Although figure 2 indicates that the floor price for corn was seldom operative in East Java, as domestic prices tended to stay well above the announced support price, in other locations the KUDs played an important role in guaranteeing a market for newly emerging market supplies of yellow corn (Timmer, 1987c).

Under tropical conditions, corn is expensive to store even for a few months, as insect infestations and aflatoxin contaminations rapidly cause deterioration in quality. All modern storage technologies require corn of low moisture content to prevent such deterioration, and this is difficult to achieve in the Indonesian corn system. Producers have small plots with tiny marketings spread over several months, primarily during the corn harvest in the rainy season when sun-drying capacity is haphazard at best. Mechanical corn dryers would probably be able to operate only sporadically, thus placing the burden of recovering capital costs on relatively small volumes. Consequently, storage costs for corn in the Indonesian environment have been very high, and without government intervention, these costs would be reflected in wide seasonal price swings.

A particularly fascinating dimension of the Indonesian corn economy historically has been the relative width of the f.o.b.–c.i.f. band relative to seasonal price movements. Prior to the early 1980s, seasonal price fluctuations usually fell within the band, and so corn behaved as a nontradable commodity. As transportation and port facilities improved, however, the

9. Some of the fluctuations in corn production apparent in published statistics are an artifact of the calendar-year nature of the statistics that straddle the corn crop year, which ends sometimes in December and sometimes in January.

10. The welfare significance of the fluctuations for the producer-consumer households was cushioned to some extent by the complementary seasonal patterns of the corn and rice harvests.

band narrowed, and in the early 1980s, Indonesia actually exported and imported corn in the same year. Sometimes this trade in corn involved subsidies in both directions. In 1984, for example, BULOG moved corn procured through the KUDs in the province of South Sulawesi directly into export markets at lower costs than would have been incurred in shipping it to Jakarta-based feed mills. Later in the year, corn imported from Thailand was subsidized for sales to those feed mills.

Part of this behavior is explained by the combination of high storage costs relative to the width of the f.o.b.–c.i.f. band between the export price and the import price. In the simple model illustrated in figure 5, the f.o.b. export price provides a floor of $120 per metric ton while the c.i.f. import price provides a ceiling of $160 per ton. With "high" storage costs ($7.50 per ton per month), the seasonal price rise is so rapid that the c.i.f. price is reached in September, after starting its climb at the end of the main corn harvest, which runs from January to April. Corn is exported from January to April, but it is imported from September to December, in the absence of any government interventions (and assuming constant world prices).

Two possible interventions, both with historical precedent, are shown in the figure. First, imports might be banned (in an effort to save foreign exchange), in which case domestic prices simply rise beyond the c.i.f. price until the new harvest starts. How high the prices climb would depend on traders' expectations earlier in the harvest and postharvest season. If procurement and consumption were based on expectations of import availability at $160 per ton, and these imports were subsequently prohibited, the price rise between September and December could be steep indeed, limited only by the purchasing power of consumers and the availability of corn substitutes in the food system.

Alternatively, and more commonly in Indonesia, the government could subsidize the import of corn to keep feed costs low and thus to stabilize the prices of poultry and eggs. In the illustration, the "normal" seasonal price rise is cut in half, and imports are roughly twice as large as they would be otherwise. The truncated seasonal price rise has a substantial impact on the private marketing sector, as there are few incentives to store corn for more than a few months. This in turn means there are few incentives to invest in the *capacity* to store corn for longer periods, which in turn means it is very expensive to try to store corn for these longer periods. A vicious circle is set up whereby government subsidies to contain the sharp seasonal price rise become more and more necessary as greater demand develops for year-round supplies, a situation that presented itself quite tangibly in Indonesia in the mid-1980s (see Dorosh, 1987; Mink, 1987a, 1987b; Timmer, 1987b, 1987c).

Breaking into such a vicious circle is not easy, but two government

FIGURE 5. The role of storage costs and government trade policy on corn price formation and the potential for imports and exports in the same crop year

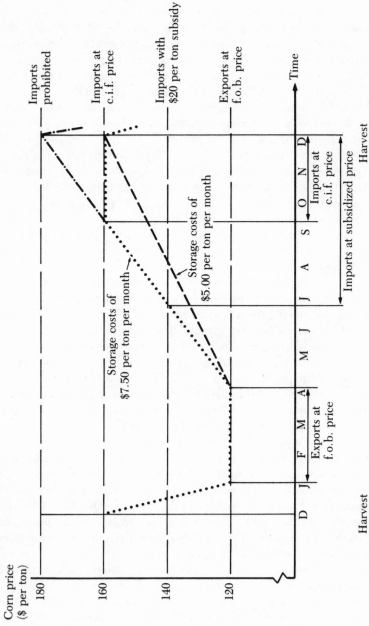

NOTE. Illustrative price and cost figures are in dollars per metric ton.
Reprinted from Timmer (1987b). Copyright © 1987 by Cornell University. Used by permission of the publisher, Cornell University Press.

initiatives were seen to be helpful. First, clearer signals on government trade policy for corn were essential for the private sector to have enough confidence to invest in improved drying and storage facilities and to incur the costs of obtaining year-round supplies from domestic sources. Such investments were particularly risky until the government announced a clear policy with respect to the circumstances in which corn imports would be used, especially if subsidized, to maintain stability in domestic poultry prices.

Second, government investments in lowering storage costs through new technology—safe, powdered insecticides that could be used at the KUD level and better dryers at the village level—could significantly alter the pattern of seasonal price formation. As figure 5 indicates, simply reducing storage costs from $7.50 to $5.00 per ton per month, under the assumptions of the model, would eliminate the need for imports.

Direct price policy for corn, although not as pervasive as for rice, was a major factor in the mid-1980s in the outlook for the corn economy. Price responsiveness of producers and consumers was modest in the short run, but proceeded in appropriate directions, so price policy affected levels of output and consumption in predictable ways (see Mink, 1987b; and Monteverde and Mink, 1987). More important, price policy affected the structure of the marketing sector and had crucial implications for the long run. Given the diversity and geographic scatter of Indonesian corn producers, a competitive and dynamic marketing sector was needed to connect growth in demand and uses for corn with farmer willingness to locate and adopt the new seed technologies available in the private sector.

Without relatively stable "rules of the game" and a well-defined price policy for both farmers and feed mills—including the possibility of a policy of nonintervention—marketing agents in the private sector were likely to continue to play the limited role in longer-term storage that they played in the past. This left a heavy burden on BULOG, both to support corn prices in locations where the private sector had little incentive (or initiative) to be involved and to guarantee corn supplies to the politically important feed mills and small-scale poultry operations. Competent as BULOG was in implementing food price policies through trade interventions, it was not a low-cost or nimble marketing agent. The Indonesian corn economy is likely to be retarded in its development until such marketing agents are widely available.

Cassava. One more step down in the consciousness of Indonesian food policy makers is cassava. A starchy root crop consumed widely in fresh form but only among the rural poor when dried, cassava products have been exported since the tapioca industry was established during the Dutch colonial period. Although tapioca is no longer a significant domestic or export product, the European Common Agricultural Policy (CAP) created a niche for gaplek (dried cassava) exports to Europe, where it is mixed with soybean meal to make "synthetic corn" and thus avoids the variable levy on feed grains established by the CAP (see Nelson, 1984). Thailand is the major exporter of dried cassava to Europe, but Indonesian exports have been fairly regular since the 1960s. They were interrupted whenever the exchange rate became significantly overvalued or when crop shortfalls led domestic prices to rise above the equivalent Thai export price. On such occasions, cassava starch and flour were imported from Thailand.

Despite periods of very low prices for cassava, no government support price for either fresh or dried cassava was implemented. The logistical difficulties of such a floor price coupled with the low political visibility of producers and consumers were probably sufficient to explain this reluctance to intervene in formation of cassava prices, but evidence that pointed toward the efficiency of existing mechanisms of price formation also helped persuade policy makers not to intervene in the cassava market. Unnevehr (1984) has demonstrated clearly that cassava prices on Java were determined almost entirely by two mechanisms: by f.o.b. export prices in the East Java port of Surabaya whenever internal prices were at or below the export price; and by levels of cassava production and rice prices (as a substitute in consumption) whenever domestic cassava prices rose above the export price. Most of the time cassava behaved as a tradable commodity, as it did in 84 of the 108 months between 1971 and 1979, the period of Unnevehr's analysis, and prices were determined by the world price. In the other months, local supply and demand conditions determined cassava prices.

These local conditions varied widely from month to month and by region on Java (and on the Outer Islands). When exports flowed from the main ports, a clear pattern of price margins was formed from the lows in the supplying hinterlands to the ports. But when domestic supply and demand conditions took over and exports stopped, the hierarchy of price margins also broke down. Consequently, correlation of cassava prices among local markets on Java was much higher when exports provided a basing point for price formation than when local conditions determined local prices. The same sort of market integration was provided by feed mills in Jakarta and Surabaya in the case of corn, and similar market fragmentation occurred when imported corn supplied the Jakarta mills, and movement of corn from East and Central Java to Jakarta ceased. Rice markets can also become disconnected when flows from rural areas are reversed under the impact of a low urban ceiling price for rice, but this has not been a significant factor since the substantial surpluses developed in the mid-1980s (Timmer, 1974).

In summary, government intervention influenced price formation for rice, corn, and cassava in direct proportion to the importance of the commodity to policy makers and to the economy. Few attempts were made to intervene in price formation by fiat or police action; even during high prices in the mid-1970s and low prices in 1985, it was not illegal to sell rice above the ceiling price or to buy it below the floor price. Nearly all price interventions have been attempted through use of the market rather than displacement of it, and this no doubt accounts for much of the success in defending the desired price levels. As a consequence, the private food marketing sector has had a relatively large role, and the structure, conduct, and performance of this sector is a crucial factor in the design and implementation of price policy in Indonesia.

Input Price Interventions

Agricultural input prices have been the subject of extensive intervention, usually in the form of explicit or indirect subsidies. Only land, farm labor, and animal power were relatively unaffected by government policy; at various times between 1968 and 1985, seeds, water, pesticides, fertilizer, fuel, and machinery had their costs to farmers reduced by specific price subsidies covered by direct budget allocations, or through credit subsidies that incurred indirect opportunity costs in revenue forgone by the national budget.

Relatively little is known about the exact costs of these subsidies because most were included in the general budget of the relevant ministries— Agriculture, Public Works, Mines and Energy, and the Central Bank. Except for fertilizer, the relative benefits of these subsidies are also poorly understood. Timmer (1985) attributed a significant share of the increase in rice production between 1968 and 1982 to improvements in irrigation and the shorter maturities of the modern, high-yielding rice seeds, but no evaluation of the impact of the *prices* of these key inputs has been conducted. Because little mechanical power was used in the production of Indonesia's food crops, subsidized fuel prices had little impact on choice of technique. Subsidized credit may have had a minor impact on the widespread use of tractors in land preparation in North Sumatra, but the relatively high wage rates characteristic of the Outer Islands were probably the major factor (Mink, 1987b).

Pesticide Subsidy. By the mid-1980s, the pesticide subsidy was very large. Farmers paid only 10 to 20 percent of the full economic cost of the most widely used pesticides, and their extremely low price led to widespread and heavy applications. Between 1979 and 1983, use of pesticides increased 35 percent per year, to an annual level of over fourteen thousand tons. Such large volumes meant that the pesticide subsidy was large in absolute budgetary terms, exceeding $100 million in the 1984–85 budget.

The benefits to be matched against these high costs were dubious. The high rates of application caused serious "downstream" ecological problems as the pesticide runoff poisoned breeding grounds for fish and shrimp in the coastal waters around Java, Sumatra, and Sulawesi. Rice paddies no longer supported a freshwater fish crop. Of most concern, however, was the biological pressure put on the small handful of insect-resistant varieties of rice, such as IR-36, Cisadane, and Krueng Aceh. Heavy spraying of pesticides caused particular insect pests, such as the brown planthopper, to evolve more rapidly into new biotypes that were capable of feeding on resistant varieties of rice. Unless this selection pressure was dramatically reduced by a new program for integrated pest management, there was significant danger of a new outbreak of pests similar to that which plagued rice production in the 1976–78 period.

Fertilizer Subsidy. In contrast to the relatively low level of knowledge about the costs and benefits of subsidies to other inputs, the fertilizer subsidy has been extensively studied. Total use of fertilizer on food crops, most of it on rice, grew 25 percent per year from 1970 to 1983. While this growth is from a small base, the rate was still 23.8 percent per year from 1979 to 1983, indicating both powerful incentives to use more fertilizer and a distribution system that was capable of delivering larger amounts to farmers each year. Most of the *potential* incentives to use fertilizer came from the new rice technology inserted into a cultivation environment made vastly more productive by massive investments in irrigation.

Fertilizer distribution was handled primarily by a competitive private sector, although a government distribution agency (P. N. PERTANI), the government-owned fertilizer producing company (P. N. PUSRI), and the village cooperatives (KUDs), also played significant roles. From the wholesale level to the farmer, however, most fertilizer was distributed by small-scale traders and village kiosks. When the government intervened in the price of fertilizer, it did so at the wholesale level and was careful to avoid any restrictions on the quantity of fertilizer that might subsequently be demanded. This combination of subsidized price with unrestricted fertilizer quantities is a crucial aspect of determining the impact of the fertilizer subsidy.[11]

If farmers carefully optimized their fertilizer use by setting its full marginal cost equal to the revenue produced by higher crop output, a price subsidy would cause distortions in resource allocation and diminished social welfare. Farmers would be better off, of course, but under these standard assumptions about the behavior of competitive economic

11. There were episodes when the government tried to monopolize the distribution of fertilizer or restrict its distribution only to the KUDs. When fertilizer use fell off each time, open competition was quickly restored (see Timmer, 1985; World Bank, 1983).

agents, the resources used to subsidize the fertilizer price could better serve society in some alternative use. Negative externalities to heavy use of fertilizer—because of nitrification of water supplies and rivers, for example—would merely emphasize the distortions introduced by the subsidy.

The very rapid growth in use of fertilizer since 1970 suggests, however, that farmers were not carefully optimizing their use of fertilizer in the manner required by the neoclassical model of resource allocation. The strong time trend suggests that significant disequilibrium existed in fertilizer use because farmers did not have full knowledge about the productivity of the new input and were highly risk averse in experimenting with progressively higher application rates. The a priori suggestion that the subsidy was inherently distorting—that it led to an allocation of resources that reduced total economic welfare—might well be wrong. The subsidy may have *reduced* distortions by bringing farmers closer to the desired equilibrium at which the marginal cost of fertilizer to the economy was equal to its marginal revenue product. The only way to find out was to examine empirically the factors determining levels of fertilizer use and the impact of that use on crop output and the rest of the economy. Such an analysis was carried out for the period 1968 to 1982 (Timmer, 1985).

The results of attempting to measure the impact of a marginal change in the fertilizer subsidy are summarized in figure 6. At the margin, the full social costs relative to the social benefits of subsidizing fertilizer are a function of two critical parameters: the social opportunity cost of rice, measured by the border price as either an import or an export, and the marginal productivity of fertilizer in terms of *gabah* (rough rice). Holding other things constant, the marginal benefit-cost ratio of using budget resources to subsidize fertilizer rises with higher opportunity costs for rice and with higher *gabah*-to-urea response rates. For two sets of assumptions about the full social cost of fertilizer (Rp 150 or Rp 200 per kilogram compared with a farm-gate price of Rp 70 per kilogram in 1982) and additional costs generated by the higher yields of rice induced by the incremental fertilizer use (*m* equal to 10 percent or 20 percent of the incremental yield), figure 6 shows a constant benefit-cost ratio of 1.0 and 2.0 as a function of the social opportunity cost of rice and the parameter indicating the *gabah*-to-fertilizer response rate.

These two parameters depend on the level of the fertilizer subsidy itself. This simultaneous relationship helps explain why the potential band between the c.i.f. import price of rice and the f.o.b. export price is so wide. Indonesia is a significant actor in the world rice market. Higher fertilizer subsidies lead to greater domestic rice production and cause a reduction in demand for rice by Indonesia from this market, and hence lower world rice prices. In addition, the marginal productivity of fertilizer declines at

FIGURE 6. Sensitivity of marginal benefit-cost ratio from fertilizer subsidy to alternative parameter values

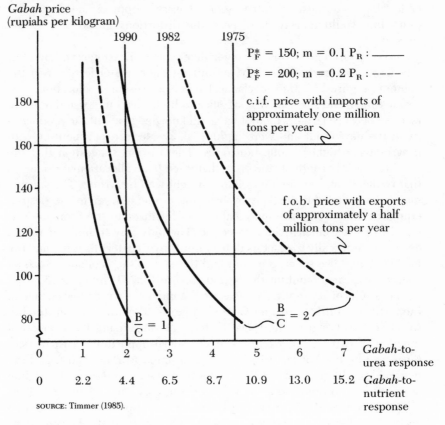

Gabah price
(rupiahs per kilogram)

$P_F^* = 150; m = 0.1 P_R$: ———

$P_F^* = 200; m = 0.2 P_R$: ----

c.i.f. price with imports of approximately one million tons per year

f.o.b. price with exports of approximately a half million tons per year

$\frac{B}{C} = 1$

$\frac{B}{C} = 2$

SOURCE: Timmer (1985).

higher levels of use, which are induced by lower fertilizer prices. The econometric results that supported this analysis showed not only that a highly significant exogenous time trend provided roughly one-half the impetus to increased fertilizer use but also that farmers were highly responsive to fertilizer prices directly, or to the *gabah*-to-fertilizer price ratio. Even at constant prices, the marginal productivity of fertilizer tends to decline over time as fertilizer use grows exogenously, but the rate of decline slows as the gap between actual and optimal use narrows.

At the margin, the fertilizer subsidy was socially profitable by a factor of 2 to 1 so long as Indonesia was importing about one million tons of rice per year and the marginal productivity of fertilizer was high (see figure 6). This was true even for the high cost assumptions shown by the dashed line in figure 6, and it remained true for the low cost assumptions at expected levels of fertilizer use in 1990. For a benefit-cost ratio of just 1.0, all reasonable coefficients of fertilizer productivity yielded social profits to a subsidy at the high import price.

The picture would change quite dramatically if a combination of agricultural investments and price policy brought Indonesia to a rice-exporting status (or if world rice prices collapsed for other reasons). At an f.o.b. price consistent with about one-half million tons of exports (and their corresponding impact on the world rice market), the fertilizer subsidy, for a wide range of assumptions about fertilizer productivity and full costs of increased use, was no longer socially profitable at the margin. For example, at the 1982 level of fertilizer productivity indicated in figure 6, a benefit-cost ratio of 2.0 was no longer available even for low-cost assumptions, and a benefit-cost ratio of 1.0 would be questionable by 1990 with high-cost assumptions. At the margin, the social profitability of the fertilizer subsidy thus depended very much on the circumstance. It had a high payoff when use of fertilizer was relatively low and Indonesia was importing rice at relatively high prices; it was a questionable investment of budgetary resources when exports lowered the price received for the rice produced by increased use of fertilizer.

Overall Effect of Input Subsidies. Input subsidies were widely used to improve the profitability of Indonesian agriculture. Some of these subsidies were sectorwide—for example, for fertilizer, pesticides, and irrigation water—and could be used on any crop. The subsidy on development and distribution of high-yielding seeds was specific to the commodity. Most of the subsidies were designed to increase rice output, and any spillover to corn, cassava, or other food crops was accidental. The input subsidies no doubt significantly affected the profitability of growing rice and perhaps corn.

Figures 1 and 2 depict rice and corn prices relative to border and floor support prices, but they do not show how these prices had changed relative to the prices of all goods and services in the economy. When deflated by the Jakarta-based consumer price index, the prices of rice, corn, and cassava all declined between 1968 and 1983. Even if the high prices in 1968 were removed as an aberration caused by the previous inflationary episode, real prices of rice remained stable at best during the rest of the period, and the declines in corn and cassava prices remained significant. For the period from 1969–70 to 1982–83, real wholesale prices for rice, corn, and cassava had a downward trend of 0.3 percent, 1.1 percent, and 1.1 percent per year, respectively. The deflated floor price of rice, however, improved slightly over this period, by 0.2 percent per year, which confirms that from 1969 real prices of rice remained approximately constant. Heavy subsidies for inputs were one important vehicle for maintaining the profitability of food crop cultivation in the face of such trends in real prices.

The relative success of the production efforts was at least partially in proportion to the degree to which the input subsidies could be utilized by producers of the individual commodities and to movements in their real prices. Over the 1969–83 period, output of rice and corn—crops that benefited substantially from input subsidies—grew by 4.9 percent and 5.3 percent per year, respectively.[12] The relatively faster growth of corn production during this period is a bit of a puzzle. Increasing commercialization and better market integration caused by more regular domestic demand from the livestock feed industry seem to account for much of the increase (Mink, 1987b; Timmer, 1987c). Very little fertilizer was used on cassava, and so the fertilizer subsidy would affect the profitability of cassava cultivation only slightly. Cassava output grew just 0.7 percent per year. Another factor contributing to these differences in output growth was the introduction of new technologies for corn and rice, but not for cassava. Rice also benefited from large-scale investments in irrigation.

The Impact of Macroeconomic and Trade Policy on the Food Sector

Indonesia's macroeconomic and trade policies reflect a curious blend of liberal market approaches and high tariff and quota barriers for most industrial products. Although efforts were made since 1980 to privatize the management of the many state-owned trading and industrial companies, ownership and the boards of directors were still in public hands in the mid-1980s. From the point of view of the food sector, three aspects of these policies are crucial: the impact of trade policy on the costs of agricultural inputs and rural household purchases from the urban sector; the net result of foreign exchange rate policy directly, and trade policy indirectly, on the effective exchange rate; and the impact of other macro prices, especially interest rates, on decisions about choice of technique in both the rural and urban sectors. The important role of budgetary and fiscal policy as they affect investments in agriculture has already been noted; it is a parallel topic to the impact of price policy, which cannot be treated in depth in this paper.[13] The impact of inflation, the last important macroeconomic variable, is felt primarily through the effective exchange rate.

Trade Policy. Roughly speaking, Indonesia's macro prices have been determined by a market orientation that reflected basic scarcity values for capital, labor, and foreign exchange. This approach has been consistently advocated by the Western-trained economists who have held key cabinet

---

12. The growth rate for corn was calculated from 1970–71 to 1980–81 using adjusted production data derived from the BULOG-Stanford Corn Project (see Mink, 1987b).

13. The comprehensive topic of macroeconomic and trade policy has been treated in detail by Dorosh (1986).

positions in the New Order government since 1968. Trade policy, on the other hand, has consistently been determined by a more nationalistic force within the cabinet, which has wished to pursue a path of import substitution and self-sufficiency, even at high costs, in a broad range of industrial products. The accommodation of both approaches under President Suharto's role as final arbiter of cabinet disputes on policy produced the curious blend of policies that seemed to tug the economy in opposite directions simultaneously, often to the considerable confusion of private and foreign investors. The balance between market forces and statism at the level of central policy has always been delicate. Profound implications for the direction of macroeconomic policy have been read into every cabinet appointment. Divining the ascendancy or decline of key individuals and the approaches they espouse has been a minor industry in Jakarta; the profitability of individual factories, of entire industries, and of the urban as opposed to the rural, sector depends critically on which approach is implemented.[14]

The mechanisms by which these key economic strategy choices ultimately affect the profitability of food crop production are complicated and only roughly understood. When domestic industry was protected and high cost, most industrial inputs into the agricultural sector were also high cost. An exception, however, has been fertilizer, the most important industrial input into agriculture. Indonesian factories using domestic natural gas have produced nearly all the nitrogen fertilizer (mostly urea) used by farmers. The plants tended to embody modern technology and were well managed; their costs of production were competitive with most producers in other countries except in periods of surplus supplies when the marginal costs of Arab Gulf producers were below those of all other suppliers. But no matter what the real costs of production were, fertilizer was heavily subsidized since the mid-1970s. This key industrial input was not responsible for any deterioration in the rural-urban terms of trade, and a similar story held for petroleum products until the mid-1980s.

Virtually every other rural input, however, had its costs raised directly or indirectly. Tools and implements, for example, were made from high-cost iron and steel. Diesel engines from domestic manufacturers cost twice their import cost; for some models there was negative value added in domestic assembly. Although this would seem to be impossible, the knocked-down kits of imported parts indeed cost more than the assembled engines themselves because of high-volume manufacturing efficiencies in Japanese factories. Trucks, the mainstay of the rural marketing sector, have been heavily protected by high tariffs.

The high cost of manufactured consumer goods also weighed against

14. Publication of a series of articles in the *Wall Street Journal* in early December 1986 revealed how sensitive these matters are and how important the debate is over trade policy: these issues of the newspaper were banned in Indonesia.

the rural sector, as would be expected unless it shared equally in the protection afforded industry. At least for the three commodities of primary concern here, such protection was clearly not the case for most of the period under analysis. The rice sector received significant protection only after 1984, and cassava and corn have traditionally been exported without subsidy even when the exchange rate was somewhat overvalued. In 1973 and 1974, the Ministry of Trade banned exports of cassava and corn to keep their domestic prices below world levels. For most of the 1968–84 period, the food crop sector received negative protection; the only significant exception was soybeans, whose domestic price has been kept well above the world price since the late 1970s.[15]

In net, trade policy provided high protection to the industrial sector and negative protection to agriculture, thus biasing the rural-urban terms of trade against the rural economy. While input subsidies compensated partially for this direct antirural bias, and rice prices in particular were held more or less constant in real terms after 1969, the overall terms of trade declined by 2.3 percent per year from 1970 to 1983, thus putting pressure on rural incomes and reducing incentives to increase output. Where new, low-cost technology was available, or price supports for specific commodities meshed with input subsidies, incentives faced by farmers were substantially positive. More neglected crops, such as cassava, did not fare as well. Hence the overall direct impact of trade policy on agriculture was negative; its indirect impact through the equilibrium value of the foreign exchange rate was probably just as negative.

Foreign Exchange Rate. The foreign exchange rate is the most important macro price influencing the profitability of agricultural production specifically and the health of the rural economy generally. From April 1970 until the devaluation of November 1978, Indonesia maintained a fixed exchange rate that was devalued as necessary (in August 1971) to maintain equilibrium in the balance of payments. After 1978, the government allowed the rate to float in a highly controlled manner. Major devaluations were announced in March 1983 and again in October 1986 when oil prices fell. The rate floated in a controlled manner in the interim periods. Market forces clearly influence the value of the rupiah, especially by determining the pressures on the rate of depreciation via the float, but macro policymakers also set the level from which the market can exert its influence. Most devaluations and the rate of float have been determined by basic market forces, but the 1978 devaluation came as a complete surprise to the market and is seen as one of the first and clearest applications of "exchange

15. Sugar is another important exception. In the mid-1980s prices of sugar in Indonesia were roughly comparable with those in the United States, about four to five times the world price.

FIGURE 7. Structure of relationships among agricultural share in GDP, oil import share, and macroeconomic variables

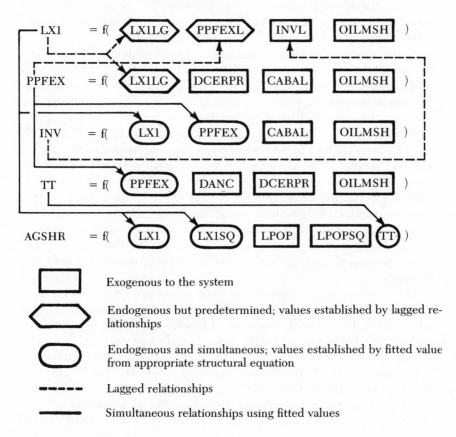

		Exogenous to the system
		Endogenous but predetermined; values established by lagged relationships
		Endogenous and simultaneous; values established by fitted value from appropriate structural equation
		Lagged relationships
		Simultaneous relationships using fitted values

SOURCE: Timmer (1984), p. 58.

rate protection" on behalf of the sectors lagging in adjustment to high oil prices (Warr, 1984).

An empirical study of the relationship among oil prices, the foreign exchange rate, and the rural-urban terms of trade in Indonesia provides direct evidence of the importance of macro price policy to agriculture (Timmer, 1984). This study uses a Chenery-Syrquin-type model to explain the declining share of agriculture in gross domestic product from 1960 to 1980 as a function of incomes per capita and country size for a sample of seven Asia-Pacific countries, including Indonesia. As shown in figure 7, the model has separate equations to explain income per capita (LX1), the purchasing power foreign exchange rate (PPFEX), investment (INV), and the rural-urban terms of trade (TT). The predicted value of the terms of trade is then added to the basic Chenery-Syrquin model explaining the share for the agricultural sector in GDP (AGSHR) to see if relative prices affected the process of structural change. The results provided powerful confirmation of this impact.

In the model, the rural-urban terms of trade—defined as the GDP deflator of the agricultural sector divided by the GDP deflator for the rest of the economy—are determined by five exogenous variables in addition to commodity-specific price and trade policy: the foreign exchange rate (lagged), the relative share of oil exports or imports in GDP (OILMSH), the current account balance as a share of GDP (CABAL), world prices for cereal grains (DCERPR), and world prices for noncereal agricultural commodities (DANC). The impact of changes in the rural-urban terms of trade on the agricultural sector can be analyzed in several ways. In the model the impact was captured via influence on the share of agriculture in gross domestic product, holding incomes per capita and population size (LPOP) constant. This influence was large and robust: an increase of one standard deviation in the rural-urban terms of trade raised the share of agriculture by 10 percent (for example, from 30 to 33 percent); other things held constant.

The structure of the model itself also contains important lessons about the role of macro prices in agricultural growth and the mechanisms by which this role is felt. The share of oil imports or exports is a significant variable in nearly all aspects of the model. For Indonesia, an oil exporter, a rise in oil prices led to more rapid income growth, larger investment, an appreciation of the real exchange rate, and a deterioration in the rural-urban terms of trade. The model shows how growth in agriculture might be stopped altogether in oil-exporting countries if differential inflation (relative to that of the United States) was combined with a fixed nominal exchange rate.

The model fit the Indonesian experience particularly well and explained the concerns of macro policy makers in 1978 over the deteriorating health of the rural economy. The combination of stagnant growth in the overall agricultural sector with problems of pests and disease in the rice economy led to a major reappraisal of food policy (Afiff, Falcon, and Timmer, 1980). The result was a threefold strategic redirection: new efforts to diversify the food economy away from rice; new incentives for rice producers through a higher (nominal) floor price and subsidized fertilizer price; and a major shift in macro prices via the 50 percent devaluation of the rupiah in November 1978, at a time when many observers felt a revaluation might be announced because of rising foreign exchange reserves.[16]

16. See Gillis et al. (1983), especially pp. 629–637, for a more complete description of this episode.

Although this modeling approach to determining the impact of changes in the rural-urban terms of trade on the agricultural sector has the advantage of generating many broad lessons about the factors affecting structural change, it does miss some of the specificity of the Indonesian experience. Fortunately, it is also possible to measure the impact of the terms of trade on agricultural growth directly. While this is somewhat more difficult because of all the additional factors influencing agricultural output, figure 8 shows how agricultural gross domestic product at constant prices compared with the rural-urban terms of trade in Indonesia from 1968 to 1983.

The rapid rise in agricultural GDP and the uneven but dramatic fall in the terms of trade are obvious, but more subtle patterns can also be discerned. In figure 9, the 1969 to 1983 time period is divided into three subperiods when the *rate of growth* in agricultural GDP varied substantially: 8.2 percent per year between 1969 and 1974; 4.3 percent per year between 1978 and 1983; and only 0.8 percent per year between 1975 and 1977. These growth rates were matched against the average rural-urban terms of trade for the same subperiods, but lagged one year (to allow agricultural producers time to respond to changed incentives). Although figure 9 has only three observations, the positive response of agricultural growth to the terms of trade is fairly clear. [17]

Other Macro Prices. Macro prices other than the foreign exchange rate have had relatively little distorting effect on agriculture. The availability of subsidized credit in the rice intensification program (BIMAS) probably helped spur fertilizer demand, but as noted, such increased demand appeared to reduce distortions rather than increase them. The widespread availability of cheap unskilled labor has prevented agricultural mechanization, even though the Asian Development Bank made some subsidized credit available for this purpose. Consequently, the major influence of macro prices on agricultural output has been through the foreign exchange rate, and this influence has been dramatic indeed.

Because of the large increases in oil prices in the 1970s, Indonesia's rural economy was severely buffeted by declining terms of trade. Price policy for rice, the fertilizer subsidy, and a more rural-oriented macro policy after 1978 helped overcome the pressures exerted by these exogenous changes

17. A regression model using annual data with the same specification and lags showed a positive and significant coefficient for the impact of the terms of trade on agricultural growth. A 10 percent change in the terms of trade led to a change in the agricultural growth rate of three percentage points. Since the fitted trend growth rate in agricultural GDP for the entire period was 4.58 percent per year, the large relative influence of the terms of trade is obvious. The equation in which this result was obtained also had a marginally significant time trend of 0.7 percent per year, implying that actions taken to alleviate the declining terms of trade were having an increasingly positive effect on agricultural growth. An equation without time had a terms of trade coefficient less than one-half as large as the first equation, and the coefficient had only marginal significance.

FIGURE 8. Rural–urban terms of trade and agricultural GDP

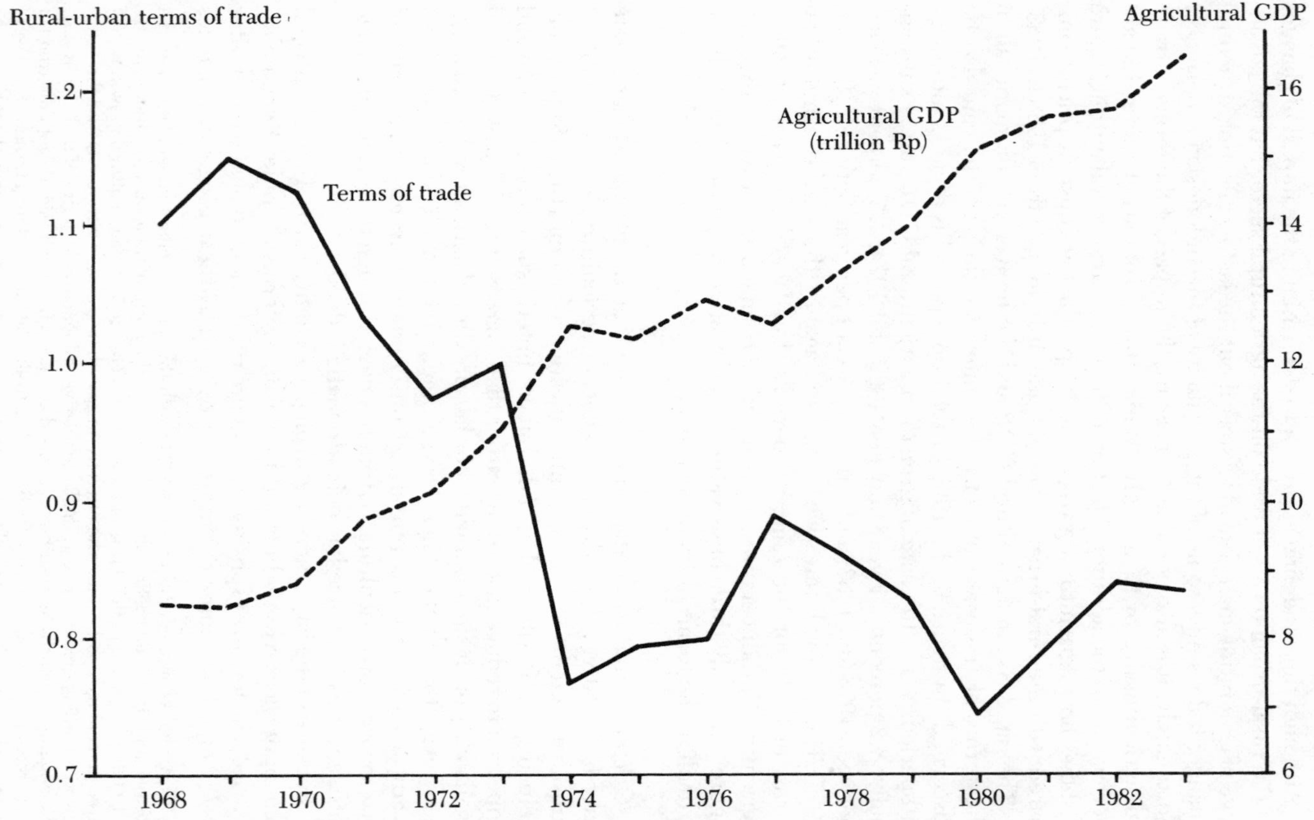

SOURCE: Data from Government of Indonesia, Central Bureau of Statistics, *Statistical Pocketbook*, various issues.

FIGURE 9. Relationship between agricultural growth rates and rural-urban terms of trade, selected periods

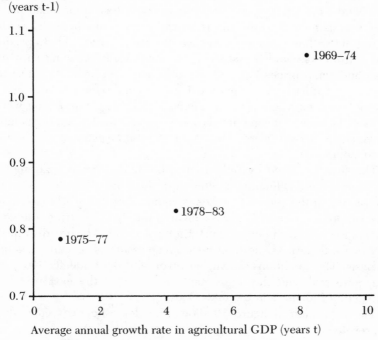

Average terms of trade
(years t-1)

Average annual growth rate in agricultural GDP (years t)

SOURCE: Calculated from data in Figure 8.

on Indonesia's macro economy. The lessons learned from these experiences have not been painless, but the pragmatic search for policies that improved rural welfare by countering the negative effects of other policies, and doing so without imposing high costs on industrial development, paid off in the early 1980s in the form of a highly dynamic rural and urban economy. The experience is especially noteworthy when compared with the experience of other oil exporters such as Mexico and Nigeria. Their management of oil revenues and macro policy led to steep declines in the health of their rural economies, in direct contrast to the Indonesian experience (Gillis et al., 1983).

Tradeoffs in Price Policy

Policy makers in all countries face four basic dilemmas over food pricing, and each involves setting relative prices: crop prices to producers relative to food prices for consumers; domestic food prices relative to unstable world prices; input prices relative to output prices; and rural prices (agricultural goods) relative to urban prices (industrial goods). There is some overlap among these four issues, but they are sufficiently discrete, with independent policy instruments available for intervention, that they provide a basis for separate analysis. None of the four dilemmas would be significant without a budgetary constraint; the interests of both producers and consumers could be satisfied, for example, by keeping farm prices high and retail prices low and by subsidizing the marketing margin in between. Similarly, each pricing issue is conditioned to an important extent by the macroeconomic and general political environment, whether it takes the form of income levels of consumers, the foreign exchange rate at which rural exports are valued, agricultural investments, or industrial trade policy.

The situation faced by Indonesia in the mid-1980s as it attempted to cope with these dilemmas is illustrated in figure 10, which shows the interaction of the Indonesian rice economy with the world rice market. The supply and demand curves shown in the figure illustrate the generic class of issues facing policy makers; they are meant to be broadly representative of Indonesian conditions rather than results of specific econometric analysis. The conditions shown, however, and the tradeoffs they present are quite real, and the figure captures many of the food price issues debated in Indonesia in the mid-1980s.

The right side of figure 10 shows the domestic rice economy. The aggregate demand curve for rice has an elasticity of -0.3, and two alternative aggregate supply curves have elasticities of 0.1.[18] These price elasticities represent the outcome of decisions by producers and consumers in the short run, perhaps within a time horizon of one year. The **bold** supply curve indicates supply conditions with the fertilizer subsidy; the lightly drawn supply curve indicates supply conditions with the fertilizer subsidy removed, thus raising the costs of production for rice farmers. Rice self-sufficiency would be reached at roughly $280 per ton with the fertilizer subsidy and at $330 per ton without it.[19]

18. Because the supply and demand curves are linear, these elasticities hold only at the initial point of intersection, and then only approximately. The elasticities themselves are based on a synthesis of a wide array of empirical studies rather than on any one equation.

19. These calculations hold many things constant. In particular, all prices are quoted in dollars per ton whether they are domestic or world market prices, which implies a fixed exchange rate no matter what happens to levels of rice imports or exports. When rice trade is small relative to domestic production and oil export revenues are robust, such an assumption is probably within the margin of error of the example. When such conditions do not hold, general-equilibrium feedback effects on the exchange rate are likely. In addition, technology, population, incomes, and so on are being held constant so that the supply and demand curves remain stationary. Lastly, other actors in the world rice market are assumed to continue their existing export and import policies rather than react to changes in Indonesian rice trade with their own strategic initiatives.

FIGURE 10. The world rice market as seen by Indonesia, circa 1984

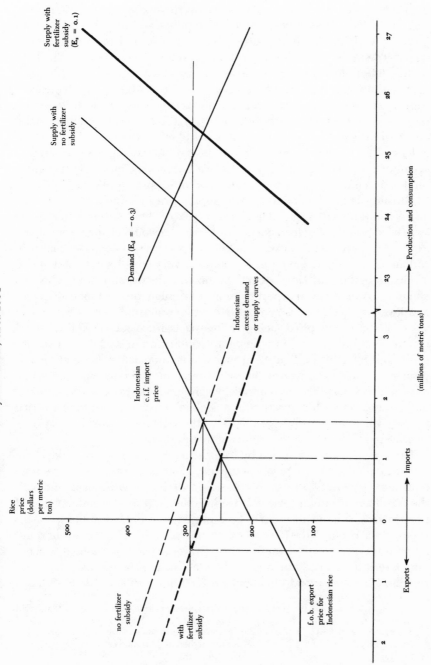

SOURCE: Reprinted from Timmer (1986b), p. 79. Copyright © 1986 by Cornell University. Used by permission of the publisher, Cornell University Press.

The left side of figure 10 shows the world rice market as seen from Indonesia. The gap between domestic supplies and demand is reflected onto the world market in the form of an excess demand and supply curve, which crosses the export-import axis at the self-sufficiency price. The **bold** dashed line reflects excess supply and demand conditions with the fertilizer subsidy; the light dashed line, without it. These alternative excess supply and demand curves depend on prices facing *domestic* decision makers, no matter what the world price is. If Indonesia maintains a price policy in the short run independent of world market prices, as it has since at least 1968, then price formation in the two markets must be treated as separate but linked issues. The link is via Indonesia's impact on the world market as a function of its import demand or export supply.

This impact is depicted as a rising supply price for Indonesian imports and a falling export price. There is a break of about $30 per ton at the switch from importing to exporting as Indonesia would change from facing a c.i.f. delivered import price to an f.o.b. export price. Given the quality of Indonesia's rice available for export and the very low elasticity of demand for rice from the world market in the short run, the export price declines to about $120 per ton at an export volume of 1 million tons and then stabilizes at a level at which rice is competitive with corn as a livestock feed. The slope of the world price facing Indonesia is thus not zero, the "small country" assumption used in most international trade models, but significantly positive. In the figure, an increase in Indonesia's demand for imports of 1 million tons raises the world price by $50 per ton. The switch between 1980 and 1985 from importing 2 million tons to exporting one-half million tons could thus account for a decline of $125 per ton in world rice prices, which is roughly equivalent to the decline in world rice prices *relative to world wheat prices* during that period.[20]

The pricing dilemmas faced by Indonesia can now be seen starkly. The starting point, reflecting policy in the mid-1980s, was a domestic rice price equivalent to about $300 per ton. As figure 10 shows, at this price and with the fertilizer subsidy in place, a surplus of about one-half million tons of rice existed. This surplus had to be dumped onto the world market at an export price of only $150 per ton, and thus a subsidy of $150 per ton would be required to dispose of the surplus. This outcome is a reasonably accurate description of the situation in 1985–86, before the devaluation of the rupiah in October 1986 from about Rp 1100 to Rp 1650 per U.S. dollar.

---

20. This can be checked by the following back-of-the-envelope calculation: in 1980 world rice prices averaged about $430 per ton, whereas wheat prices were $170 per ton, a ratio of 2.5:1. In 1985, rice prices were about $220 per ton and wheat prices were $130 per ton, a ratio of only 1.7:1. If rice prices had been $125 per ton higher (and this had caused wheat prices to be $10 higher), the ratio would have been 2.5:1, the same as in 1980. This calculation abstracts from long-run structural changes in competitiveness of wheat relative to rice, whether from changing technologies or demand patterns.

Such an outcome was unsatisfactory for at least two reasons: fertilizer subsidies were paid to induce farmers to grow rice that had no domestic use, and the rice was then exported at a further subsidy. What were the alternatives? A base case might start without any interventions—no rice price policy and no fertilizer subsidy. With these assumptions, the world market and the Indonesian market clear at the same price of about $280 per ton, and Indonesia imports 1.6 million tons of rice. This "no intervention" case is very revealing even in the partial-equilibrium version shown in figure 10. Self-sufficiency in rice, the long-sought goal of Indonesian rice policy, depends crucially on two pricing interventions—the fertilizer subsidy and the protection of rice farmers from lower world prices. Keeping the fertilizer subsidy, while allowing free trade in rice, would reduce imports to just 1 million tons a year and lower the world (and domestic) price to $250 per ton.

Despite the high budgetary costs of rice price policy in the mid-1980s, it is easy to understand how it came about and why the policy was difficult to change. Any normative implications of the "pure" border pricing paradigm were undermined by the demonstrated social profitability of the fertilizer subsidy when Indonesia was a rice importer and by the sharp instability in rice prices in world markets. Price policy thus had to be based on a pragmatic empirical analysis of perceived costs and benefits to alternative interventions rather than on a simplistic market ideology. This obviously complicates matters. In each of the four major areas of pricing dilemmas, the costs and benefits of different approaches are hard to identify clearly, much less measure accurately enough that policy makers can use the results with confidence in a cabinet debate. What follows is a rough attempt to consider the costs and benefits relevant to each of the four pricing dilemmas.

As figure 1 indicates, since 1974 the difference between nominal prices of rice in the world market and Indonesian prices has narrowed. Since real prices of rice in Indonesia have remained roughly constant since 1969, this convergence of prices implies a fall in world prices to Indonesian levels rather than a rise in Indonesian prices to world levels. By the mid-1980s, world prices had in fact plummeted to less than $200 per ton from their peak of nearly $500 per ton in 1982, a degree of instability that perhaps confirmed Indonesia's judgment (since the mid-1970s) not to follow world prices very closely. Rice producers were *relatively* better off in 1986 compared with the world market price than they were in 1974 or 1982, but their rice sales earned them no more income in real terms relative to other *domestic* opportunities. Most additional incentives since 1978 to grow rice came from input subsidies, especially for fertilizer.

Because of the constant real price of rice, consumers were no worse off than before. If their incomes were higher, they were better off. But many poor consumers might not have had higher incomes and were inadequately fed in the mid-1970s. How did price policy affect them? The two primary staples of the very poor, cassava and corn, became cheaper over time, thus widening the opportunity of poor consumers to expand their consumption of these food sources of last resort. Perhaps more important, the price indicator for average-quality rice used in the analysis of price changes masked an important structural shift in the Indonesian rice market since the mid-1970s—the significant increase in the array of qualities available in most retail markets.

These range from the *beras pegawi* found in large urban markets—the rice received from BULOG by civil servants and traded for higher-quality rice on a 2:1 or even 3:1 basis—to *beras ciandjur*, the long-grain, scented traditional variety grown in parts of West Java, which often sells for twice the price of the average-quality rice that is used as an indicator by the Bureau of Statistics and BULOG. Consequently, in many markets one quality of rice is available for less than one-half the price of the average-quality rice, and other qualities for more than double the price. The availability of the low-quality rice in particular had significant welfare implications for the poor. The social prestige associated with eating rice as a staple could be garnered at a cost nearly as low as corn or cassava.

It is easy to see that the fertilizer subsidy in 1986 was somewhat too large, that irrigation water cost too little, and that pesticides should have priced at least at their full economic cost. Thus input subsidies should have been reduced. But by how much? Analysis conducted late in 1985 and early in 1986 suggested that the Indonesian rice economy was delicately balanced, with the gap between production and consumption capable of shifting over time toward large imports or exports in the face of relatively modest changes in fertilizer prices (Timmer, 1986a). What gave Indonesian policy makers pause in altering the policy was the lack of solid answers to a series of questions about the dynamics of the rice economy: future growth in rice consumption, the direction of future trends in world rice prices, and the extent of built-in momentum in rice production due to past investments in irrigation and varietal research. Even apart from concerns over farmer welfare at a time when BULOG was unable to defend the floor price and over the weakness of the rest of the economy due to falling oil revenues, a cautious approach to raising fertilizer prices simply revealed an incremental approach to finding out how the economy responds to policy initiatives.

From the point of view of the food sector, the most troublesome issue facing Indonesian policy makers in early 1986 was the rural-urban terms of trade. Although all the issues already discussed contribute to the value of this indicator, broader strategic decisions dominate its determination. In particular, trade orientation for the manufacturing sector, oil exports, and exchange rate policy are the three main factors that ultimately determine the relative profitability of production and incomes in rural areas. Since three-quarters of Indonesia's population live in rural areas and are directly or indirectly dependent on the health of the rural economy for their well-being, how these three factors work out is crucial to the standard of living for the vast majority of Indonesians.

Policy makers could do relatively little about oil prices, but expanding the volume of oil exports might recoup some lost oil revenues. With a strong determination to maintain a competitive exchange rate, policy makers allowed the rupiah to follow the dollar down in value since early 1985 and then devalued it sharply in October 1986 because of the massive loss in export earnings due to price declines for oil and other primary commodities. One intent of the devaluation was to stimulate rural incomes and spur additional exports, especially for crops such as cassava and corn, which were within the c.i.f.-f.o.b. nontradable band. In addition, the higher price for foreign exchange would reduce imports through market pressures, thus allowing the government to rely less on tariffs and quotas as a way of bringing balance to the current account.

This approach permits a less protective approach to manufactures; historically, industrial protection seems to have been an important factor in turning the terms of trade against the rural sector. A "state-managed" approach to restoring balance in the trade account, rather than a "market-induced" approach, would place a heavy burden on the rural economy, and clearly there was a danger that much of the dynamism of the 1978–85 period might be stifled. In addition, the historical record indicates that protection has not turned the Indonesian industrial sector into an alternative "engine of growth," and the prospect that such a trade strategy might prevail was very worrisome indeed.

The Role of Prices

What has been the overall role of prices in the development of Indonesia's food crops? Because Indonesia has intervened into price formation for crops, agricultural inputs, and macro prices, the issue is whether such interventions created distortions in the allocation of economic resources, thus slowing growth, or whether the interventions successfully removed existing distortions in the economy, thus permitting a more efficient allocation of resources and faster growth in output. Implicit in framing the question this way is the argument that price interventions *alone* do not necessarily create a distortion in resource allocation. The intervention might have the effect of reducing a distortion in resource use caused by another factor—lack of knowledge or risk aversion, for example. The potential distorting effect of price interventions must be judged only empirically, not on a priori grounds (see Timmer, 1986b).

Such an empirical judgment of the overall impact of price policy is made at three levels. The first is the role of price policy for individual commodities in the growth in output of those commodities. If the analysis is restricted to the impact of output prices per se, their role was relatively modest simply because the prices themselves changed in real terms only slightly over the period under investigation (see appendix table A). At the same time, output of rice and corn increased fairly dramatically, and cassava output increased slightly. But if commodity prices are measured relative to the fertilizer price, the contribution of commodity-specific price policy to growth in output could have been quite significant, especially for rice and corn.

For rice, the most important crop in the entire rural economy, roughly one-half the rate of growth of 5 percent from 1968 to 1984 is attributable to improved financial incentives generated by the massive fertilizer subsidy. Growth in output for corn also benefited to some extent from this subsidy, but total use of fertilizer on corn remained small relative to its use on rice. Cassava output seems to have been little affected directly by the fertilizer subsidy, although a negative relative effect may have been felt through the improved profitability of more fertilizer-intensive crops such as rice, corn, and vegetables.

The second level of price impact is sectoral. How did the terms of trade between the rural and urban sector contribute to growth in output of food crops? These terms of trade are partially composed of individual commodity prices, but they also include the influence of the entire range of prices of farm inputs, consumption items in rural household budgets, and prices other than those of rice, corn, and cassava. Such a broad measure of the profitability of rural activities is thus determined by agricultural price policy directly and by a host of other, more macro, factors indirectly. Most important of these is the foreign exchange rate, which in Indonesia was heavily influenced by petroleum prices.

Indonesia's experience with the impact of booming oil revenues on its agricultural sector is now recognized as a classic case of Dutch Disease. The "treatment" administered in 1978, a dose of exchange rate protection, almost certainly explains much of the divergent path of agriculture in Indonesia compared with the experience of Nigeria or Mexico (Corden and Warr, 1981; Warr, 1984; Gillis et al., 1983; and Timmer, 1984). The specific concern for rural profitability and incomes reflected in macroeconomic decision making after 1978 thus complemented (and incorporated) the commodity-specific pricing policies.

The third level of impact of prices on food crop development is at the macroeconomic level. How do interventions into macro prices and other key signals affect decision makers who allocate resources? Part of their impact is picked up directly in the rural-urban terms of trade and their effect on sectoral output, but the dynamic allocative efficiency of the entire macro economy has an additional impact on agriculture through the growth linkages first spelled out by Johnston and Mellor (1961). If interventions create distortions that slow the growth of total economic output, they will also tend to impede the development of these linkages and hence have a doubly dramatic effect on agricultural growth.

Using data from the *World Development Report 1983*, Dapice carried out an extremely interesting, if crude, test of the impact the overall level of price distortion in an economy has on agricultural growth. His results, which show a strong inverse relationship between distortion and growth in agricultural output, are striking and surprisingly robust given the limited sample (thirty countries, with eight in sub-Saharan Africa) and the obvious difficulty in specifying a single measure of price distortion that would be applicable to all thirty countries.[21]

In the Dapice model, the rate of growth in agricultural output is a function of independent variables including population growth, a regional dummy, and the distortion index. The distortion index is meant to capture the impact of "bad" pricing policies. It ranges from a low of 1.14 for Malawi to a high of 2.86 for Ghana; the Indonesian value of 1.86 is roughly in the middle of the sample. A dramatic policy shift from "bad" to "good" might realistically involve a change in the distortion index of one full point. Consequently, the highly significant negative coefficient of about 2.4 attached to this distortion index implies that the difference between bad and good economic policy accounts for 2.4 percentage points of agricultural growth per year. Since the average agricultural growth rate for the entire sample of countries was only 2.9 percent per year, price distortions clearly play a major role in explaining differential rates of agricultural growth.[22]

21. Distortions in the World Bank analysis were measured in a fairly crude and impressionistic fashion. Price distortions in foreign exchange pricing were measured for the exchange rate, degree of protection of manufacturing, and protection or taxation of agriculture. Distortions in factor pricing were measured for capital and labor prices. Distortions in product prices were measured for power tariffs and through the rate of inflation. All of these elements were weighted equally into a three-step measure of overall price distortions—high, medium, and low—which took on the value of 3, 2, and 1, respectively, in the statistical analysis. In all cases, deviations from free-market prices were recorded as distortions.

22. A simple equation with the rate of growth in agricultural output from 1970 to 1982 as the dependent variable, and with population growth, the distortion index, and a dummy for the sub-Saharan African countries as independent variables indicated that about 80 percent of population growth is directly reflected in aggregate agricultural growth. When the equation is then specified in per capita terms, a dummy variable equal to one when population growth rates are in excess of 2.5 percent per year has a negative coefficient of about 0.7, which is marginally significant even in the presence of the other two variables. Holding all other variables constant, the dummy variable for sub-Saharan African countries is consistently

The Indonesian economy in the mid-1960s must have been among the worst distorted in recent comparative history, perhaps rivaling the 2.86 distortion index measured for Ghana during the mid-1970s. This starting point implies that Indonesia's economic policies within these definitions improved by a full point, from 2.86 to 1.86, thus contributing perhaps 2.4 percentage points per year to the agricultural growth rate over this period. (Indonesia averaged 3.8 percent per year during the time period of the World Bank sample and 4.6 percent per year from 1968 to 1983.) Some of this impact is transmitted through improved commodity price policy and in better rural-urban terms of trade, and it would be double counting to add this entire 2.4 percent to the 2–3 percent accounted for by those price factors in order to find the total contribution of price policy at all three levels.[23] But there was also likely to have been some additional contribution from the vastly improved macro and trade policy environment. The implication is that micro and sectoral projects and programs, independently of both the specific and overall price environment, can explain relatively little of aggregate growth performance for food crops.

Indonesia's story of food crops has a conclusion identical to that reached in 1973 with respect to choice of technique in rice milling on Java: " 'Getting prices right' is not the end of economic development, but 'getting prices wrong' frequently is" (Timmer, 1973, p. 76). For agricultural projects and programs to be effective in generating sustained growth in output, they must be inserted into a favorable agricultural and macro price environment. There is nothing in the Indonesian record to suggest, however, that this favorable price environment *alone* generates a dynamic rural economy. For this, an active research and investment program on behalf of agricultural producers (and consumers) is also needed. But the Indonesian evidence is quite powerful in suggesting that there is little return to such programs for research and investment in the absence of a favorable price environment. Even more powerful, perhaps, is the implication that the favorable price environment itself is defined to a large extent by macro price policies and not just by commodity and sectoral price policies. Agricultural development is thus the joint responsibility of macroeconomic policy makers and the Ministry of Agriculture.

---

negative and significant with a coefficient in the range of 1.0 to 1.4, thus confirming that Africa's poor performance in agricultural growth stems from more than just bad policies.

23. It should be noted, however, that in the World Bank definition of distortions the fertilizer subsidy in Indonesia would count as a distortion. In fact, the subsidy helped to remove a distortion (the failure of farmers to equate the marginal cost of fertilizer with its marginal revenue due to a lack of knowledge and the private risk of losing their investment), as the empirical evidence presented in Timmer (1985) indicates.

References

Afiff, Saleh, and C. Peter Timmer. 1971. "Rice Policy in Indonesia." *Food Research Institute Studies in Agricultural Economics, Trade, and Development* 10(26): 131–59.

Afiff, Saleh, Walter P. Falcon, and C. Peter Timmer. 1980. "Elements of a Food and Nutrition Policy in Indonesia." In Gustav Papanek, ed., *The Economy of Indonesia*, 406–28. New York: Praeger.

Anderson, Kym, and Yujiro Hayami, with associates. 1986. *The Political Economy of Agricultural Protection: East Asia in International Perspective*. London: Allen & Unwin.

Badan Urusan Logistik (BULOG). 1971. *Seperempat Abad Bergulat dengan Butir-butir Beras*. (A quarter century's struggle with rice.) Jakarta.

Chenery, Hollis B., and Moise Syrquin. 1975. *Patterns of Development, 1950–1970*. London: Oxford University Press.

Corden, W. M., and Peter G. Warr. 1981. "The Petroleum Boom and Exchange Rate Policy in Indonesia." *Ekonomi dan Keuangan Indonesia* (Economics and finance in Indonesia) 29(3): 335–59.

Dorosh, Paul A. 1986. "Macroeconomic Policy and Agriculture in Indonesia." Dissertation, Stanford University.

———. 1987. "International Trade in Corn." In C. Peter Timmer, ed., *The Corn Economy of Indonesia*, 235–250. Ithaca: Cornell University Press.

Falcon, Walter P., and Eric A. Monke. 1979–80. "International Trade in Rice." *Food Research Institute Studies* 17(3): 279–306.

Falcon, Walter P., William O. Jones, Scott R. Pearson, and others. 1984. *The Cassava Economy of Java*. Stanford: Stanford University Press.

Gillis, S. Malcolm, Dwight H. Perkins, Michael Roemer, and Donald R. Snodgrass. 1983. *Economics of Development*. New York: Norton.

Johnston, Bruce F., and John W. Mellor. 1961. "The Role of Agriculture in Economic Development." *American Economic Review* 51(4): 566–93.

Mears, Leon A. 1959. *Rice Marketing in the Republic of Indonesia*. Jakarta: Institute for Economic and Social Research, University of Indonesia.

———, and P. T. Pembangunan. 1981. *The New Rice Economy of Indonesia*. Yogyakarta: Gadjah Mada University Press.

Mink, Stephen D. 1987a. "Corn in the Livestock Economy." In C. Peter Timmer, ed., *The Corn Economy of Indonesia*, 142–174. Ithaca: Cornell University Press.

Mink, Stephen D., and Paul A. Dorosh. 1987b. "An Overview of Corn Production." In C. Peter Timmer, ed., *The Corn Economy of Indonesia*, 41–61. Ithaca: Cornell University Press.

Monteverde, Richard, and Stephen D. Mink. 1987. "Household Corn Consumption." In C. Peter Timmer, ed., *The Corn Economy of Indonesia*, 111–141. Ithaca: Cornell University Press.

Nelson, Gerald C. 1984. "Gaplek." In Walter P. Falcon et al., *The Cassava Economy of Java*, 110–135. Stanford: Stanford University Press.

Schwartz, Robert. 1986. "Trends in Agricultural Commodity Prices: An Exploration in Search of Optimal Predictors." Manuscript, Harvard Business School, December.

Siamwalla, Ammar, and Stephen Haykin. 1983. *The World Rice Market: Structure, Conduct, and Performance*. International Food Policy Research Institute Research Report no. 39. Washington, D.C.

Timmer, C. Peter. 1973. "Choice of Technique in Rice Milling on Java." *Bulletin of Indonesian Economic Studies* (Canberra) 9(2): 57–76.

——. 1974. "A Model of Rice Marketing Margins in Indonesia." *Food Research Institute Studies* 13(2): 145–167.

——. 1975. "The Political Economy of Rice in Asia: Indonesia." *Food Research Institute Studies* 14(3): 197–231.

——. 1984. "Energy and Structural Change in the Asia-Pacific Region: The Agricultural Sector." In Romeo M. Bautista and Seiji Naya, eds., *Energy and Structural Change in the Asia-Pacific Region: Papers and Proceedings of the Thirteenth Pacific Trade and Development Conference*, 51–72. Manila: Philippine Institute for Development Studies and the Asian Development Bank.

——. 1985. "The Role of Price Policy in Rice Production in Indonesia, 1968–1982." Harvard Institute for International Development Discussion Paper no. 196. Cambridge.

——. 1986a. "Rice Price Policy in Indonesia: 'Keeping Prices Right.' " Draft paper prepared for the Economic Development Institute of the World Bank Workshop on Agricultural Price Policy, April. Amsterdam.

——. 1986b. *Getting Prices Right: The Scope and Limits of Agricultural Price Policy.* Ithaca: Cornell University Press.

——, ed. 1987a. *The Corn Economy of Indonesia.* Ithaca: Cornell University Press.

——. 1987b. "Corn in Indonesia's Food Policy." In C. Peter Timmer, ed., *The Corn Economy of Indonesia*, 253–285. Ithaca: Cornell University Press.

——. 1987c. "Corn Marketing." In C. Peter Timmer, ed., *The Corn Economy of Indonesia*, 201–234. Ithaca: Cornell University Press.

——. 1988. "The Agricultural Transformation." In Hollis B. Chenery and T. N. Srinivasan, eds., *Handbook of Development Economics*. Amsterdam: North-Holland.

——, Walter P. Falcon, and Scott R. Pearson. 1983. *Food Policy Analysis.* Baltimore: Johns Hopkins University Press for the World Bank.

Unnevehr, Laurian J. 1984. "Transport Costs, Tariffs, and the Influence of World Markets on Indonesian Domestic Cassava Prices." *Bulletin of Indonesian Economic Studies* (Canberra) 20(1): 30–43.

Warr, Peter G. 1984. "Exchange Rate Protection in Indonesia." *Bulletin of Indonesian Economic Studies* (Canberra) 20(2): 53–89.

World Bank. 1983. *Indonesia: Policy Options and Strategies for Major Food Crops.* Washington, D.C.

APPENDIX TABLE A

Year	Consumer price index[a]	GDP deflator[a]	Terms of trade[b]	Real GDP, 1980 prices[a]	Agshare at current prices (percent)[a]	AgGDP (constant prices)	AgGDP at constant terms of trade
1968	14.96	11.34	1.102	18.49	51.00	9.43	8.56
1969	17.56	13.73	1.150	19.80	49.27	9.76	8.48
1970	19.72	15.84	1.127	21.09	47.16	9.95	8.83
1971	20.64	16.28	1.033	22.56	44.83	10.11	9.79
1972	21.93	18.49	0.975	24.69	40.25	9.94	10.19
1973	28.76	24.58	1.000	27.48	40.13	11.03	11.03
1974	40.40	36.21	0.769	29.58	32.66	9.66	12.56
1975	48.10	40.72	0.794	31.05	31.67	9.83	12.38
1976	57.63	46.61	0.800	33.19	31.11	10.33	12.91
1977	64.02	52.67	0.891	36.09	31.07	11.21	12.58
1978	69.22	58.44	0.862	38.93	29.48	11.48	13.31
1979	84.37	77.43	0.829	41.36	28.09	11.62	14.01
1980	100.00	100.00	0.747	45.45	24.84	11.29	15.11
1981	112.20	110.20	0.795	49.05	25.25	12.39	15.58
1982	122.90	118.90	0.841	50.15	26.27	13.17	15.67
1983	137.40	136.90	0.837	52.25	26.36	13.77	16.46
Average annual percent change 69–70 to 82–83	16.12	18.05	(2.32)	7.32	(4.55)	2.44	4.87

APPENDIX TABLE A (cont.)

Year	Rice price East Java[c] Rp/kg	Paddy floor price Rp/kg	Corn price East Java[c] Rp/kg	Cassava price East Java[c] Rp/kg	Farmgate urea price Rp/kg	Deflated rice price Rp/kg	Deflated paddy floor price Rp/kg	Deflated corn price Rp/kg	Deflated cassava price Rp/kg	Paddy floor price to urea price ratio
1968	41.20	23.00	16.70	12.80	40.00	275.40	153.74	111.63	85.56	0.58
1969	31.80	20.90	20.10	11.10	31.50	181.09	119.02	114.46	63.21	0.66
1970	38.70	18.00	19.60	14.20	26.60	196.25	91.28	99.39	72.01	0.68
1971	37.80	20.90	19.40	13.30	26.60	183.14	101.26	93.99	64.44	0.79
1972	47.40	20.90	26.30	19.10	26.40	216.14	95.30	119.93	87.10	0.79
1973	68.50	30.40	33.50	20.50	40.00	238.18	105.70	116.48	71.28	0.76
1974	75.10	41.80	44.60	20.20	60.00	185.89	103.47	110.40	50.00	0.70
1975	97.50	58.50	58.60	28.80	80.00	202.70	121.62	121.83	59.88	0.73
1976	121.40	68.50	70.90	50.20	70.00	210.65	118.86	123.03	87.11	0.98
1977	120.90	71.00	61.70	36.70	70.00	188.85	110.90	96.38	57.33	1.01
1978	127.90	75.00	64.40	23.30	70.00	184.77	108.35	93.04	33.66	1.07
1979	159.90	85.00	92.10	54.70	70.00	189.52	100.75	109.16	64.83	1.21
1980	183.40	105.00	103.30	59.10	70.00	183.40	105.00	103.30	59.10	1.50
1981	201.90	120.00	99.80	39.80	70.00	179.95	106.95	88.95	35.47	1.71
1982	227.30	135.00	117.10	50.20	70.00	184.95	109.85	95.28	40.85	1.93
1983	244.10	145.00	122.90	104.90	90.00	177.66	105.53	89.45	76.35	1.61
Average annual percent change 69–70 to 82–83	15.74	16.40	14.84	14.97	8.10	(0.31)	0.18	(1.12)	(1.09)	7.76

[a] Dorosh (1986).
[b] Timmer (1984) updated from Central Bureau of Statistics, *Statistical Pocketbook, 1985* (Jakarta, Indonesia).
[c] Nominal wholesale prices in rupiahs per kilogram from Dorosh (1986).

3. Thailand: The Experience of a Food Exporter

Theodore Panayotou

Over the past three decades, the Thai economy has grown at the remarkable rate of 7.5 percent per annum in real terms while population growth has been reduced from 3.3 percent in the mid-1950s to under 2 percent in the mid-1980s. Agriculture has been the dominant sector that, despite a steady decline in its relative share, continues to contribute a quarter of GDP, 60 percent of exports, and 70 percent of employment. Agriculture has also been the main source of investable surplus, foreign exchange, and low-cost food and industrial labor, as well as backward and forward linkages that have fueled industrial growth. The agricultural sector grew at rates of 4–5 percent per annum and diversified into new crops, making Thailand, with a population of 50 million, not only self-sufficient in food but also the supplier of 30 percent of rice, 90 percent of cassava, 15 percent of rubber, 5 percent of sugar, and 4 percent of maize traded in world markets.

This remarkable performance of Thai agriculture over the past three decades has taken place in an unfavorable price policy environment that included heavy agricultural export taxes, industrial protectionism, and adverse macro policies that resulted in adverse terms of trade for agriculture. Obviously "getting prices wrong" at the expense of agriculture has not retarded agricultural growth in Thailand. This is not to say that price policies had no impact on agricultural growth but that there have been compensatory factors offsetting the effects of unfavorable price policies. Arable land drawn from reserved forests grew at 4.6 percent per annum during the 1960s and at 3.0 percent per annum during the 1970s at little or no cost to the individual farmer. The irrigated area has tripled over the past twenty years making a dry season crop possible, again at little direct cost to the farmer. Past agricultural growth has been accomplished largely through land expansion rather than yield improvement, thus circumventing to a large extent the unfavorable price policies.

However, the past rate of expansion is no longer possible because of the increasing cost of bringing new land into cultivation either by clearing forest land or increasing the irrigated area. As Thai agriculture moves up on a rising supply curve, pressures are building for lowering taxation on agriculture and providing price and income support for farmers, especially in times of depressed commodity prices. Policy changes are becoming increasingly likely as the importance of agricultural taxation as a source of government revenues declines, as the share of food in the consumer's budget falls, and as the political power shifts from urban consumers to rural producers. Moreover, policy reform is needed to stimulate new sources of growth and to maintain Thai agriculture's comparative advantage in world markets.

While growing under "wrong" prices in the past has not been without cost, as resource depletion and the widening rural-urban gap suggest, getting prices "right" in the future would not automatically generate new sources of growth unless the necessary institutional reforms and technical change take place to translate price incentives into increased agricultural productivity. But growth has not been, and is not likely to be, the only or even the primary objective of Thai price policy. Successive Thai governments have used with varying success a multitude of policy instruments (such as export taxes, subsidies, and price supports) to accomplish an array of not always explicit and often conflicting objectives (such as price stability, government revenues, export earnings, improved income distribution, and growth) without predetermined priorities and tradeoffs.

The purpose of this chapter is to analyze the objectives, instruments, and effects of past and present Thai policies toward the agricultural sector in the dynamic context of a rapidly growing and changing economy and to draw out some policy implications and lessons for Thailand and other developing countries. However, not all relevant policies will be addressed. The focus is on price policies affecting the food sector including sectoral and macro policies that have indirect, often unintended, but powerful effects on the food system. Nonprice policies such as irrigation infrastructure, research, and extension, and nonfood crops such as rubber and kenaf will be touched on only to the extent that they relate to food price policies. Special attention is paid to rice, which is Thailand's most important, and most heavily taxed, food crop, grown by 98 percent of Thai farmers and accounting for 40 percent of agricultural GDP, 30 percent of agricultural exports, and over 50 percent of the calories in the Thai diet.

One important finding of this study is that rice export taxation, Thailand's single most important food price policy instrument, has been decisively successful in keeping consumer prices low and stable, but it has done so at the expense of farmers' incomes and productivity growth. On the other hand, the consumption subsidy, the price support, and fertilizer subsidy, all financed from rice taxation, have been largely unsuccessful in improving income distribution and raising farmers' incomes at the same time that they have produced unintended outcomes and leakages. Free land and water and the undervaluation of labor resulting from rice taxation have been far more effective than the explicit price support and fertilizer subsidies in promoting agricultural growth and raising farmers' incomes in the otherwise unfavorable price policy environment. Another finding is that trade policies, industrial protection in particular, have reinforced the adverse effects of rice taxation on agriculture's terms of trade, whereas macro policies have been more benign to agriculture with the notable exception of the interest rate controls that have limited rural credit.

The following four sections of this chapter are devoted to stating the objectives of food price policy at different stages of Thailand's development; describing the various price policy instruments; assessing the effects of these instruments on policy objectives; and analyzing the tradeoffs in price policy. The concluding section examines the implications of the findings and outlines the key pricing issues for the future and the appropriate role of the government.

Food Policy Objectives

The objectives of food policy in Thailand have evolved from raising (or saving) government revenues in the immediate post–World War II years, to maximizing export revenues and keeping consumer prices low and stable in the 1960s and 1970s, to raising farmers' income and promoting agricultural growth in the 1980s. As new objectives were added and gathered momentum, the added objectives continued to play a collateral role in price policies and occasionally to override the new objectives. This section describes briefly the evolution of the food policy objectives since World War II.

The history of food policies in Thailand dates back to the nineteenth century. Before the mid-1850s all rice exports were banned. In 1851 King Rama IV lifted the ban which opened up Thailand to the rest of the world. In 1856 the Bowring Treaty with the British was signed, inaugurating an eighty-year period of free trade. Following World War II, Thailand found itself on the losing side and was forced to pay war reparations in the form of 1.5 million tons of rice. This obligation marked the government's entry into the rice trade through the establishment of the Rice Office, a government monopoly that tried to depress domestic rice prices and shift part of the burden back to the farmers. The objective of government intervention in these earlier postwar years was clearly to procure sufficient quantities of rice to meet Thailand's obligations for war reparations without expending scarce government revenues.

While Thailand's rice supply obligation was lifted in 1949, the government retained the Rice Office because it saw the opportunity to raise government revenues by keeping domestic prices below world prices. The objective of food policy shifted from rice procurement for international reparations to raising government revenues for both recurrent and development expenditures, since at that early stage of Thailand's development there was little else that could be taxed besides rice exports.

A collateral objective of government intervention in the rice market was to keep food prices low for civil servants whose salaries were eroded by postwar inflation. Because for fiscal reasons the government was unable to raise their salaries, a cheap rice policy was pursued as a substitute for a salary increase (Siamwalla, 1975).

Thus all immediate postwar food policies (which were basically rice policies) had either direct or indirect fiscal objectives, that is to raise or save government revenues. Rice taxation continued to be an important source of government revenues throughout the 1950s and the 1960s, but its relative contribution declined steadily from 32 percent of the budget in 1953 to only 7 percent in 1969. Even then the rice premium alone contributed 1.25 billion baht (B 1.25 billion) to government revenues (US\$ 1 = B 25).

In the 1970s and 1980s, because of the development of new sources of tax revenues and the emergence of new objectives of food policy, government revenues were no longer considered the primary objective of food price policies, although the role of the rice premium as a source of unchallenged funds for farm support programs assumed an importance of its own to which other objectives are occasionally sacrificed. As early as the late 1940s, the government began using rice export taxation as a means to improve Thailand's terms of trade and increase foreign exchange earnings. The rationale for this objective was the perception on the part of the policy makers that Thai rice enjoys a monopolistic position in the world market, and therefore the burden of taxes would be borne by the foreign consumer. Whether this is in fact the case is a major controversy in Thailand, which we will discuss when we assess the effectiveness of the policy instruments used to accomplish this objective.

As with government revenues, the relative importance of this objective declined over time from a primary objective in the 1950s and 1960s, to a collateral objective in the 1970s and 1980s. This is a reflection of the diversification of exports, stimulated in part by rice taxation, and the emergence of other more important objectives of food policy rather than the result of a change in the policy makers' perception of Thailand's position in the world rice market. Rice export taxation is still partially justified as a means of maximizing export earnings or at least preventing price undercutting among competing Thai rice exporters.

Another concern which gathered momentum in the 1950s and became a primary objective of food policy in the 1960s and 1970s is urban consumers' welfare. While, always, it has been in the interests of the urban elite to maintain low food prices, the industrialization effort and the concomitant urbanization that began in the 1950s heightened the importance of low and stable food prices for both political stability and industrial growth. At a time when urban consumers spent almost 50 percent of their income on food, and derived over 50 percent of their calories from rice, the price of rice was the main determinant of the cost of living and the consumers' real income. The success of cheap rice policy in forestalling increases in the salaries of civil servants in the immediate postwar years provided the model for forestalling demands for higher wages in the rest of the urban sector, particularly among industrial workers. Ignoring such demands would have led to political instability, whereas meeting them would have reduced profits and slowed down industrial growth. Again, a cheap rice policy was the easy way out. Such policy effected through export taxation was compatible with other concurrently important objectives such as raising government revenues or exploiting Thailand's perceived monopolistic power in world rice markets.

Price stability has been a distinct major objective of food policy but not independent of the desire to maintain low food prices. Price stabilization practiced even during years of great stability in the world rice market (1955–66) had a definite downward bias, the benchmark always being the price level prevailing during the preceding one or two years rather than the long-term trend in world prices. According to Siamwalla (1975): "Stabilizing prices meant essentially lowering prices when they were high rather than raising them when they were low" (p. 240). This asymmetry in the price stabilization policy, which results from the concurrent objective of maintaining low food prices for urban consumers, has been embodied in legislation (the 1974 Farmers' Aid Fund Act) that authorizes export taxation but no export subsidies. Thus while there are no limits to the government's ability to pursue price stability against the upside risk, there is little the government can do against the downside risk beyond reducing export taxation to zero. To the extent that the government is pursuing other conflicting objectives through export taxation (such as raising government revenues), even its ability to reduce export taxation may be limited.

In any case, the government has not been particularly concerned with the downside risk and the asymmetrical effects of its stabilization policies between rice consumers and rice producers because producers' welfare was not considered to be critical to political stability and economic growth. In contrast to the government's preoccupation with the welfare of urban consumers, the welfare of farmers received only lip service. For instance, in 1965 the government introduced for the first time a farm price support program, but the support prices were set below the market prices. As expected, little rice was sold to and bought by the government, and therefore the program had no impact on farm prices. In 1967, when government policies failed to forestall a domestic price increase by 50 percent in a single year, the government justified the high prices as benefiting the farmers. However, two years later when prices fell again, the government failed to provide the subcommittee in charge of the price support program with sufficient funds, manpower, and facilities to be effective in supporting farm prices.

It was not until 1974 that the government began to pay serious attention to the farmers' interests by requiring that the revenues from the premium be placed in a special fund, the Farmers' Aid Fund, to be spent for the improvement of farmers' welfare through price support and other programs. But even then, it was not clear that farmers' welfare became a primary objective of food price policy since export taxes continued to be levied concurrently with price support, and the government negated the program by releasing rice back to the market soon after procuring it (Siamwalla, 1975). It is true, however, that in recent years there has been an increasing shift among policy makers from a preoccupation with consumers' welfare to a concern for farmers' incomes and production incentives, although no effective program has yet been introduced to translate this concern into action.

The differential taxation of the food sector—that is, the high taxation of rice compared to other crops—was undoubtedly due to the prominence of rice as the major wage good and most important export crop. Rice exports are easy to tax while domestic rice prices constitute an important political and economic parameter. With the exception of rubber, Thailand's second most important export crop, which is also heavily taxed, other nonrice crops were not taxed except through the regular export tax. Even in recent years, when nonrice crops such as maize and cassava have become important export crops, their taxation remains low by comparison to rice.

It may be argued that the objective behind the differential taxation of rice is promotion of diversification away from rice and/or improvement in income distribution since rice exports originate mainly in the wealthy central plain while the export of cassava and many other upland crops originate in the poorer regions of the northeast and the north. However, the distribution hypothesis is contradicted by the relatively heavy taxation of glutinous rice grown in the northeast and the low taxation and occasional subsidies for sugar mostly grown in the central plain. The diversification hypothesis is more credible, although it is not clear why Thailand should depress its international comparative advantage in rice production and force diversification into less profitable crops. However, crop diversification as an objective of food policy is compatible with the policy makers' perception of inelastic world demand for Thai rice.

Similarly the differential taxation of agriculture and industry (the former is taxed and the latter is protected) could be ascribed to a deliberate policy objective to promote industrialization through cheap wage goods and the squeeze of investable surplus out of agriculture. Certainly the industrial trade policies that provided heavy protection for the manufacturing sector aimed to promote import substituting industrialization, which began in the 1950s and continued through the 1970s. Regardless of the intentions of the policy makers, the cheap rice policy must have been conducive to industrial growth, although to the extent that low rice prices have reduced farming incomes, and hence the purchase of industrial goods, there has also been a negative effect on growth.

To what extent were these other objectives or outcomes the intention of the Thai government is a moot point. According to Siamwalla (1975), who has studied the Thai rice policies very closely and with a historical perspective,

> There were also various attempts to relate the question of the premium to broader development issues, for example, the desirability of having cheap wage-goods for industrialization, the desirability for Thai agriculture to diversify away from rice, and the question of income distribution, among others. But these issues were largely raised in abstract debates conducted away from the realms of policy making. The aim of policy makers in Thailand has generally been to maintain the prices of rice at levels which are politically acceptable, which usually means not too different from that prevailing in the previous one or two years. (p. 241)

In conclusion, the objectives of food price policy in Thailand have been many and varied. The dominant objectives shifted from government revenues and export earnings in the 1950s, to consumer welfare, price stability, and industrial growth in the 1960s and 1970s, and to farmers' incomes and agricultural growth in the 1980s. Other objectives such as diversification of agriculture, structural change of the economy, income distribution, and nutrition may have also been in operation, but they did not dominate the policy debate. Food self-sufficiency is not an operational objective, since Thailand is more than self-sufficient in rice (and other foods), whereas food security has the special meaning of retaining sufficient quantities of rice for domestic production to prevent politically unacceptable increases in rice prices and the general cost of living.

Food Policy Instruments

There is a variety of price (and nonprice) policy instruments with which a government may attempt to achieve its policy objectives. Some are more direct and visible than others, and the government's choice depends partly on political considerations and partly on budgetary costs and administrative constraints. Over the years Thailand has adopted a portfolio of policy instruments that include export taxes, quantitative controls, consumption subsidies, farm price supports, and input taxes and subsidies. In addition, the Thai government employed industrial trade and macro policy instruments such as import tariffs, interest rate controls, and exchange rate adjustments, which, though aimed at broader socioeconomic objectives, had pronounced effects on the food sector. Looked at ex post, the combination of instruments appears ad hoc and overly complicated because the rationale for some of the instruments disappeared as circumstances changed, and new instruments were introduced to remedy unfavorable effects of old instruments or to pursue new objectives without discontinuing old instruments that created vested interests. There has also been the tendency to use different instruments to pursue different objectives rather than to formulate a coherent and consistent set of instruments to pursue a set of objectives with explicit tradeoffs and priorities.

Export Taxes

In the immediate postwar years, while all rice exports were made in the name of the Rice Office, private merchants were granted export licenses on a quota basis issued by the Ministry of Commerce. In 1950 a premium was imposed as a fee for obtaining a license to export different grades of rice. A second policy instrument through which rice exports were taxed in the immediate postwar years was the multiple exchange rate system. While the exporters of all other goods could sell their foreign exchange on the free market at B 60 per pound sterling, rice exporters were required to sell their foreign exchange earnings to the Bank of Thailand at B 40 per pound sterling. This requirement alone amounted to a 33 percent tax rate on rice exports.

The system of rice export taxation was reformed and simplified in 1955: the multiple exchange rate system was abolished and a premium of B 400 per ton for all grades except brown rice (B 200 per ton) was imposed by the Ministry of Commerce on licensed exporters. This reform marks the beginning of the modern era in rice export taxation.

The rice premium was used as a flexible tool of market intervention for the attainment of a variety of objectives: keeping domestic prices low and stable, improving the terms of trade for Thailand, and raising government revenues. To accomplish these objectives the government had to adjust the premium often, almost monthly. Yet the rice premium alone was considered insufficient for the task. Two additional policy instruments were introduced to control domestic rice prices at low and stable levels: a quantitative control of exports and a rice reserve requirement ratio. Both the premium and the quantitative controls of export were based on the perception of inelastic world demand for Thai rice. Moderate increases in the premium were expected to be absorbed by foreign buyers without significantly lowering domestic consumer prices. Quantitative control of export was then thought to be necessary to accomplish this while putting additional upward pressure on export prices. While the combination of quantitative controls and export premiums was keeping domestic prices well below world prices, beginning in 1966 a rice reserve requirement was also imposed on exports to procure rice for a direct consumer subsidy. For every ton exported, the rice exporter was required to sell a fixed proportion, known as the rice reserve ratio, to the Public Warehouse Organization (PWO) at below market prices set by the government. The rice reserve ratio requirement implied significant additional taxation for rice exports ranging between B 400 and B 2,500 per ton in the mid-seventies. In the early eighties (1980–81) the reserve requirement implied a tax of B 1,000–2,200 per ton. It was suspended in 1982 in response to a decline in rice prices.

In addition to the export premium and the reserve requirement, the government also imposed regular export taxes on rice at about 5 percent of the f.o.b. export price. Table 1 presents an account of the various levies on exported rice and the implied tax rate in recent years. The total levies ranged between B 725 per ton in 1983 to B 3,409 per ton in 1981 amounting to 11 percent and 30 percent, respectively, of the export price (f.o.b.).

As shown in figure 1, variations in the tax burden closely follow variations in the export price.[1] Table 2 computes and compares the tax burden of the rice sector for 1981 and 1983, two very different years in world market conditions. As indicated in this table, in response to a 45 percent drop in the export price, export taxes were reduced by 90 percent, a response that had stabilizing effects on domestic prices and destabilizing effects on world prices.

Export taxes are levied on virtually all exported or exportable commodities with the notable exception of maize. However, for most crops export taxes are minimal, rarely exceeding 2 percent of f.o.b. price or 6 percent of the farmgate price (see table 3). Two important exceptions are sugar among the food crops and rubber among the nonfood crops.

A sugar premium rate is set annually to vary according to the f.o.b. price. For a price under B 7,000 per ton the premium was set at zero for the period 1979–83. At higher prices the premium varies from 20 percent to 100 percent of the f.o.b. price, depending on the price level. Since the threshold price is set to cover production cost and allow for a "normal" return and since Thailand is a high-cost producer of sugar, sugar premiums are rarely collected. Under depressed or even normal world market conditions, Thai sugar enjoys protection (import tariffs) and export subsidies. Only during boom conditions, such as during 1973–76, a significant amount of premium revenues (37 percent of the export value) was collected. In a pattern parallel to rice taxation, in 1972 the government introduced a sugar reserve requirement for sale of 7 percent of output at 10 percent below market prices to the government, for resale to civil servants

---

1. The tax burden we are discussing here is an "accounting" or "apparent" burden, and as such it does not reflect the opportunity cost or forgone revenue from the changes in quantities and prices caused by the various taxes and quotas.

TABLE 1.   Official levies on exported rice, 1979–83 (in baht per ton)[a]

End of period	Rice premium	Export tax	Reserve requirement	Total levies	As % of export price, f.o.b.
1979					
March	900	275	531	1,706	26.6
June	900	285	626	1,811	27.4
September	900	310	955	2,165	29.3
December	900	320	868	2,068	26.5
1980					
March	900	365	1,068	2,333	27.5
June	900	405	1,136	2,441	27.2
September	900	410	1,116	2,426	26.8
December	700	450	1,481	2,631	27.1
1981					
March	700	460	1,943	3,103	29.9
June	700	500	2,124	3,324	29.6
September	700	525	2,184	3,409	30.3
December	400	475	1,226	2,101	23.7
1982					
March	400	400	350	1,150	15.4
June	400	370	—	770	11.5
September	400	350	—	750	12.1
December	400	325	—	725	11.9
1983					
March	400	325	—	725	11.2
June	400	325	—	725	11.7
September	400	325	—	725	10.6
October	200	162.5	—	362.5	n.a.

SOURCE: Pinthong (1983), p. 26.
[a]Milled white rice, 5% broken.

TABLE 2.   Rice export taxes in 1981 and 1983

	June 1981		October 1983		
	$ per ton	% of f.o.b.	$ per ton	% of f.o.b.	% change
F.o.b. price	545.00		300.00		−45
Premium	33.49	6.1	8.74	2.9	−74
Export duty	23.92	4.4	7.10	2.4	−70
Reserve requirement	95.36	17.5	nil	0	—
Total taxes	152.77	28.0	15.84	5.3	−90

SOURCE: Kim (1984), p. 6.

and low-income consumers who would otherwise have had to pay the higher prices of the protected domestic market. The central feature of the government policy toward sugar has been a cross-subsidization between the domestic and export markets aiming to secure an "adequate" return to the producers. The cross-subsidy took different forms over the years

FIGURE 1. Export and wholesale prices and tax burden for 5 percent rice

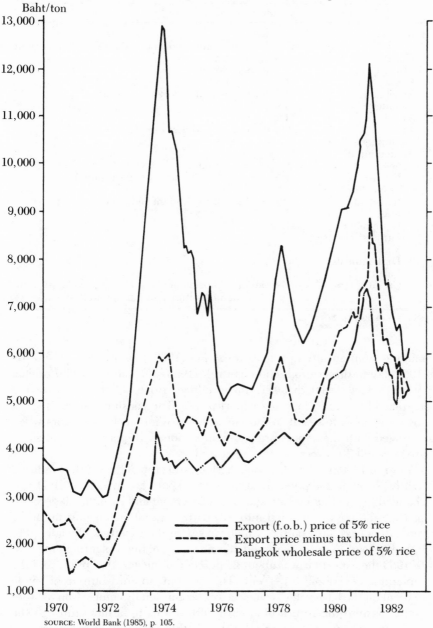

Baht/ton

Export (f.o.b.) price of 5% rice
Export price minus tax burden
Bangkok wholesale price of 5% rice

SOURCE: World Bank (1985), p. 105.

TABLE 3.   Taxes and subsidies on farm products and inputs 1981

Taxes (+) and subsidies (−) as % of farmgate prices

Products		
Paddy	52.3	(premium and export tax and reserve requirement)
Corn	2.9	(export tax)
Mung bean	3.2	(export tax)
Cassava	4.3	(export tax)
Sugarcane	2.3	(premium and export tax—subsidies)
Peanuts	5.9	
Kenaf	4.2	
Rubber	30.0	(export tax and cess—replanting subsidy)
Farm inputs		
Traded inputs		
Seed	*	(same as product)
Fertilizer	1.5	(net effect of import tax and subsidy)
Pesticides	6.9	
Irrigation	*	(subsidy of investment and operating cost)
Fuel	35	
Equipment	42	
Nontraded inputs		
Manure	0	
Draft animals	0	
Labor	0	
Credit	*	(implicit subsidy of about 6% for the clients of the Bank of Agriculture and Agricultural Cooperatives)

SOURCE: Kim (1984), p. 20.

ranging from an attempt at cartelization (1960–61), a cess and subsidy (1962–66) to direct production controls (1968–83), and the 70/30 pricing system (since 1984) that sets the producer price at 70 percent of the average of the consumer and export prices. The consumer price is set at such a level as to result in "adequate" return for sugar producers when averaged with the export price and apportioned 70 percent to the sugar growers and 30 percent to the sugar millers.

Prior to 1960, rubber, the main agricultural crop of the south, was taxed lightly through a 7 percent ad valorem export tax, which in 1960 was changed to a sliding tax rate starting at 5 percent and rising to 20 percent. In 1968 the tax was divided into two parts: a traditional export tax and a replanting cess (tax), both of which vary with the gazetted (officially published) prices, in order to provide for financing of the replanting program. In 1983 the export tax was about 22 percent of the gazetted price, and the replanting cess about 8 percent. This amounts to a tax burden of 35–40 percent on the farm value, a very heavy tax burden by comparison to other crops, despite the return of about a fifth of this to farmers through the replanting program. On the other hand, the main rubber-producing region of Thailand is the south, which is rice deficient and therefore not significantly affected by rice taxation. In this sense, rubber export taxation is a supplement of rice taxation for the south.

Quantitative Controls

Historically, quantitative restrictions and export quotas have been important policy instruments, used either independently or in combination with export taxes to limit exports and lower or stabilize domestic prices. Quantitative restrictions took the form of either export quotas allocated among exporters based on past performance or simply a limit in the number of export licenses issued.

The justification offered for quotas includes: inadequacy of export taxation to limit exports (because of inelastic export demand as in the case of rice), nonfulfillment of contracts by certain exporters (maize), quality control (cassava and maize),[2] cartel obligations and international agreements (sugar and cassava), and price undercutting among exporters (all crops). The true effect of quantitative restrictions has usually been the creation of economic rents for the lucky few who are able to obtain export quotas, and for those who have opportunities for corruption in creating and protecting these rents.

The quotas for rice and maize exports were abolished in 1981. The export quotas for sugar and cassava were retained because of Thailand's membership in the International Sugar Organization and its tapioca limiting agreement with the European Economic Community (EEC), respectively, both of which are currently under review and revision. Similarly the policy of setting minimum export prices for rice, rice bran, and maize was abolished in 1981. The objective of this policy, which was periodically introduced but proved difficult to enforce, was to prevent exporters from undercutting each other to secure buyers and increase their market share.

Consumption Subsidy

In addition to the implicit consumption subsidy provided by the export taxes that kept the domestic retail price of rice well below world prices, the government introduced direct rice price subsidies for urban consumers through the rice reserve requirement imposed in 1962 and institutionalized in 1966. Rice exporters were forced to sell the government rice at below market prices in proportion to their exports. Thus, the burden of the consumer subsidy was borne by the rice exporters and ultimately by the rice farmers (and possibly the foreign consumers).

The collected rice was then resold by the Public Warehouse Organization to selected shops,[3] which, in turn, sold it to consumers, as long as they showed their identity card and their housing registration in the district of the shop. This requirement automatically excluded large numbers of poor

2. Fulfillment of contracts and quality control are enforced through the "past performance" criterion for allocating quotas or issuing export licenses. Those who have not fulfilled their past contracts or have exported poor quality products have their quotas reduced.

3. While we found no comparable data on procurement and resale prices, the idea was that the subsidy does not impose a burden on the government budget.

people and migrants who did not have these documents in order (Siamwalla and Setboonsarng, 1986), with obvious distributional implications. The amount of rice allowed per transaction was fixed, but no limit was placed on either the number of transactions or the total supplies sold by each shop, and in effect, a considerable amount of the subsidized rice was diverted back to the free market and part of it was exported.

The leakage of subsidized rice became especially problematic during the mid-seventies. As domestic prices rose with world prices, this second-tier consumer subsidy increased from 10 percent during 1966–68 to 25–30 percent during 1973–74. The incentives for leakage and diversion also increased accordingly, and long lines formed outside the rice shops. The government responded by releasing additional quantities of cheap rice and increasing the rice reserve requirements (a ton per ton exported) to replenish its stocks. Fearing political unrest, the government banned exports in June 1973, which also cut off the replenishment of the cheap rice stocks. Although this was a short-lived crisis, according to Siamwalla (1975) "the rice crisis of mid-1973 was both a consequence of, and in turn had its effect on, the political crisis which led to the downfall of a very long established regime" (p. 245).

In the early 1970s the bulk of cheap rice (80–90 percent) was sold in Bangkok. Since 1974 over five hundred thousand tons of cheap rice was supplied, but still 70 percent was retained in Bangkok. Only as late as 1978 did more than nominal amounts of cheap rice begin to arrive in the provinces.

In 1979, in order to stop the leakages into the free market as well as get rid of a rising surplus of glutinous rice, the government differentiated the product from regular rice by introducing osha rice, an 80–20 mixture of nonglutinous rice (15 percent broken) and glutinous rice (10 percent broken). The leakages into the free consumer market were thus successfully blocked, but new leakages occurred toward the animal feed market since this low-quality, low-price mixture was competitive with other feeds. Moreover, as Siamwalla and Setboonsarng (1986) point out, "as the cheap rice program became more diffused [to rural areas] its command of political support began to decline" (p. 16). In 1981 the Commerce Ministry converted the rice reserve requirement from kind to cash and scrapped it altogether in 1982 as rice prices in the world market began their downward slide, thus eliminating the direct subsidization of rice consumption. Of course, the indirect subsidization through the rice export premium, which has been more effective, continued.

Farm Price Support Program

As the consumption subsidy through cheap rice sales became the outlet for the rice collected through the reserve requirement, the farm price support program became a partial outlet for tax revenues collected through the rice premium. Although nominal price support programs have existed since 1965, it was not until 1974, when the Farmers' Aid Fund was created, that serious efforts (at least in terms of expenditure) were made to support the farmgate price of rice above the market price. The idea behind the price support programs was for the government to buy rice from the farmers at prices above the market in sufficient quantities to force the market prices up to the support level. Since farmers know that they can always sell their rice to the government at the higher support price, they will not supply it to the market until the market price rises to the support level.

Such was the theory behind the support programs. In practice the program has not worked well for several reasons. By the time the price-support price is agreed upon and implemented, many farmers are forced by cash needs and debt to sell their output to traders, who then benefit from the price support. Furthermore, the budget is limited and never adequate to purchase sufficient quantities to influence the market price (buying 100,000 tons out of an output of 17 million tons would make little difference). Another reason the program has not worked is the limited funds and lack of storage capacity—the funds are rolled over by releasing the rice stocks back into the market soon after they have been procured, thereby defeating the purpose of the program. Finally, because of their limited manpower and skills, the Marketing Organization of Farmers (MOF) and Public Warehouse Organization (PWO), which are in charge of the implementation, rely on rice mills that have the skill and the storage capacity to act as government agents for the programs and expropriate most of the benefits from the program for themselves.

A limited scheme of price support for maize has also been operational since 1975–76 with the Marketing Organization of Farmers intervening in the local markets to influence prices. Although this policy did not meet its target in terms of volume and value of purchased output and had little effect on the average farmgate price, it did have some effect on local prices.

In recent years, the government has proposed price support programs for virtually all the major crops (maize, cassava, sugarcane, tobacco, and cotton), along the lines of the rice support program. If implemented, these programs are unlikely to last because the margin between the domestic and world prices of these crops is not large enough to cover the price support costs, unlike the rice price support and the rubber replanting programs, which are financed from the rice premium and the cess tax, respectively.

A form of price support that has more resemblance to the rubber cess-financed replanting program than to the rice price support is the sugar cess-export subsidy, which was introduced in the early 1960s to secure the continued viability of the industry in the face of depressed export prices without a drain on government budget. A cess on the production of centrifugal sugar was to finance an export subsidy for raw sugar. Bertrand (1980) demonstrated that this system was superior to a straight export subsidy in that it involved a lower loss to the economy and less of a drain on government revenues. The scheme worked well until 1965 when a severe sugar slump "made it difficult to find a package of tax-subsidy rates that would be both self-supporting and move large amounts of Thai sugar into world markets" (Bertrand 1980, p. 58). In 1966, in an attempt to reduce the surplus resulting from heavy protectionist policies, the cess-export subsidy system was replaced by a combination of measures including selective export subsidies and production controls, access to the U.S.-protected market, and entrance into the International Sugar Organization.

A sudden boom in the world sugar market during 1973–76 brought about a total reversal in sugar policy: the domestic price floors and export subsidies were replaced by domestic price ceilings and export taxes, including a sugar export premium that accounted for 37 percent of the value of exports. However, the new policy was short-lived. Since Thailand is a high-cost sugar producer, a return of world prices to normal levels in 1976–77 saw the return of protection of the domestic sugar market, production controls, and export subsidies, albeit at low levels.

The rationale of government policies toward the sugar sector has been to protect the processing industry (which is partly government owned and politically powerful) and to regulate its relationship to sugarcane growers. The Sugar Act of 1968 gave the "Committee for Policy Counseling and for Maintenance of Price Level of Sugarcane and Sugar" the right to set the price of sugarcane. The sugarcane price is now set annually one month before the harvest season through a formal bargaining process among cane growers, sugar millers, and the government, based on the export price of refined sugar and an agreed income sharing formula of 70:30 for growers and millers, respectively.

Input Taxes and Subsidies

The most significant interventions in the agricultural input market have been the taxation of imports of nitrogen fertilizer and more recently the introduction of indirect fertilizer subsidies. An implicit subsidy is also involved in the provision of free irrigation water from irrigation systems constructed with public funds, including the proceeds from export taxation. A second implicit subsidy to agriculture, and to all labor-using activities, is the undervaluation of the opportunity cost of labor resulting from the taxation of rice, which partly offsets the effect of taxation on production incentives (Bertrand, 1980). A third implicit and certainly unintended subsidy is the availability of public forest land free of charge for agricultural expansion. Implicit subsidies are also provided through other public investments and programs such as research and extension and agricultural credit, but their cost and impact have been limited by comparison to the implicit irrigation, labor, and land subsidies.

Fertilizer policies date back to the 1968–74 period when the government promoted import substitution for nitrogen fertilizer through heavy protection of local production by means of an import monopoly for nitrogen-based fertilizers granted to the Thai Central Chemical Company, a local fertilizer-producing company. The monopoly resulted in high domestic fertilizer prices (68 percent above world prices), which in turn reduced fertilizer use and directed fertilizer imports to less suitable, non–nitrogen-based compound fertilizers. Despite the heavy protection, the domestic fertilizer plant failed and production was discontinued. The monopoly, however, was not abolished, but continued to sell imported brand-name compound fertilizers. While other smaller importers have entered the fertilizer importing and mixing industry in recent years, the Thai Central Chemical Company continues to control 50–70 percent of the market. With the formation of the Thai Fertilizer Importers Association by smaller importers, the industry assumed an oligopolistic structure.

At present, there are no trade restrictions on fertilizer imports, and only a minimal import tax of 1.8 percent is levied on them. However, urea imports are still subject to an additional 17 percent import duty or a total tax rate of 19 percent because the government intends to tax the industrial use of urea but is unable to separate it from its agricultural use. Though the least costly and most suitable fertilizer for Thai soils, urea is at a considerable disadvantage vis-à-vis other fertilizers, partly because of the import duty and partly because of the dominant position and brand loyalty that compound fertilizers enjoy as a result of past protectionist measures. These factors account for the exceptionally low use of urea in Thailand (only 2.5 percent of the total fertilizer use) and—in conjunction with the high rice taxation, poor water control, and free land for expansion—they explain why Thailand is among the lowest fertilizer users in Asia.

Most fertilizer is used in the irrigated areas of the central and northern regions (30–40 kg/hr) with good water control where crop production risks are small, and even a 1.5 value/cost ratio constitutes sufficient incentive. In flooding areas, such as the lower central plain, and in rainfed areas such as the northeast, very little fertilizer is used; because of higher risk, a much higher value/cost ratio is necessary to induce fertilizer use in these areas.

The government's response to the low fertilizer use and increasing need for intensification of agriculture has been to distribute subsidized fertilizer through the MOF. The purpose of the MOF fertilizer distribution operations introduced through the Fertilizer Act of 1975 has been to moderate the tendency of fertilizer firms to manipulate prices and to encourage farmers to use more fertilizer by making it available at a lower (subsidized) price.

The fertilizer subsidy has three components. First, MOF distributes fertilizer to the farmers at the Bangkok wholesale cost, absorbing all transportation and distribution costs, which is ultimately drawn from the Farmers' Aid Fund. Second, MOF receives interest-free working capital on its retail sales. Third, MOF provides subsidized credit (six months interest-free loans) to its target beneficiaries and absorbs all lending and other financial losses.

The subsidy costs the Farmers' Aid Fund about $15 per ton directly for distribution and $60 per ton indirectly for subsidized credit, defaults, and other losses. The total subsidy amounts to 35 percent of the wholesale price, but less than half of this reaches the farmer (World Bank, 1985); the rest goes to intermediaries. However, MOF fertilizer distribution amounts to only 13 percent of all fertilizer sales, and over 85 percent of the subsidized fertilizer flows to larger, more affluent farmers in the irrigated areas of the central plain.

The MOF is not directly involved in the importation and mixing of fertilizer; nor has it shown much interest in the promotion of low-cost straight nitrogen fertilizer or in quality control and regulation of brand-name mixed fertilizers. To the contrary, MOF has promoted the use of mixed fertilizers by purchasing them from local oligopolists and distributing them to the farmers at a subsidized price.[4]

Industrial and Trade Policies

Thai industrial trade policies, while aiming to foster industrialization, have had significant effects on the agricultural sector by causing further deterioration of the terms of trade for agriculture. The main instruments of industrial development and trade policy in Thailand have been import tariffs and investment and export incentives. In the 1960s, the nominal tariffs ranged between 25–30 percent for intermediate products and consumer goods, and 15–20 percent for machinery and equipment. Nominal rates for consumer goods rose to a range of 30–55 percent in 1971, were selectively reduced in 1974 to control inflation, and rose again to reach 30–60 percent in 1978. The effective rate of protection of manufactured products averaged 87 percent in 1971, declined to 19 percent in 1974, and rose again to 70 percent in 1978 (World Bank, 1984).

In 1982 there was a major change in the import tariff structure that reversed past trends of increasing protection and reduced trade distortions through lower and more uniform tariff levels. The overall rate of effective

4. The MOF buys mixed fertilizer from the Thai Central Chemical Company, which imports the ingredients including nitrogen (free of import duty), mixes them at a large fertilizer mixing plant, and sells only compound fertilizers to avoid the import duty, to utilize its excess capacity, and to exploit farmers' brand loyalty.

protection declined to 40 percent (47 percent for nonimport competing industries, 43 percent for export industries, and 32 percent for import competing industries). These rates of protection, although half their 1971 levels, imply considerable protection of industry when compared with the negative effective rates of protection of agriculture, which for 1981 averaged −65 percent for rice, −22 percent for maize and cassava, and −12 percent for sugarcane (Kim, 1984).

Other protective instruments employed in Thailand include price controls (minimum prices), heavily used in the 1970s and relaxed in the 1980s (except for sugar, milk, and petroleum products), and quantitative controls on imports including import bans for certain products. In 1982 there were forty-six products under import control and several industries under minimum domestic content requirements. The effect of these restrictions is similar to that of tariffs, that is, reduced market competition, higher production costs, and higher consumer prices.

The government also provides investment and export incentives, such as exemptions from duty on imported machinery and from corporate income taxes, and protection against competing imports to foster labor-intensive, export-oriented regionally decentralized industries. These incentives amount to a considerable capital subsidy encouraging the excessive use of scarce investment resources and involving a significant drain on fiscal revenues: duty and business tax exemptions for promoted industries accounted for 13 percent of the central government cash deficit in 1981. The supported investments have been less profitable, more centralized, more capital intensive, and not more export oriented than the average new investments of the sector as a whole (World Bank, 1984). Export incentives are ineffective because the protective structure favors production for import substitution rather than for exports.

The effect of these industrial policies is perhaps even greater on other sectors. Protection-induced price distortions raise the costs to agriculture and other nonindustrial sectors, reducing their competitiveness in the world market. The World Bank (1980) estimates that "protection and other distortions can reduce an exporter's value added by up to 30% compared to a situation with no distortions" (p. 32). Furthermore, as a result of the higher production costs and higher prices for industrial consumer goods caused by industrial protection, farmers' welfare was reduced and the rural-urban income distribution worsened.

Macro Price Policies

With the notable exception of interest rate ceilings and credit policies, macro price policies have had little adverse effect on the food sector because macro prices have either been kept close to their equilibrium values (exchange rate) or have been ineffective (minimum wages).

Thailand, by comparison to other developing countries, has followed rather prudent macroeconomic policies. The inflation rate during 1970–82 averaged 9 percent per annum compared to 20 percent in Indonesia and 13 percent for middle-income economies as a group. In 1983 the inflation rate was below 4 percent and in 1984 below 1 percent. During the past twenty-five years two-digit inflation was limited to four years of oil price stocks: 1974–75 and 1980–81. Of course, the control of the price of rice through the rice export taxation and the rice consumption subsidy as well as the control of the prices of petroleum products have contributed to general price stability. In general, however, there has been little divergence between domestic and international rates of inflation.

For the past twenty-five years (1960–84) Thailand has maintained a fixed exchange rate interrupted only by small periodic devaluations in recent years. While the nominal exchange rate in relation to the U.S. dollar remained at about B 20 for the entire 1960–80 period, the real effective exchange rate moved within a band of +10 percent. The rising strength of the U.S. dollar in the early 1980s and the inflation of 1980–81 resulted in an overvalued exchange rate. The government responded by periodic small devaluations, which brought the nominal exchange rate to B 23.4 to the dollar and the effective rate to B 24.7 in 1984. In November 1984 the baht was devalued by 16 percent, the fixed exchange rate system was abandoned, and the baht was pegged to a basket of currencies structured to reflect the country's trade patterns, the state of the economy, and international exchange rates. While the value of the baht was allowed to float within a band vis-à-vis the U.S. dollar, the fall of the dollar against other currencies since September 1985 caused a 3 percent appreciation of the baht against the dollar. The government responded by a new devaluation of the baht against the dollar in December 1985.

Thus, through a combination of a strong economy, low inflation, and successive exchange rate adjustments, Thailand managed to maintain a fairly realistic exchange rate, thereby minimizing the damage to its export performance from overvalued exchange rates. Except for the immediate post–world war years, when the government used foreign exchange controls and multiple exchange rates as instruments for taxing agriculture, the exchange rate policy has been fairly neutral toward the agricultural sector, although temporary exchange rate disequilibria have affected agriculture disproportionately because of its export orientation and absence of protection.

Interest rate ceilings and implicit interest rate subsidies for promoted industries have been the main interest rate distortions affecting the agricultural sector and the rural economy in general. Despite a central bank provision that a certain percentage (13 percent in recent years) of commercial banks' deposits be lent to agriculture, fewer than 40 percent of the farmers have access to institutional credit, and default rates on such loans are as high as 50 percent. Noninstitutional rates of 60 percent per annum are not uncommon. Credit policy relies on mandates, quotas, interest rate ceilings and constrained use of loan proceeds while there is growing evidence that farmers would prefer more flexible terms and increased credit availability even if they had to pay higher interest rates. While the decline in inflation since 1982 and the fall in nominal interest rates worldwide have rendered interest rate ceilings ineffective (nonbinding), the government has reaffirmed, as recently as March 1986, its interest rate policy by lowering the ceilings on commercial interest rates. Minimum wages were first introduced in 1973 for Bangkok and subsequently expanded to cover the whole country. Minimum wages are set annually at different levels for different regions and apply to all sectors except agriculture and government administration. In earlier years, minimum wage adjustments exceeded the rate of inflation but in recent years they have barely maintained constant real wage levels. To the extent that minimum wages have raised nonagricultural wages and limited nonagricultural employment, the farming sector would have benefited from low labor costs, while rural labor would have suffered from depressed rural wages. Because of low general compliance and the nonbinding levels at which minimum wages were set in recent years, however, any minimum wage effects are likely to be small.

Food Policy Outcomes

The degree to which the policy instruments have achieved the intended policy objectives is only one aspect of policy analysis and evaluation. Another important aspect is the cost of the policy instrument compared to the benefits generated and to the costs of alternative instruments for attaining the same objective. A third aspect of policy evaluation concerns the side effects or unintended outcomes of the policy. This section assesses the outcomes of various policy instruments in terms of the main policy objectives discussed in the second section of this chapter: government revenues, export earnings, consumer welfare, farmers' incomes, static efficiency, dynamic efficiency and growth, crop diversification, price stabilization, and income distribution. Budgetary costs and side effects are discussed as they relate to these objectives.

Government Revenues

During the early postwar years rice taxation contributed between a quarter and a third of total government revenue. In the 1960s, the share of rice export taxes in total government revenue declined to about 10 percent, in the 1970s to 4 percent, and in 1982 it was only 2 percent. The projected share for the 1980s is below 1 percent. This precipitous decline in the contribution of rice export taxation to government revenues from 32 percent in the early 1950s to under 1 percent in the early 1980s is due mainly to the development of other sources of government revenues. But low world rice prices, and therefore low export taxes, also played a role since 1982. These trends indicate that government revenue is no longer a primary objective of export taxation.

Despite its quantitative decline, the rice export premium has nevertheless assumed importance as a source of unchallenged funds for politically visible interventions in the farm sector. Revenues from the export taxation are deposited in the Farmers' Aid Fund and earmarked for agricultural purposes, where they can be and are used for projects and programs such as the rice price support and the fertilizer subsidy that "would have never passed the scrutiny of the Finance Ministry or the Budget Bureau" (Siamwalla and Setboonsarng, 1986). With the notable exception of rubber, the contribution of other crops to government revenues has been negligible.

Export Earnings

The success of export taxation and quota restrictions in increasing export revenues depends on the elasticity of demand for Thai rice in world markets. Tsujii (1973) estimated this elasticity to be slightly less than one (−1.0), which supports the proponents of the premium. More recently, Wong (1978) estimated the price elasticity of world demand for Thai rice to be about −4.0, while the World Bank (1983) believes in a short-term elasticity of about −4.0 and a long-term elasticity of at least −10.0. These later estimates suggest that most of the burden of the export premium is shifted onto farmers rather than foreign consumers. Siamwalla (1975) argues that the short-run elasticity of demand for exports is not constant but changes with fluctuations in export supplies and input demand, becoming more elastic as price falls under the pressure of excess supply, implying a kinked export demand.

The world elasticity of demand for Thai rice is in part determined by Thailand's share of the world output and trade. Usher (1967) argues that the elasticity is high because of Thailand's small share of world output (about 3 percent), while Siamwalla (1975) considers Thailand's share in the total volume of traded rice as a more appropriate indicator of Thailand's market power because of various barriers in the world rice market.

If we accept an elasticity estimate of 4.0 and Thailand's share in world rice trade as the relevant indicator of Thailand's market power in the short run, it is reasonable to conclude that Thailand did benefit from restricting rice exports at times of excess demand in the world market. However, in the long term, when both the world demand for Thai rice becomes more elastic and Thailand's share in world rice production (not trade) becomes more relevant, monopolistic behavior would be to Thailand's disadvantage. Bale and Lutz (1981) estimated that in 1976 Thailand lost U.S. $110–320 million in foreign exchange earnings from rice as a result of price distortions, the exact figure depending on the elasticity estimate.

Consumers' Welfare, Farmers' Incomes, and Static Efficiency

Domestically, consumers have clearly benefited and farmers have lost from rice export taxation. The question is, How much? The extent of gains and losses once again depends on the elasticities of foreign demand, domestic demand, and domestic supply. The first, as we have seen, is the most controversial. Table 4 computes the efficiency and distributional effects of rice export taxation for 1981 (a good year) given alternative foreign demand elasticity values. Under a low demand elasticity of −4.0 (short run, or conditions or excess demand), nonfarm consumers gained B 5.04 billion as a result of reduced rice prices, whereas farmers lost B 8.40 billion as a result of low farmgate prices for paddy. The government, which collected B 6.0 billion in tax revenues, was a second beneficiary of the export tax, whereas foreign consumers bore a tax burden of B 2.6 billion. Of course, from the standpoint of Thailand, the latter is a benefit rather than a cost, pursued as one of the objectives of the export tax policy on the assumption of inelastic demand.

These do not, however, yield a net benefit because the export tax has caused certain efficiency losses by artificially encouraging less production and more consumption than that warranted by the social opportunity costs of resources involved. The estimated production loss is B 1.05 billion (based on a supply elasticity of 0.6), and the consumption loss B .04 billion (based on a domestic demand elasticity of 0.02). After deducting these losses, Thailand's total net benefit from export taxation was B 1.55 billion. This figure would appear to justify the export taxation.

Very few, however, would accept an elasticity of −4.0 as more than temporary. Under the medium- to long-run elasticities of −10.0 to −100.0, the gains to consumers are considerably higher, but the burden on producers is disproportionately higher because foreign consumers can obtain their rice supplies from alternative sources and so bear virtually no tax burden. Rice output is 3.5 to 4.5 million tons lower than it could be, and the economy suffers a net efficiency loss of B .56 to 3.3 billion.[5]

The results of the price support program should be evaluated based on both its ability to raise farm prices close to the support price level in years when demand was weak and prices low, and its ability to give farmers a share in the benefits generated by the program. Table 5 compares the farm

5. While the producers have lost from export taxation, they have gained from price support and the fertilizer subsidy, both of which are financed from export taxation. The question is, How much of what has been taken away from them was returned to them through these programs?

TABLE 4.   Estimates of the efficiency and distributional effects of rice export taxation, Thailand, 1981

	Low demand elasticity	Medium demand elasticity	High demand elasticity
Estimate of the elasticity of demand for Thai rice on world markets	−4	−10	−100
Changes in export price as a ratio of export tax	.44	.24	.03
		(billion baht)	
Tax imposed on foreign consumers	2.64	1.44	.20
Government	6.00	6.00	6.00
Transfer from farmers	8.40	11.40	14.55
Transfer to nonfarm consumers	5.04	6.84	8.73
Net efficiency loss:			
Production	1.05	1.94	3.30
Consumption	.04	.06	.08
Total benefit of export tax	1.55	−.56	− 3.28
		(million tons)	
Production of paddy:			
With export tax	17	17	17
Without export tax	19.5	20.4	21.4

Underlying assumptions for calculations:
  Elasticity of domestic supply = .6
  Elasticity of domestic demand = .02
  Domestic production = 17 million tons
  Domestic on-farm consumption = 6 million tons
  Domestic off-farm consumption = 7 million tons
  Farmgate paddy price = B 3,400/ton
  Consumer price = B 3,600/ton
  Export tax on paddy = B 1,500/ton

SOURCE: Krongkaew (1985), p. 342.

price to the support price for the crop years 1969–70 to 1982–83. Only in years of strong demand and high world prices such as 1976–77, 1977–78, and 1980–81 were farm prices anywhere close to the support prices. In deflated terms, the program failed to maintain farm prices (and therefore real farming incomes) even at a constant level: real farm prices have declined steadily since 1973. The failure of the program is hardly surprising since procurement in most years was about 1 percent of production and only in 1980–81 and 1981–82 exceeded 10 percent. Yet the farm price in 1981–82 was only 77 percent of the support price. The higher ratio of farm to support prices in 1980–81 was due to partial transmission of high export prices despite the upward adjustment of the export taxes. In 1982–83 the high ratio was due to the downward adjustment of the support price.

TABLE 5. Prices received by farmers, minimum guaranteed price, and government procurement of paddy

	Farm price[a]	Support price[b]	Ratio of farm to support prices	Deflated farm prices[c] (baht/ton)	Procurement by: MOF	PWO (thousand tons)	AFCT	Total[d]	Procurement as percent of production
	(U.S. $/ton)								
1969–70	45	63	72	933	—	—	—	69	1
1970–71	36	63	57	728	—	—	—	117	1
1971–72	47	54	87	927	—	—	—	200	1
1972–73	76	—	—	1,316	—	—	—	—	—
1973–74	105	—	—	1,473	—	—	—	—	—
1974–75	109	137	79	1,460	249	—	—	249	2
1975–76	100	130	77	1,282	37	—	—	156	1
1976–77	104	110	94	1,228	15	—	—	15	—
1977–78	118	118	100	1,277	4	—	—	5	—
1978–79	123	132	93	1,205	187	—	—	213	7
1979–80	145	167	88	1,203	1,084	—	—	1,146	7
1980–81	167	170	98	1,217	—	1,807	94	1,901	11
1981–82	140	182	77	n.a.	139	1,840	233	2,212	12
1982–83	145	160	91	n.a.	525	640	155	1,320	8

NOTE: MOF = Marketing Organization of Farmers
PWO = Public Warehouse Organization
AFCT = Agricultural Federation of Cooperatives in Thailand

SOURCE: World Bank (1985), p. 15.

[a] Average farm price 1st grade paddy calendar year (second year shown)
[b] Minimum guaranteed price 100%, 1st grade
[c] Deflated by cost-of-living index, Bangkok, 1970 = 100
[d] Including purchase made directly by the government in earlier years

Table 6 shows how the extra margins generated by the price support program were shared among the primary beneficiaries (farmers) and various intermediaries. Of B 236 million of extra margins created by the price support program, only 13 percent was received by farmers. The remaining 87 percent went to intermediaries such as millers, exporters, MOF and its officials, politicians and local-level officials, and farm leaders. Moreover, the farmers who benefited from the program were mainly large commercial farmers in easily accessible provinces, particularly in the central plain.

The experience with the fertilizer subsidy has been strikingly similar to that of the price support program: it has had little impact on the general level of fertilizer prices, in the same way the rice support price had little effect on farmgate prices of rice; only a fraction of the government's subsidy costs have reached the farmers; and only a small number of large, accessible, and well-off farmers have benefited (see World Bank, 1985, pp. 22–23).

Furthermore, the fertilizer subsidy has failed to increase fertilizer use and crop yields. The reasons are many. First, government sales have simply replaced private sales. Second, the tax on urea is still in effect, and the subsidy, to the extent that it has been effective, has promoted the use of the more costly, less appropriate mixed fertilizers. Third, the few farmers reached by the subsidy have been those who were using fertilizers before the subsidy. Fourth, the main causes of low fertilizer use—loss of water control, poor fertilizer quality, and insecure land ownership—have not been remedied. Thailand continues to be among the lowest fertilizer users in the world.

Of course, low fertilizer use does not necessarily imply loss of efficiency if extensive agriculture is socially more profitable than intensive agriculture in Thailand. However, the simultaneous taxation and subsidization of agriculture has severe efficiency and distributional implications, especially when taxation is as general and as effective as the rice export premium, while subsidization is as partial and ineffective as the price support and the fertilizer subsidy. The World Bank (1983) has estimated the direct income impact on farmers of rice taxation to be between B 8.4 and 14.5 billion annually and of rubber taxation B 3.3. billion and concluded that "these direct income effects of the pricing policies alone take out as much or more from the rural areas as the combined rural development expenditures for agriculture and non-farm activities" (p. 16).

While economically ineffective and costly, the price support and the fertilizer subsidy, like the consumption subsidy, have been very successful politically because they constitute a visible government concern, they benefit those who have political power, and they have no budgetary opportunity costs since they use earmarked funds from export taxation.

In economic terms, implicit and perhaps unintended subsidies have

TABLE 6. Share of extra margins generated by the 1982–83 price support program, indicating "leakages"

Beneficiaries	Share of extra-margins generated (%)		
	Farmers' paddy	Millers' paddy	Total[b]
Millers	8.4	16.9	25.3
Exporters	8.4	20.0	28.4
MOF[a] and its officials	4.4	16.1	20.5
Local-level officials	—	6.3	6.3
Farm leaders	—	6.3	6.3
Farmers	8.5	4.7	13.3
Total	29.7	70.3	100.0

SOURCE: World Bank (1985), p. 49.
[a]MOF = Marketing Organization of Farmers
[b]These percentages may not add up to exactly 100 because of rounding error.

been more effective in raising agricultural production and supporting farmers' income than explicit and highly publicized input subsidies and price support programs. The supply of water free of charge from publicly funded irrigation facilities is an important subsidy to the agricultural sector. Bertrand (1980) has estimated the implicit irrigation subsidy at B 200–700 per hectare for paddy (depending on location and season), at B 400 per hectare for sugarcane, B 300 for tobacco, and B 150 for maize. This subsidy has both positive and negative efficiency (and distributional) implications. On the positive side, the implicit irrigation subsidy offsets part of the price distortion and disincentive to agriculture in general and rice in particular introduced by export taxes. On the negative side, the supply of water free of charge results in inefficient use and waste. Irrigation efficiency is as low as 15 percent of the potential and the "total area of the second and third crops is estimated at no more than 25 percent of the area irrigated . . . the early investments in large-scale irrigation did not yield the planned return" (Rijk and Van Der Meer 1984, pp. x–xix).

A substantial input subsidy for the labor-using nonrice agricultural and nonagricultural sectors is implied by, and partly affects, the disincentives created by rice taxation, which undervalues the opportunity cost of labor. Bertrand (1980) estimates this undervaluation (or subsidy) to be 16 percent of the market wage during the wet season in all regions except for the south where 8 percent adjustment is used because of the smaller role played by rice in the south.

The most significant and least quantifiable implicit subsidy is the availability of free public forest land for agricultural expansion. Barker, Herdt and Rose (1985) report that 75 percent of the rice production growth during 1967–72 and 86 percent during 1972–77 was due to area expansion. For upland crops the contribution of land area to growth has been almost 100 percent. In the same way that free water has benefited farmers in irrigated areas, free land has benefited farmers in the rain-fed areas. Again, in terms of efficiency there are positive and negative aspects. On the one hand, the availability of free land has offset part of the distortion and disincentive introduced by export taxation, and part of the efficiency and distributional distortion introduced by the supply of free water in irrigated areas. On the other hand, the failure to account for the social opportunity cost of land and forests and related externalities (see Panayotou, 1983) and the underinvestment resulting from insecure ownership (almost 50 percent of agricultural land is not securely titled) imply considerable efficiency losses (see Onchan and Feder, 1985).

Income Distribution and Nutrition

The distributional effects of food policies have been considerable but not in line with the declared national objectives of reducing rural-urban inequalities. As we have seen, about B 5.0 billion were transferred in 1981 from farmers to nonfarm consumers and B 3.4 billion to the government, a fraction (not more than 50 percent) of which was returned to selected farmers in the form of price support or other interventions.

We have already seen the effects of the rice reserve requirement as a tax burden on the producers and as an indirect subsidy on the consumers through its effect on domestic prices via the reduction of exports. The reentry of these rice reserves into the market as cheap rice had a further depressing effect on domestic prices. Coupled with the fact that most of the cheap rice was distributed and consumed in Bangkok, this further exacerbated inequalities between urban and rural households. Moreover, since many of the urban poor did not meet the documentation requirements of the program while wealthy urban consumers had free access to the program, urban-urban inequalities were also widened.

Rice export taxation, however, had positive effects on rural-rural and possibly on urban-urban income distribution. Only 30–50 percent of total production is marketed. Fifty percent of paddy farmers sell less than 10 percent of their rice production, and many are net purchasers of rice. Trairatvorakul (1984) has estimated the elasticity of marketable surplus to be positive, ranging from .08 to .12, and the price elasticity of rice consumption among farmers to be negative, ranging from −0.3 to −0.8. He infers that when the price of rice rises, small farmers sell more and eat less without substituting other foods for rice, thus experiencing a decline in calorie intake and nutritional status. Trairatvorakul, having researched in depth the effects on income distribution and nutrition of rice price policies, concludes that elimination of rice export taxation would benefit the large commercial farmers (the top three deciles of rural households) who will receive about 50 percent of the net gains to the rural sector, while the bottom three deciles would receive only 13 percent of the gains.

When the gains from the supply response (short-run elasticity of 0.36) and the rise in wages are included, the distribution of total net gains improves (37 percent versus 27 percent), but it is not reversed. At the same time, higher rice prices would reduce the real incomes and the nutritional status of vulnerable socioeconomic groups such as small paddy farmers, small farmers of other crops, fishermen, and farm workers who are net buyers of food.

Urban-urban distribution would also worsen since urban poor spend a larger proportion of their income on food than urban high-income consumers. By implication, while rice export taxation has widened the rural-urban income gap, it has reduced this gap within each area and has probably made a modest contribution toward the alleviation of the worst forms of poverty and malnutrition. Nationwide, however, rice export taxation has raised the number of households in poverty. Trairatvorakul calculates that an increase in rice prices by 50 percent would reduce the percentage of poor households among rice growers from 34 percent in 1975–76 to 27 percent, and increase it among the rest of the population from 16 percent to 20 percent. Overall poverty would be reduced from 26.0 percent to 23.6 percent.

The rice price support, the fertilizer subsidy, the protection and subsidization of the sugar sector, and the implicit irrigation subsidy have all benefited the larger, more affluent farmers of the central region and had little effect on the rain-fed rice and cassava growers of the northeast, thereby exacerbating further an already wide regional income gap. The main countervailing force that kept the widening of this gap in check, and has in fact contributed to a reduction in "absolute" poverty, has been the free access to public forest land for expansion of cultivation in conjunction with the almost free access of Thai cassava to the EEC animal feed market.

Finally, the industrial trade policies that protected domestically produced manufactures from foreign competition have contributed to a widening of the rural-urban income gap by raising the costs of agricultural inputs and consumer goods purchased by farmers, and to further deterioration of agriculture's terms of trade with industry.

Price Stability

In terms of price stability, the acclaimed objective of price intervention during the late 1960s and the 1970s, export taxation performed well. World rice prices are extremely volatile because most rice production is rain-fed and therefore subject to the variability of weather, and because only 3 percent of world rice production is traded internationally.

The Thai government has attempted to insulate domestic prices from world price fluctuations by varying the export premium. The coefficient of variation of the domestic price of rice during 1961–80 was only 12.3

compared to 20.3 in the world market. This price stability compares favorably with that of other developing countries for the same period, for example Indonesia (30.2), Burma (28.2), Sri Lanka (35.7), and Bangladesh (17.7). In constant prices for the period 1970–82, the coefficient of variation was only 0.115 with a mean price of B 6.5 per kilogram, which implies considerable stability in consumers' real incomes. Figure 2 shows trends in Bangkok wholesale prices and farm paddy prices, which are relatively stable, especially in comparison to the extreme variability of the f.o.b. export price (see figure 1). It is also worth noting that farm prices have been relatively more stable than Bangkok wholesale prices. The variance of the farmgate price during 1967–80 was 78 percent of the variance of the Bangkok wholesale price, and only 26 percent of the variance of the export price. The variance of the Bangkok wholesale price of rice averaged only 33 percent of the variance of the export price (see table 7). The adjustment of the rice export tax during this period was the main factor reducing the variation of the Bangkok wholesale price. While the government deserves full credit for price stabilization, this stabilization has been attained at high cost. Since prices were stabilized at low rather than high or intermediate levels, farmers' production incentives were dampened and resource allocation suffered. Price stability around a long-term price trend would be a preferable strategy to the almost complete insulation from market forces caused by export taxation, which averaged almost 40 percent of the f.o.b. price for a thirty-five-year period.

The World Bank (1985) proposed for Thailand a "policy which introduces taxes and subsidies in an automatic way only when the world price exceeds or falls short of certain thresholds and only for so long as the world price continues to remain beyond these thresholds" (p. 27). Almost the same degree of domestic price stabilization for the years 1970–82 could have been accomplished with an export tax for 1973–74 and an export subsidy for 1971 and 1982 and no intervention for the remaining nine years. The effect on the government budget would have been positive, and farm prices would have been allowed to rise steadily with the long-term trend of world prices. Consumers, however, would have had to pay higher rice prices (averaged B 10.67/kg compared to the actual of B 6.56/kg).

The export prices of the other major crops, such as maize, cassava, and sorghum have been considerably more stable than rice prices. However, because of the absence of government stabilization efforts or other interventions that cut the linkage between the world and domestic markets, a larger percentage (55–85 percent) of the export price variation was transmitted to the Bangkok wholesale market (see table 7). On the other hand, the transmission of price variations from the wholesale market to the farm was lower for upland crops than for rice because of a lower degree of competitiveness in local markets.

One argument for price stabilization is that price instability discourages

FIGURE 2. Wholesale and farmgate prices of rice (current year prices)

Baht/ton

- - - - - Bangkok wholesale price of 5% rice
———— Farmgate price of paddy

Year

SOURCE: World Bank (1985), pp. 105–106.

TABLE 7. Variances of export, wholesale, and farmgate prices of major crops (based on 1967–80 figures)

Crop	Export price	Wholesale price	Bangkok farmgate price
Rice	4.75	1.58 (33%)*	1.24 (26%)* (78%)**
Maize	0.57	0.49 (85%)*	0.30 (52%)* (61%)**
Cassava	0.54	0.34 (62%)*	0.1833 (52%)**
Mung bean	0.86	6.15 (76%)*	1.65 (20%)* (27%)**
Sorghum	0.65	0.36 (55%)*	0.21 (32%)* (58%)**

SOURCE: Kunwatanusorn (1983).
    *percent of variance of export price
    **percent of variance of Bangkok wholesale price

investment and slows down production growth. Kunwatanusorn (1983), who has studied the effect of instability of world prices on the production of major food crops in Thailand, found little responsiveness among farmers to farmgate price fluctuations. He concludes that a policy of raising crop prices would be more effective in stimulating output growth than a policy of stabilizing prices at a lower average level.

Crop Diversification

A suggested objective of rice export taxation has been to promote crop diversification away from rice. Although there is apparently no quantitative study that relates the expansion of nonrice crops to rice export taxation, the heavy taxation of the rice sector—about 52 percent of the farmgate price—compared with the light taxation of the upland crops—3–6 percent of their farmgate price (see table 3)—has undoubtedly contributed to a rapid expansion of the upland crop area and a slower expansion of paddy area. Between 1965 and 1980 paddy area increased by only 44 percent compared to a 300 percent increase in the area planted to maize and sugar and an 800 percent increase in the area planted to cassava. In terms of output, the contribution of rice to crop GDP declined from 53 percent in 1960 to 39 percent in 1980, while that of all upland crops increased from 8 percent in 1960 to 19 percent in 1980 (World Bank, 1982). The share of the two traditional export crops, rice and rubber, in total agricultural exports dropped from 66 percent in 1962 to 30 percent in 1975, while that of sugarcane, cassava and maize increased from 13 percent to 51 percent during the same period.

The extent to which considerable diversification was caused by differential export taxation depends on the cross-price elasticities of supply, which in turn depend partly on climatic, soil, and water conditions. Wong (1978) estimated the cross-price elasticity between rice and other crops to be -0.28 in the short run and -0.63 in the long run. These elasticities imply considerable scope for crop substitution in response to price incentives. Therefore, it is likely that export taxation on rice is responsible for a significant portion of observed crop diversification. These output price effects would be reinforced by implicit land and labor subsidies for nonrice agriculture due to export taxation's depressing effect on the opportunity cost of land and labor taken out of the rice sector.

As we have seen earlier, rice production would have been up to 4.5 million tons larger without export taxation. To the extent that prime paddy land less suitable for upland crops has been switched out of rice production, or has been used less intensively in response to rice export taxation, there has been a loss in both efficiency and growth in aggregate agricultural output. For example, the switching of land from rice to sugarcane that has occurred in the central region as a result of the taxation of the rice sector and the protection of the sugar industry constitutes a misallocation of resources because Thailand has a clear comparative and absolute advantage in the production of rice. Sugarcane would not have been a major crop in Thailand without the combined effect of sugar protection and rice taxation.

In conclusion, rice taxation has been successful in promoting the diversification of Thai agriculture and structural change for the economy as a whole, but it is not clear that the benefits from diversification outweigh the forgone benefits of specialization. Moreover, the diversification was accomplished "through policies that have worsened the distribution of income by transferring substantial resources from the agricultural to the non-agricultural sector" (Bertrand, 1980, p. 80).

Dynamic Efficiency, Structural Change, and Growth

Food price policies have important effects on dynamic allocative efficiency and economic growth, which could prove to be more significant than their static effects on welfare. On the consumption side, distorted food prices lead to distorted patterns of demand growth, and therefore distorted patterns of investment and structural change. To the extent that they affect nutrition, they also have implications for the development of human capital (Timmer, 1986). On the production or supply side, price expectations influence investment decisions and technological change.

Tolley, Thomas, and Wong (1982) have calculated that the benefit-cost ratio of shifting from traditional varieties (TV) to high yielding varieties (HYV) in well-irrigated areas of Thailand is reduced from 4.04 to 3.30 and in less well-irrigated areas from 3.76 to 3.08 because of the rice export premium. Thus the effect of export taxation on dynamic efficiency is negative but small if we consider only technology adoption. However, this negative effect is likely to be considerably larger if we consider the effect of the taxation on investment in land development and water control, which is necessary if the high risk of crop failure with HYVs is to be reduced.

The combination of low rice prices, high fertilizer prices, and insecurity of land ownership is at least partially responsible for the observed underinvestment in land improvement and on farm irrigation. Poor water control coupled with high cost of low-response fertilizer is not conducive to the adoption of HYVs. Only in well-irrigated areas with adequate drainage and only during the dry season have HYVs of rice been adopted covering only 9 percent of the paddy area. In contrast, sugarcane policies (protection of the domestic market and export price subsidies) have encouraged rates of investment in production and processing that are unjustified by Thailand's comparative disadvantage in sugar production and the unfavorable long-term prospects of the industry.

The dynamic effects of food prices work their way not only through technological innovation and investment but also through changes in the resource base. High fertilizer prices combined with relatively attractive upland crop prices have contributed to the deforestation of watersheds (see Panayotou, 1983) and the cultivation of marginal lands now experiencing second-generation problems of floods, droughts, and soil erosion, which in turn will alter the future crop mix and cropping pattern. Flooded areas in the central plain are being converted to deep-water rice and fish farming, while cassava land in the east is being converted to rubber. This foreclosure of options involves losses in terms of dynamic allocative efficiency.

At a sectoral level, low food price policies combined with industrial protection have turned the terms of trade dramatically against agriculture and in favor of manufacturing, inducing an artificially rapid rate of structural change that does not reflect the true state of development of the economy. The share of agricultural employment in total employment has declined very slowly (over 70 percent of the labor force is still employed in agriculture), whereas the share of agriculture in GDP has dropped rapidly to less than a quarter. While agriculture's relative contribution to the economy declines and that of industry rises as a natural and inevitable outcome of the development process, price policies have accelerated the process.

The dynamic efficiency effects of price policies have important implications for both the rate and the pattern of growth. Delayed technological change, underinvestment in some crops and industries and overinvestment in others, degraded resource base and accelerated structural change, all imply a waste of resources and reduced overall productivity and result in slower sustainable growth than would have been possible otherwise. Amranand (1983) using the SIAM2 computable general equilibrium model, which captures only some of these dynamic effects, found that, depending on the elasticity of world demand for Thai rice, a reduction of the rice export tax by 5 percent would increase GDP by 0.16–0.24 percent, while a B 5 billion worth *effective* price support would increase GDP by 0.26–0.72 percent. These are admittedly small gains, but they are only a partial indication of the dynamic response to changes in price policies.

Food Policy Tradeoffs

Food price policy inevitably involves dilemmas and tradeoffs, and despite Thailand's sizable food surplus, Thai food policy is no exception. The most important tradeoffs facing Thai policy makers have been (1) domestic consumption versus exports; (2) consumers' versus producers' welfare; (3) price stability versus price incentive transmission; (4) domestic versus international price stability; (5) government revenues versus export earnings; (6) pricing policies versus budgetary considerations; (7) crop specialization versus crop diversification; (8) agricultural growth versus industrialization; and (9) short-run gains versus long-run considerations (sustainability of the growth process). The way these tradeoffs and conflicts are resolved, whether deliberately or by default, is critical to the efficiency, equity, and growth outcomes of food price policy.

Domestic Consumption versus Exports

Thai food price policies have had a domestic consumption bias. An important consideration since the early sixties has been the availability of sufficient quantities of food for domestic consumption to meet a growing demand without politically unacceptable price rises. Food security in this special sense has been pursued by restricting food exports rather than by promoting food production, either because policy makers believed that any increase in production will be exported (since export prices always exceeded domestic prices) or because they assumed near zero price elasticity of food supply. While policy makers perceived the problem as simply one of allocation of a given production between the domestic and world markets, in fact, food production and the supply of marketable surplus are not independent of the instruments used in effecting this allocation. Rice export taxation in particular has affected production incentives and reduced domestic production. As depicted in table 8, an increase in domestic rice consumption by 139,000–323,000 tons was accomplished at the expense of 371,000–1,165,000 tons of rice production and 509,000–1,488,000 tons of rice exports, depending on whether low (short-run) or high (long-run) demand and supply elasticities are used (see appendix table). The social loss in production from price distortions in four major crops (rice, maize, sugar, and rubber) in 1976 was estimated in the range of U.S. $23–70 million while the social gain in consumption was only $4–9 million implying a net social loss of $14–42 million. In addition, $111–324 million in foreign exchange was lost in a single year. Thus the policy dilemma was resolved in favor of consumption and against production and exports, although it was possible to reconcile the conflict by using more neutral policy instruments or by providing compensatory production incentives. However, this would have involved another tradeoff between pricing policy and budgetary considerations.

Consumers' Welfare versus Producers' Welfare

The resolution of the production-consumption-exports tradeoff in favor of consumption through export taxes, and the resulting low food prices without compensatory production incentives or income transfers for producers, imply a policy choice in favor of consumers and against producers. The consumption subsidy has provided additional welfare gains to con-

TABLE 8.   Real effects of price distortions in Thailand, 1976

Estimate change in	Rice	Maize	Sugar	Rubber
Production (thousand tons)				
Low	−371	5	55	−37
High	−1,165	16	166	−117
Consumption (thousand tons)				
Low	139	0	−37	0
High	323	−1	−112	1
Exports (thousand tons)				
Low	−509	6	93	−37
High	−1,488	17	278	−117
Employment (workers)				
Average coefficient				
Low	−49,467	400	6,197	−666
High	−155,333	1,230	18,703	−2,106
Marginal coefficient				
Low	−71,727	800	9,295	−999
High	−225,233	2,560	28,054	−3,159

NOTE: *Low* refers to low elasticity estimates; *high* refers to high elasticity estimates. See appendix table A for the basic data used in the calculations of high elasticity estimates.
SOURCE: Bale and Lutz (1981), p. 15.

sumers, also at the expense of producers since the source of the subsidy has been the rice reserve requirement imposed on rice exporters and ultimately borne by the farmers. In contrast, the price support program and the fertilizer subsidy have been generally underfunded and ineffective, and in any case, the funds came from agricultural taxation (Farmers' Aid Fund).

In the last decade there has been a perceptible policy shift toward a more balanced resolution of the conflict between consumers and producers, but no effective instruments have yet been introduced. While on average consumers gained and producers lost as a result of government policies, the direction of gains and losses has varied across crops. Bale and Lutz (1981) have estimated that when all major crops are considered, in a single year (1976) consumers gained over $600 million and producers lost over $700 million from price distortions (see table 9). In the case of rice, price distortions have resulted in a welfare gain for rice consumers of about $750 million and a welfare loss for rice producers of about $850 million in a single year (1976). In contrast, sugar consumers incurred a welfare loss of about $130 million, whereas sugar producers enjoyed a welfare gain of about $330 million because of the protection and subsidies provided to the sugar industry. (More recently, sugar protection and subsidies have been reduced and in price boom years an export premium was imposed.)

Price Stability versus Price Transmission

Policy makers faced with a choice between stable domestic prices insulated from world market fluctuations, and fluctuating prices in response to

TABLE 9. Net social losses and monetary effect of price distortion in Thailand, 1976 (in thousand U.S. dollars)

	Rice	Maize	Sugar	Rubber	Total
Net social loss in production					
Low	10,503	6	5,363	6,641	22,513
High	33,008	18	16,088	20,659	69,773
Net social loss in consumption					
Low	3,926	0	3,623	0	7,549
High	91,161	1	10,868	100	20,180
Total net social loss					
Low	14,429	6	8,985	6,641	80,061
High	42,169	19	26,955	20,759	89,903
Welfare gain of producers					
Low	−864,557	61,146	334,968	−148,421	−671,864
High	−887,062	6,134	324,243	−162,439	−719,124
Welfare gain of consumers					
Low	741,019	−660	−126,235	9,570	623,694
High	735,784	−661	−133,480	9,471	611,114
Government revenues	109,109	−5,492	−217,791	132,210	18,108
Foreign exchange earnings					
Low	−110,989	636	27,647	−26,041	−108,747
High	−324,376	1,907	82,408	−81,408	−302,935

NOTE: *Low* refers to low elasticity estimates; *high* refers to high elasticity estimates. See appendix table A for the basic data used in the calculations of high elasticity estimates.
SOURCE: Bale and Lutz (1981), p. 18.

world market conditions, opted for the former on the grounds that price stability benefits both consumers and producers. However, since prices have been stabilized below their long-term trend, price stability cannot be said to have benefited food producers. Moreover, where the government severed the link to the world market, price signals reflecting changes in world market demand and supply and the opportunity costs of resources have not been accurately transmitted to producers, resulting in a distorted allocation of resources. As indicated in table 10, the transmission coefficients between export prices and domestic prices are lowest in the case of rice (75 percent) and sugar (55 percent), where government interventions have been the greatest. The stabilization of domestic rice prices at low levels and of sugar prices at high levels, compared to world prices, has distorted Thailand's comparative advantage against rice and in favor of sugar.

Domestic versus International Price Stability

Thailand, as a major world exporter of rice, could have helped stabilize the world rice market by increasing rice exports during world rice shortages and reducing exports during world rice surpluses to reduce world

TABLE 10. Price transmission coefficients among export prices, Bangkok wholesale prices, and farmgate prices

Crop	Export to Bangkok wholesale		Bangkok wholesale to farm	
	r_{xw}[a]	E_{xw}[b]	r_{wf}[c]	E_{wf}[d]
Rice	0.75 (t_0)	0.65 (t_0)	0.98 $(t_{1/2})$	0.99 $(t_{1/2})$
Maize	0.94 $(t_{1/2})$	0.87 $(t_{1/2})$	0.93 (t_1)	1.0 (t_1)
Sugar[e]	0.55 $(t_{1/2})$	0.35 $(t_{1/2})$	0.85 (t_1)	0.97 (t_1)
Cassava[f]	0.96 (t_0)	1.0 (t_0)	0.92 (t_0)	1.1 (t_0)

NOTE: Items in parentheses indicate the associated time lag (in months). For example, t_0 indicates the same month, $t_{1/2}$ a half-month lag, etc. The time lags selected are the ones with the highest value of r and E.
SOURCE: World Bank (1985), p. 66.
[a] r_{xw} represents the proportion of Bangkok wholesale price changes explained by changes at the export price level.
[b] E_{xw} represents the % change in wholesale price following a 1% change in the export price.
[c] r_{wf} represents the proportion of farm price changes explained by changes at the Bangkok wholesale price level.
[d] E_{wf} represents the % change in farm price following a 1% change in the Bangkok wholesale price.
[e] Raw sugar at export to Bangkok wholesale level. Sugarcane at the Bangkok wholesale to farm level.
[f] Cassava pellets.

price fluctuations. Instead the Thai government chose to stabilize domestic rice prices at the expense of international price stability. During times of world rice shortages and high export prices (e.g., 1981) the government raised export taxes and restricted rice exports to prevent a rise in domestic prices, thereby putting further upward pressure on world prices. During times of world rice surpluses and low export prices (e.g., 1983), export taxes were lowered and exports promoted putting further downward pressure on world prices. Therefore, the Thai price stabilization policies have had a destabilizing effect on world rice prices.

Government Revenues versus Export Earnings

Export taxation has been justified partly as a means of increasing Thailand's export earnings by raising export prices more than reducing export quantities. However, the government has been reluctant to eliminate or reduce sufficiently export taxation when it was obvious that such a move would increase export earnings without a significant effect on domestic rice prices. In earlier years, collection of government revenues was a major objective of food policy. In recent years, replenishment of the Farmers' Aid Fund for financing politically visible programs such as the crop price support and the fertilizer subsidy occasionally has taken precedence over export earnings when the two are in obvious conflict (e.g., 1983). Bale and Lutz (1981) estimated that in 1976 price distortions earned the government $109 million and deprived the country of $111–324 million in foreign exchange earnings.

Pricing Policies versus Budgetary Considerations

In formulating its food price policies, the government has made a deliberate effort to minimize the burden on government budget. Subsidies have been set in forms and levels that could be self-financed, with little or no obvious drain on the budget. For instance, the rice consumption subsidy was provided from the rice reserve requirement imposed on rice exporters; the farm price support and fertilizer subsidy have been financed from export taxation (Farmers' Aid Fund), although export taxes were not initially intended to fund farm support programs; and the sugar export subsidy and the rubber replanting program have been financed through cess taxes. The government has generally avoided setting prices or subsidies at levels that would require direct government outlays. Of course, even self-financed subsidies constitute an indirect drain on the budget not only because tax revenues are to some degree fungible but also because the government has a limiting tax-collecting ability, and therefore the government must make choices among competing earmarked tax programs.

Specialization versus Diversification

Despite Thailand's considerable comparative advantage in rice and rubber production, the government has promoted crop diversification both through rice and rubber taxation and through assistance to other crops, especially sugar and cotton in which the country has no comparative advantage. Other upland crops such as maize and cassava have also been promoted through relatively little or no taxation. The high taxation on rice is equivalent to a land-and-labor subsidy for other crops and has been explicitly justified as a deliberate policy to promote diversification of Thai agriculture away from rice. While this is consistent with the policy makers' perception of the world demand for Thai rice as inelastic, it is not clear that the benefits from diversification outweigh the forgone benefits from specialization.

Agricultural Growth versus Industrialization

In the same way that Thailand tried to diversify away from rice, it has tried to diversify away from agriculture in general, through taxation of agriculture and promotion and protection of industry. While industrialization is part and parcel of the development process, concurrent agricultural growth is equally important both in its own right and as a source of food, labor, raw materials, and savings for industrial growth. The combination of agricultural commodity and industrial trade policies suggests a strong bias in favor of rapid industrialization and forced structural change. As with crop diversification, it is not clear that the gains from faster structural change exceed the costs of slower agricultural growth, especially when the promoted industries are capital intensive.

Short Run versus Long Run

While agricultural growth in Thailand has not been slow by comparison to other countries, it is important to consider that 90 percent of this growth came from expansion of the area under cultivation rather than from productivity growth. This is not necessarily undesirable given Thailand's relative factor endowments. Since the land frontier has been virtually exhausted, however, future growth must come from productivity growth. In addition, since expansion into forest areas and marginal lands has impaired the resource base of agriculture, considerable productivity improvement will be necessary simply to maintain production, let alone to induce further growth. Unfortunately, insecure ownership over almost 50 percent of the agricultural land, resulting from forest encroachment, is not conducive to making the necessary investments for productivity growth (Onchan and Feder, 1985).

Because institutional reform, technological change, and rehabilitation of the resource base are lengthy and costly processes, it does appear that past growth through uncontrolled land expansion has been partly attained at the expense of future growth. Long-term sustainability would have dictated a more regulated land expansion combined with gradual productivity improvement. Past agricultural policies apparently have adopted a short-term view of agricultural growth, though probably not deliberately.

Summary and Conclusion

Since the end of World War II, Thai policy makers have employed a panoply of price policy instruments to attain a combination of conflicting food policy objectives, including government revenues, export earnings, low and stable food prices, crop diversification, income distribution and nutrition, structural change and growth, and higher farming incomes. While there has been a gradual shift in emphasis from government revenues to consumer welfare and price stability, and more recently to farming incomes, all these objectives continue to play a role in current food price policy.

The inevitable conflicts and tradeoffs between objectives have on balance been resolved, either deliberately or by default, in favor of urban food consumers, nonrice farmers, in particular sugar farmers, industrial producers, the government budget, domestic price stability, and short-term growth. Rural food producers (especially rice farmers), industrial goods consumers, foreign exchange earnings, international price stability, and long-term sustainable growth have suffered.

Policy instruments that have been employed include export taxes and quotas, consumption subsidies, farm price supports, input taxes and subsidies, industrial protection, interest rate ceilings, and minimum wages.

Of all these, rice export taxation stands out as the most important instrument in terms of its impact on both the food sector and the rest of the economy. Consumers' welfare and farmers' incomes, government revenue and export earnings, crop diversification and structural change, growth and income distribution, have all been among the objectives and effects of rice export taxation. Rice and rubber taxation have combined with industrial protection in turning the terms of trade decisively against agriculture and inducing rapid structural change and industrialization. That is, industrial trade policies (cf. protection) have compounded the effects of agricultural trade policies (cf. export taxation).

Of the remaining policy instruments, the most effective have been sugar protection and export subsidies, and fertilizer protection and import taxes. The former resulted in a rapid expansion of the sugar industry, and the latter slowed growth in fertilizer use. The rice consumption subsidy, the farm price support, and the fertilizer subsidy have been generally underfunded and ineffective in attaining their acclaimed objectives. Their main effects have been the creation of extra margins and rents for a long chain of intermediaries and a small group of well-positioned beneficiaries, at a significant cost to the rest of the rice sector which paid part of the cost (through taxation). In political terms, however, these policy instruments have been more effective than either rice export taxation or industrial protection because they constitute a visible government concern for the welfare of both consumers and producers. It could even be argued that these economically ineffective but politically powerful instruments have been used as a smoke screen to disguise the heavy burden imposed on food producers and industrial good consumers through export taxation and industrial protection.

In contrast to the considerable price distortions introduced by agricultural and industrial trade policies, macro price policies have had relatively little adverse effect on the food sector, either because they have been kept close to their equilibrium values (exchange rate) or because they have been ineffective (minimum wage rate). The main exception has been interest rate ceilings, which have limited formal rural credit and forced farmers into higher-interest, informal markets, thereby distorting the pattern of investment against agriculture and in favor of industry.

Despite the heavy direct and indirect taxation, Thai agriculture has managed to grow at a rate of 4–5 percent per annum and to remain competitive in world markets through a combination of free land available for expansion in the north and the northeast, and free irrigation water available for intensification and multiple cropping in the central plain, as well as through relatively abundant low-cost labor. These implicit land, water, and labor subsidies have been far more effective in promoting agricultural growth and raising farmers' incomes in the otherwise unfavor-

APPENDIX TABLE A.   Basic data used in the estimation of price distortions in Thailand, 1976

	Rice	Maize	Sugar	Rubber
Border price (U.S. $/ton)	218	115	298	695
Nominal protection coefficient	.74	1.02	1.65	.49
Supply elasticities				
Low	.07	.10	.08	.09
High	.22	.30	.24	.28
Demand elasticities				
Low	−.03	−.05	−.15	.00
High	−.07	−.15	−.45	−.02
Production (thousand tons)	15,063	2,675	1,757	400
Consumption (thousand tons)	13,143	287	633	27
Exports (thousand tons)	1,925	2,388	1,124	373
Labor coefficient (man-hrs/ton)				
Average	400	240	338	54
Marginal	580	480	507	81

NOTE: *Low* refers to low elasticity estimates; high refers to high elasticity estimates.
SOURCE: Bale and Lutz (1981), p. 13.

able price environment than have the explicit price support and fertilizer subsidies.

However, the future cannot be a simple projection of the past because of the approaching land frontiers and the rising private and social costs of bringing new land into cultivation and of expanding the area under irrigation. Moreover, today's agriculture has inherited some of the legacies of the past uncontrolled expansion, including a degraded resource base and insecure land ownership. Under these circumstances there would be little to compensate for the continued heavy taxation of agriculture. Policy reform and institutional change to improve efficiency in resource use and provide incentives for productivity improvement are needed both to stimulate new sources of growth and to maintain Thailand's comparative advantage in world food markets. Policy changes that would improve agriculture's terms of trade are becoming increasingly likely as the share of food in the consumer's budget falls and political power shifts from urban consumers to rural producers.

In light of these considerations, the key pricing issues for the future will include the following: the elimination of existing price distortions; the design of an appropriate incentive structure to stimulate productivity improvement; the pricing of irrigation water to promote efficient use; the reform of fertilizer price structure to promote the use of nitrogen fertilizer; and the design of a new price stabilization system that would allow transmission of long-term price signals from the world market to the domestic economy. To be effective such price policy reform should be accompanied by institutional reform to provide security of land ownership and protection of the resource base. In addition, investment in appropriate (seed) technology for the flooding and rain-fed areas of the country would be helpful. Obviously, this is a long list of policy reforms. Nevertheless, such reforms would help raise efficiency, stimulate growth, and improve income distribution. Although it would be unrealistic to expect all these policy reforms and institutional changes to take place at once, recent government efforts to reduce rice taxation, promote fertilizer use, issue land titles, and improve irrigation efficiency justify a degree of optimism that these reforms can and will be made in the foreseeable future. The reform of trade and industrial policies appear less likely.

The main lesson to be derived from the Thai food price policy experience is that "getting prices right" is neither a necessary nor a sufficient condition for agricultural growth. Getting prices "wrong" in the past has not retarded agricultural growth because there were other important compensating factors: free irrigation water and free land for expansion. Getting prices "right" in the future would not automatically generate new sources of growth if the necessary institutional reform and technical change do not take place. However, growing under "wrong" prices is not without costs as the excessive diversification, resource depletion, and widening of the rural-urban gap in Thailand suggest.

References

Amranand, P. 1983. "Impact of the Price Support Programme for Rice." *The Siam Project on Macro Economic Management of the Thai Economy.* Bangkok: National Economic and Social Development Board and World Bank.

Bale, M. D., and E. Lutz. 1981. "Price Distortions in Agriculture and Their Effects: An International Comparison." *American Journal of Agricultural Economics* 63:8–22.

Barker, R., R. W. Herdt, and B. Rose. 1985. *The Rice Economy of Asia.* Washington, D.C.: Resources for the Future.

Bertrand, T. 1980. *Thailand: Case Study of Agricultural Input and Output Pricing.* World Bank Staff Working Paper no. 385. Washington, D.C.

Kim, H. 1984. "Financial and Economic Analysis of Farm Enterprise Models." Background Paper no. 1 for *Thailand: Pricing and Marketing Policy for Intensification of Rice Agriculture,* World Bank Country Study. Washington, D.C.: World Bank.

Krongkaew, M. 1985. "Agricultural Development, Rural Poverty and Income Distribution in Thailand." *The Developing Economies* 23(4).

Kunwatanusorn, S. 1983. "Effects of Instability of World Prices of Major Food Crops on Their Production: A Case Study of Thailand." Thesis, Thammasat University, Bangkok.

Onchan, T., and G. Feder. 1985. "Land Titling and Agricultural Development of Thailand: Some Current Research Results." Paper presented at the Seminar on Managing Renewable Resources: Historical and Contemporary Perspectives, June 24–28, Sapporo, Japan.

Panayotou, T. 1983. "Renewable Resource Management for Agricultural and Rural Development in Southeast Asia: Research and Policy Issues." Paper presented at

108   THEODORE PANAYOTOU

the Fifth Biennial Meeting of the Agricultural Economics Society of Southeast Asia (AESSEA), November 16–19, Bangkok.

——, ed. 1985. *Food Policy Analysis in Thailand*. Bangkok and New York: Agricultural Development Council.

Pinthong, C. 1983. "Evaluation of Government's Rice Procurement Policy in 1982/83—The Operation of the Marketing Organization of Farmers." Background Paper 6 for *Thailand: Pricing and Marketing Policy for Intensification of Rice Agriculture*. World Bank Country Study. Washington, D.C.: World Bank.

Rijk, A. G., and C. L. J. Van Der Meer. 1984. *Thailand Agricultural Assessment Study*. Manila: Asian Development Bank.

Siamwalla, A. 1975. "A History of Rice Policies in Thailand." *Food Research Institute Studies* 14(3): 233–249.

——, and S. Setboonsarng. 1986. "The Political Economy of Agricultural Pricing Policies in Thailand." Paper prepared for the World Bank Thailand Development Institute.

Timmer, C. P. 1986. *Getting Prices Right: The Scope and Limits of Agricultural Price Policy*. Ithaca: Cornell University Press.

——, W. P. Falcon, and S. R. Pearson. 1983. *Food Policy Analysis*. Baltimore: Johns Hopkins University Press for the World Bank.

Tolley, G. S., V. Thomas, and C. M. Wong. 1982. *Agricultural Policies in Developing Countries*. Baltimore: Johns Hopkins University Press.

Trairatvorakul, P. 1984. *The Effects on Income Distribution and Nutrition of Alternative Rice Price Policies in Thailand*. Research Report 45. Washington, D.C.: International Food Policy Research Institute.

Tsujii, H. 1973. "An Econometric Study of the Effects of National Rice Policies and the Green Revolution on National Rice Economies and International Rice Trade among Less Developed Countries: With Special Reference to Thailand, Indonesia, Japan, and the U.S." Dissertation, University of Illinois.

Usher, D. 1967. "The Thai Rice Trade." In T. H. Silcock, ed., *Thailand: Social and Economic Studies in Development*, chap. 9. Canberra: Australia National University Press.

Wong, C. M. 1978. "A Model for Evaluating the Effects of Thai Government Taxation on Rice Exports on Trade and Welfare." *American Journal of Agricultural Economics* 60(1): 65–73.

World Bank. 1980. *Thailand: Coping with Structural Change in a Dynamic Economy*. Report no. 31–TH. Washington, D.C.: World Bank.

——. 1982. *Thailand Program and Policy Priorities for an Agricultural Economy in Transition*. Report no. 3705a–TH. Washington, D.C.: World Bank.

——. 1983. *Thailand: Rural Growth and Employment*. Washington, D.C.: World Bank.

——. 1984. *Thailand: Managing Public Resources for Structural Adjustment*. World Bank Country Study. Washington, D.C.: World Bank.

——. 1985. *Thailand: Pricing and Marketing Policy for Intensification of Rice Agriculture*. World Bank Country Study. Washington, D.C.: World Bank.

4. Korea: A Case of Agricultural Protection

Kym Anderson

After the devastation of the Korean War, the economy of South Korea was one of the world's poorest in terms of income per person. It was also one of the poorest in terms of physical capital and natural resources since most of the factories and mineral wealth were located in the northern half of the peninsula. Like Japan, it is among the world's most densely populated countries with twelve times as many people per hectare as in the rest of the world (or twenty times if only arable land is considered, because much of the peninsula is mountainous). Despite its poor resource endowments, however, the Korean economy has grown at twice the global average over the past twenty-five years, due primarily to a massive expansion in industrial production and exports.

An important consequence of these two features of the Korean economy—its poverty of natural resources per capita and its extremely rapid growth and industrialization—is that Korea's comparative advantage in agriculture has declined rapidly since the 1960s. Even within the agricultural sector there have been pressures for major structural adjustments associated with changes in relative input and output prices.

These pressures for structural adjustments and decline in Korea's rural sector have generated demands for a new food policy.[1] In the 1950s Korea was not unlike many other poor, agrarian economies in taxing agriculture (its export sector), protecting manufacturing from import competition, and growing rather slowly. Today it is a rapidly growing, upper-middle-income industrial economy that exports manufactured goods and is heavily dependent on imports of food and feed; and like Japan and Western Europe's advanced industrial economies, it now protects agriculture highly relative to manufacturing.

Financial assistance from the Rockefeller Brothers Fund and Stanford University's Food Research Institute is gratefully acknowledged. I also thank Ahn In-Chan for providing some recent data and Rod Tyers for simulation results on some of the effects of Korea's policies. This paper was completed while Kym Anderson was a Visiting Fellow at the Institute for International Economic Studies, University of Stockholm.

1. Food policy is virtually synonymous with agricultural policy in Korea. Its harsh climate, ranging from freezing winters to warm, humid summers, ensures that in winter agricultural production is very limited and in all seasons it is confined to temperate food products. Cereals account for nearly half the value of agricultural production (41 percent in 1984), followed by livestock products (28 percent), and fruits and vegetables (24 percent).

The purpose of this chapter is to examine the nature, causes, and effects of this dramatic change in Korea's food price policy, from taxing to subsidizing agriculture relative to manufacturing, and to draw out some policy implications and lessons from this experience for Korea and for less-developed economies.

The first section of the chapter discusses briefly the government's stated objectives of food price policy at different stages in Korea's development, together with the historical contexts in which those objectives evolved and the instruments used to achieve them. The section begins with the period of Japanese occupation, when expanding rice exports to Japan was the prime objective of imperial policy, and proceeds to the 1950s, the period of import-substituting industrialization and taxation of agriculture, when the key objective was to maintain low food prices; the mid-1960s, a time of market liberalization and export-oriented industrialization, when distortions against agriculture were removed; and the seventies and eighties, a period of growing agricultural protectionism, when the key aim of food policy was to ensure that farm incomes kept pace with nonfarm incomes and that self-sufficiency in rice was maintained. The remaining two sections of the chapter quantify the effects of recent food policies on domestic food prices, on food production, consumption, and trade, and on the welfare of farmers and others. The key effect of policy during the past two decades has been an increasing divergence between Korea's domestic and border prices for food, associated with which are the usual adverse trade and welfare effects of protection.

In short, Korea has condensed into two decades a policy transformation that took seven or eight decades in Japan and even longer in Western Europe. More than that, it now has one of the most protected agricultural sectors in the world. The chapter concludes with a summary of the findings, a discussion of the policy alternatives for Korea, speculation on the prospects for reform, and some lessons for developing economies.

Objectives and Instruments of Food Price Policy
Colonial Period

During the period of Japanese occupation (formally 1910–45), the prime objective of food policy in Korea was to expand rice exports to Japan. In 1918, following a large rise in the price of rice, riots broke out in a number of Japanese cities. The government of the day responded by pledging to eliminate Japan's dependence on foreign (noncolonial) rice by promoting rice production not only in Japan itself but also in the colonies of Korea and Taiwan. The objective of this so-called imperial self-sufficiency policy was achieved remarkably quickly: by the 1930s the Japanese Empire was 100 percent self-sufficient in rice, with the two colonies supplying about one-sixth of Japan's needs (Anderson, 1983a, p. 330).

This objective was achieved in part by large-scale investments in rice research, extension, irrigation, and related infrastructure by the Japanese in Korea (Suh, 1978). But another important form of rural assistance involved protecting rice producers from competition outside the Japanese Empire. Both tariffs and quantitative restrictions on imports were used, the effect of which was to allow rice prices within the empire to rise increasingly above international levels as domestic demand grew faster than supply. To understand this requires recognizing that the Japanese and Koreans distinguish between two types of rice: the preferred Japonica type produced in Japan and Korea and not traded outside the empire at that time, and the Indica type produced in Southeast Asia and Taiwan (Chailai variety). There was a considerable price difference between the two types, but little according to the country source of each type, as is clear from a comparison of columns 2 and 3 with column 4 of table 1. Also, there was little difference between the empire's import price and the Thai export price, allowing for transport costs (columns 5 and 6). Thus, although very little rice was imported by the empire from the late 1920s, the domestic and border prices for Southeast Asian rice shown in columns 4 and 5 are sufficiently representative to provide an indication of the nominal rate of protection in Japan and Korea for Indica rice (defined as the percentage by which the domestic price exceeds the border price). The protection rate for all rice would be slightly lower than for Indica rice, given that Japonica and Indica are less than perfect substitutes; but the changes in the Indica rate would be reasonable proxies for changes in overall rice protection (and possibly for agriculture as a whole, since rice accounted for well over half the value of all agricultural production in Japan and Korea prior to the 1950s). And the rate of protection in Korea was very similar to that in Japan because of the free operation of the rice market within the empire, as is clear from the price data in table 1: domestic prices for Korean rice were virtually the same in Japan and Korea, allowing a little for transport costs (cf. columns 1 and 3). This apparent rate of protection rose steadily until about 1920, during which time the share of the empire's rice consumption imported fell from 8 percent to 1 percent. This trend reversed during the 1920s because the ad valorem equivalent of the specific tariff fell as the international price for Indica rice rose from 1918, but resumed again in the Great Depression of the 1930s when international food prices collapsed. By the mid-1930s, when foreign imports were prohibited, the rate of protection averaged 45 percent and was as high as 60 percent in some years (column 7).

Thus food policy in Korea during the colonial period certainly boosted rice production and exports.[2] This is not to say, however, that the people of

2. Agriculture was also assisted by attempts by the Japanese government to inhibit the development of manufacturing industries in Korea, at least until the mid-1930s (Suh, 1978, chapter 8).

TABLE 1. Rice prices and the nominal rate of protection in Korea and Japan, 1903–38 (sen/kg, polished equivalent)

| | Korea | Japan | | | | Thailand | Apparent nominal rate of protection (%)[a] (7) |
| | Wholesale (at Seoul) | Wholesale (at Kobe) | | | Import | Export (all rice) (6) | |
	Korean medium-quality rice (1)	Japanese standard rice (2)	Korean third-class rice (3)	Southeast Asian rice (4)	Southeast Asian rice (5)		
1903–07		10.1	8.9	8.2	7.5	5.8	9
1908–12		11.8	10.4	9.3	7.7	7.3	21
1913–17	11.5	12.4	10.9	10.3	8.1	5.4	27
1918–22	26.0	28.6	25.9	18.8	16.5	10.7	14
1923–27	25.3	28.0	25.3	16.3	14.7	11.3	11
1928–32	17.7	18.7	17.9	14.4	11.4	8.9	26
1933–37	19.7	20.4	20.3	16.2	11.2	8.9	45
1938	23.2	25.0	25.0	20.4	11.1	9.8	84

SOURCE: Anderson, Hayami, and others (1986), table 2.2.
a[(column 4/column 5) − 1] × 100

Korea benefited from that policy at the time. Many of Korea's paddy fields were controlled by Japanese landlords. Land-tax and rent payments were made in rice, much of which was exported to Japan because the local people could not afford to consume much rice at the higher prices. During the period between the two world wars, annual rice consumption per person fell by about a third in Korea (while Japanese consumption per capita was maintained at between 160 and 170 kilograms), and this decline was only partially offset by increased consumption of other foods (see Johnston, 1953, chapter 4; Hayami and Ruttan, 1985, chapter 9).

Industrial Protection Phase

The 1940s and early 1950s were of course chaotic in Korea with the Pacific War being closely followed by the Korean War. (Details of the numerous changes in food policy during this period appear in Moon, 1975, pp. 385–90.) The government's prime objective was to keep down the price of food staples. Because farmers were required to sell grain to the government at prices well below what would have prevailed in a free market, black markets flourished during the period 1948–55; for example, the black market price for rice was usually more than double the official government price (Ban, Moon, and Perkins, 1980, p. 240). Farmers were also required to barter grain for fertilizer at an exchange rate that further taxed grain production.

In 1955 the Rhee Government signed the U.S. Farm Surplus Importation Agreement, allowing imports of PL480 shipments of grains and soybean (plus raw cotton and tallow) from the United States at little or no real cost to Korea. These shipments supplied almost one-tenth of Korea's grain consumption and accounted for 90 percent of all grain imports in the 1950s and early 1960s, thereby helping to balance food supply and demand at the government-set low price levels.

Had the exchange rate not been grossly overvalued and had domestic food prices been as high as international prices (valued at the shadow exchange rate), it is possible that Korea would have been a rice exporter in the latter 1950s and early 1960s. But instead the government chose to maintain low domestic prices for staple foods throughout this period. One reason for this decision was to keep down living costs and thereby the wages that industrialists and the government had to pay workers, since rice alone accounted for more than a third of urban household expenditure in the mid-1950s. Another reason was to lower the government's compensatory payments to landlords dispossessed of their land during the land reform program instituted in 1949: payments were made in government bonds, the value of which depended on the price of rice (ostensibly as a hedge against inflation).

Policy Transition Phase

In the 1960s, after the settling in of the new government under President Park Chung Hee, major economic policy reforms were introduced (Frank, Kim, and Westphal, 1975; Kim and Roemer, 1980; Krueger, 1979). The liberalization of the international trade and payments regime in the first half of the 1960s heralded in a new industrialization policy aimed at boosting export-oriented manufacturing production. This induced unprecedented real rates of growth of industrial production, exports, and urban wages. Between 1963 and 1979, manufacturing output grew at 20 percent per annum, export volumes grew at 25 percent, and real per capita incomes grew at almost 8 percent (compared with only 1 percent during the period 1954–63). Even since 1979 Korea's growth has continued to be rapid despite the slowdown in the rest of the world economy (Aghevli and Marquez-Ruarte, 1985).

As a result of this industrialization strategy, there has been a remarkable transformation of what was a poor, agrarian economy to what is now a highly industrialized, upper-middle-income economy. In the early 1950s agriculture accounted for almost half of GNP and two-thirds of employment; by the mid-1980s it accounted for only one-seventh of GNP and one-quarter of employment (table 2). Almost all Korea's exports in the 1950s were primary products, whereas today over 95 percent of exports are manufactured goods. Self-sufficiency in a number of foods and feeds has fallen substantially, most notably in wheat, corn, soybeans, and ruminant meat (table 3). And, most telling of all, the number of people living in farm households has almost halved since the late 1960s.

These changes suggest a marked switch in comparative advantage away from agriculture toward manufacturing, a change that is not surprising given Korea's land scarcity and rapid economic growth (Anderson, 1983b). The switch can be summarized using Balassa's (1965) "revealed" comparative advantage index, which is defined as the ratio of a commodity group's share of the country's exports relative to that commodity group's share of world exports. For Korea, this index fell for agriculture (including fish and other processed food) from 2.3 to 0.7 between 1960 and 1980 and rose for nonfood manufacturing during the same period from 0.4 to 1.5.

In addition to these intersectoral adjustments, a number of major structural changes have occurred within the agricultural sector. On the output side, the share of farm income from fruits, vegetables, and livestock products has risen rapidly, with these products increasingly supplementing cereals in the Korean diet. Furthermore, one-third of farm household income now comes from nonfarm sources, double the share during the early 1960s. On the input side, cultivated land area per farm household has been increasing, albeit rather slowly, and increases in machinery and fertilizer use have been rapidly boosting the capital intensity and produc-

TABLE 2. Structural adjustment indicators, Korea, 1963–84

	1963	1968	1973	1978	1984[a]
Share of agriculture (%) in:					
GNP (1975 prices)	44	34	26	19	15
Labor force	61	50	47	37	26
Exports	13	4	3	4	1
Share of manufacturing (%) in:					
GNP (1975 prices)	10	15	24	32	35
Labor force	8	13	16	22	23
Exports	52	77	88	90	95
Number employed in agriculture (million)	4.6	4.6	5.3	4.9	3.7
Farm population (million)	15.3	15.9	14.6	11.5	9.0
Share of net farm household income from off-farm sources (%)	18	24	19	28	33
Share of gross agricultural receipts (%) from:					
Cereals	74	57	56	48	41
Vegetables and fruit	9	14	13	23	24
Livestock products	7	14	16	21	28
Other farm products	10	15	15	8	7
Cultivated area per farm household (hectares)	.86	.90	.92	1.00	1.08
Farm machinery, fertilizer, and labor use per thousand hectares of cultivated area:					
Power tillers	0	2	12	65	250
Power threshers	3	8	28	62	133
Water pumps	4	12	20	60	127
Chemical fertilizers	97	145	260	289	354
Farm workers[b]	n.a.	3,200	2,930	2,620	2,390[c]

SOURCES: Economic Planning Board (1985a and earlier; 1985b and earlier); Ministry of Agriculture and Fisheries (1985 and earlier).
[a]Preliminary.
[b]Adult male equivalent, from World Bank (1984), table A.12.
[c]1981.

tivity of farming (table 2). This increased use of purchased inputs relative to labor and land is a response to the rapid rise in wages and land values relative to other input prices.

These structural adjustments and decline in agriculture's role in the economy would have been even greater had the government not changed its food price policy in the 1960s toward providing increasing degrees of assistance to farmers. Initially the new government tried to maintain controls on prices of food even though those on most other commodity prices were removed in July 1961. But a serious crop failure in 1962–63 sent unofficial prices soaring. This forced the government to progressively raise the food price ceilings and eventually to abandon them in 1964. This was followed by sharp falls in farm incomes relative to urban wage earners' incomes in the mid-1960s, when the former averaged only two-thirds the latter. Then in the late 1960s the United States announced that its food aid

TABLE 3.   Food self-sufficiency and income parity, Korea, 1955–84 (percent)

	1955–59	1960–64	1965–69	1970–74	1975–79	1980–84
Self-sufficiency[a]						
Rice	99	100	95	89	96	88
Barley	92	95	100	90	96	100
Wheat	38	28	21	9	3	3
Corn	54	22	40	15	6	4
Soybeans	82	89	94	81	66	29
Beef & Mutton	100	100	100	94	73	67
Pork	100	100	100	102	99	100
Chicken	100	100	100	100	100	100
Eggs	100	100	100	100	100	100
Milk	100	100	100	100	98	98
Sugar	0	0	0	0	0	0
Rural/urban income	n.a.	105[c]	74	84	97	97
(consumption) parity[b]	(n.a.)	(n.a.)	(56)[d]	(63)	(83)	(90)[e]

SOURCES: Australian National University's agricultural trade data bank (based on official government publications); Economic Planning Board (1985b and earlier).

[a]Food self-sufficiency is production divided by production plus net imports minus change in stocks, expressed as a percentage.

[b]Average income (consumption expenditure) of rural households as a percentage of the average household income (consumption expenditure) of urban wage and salary earners.

[c]1962–64.

[d]1967–69.

[e]1980–82.

shipments would be phased out, which meant that the food import bill would rise dramatically if food imports were to continue. Together these changes led to demands for a new food policy.

Growth of Agricultural Protection

Since the late 1960s the two key objectives of Korea's food price policy have been to maintain an adequate degree of food security and to ensure that farm household incomes catch up to the incomes of urban workers. Little more than lip service has been paid to consumers' interests in keeping down the level of food prices, though there has been some attempt to reduce inter- and intrayear fluctuations around trend levels. Also, the concern with the foreign exchange costs of importing food continues to diminish as industrial export earnings expand.

If the new food policy was judged solely by the extent to which the government's stated objectives have been achieved, then Korea might be considered a success story. According to official statistics, incomes of farm households caught up with those of urban wage and salary earners in 1974, and except for the 1979–80 period of low crop yields, the two have remained within 4 percent of each other ever since. A similar picture emerges from the data on consumption expenditure (table 3).

The food security objective has been perceived as requiring 100 percent self-sufficiency in rice and a high degree of self-sufficiency in other foods.

TABLE 4.   Use of formula feedstuffs in livestock production, Korea, 1970–84

	Total consumption (kt)	Formula feed consumed per animal (kg per year)			
		Beef and native cattle	Pigs	Poultry	Dairy
1970	508				
1975	901	.02	.11	.004	1.76
1976	1,382	.03	.11	.006	1.93
1977	1,896	.06	.24	.008	2.43
1978	2,693	.14	.29	.011	2.36
1979	3,880	.17	.40	.014	2.69
1980	3,463	.22	.44	.012	2.64
1981	3,490	.32	.42	.013	2.43
1982	4,420	.45	.53	.014	2.60
1983	5,852	.45	.55	.016	2.58
1984	5,985	.46	.67	.014	2.56

SOURCE: Ministry of Agriculture and Fisheries (1985 and earlier).

Again, a glance at table 3 suggests this too has been achieved, with due allowance for the severe crop failure around 1980. On closer inspection, however, it is clear that self-sufficiency in wheat is low, and for ruminant meat (primarily beef) it has fallen considerably since the early 1970s. Furthermore, self-sufficiency in rice and barley has been possible only with imports of raw material for chemical fertilizers, and self-sufficiency in livestock products has required an increasing reliance on feedstuffs (see table 4), most of which have been imported. Thus the decline in Korea's capacity to be self-reliant in food supplies is greater than a quick glance at table 3 might suggest.

Moreover, even this qualified success in achieving the two key objectives of the new food policy—maintaining farm/nonfarm income parity and staple food self-sufficiency—has been possible only because domestic food prices have been raised progressively during the past twenty years via food import restrictions to counter the effects of Korea's declining comparative advantage in agriculture. The latter has occurred despite rapid growth in agricultural production and productivity in Korea relative to other developing countries (induced in large part by the increases in domestic food prices).

Extent of Protection Growth

The combined impact of Korea's price and trade policy instruments in driving a wedge between domestic and international prices for various foods is summarized in table 5 and detailed in appendix A. The final row shows clearly the transformation in incentives faced by farmers. In the 1950s domestic food prices were set by the government at below interna-

TABLE 5. Nominal rates of agricultural protection, Korea, 1955–85[a] (percent)

	1955–59		1960–64		1965–69		1970–74		1975–79		1980–84		1985	
Rice	−4	(−12)	1	(−4)	16	(4)	75	(46)	156	(131)	198	(179)	271	(245)
Barley	−4	(−4)	17	(10)	4	(−6)	55	(20)	97	(11)	149	(67)	220	(169)
Wheat	−12	(−5)	2	(−20)	28	(19)	36	(−2)	60	(6)	143	(21)	107	(31)
Corn[b]	n.a.		41		27		63		87		134		187	
Soybeans[b]	−13	(−20)	12	(8)	61	(52)	83	(40)	129	(68)	243	(254)	275	(252)
Beef	−14		−15		29		57		217		344		216	
Pork	−11		−5		82		111		113		133		190	
Chicken	−27		7		132		103		153		168		161	
Milk	n.a.		n.a.		173		109		185		180		128	
Sugar[c]		(116)		(170)		(358)		(112)		(160)		(209)		(193)
Average[d]	−6	(−11)	3	(−2)	18	(11)	75	(41)	146	(98)	195	(152)	239	(179)

SOURCES AND METHODOLOGY: See appendix A.

[a] Defined as the percentage by which the producer price exceeds the border price. Numbers in parentheses refer to the percentage by which the consumer price exceeds the border price in cases where it differs from the producer price distortion. The 1985 estimates are preliminary.

[b] Wholesale prices of corn for feed mixes were not available but are below producer prices, so for the purpose of obtaining weighted averages, the nominal rate for consumers of corn is assumed to be the same as for wheat. Also soybean meal for livestock feed mixes is not subjected to the high rates of taxation (shown in parentheses) that apply to the use of soybeans as a food; again the consumer wheat price distortion is assumed to apply for feed users of soybean.

[c] Because sugar is not produced in Korea, only consumer price distortions are shown.

[d] The weights used to obtain the averages are based on domestic production (consumption) valued at border prices.

tional prices, but from the late 1960s those domestic prices have been allowed to increase rapidly relative to international prices. As of the early and mid-1980s, food prices in Korea averaged about three times international food prices, according to the estimates in table 5.

Rice has been the most protected of the grains. Although barley, wheat, and corn protection is almost as great, rice protection is far more significant partly because rice constitutes over 80 percent of Korea's grain production and direct consumption, and partly because consumer prices are not distorted as much for other grains as for rice.

Livestock product prices are even more distorted than grain prices. Domestic prices for beef have been as much as four times international prices for similar quality beef in recent years, double the extent of distortion in the 1970s. Pork and chicken price distortions, by contrast, have increased only slightly since the 1970s, reflecting the fact that Korea's intensive livestock sector is becoming more efficient as it adopts imported management techniques.

Sugar is not produced in Korea, but imported raw sugar is refined locally. The very considerable degree of taxation of sugar consumers, who have been paying three times the international price for refined sugar, reflects both the tariff and other restrictions on raw sugar imports as well as either monopoly rents and/or inefficiency on the part of local refiners.

As indicated in table 2, the products listed in table 5 account for about 70 percent of Korea's agricultural production, with most of the remainder accounted for by fruits and vegetables. It is difficult to obtain international prices for many fruits and vegetables, since they are usually traded in small quantities and have widely varying qualities. Therefore, their protection rates cannot easily be estimated. Nevertheless, it is noteworthy that the indexes of prices received by Korean farmers for fruit and vegetable products have risen at even faster rates than the price of rice. These rates have been considerably faster than the rates of increase of farm prices for this product group in other countries: for example, fruit and vegetable producer prices approximately doubled in the United States during the two decades to 1980, whereas they increased six to eight times in Korea (in current U.S. dollar terms—see Anderson, 1983a). Insofar as many of these products (or close substitutes) would be internationally traded in the absence of import restrictions, these price indexes suggest that rates of protection for fruits and vegetables may have grown at least as rapidly as those for the grain and livestock products shown in table 5.[3]

To avoid raising consumer prices of rice as rapidly as producer prices,

3. During 1978–82, imports were allowed to make up for domestic production shortfalls of three important vegetables, namely, sesame seed, red pepper, and garlic. The domestic producer prices of those vegetables averaged, respectively, 6.2, 4.8, and 1.7 times the average price paid for imports during that five-year period.

the government instructed its monopoly grain marketing agency to sell grains at less than cost. Thus a wedge has been driven between the purchase price and marketing costs on the one hand, and the selling price for rice and barley on the other, the difference being paid by the government. On average during the 1970–84 period the consumer price was below the producer price by 20 percent in the case of rice and almost 40 percent in the case of barley (figure 1). The government's loss associated with this reselling of grain at less than cost, and with attempting to time purchases and sales so as to reduce intrayear fluctuations in grain prices, became an increasingly significant item in the budget. During the 1970s the deficit in the Grain Management Fund (including interest on accumulated debt) amounted to 4 or 5 percent of central government expenditure.

The reason for providing a larger reduction in the consumer price for barley than for rice was to encourage the substitution of barley for rice in consumers' diets. Even though barley is much less preferred as a staple, the government is keen to encourage its continued production (in winter, when land would otherwise be idle) and consumption so as to reduce the need to import rice. In addition to altering the consumer price ratio, the government from time to time has required restaurants and school-lunch providers to mix barley with rice and to serve no rice at all on certain days of the week.

Farm product price distortions are of course not the only form of assistance to farmers. Subsidies on farm inputs also play a role in encouraging resources to remain in agriculture, while assistance policies for non-agricultural sectors have the opposite effect. Irrigation, land reclamation, and other infrastructural developments at government expense have lowered farmers' costs over the years. Also, agricultural credit has been provided by the National Agricultural Cooperatives Federation at less than market rates of interest, with the government compensating the Federation for losses on these loans (Ban, Moon, and Perkins 1980, chapter 7). The government has in addition subsidized the use of fertilizer by offering it to farmers for less than the price paid by the marketing agency to the manufacturers. This subsidy amounted on average to 1.4 percent of government expenditure during the period 1970–82. However, fertilizer production in Korea has been heavily protected from import competition, and this "subsidy" in some years has been insufficient to offset the effective tax on fertilizer consumption due to protection of manufacturers of fertilizer. The net subsidy to farmers averaged 24 percent in 1971–73, but in 1976–78 farmers faced an implicit tax on fertilizers of almost 60 percent. With the subsequent rise in international prices for fertilizer, however, this implicit tax was reduced to almost zero in 1979–81 (Anderson, 1983c). The government's contractual obligation to the protected fertilizer producers terminates in 1987, from which time a less interventionist policy is ex-

FIGURE 1. Government selling price and purchase cost for polished rice and barley, Korea, 1970–84[a] (thousand current won per tonne)

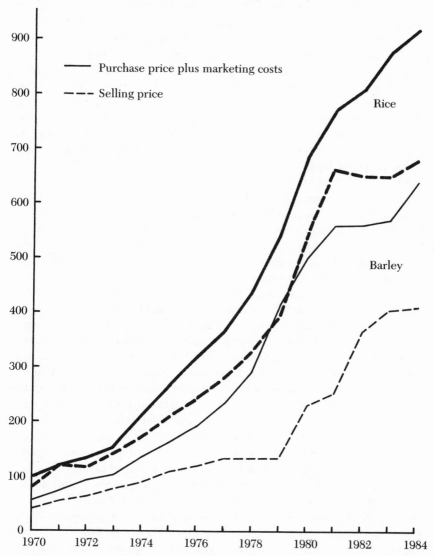

[a]Rice prices are for the rice year beginning November 1, barley prices are for the barley year beginning July 1.
SOURCE: World Bank (1984), tables A.9 and A.10, based on unpublished data from the Economic Planning Board, Seoul. (Updated from EPB sources.)

pected to be adopted. This will lead the way to an even more favorable fertilizer/grain price ratio in Korea, despite the fact that it is already one of the lowest in the world. In the mid-1980s the nitrogen/paddy price ratio was just below unity, having fallen from 3 in the 1950s and 2 in the 1960s.

It is possible to combine the measurement of the effect of distortions on output prices with distortions on input prices by estimating what is known as the effective rate of protection. This is defined as the percentage by which the return to the farmer's own resources (his land, labor, and other capital) is raised by policies affecting prices of farm output and purchased inputs. Unfortunately, careful estimates of the effective as distinct from nominal rate of assistance to Korean agriculture as a whole are not available. One set of estimates available for rice and barley, however, suggests that the effective rates rose from 15 to 300 percent for rice and from 7 to 450 percent for barley between the periods 1967–69 and 1977–79 (Ahn, 1982, tables 5.1 and 5.7).

For livestock products the effective rates depend heavily on the distortion to prices of purchased feedmixes. Korea's feedmix producers do not have to pay the high prices faced by final consumers of coarse grains, but their inputs are subject to import tariffs, stabilization levies, and restrictions on the types of ingredients to be included. Although it is difficult to estimate accurately the effect of these policy instruments on the price farmers pay for feedmix, feed industry sources in Korea guess that in recent years they have inflated that price by about 20 percent. The combined effect of this input price distortion and the distortions to livestock product prices is shown in table 6. Column 4 confirms the evidence in table 4 showing that purchased feedmix is an increasingly important input into livestock production in Korea: at domestic prices it accounted for half of the value of meat and milk production in 1984, up from 26 percent in 1980. More important, however, are the final two columns of table 6. Even assuming a 40 percent consumer tax equivalent on feedmix (twice the "guesstimated" rate just mentioned), the value of meat and milk production at border prices has been little more than the value of the feed input in recent years, and in fact slightly less than the cost of feed in 1984. That is, if in 1984 feed imports were halted and these industries were closed down overnight, the economy as a whole would have been just as well off, *even if none of those resources employed in livestock production found alternative employment.* Such is the extent of assistance to Korea's livestock sector. And given the apparent degree of import protection to fruits and vegetables already mentioned, this may well be the case in parts of that sector as well.

Overall, therefore, it is clear that food production in Korea has been increasingly assisted and food consumption increasingly taxed since the mid-1960s, notwithstanding some consumer tax relief for rice and barley.

| | Nominal protection coefficient (1) | At domestic prices: | | | Value of output (5) | At border prices: | | | |
| | | Value of output (2) | Value of feed input (3) | (3)/(2) (4) | | Value of feed input assuming: | | (6)/(5) (8) | (7)/(5) (9) |
						20% tax (6)	40% tax (7)		
Beef									
1980	2.73	462	38	.08	169	32	27	.19	.16
1981	3.60	510	65	.13	142	54	46	.38	.32
1982	4.93	561	104	.19	114	87	74	.76	.65
1983	5.63	643	135	.21	114	113	96	.99	.94
1984	5.32	716	190	.27	135	159	136	1.18	1.01
Pork									
1980	2.09	492	112	.23	235	93	80	.40	.34
1981	2.70	763	182	.24	283	152	130	.54	.46
1982	2.40	865	210	.24	360	175	150	.49	.42
1983	2.40	913	387	.42	380	323	276	.85	.73
1984	2.08	732	434	.59	352	362	310	1.03	.88
Chicken									
1980	2.46	126	80	.63	51	67	57	1.31	1.12
1981	3.12	139	127	.91	45	106	91	2.36	2.02
1982	2.69	163	149	.91	61	124	106	2.03	1.74
1983	2.60	218	192	.88	84	160	137	1.90	1.63
1984	2.52	258	162	.63	102	135	116	1.32	1.13
Milk									
1980	3.23	104	69	.66	32	57	49	1.78	1.54
1981	2.94	157	78	.50	54	65	56	1.20	1.03
1982	2.69	180	95	.53	67	79	68	1.18	1.01
1983	2.53	223	123	.55	88	102	88	1.16	1.00
1984	2.59	263	165	.81	102	137	118	1.34	1.16
Total meat and milk									
1980	2.58	1,184	309	.26	459	258	221	.56	.48
1981	3.14	1,569	452	.29	500	377	323	.75	.65
1982	3.03	1,769	558	.36	583	465	399	.80	.68
1983	3.09	1,997	837	.42	647	698	598	1.08	.92
1984	2.93	1,969	951	.50	676	793	679	1.22	1.01

SOURCE: Nominal protection coefficients (the ratio of the domestic price to the border price of a product) are from appendix A. The volumes of production (carcass or fluid milk weight) are from the Food and Agriculture Organization (1984 and earlier). The per unit values of production and of the feedmixes for each industry are from the National Agricultural Cooperatives Federation (1985) assuming liveweight-to-carcass conversion factors of .55 for beef and pork and .75 for chicken. The volumes of feedmix used by each industry are from the Ministry of Agriculture and Fisheries (1985).

This contrasts with virtually no growth in assistance to the other main tradables sector, manufacturing. According to Nam (1981) and Young et al., (1982), the nominal rate of assistance to manufacturing averaged 12 percent in 1968 and 19 percent in both 1978 and 1982. The effective rate of assistance to manufacturing in the latter two years was less than 30 percent, or less than one-tenth the rate for agriculture.

The current rate of agricultural protection in Korea now rivals that of the most protectionist industrial countries. According to the data in table 7, the overall nominal protection level in Korea in the early 1980s was as high as that in Japan and well above that in the member countries of the European Free Trade Association and the European Community. It is true that effective protection of agriculture may be higher in these advanced industrial countries, because their value-added share of output is smaller than Korea's,[4] and that the impact of their protectionism on international food markets is greater than Korea's, because their food economies are so much larger.[5] But one would expect the impact of Korea's policies on its domestic food economy to be of a similar order of magnitude to that in Western Europe and Japan, and hence the welfare cost of these policies as a percentage of GNP to be much larger for Korea, given that the average income in Korea is only one-fifth that of advanced industrial countries and that food represents a much larger proportion of Korea's GNP and expenditure. These expectations are in fact supported by recent empirical evidence derived from a simulation model of world food markets, discussed in the next section.

Before turning to the effects of Korea's protectionism, however, a brief comment is warranted on why agricultural protection has grown so rapidly and to such a high level in Korea as compared with higher-income industrial countries (an elaboration of which can be found in Anderson, Hayami, and others, 1986). As mentioned in the introduction, Korea has condensed into two decades a policy transformation that took seven or eight decades in Japan and even longer in Western Europe, and now has one of the most protected agricultural sectors in the world. One of the key reasons for this stems from the fact that economic growth has been more rapid in Korea than in any of the earlier-industrializing economies, including Japan. As a consequence of rapid growth in this densely populated economy, there

4. The value-added share of output (the percentage of the gross return not spent on purchased inputs) in 1980–83 in Korean agriculture was 0.67, compared with 0.54 in Japan and 0.46 in the European Community (Tyers and Anderson, 1986, table 10). If there are no input price distortions, the effective rate of protection is simply the nominal rate divided by the value-added share of output, and so the smaller the value-added share, the larger the effective, relative to the nominal, rate of protection, ceteris paribus.

5. The value of food production and consumption in Korea is roughly one-quarter that of Japan and one-twelfth that of the European Community (Tyers and Anderson, 1986, tables 7 and 8).

TABLE 7. Nominal rates of agricultural protection, various industrial countries, 1980–82[a]

	Wheat	Coarse grain	Rice	Ruminant meat	Nonruminant meat	Dairy products	Sugar	Weighted average
Australia	5	0	15 (70)	0	0	30 (40)	5 (40)	5 (10)
Canada	15	0	0	10	10	95	25 (50)	19 (26)
European Community (10)	40 (45)	40	40	95	25	75 (80)	50	55 (60)
EFTA[b] (5)	65	55	0	130	40	145	55	90 (93)
Japan	290 (25)	330 (25)	235 (190)	180	50	190	200 (160)	133 (114)
New Zealand	0	0	0	0	0	0	0	0 (0)
Spain & Portugal	35	30	15	65	10	75	65	35 (36)
United States	15 (0)	0	31 (0)	10	0	100	40	18 (23)
Weighted average of above	25 (29)	13 (13)	152 (143)	50 (53)	18 (18)	88 (93)	48 (58)	41 (49)
Korea	145 (45)	130 (30)	150 (140)	275	150	195	0 (190)	159 (135)

SOURCES: Appendix A and revisions of estimates in Tyers and Anderson (1986), table 9.
[a]The percentage by which the producer price exceeds the border price. In cases where the consumer price distortion differs from the producer price distortion, the latter is shown in parentheses. The weighted averages are calculated using 1980–82 production (consumption) valued at border prices for weights.
[b]The European Free Trade Area, comprising Austria, Finland, Norway, Sweden, and Switzerland.

have been unprecedented pressures for structural adjustment away from agriculture. Rapid increases in agricultural protection were deemed necessary to reduce the stress on society that would accompany such adjustment. More efficient instruments such as producer subsidies or income supplements to farmers were not considered because they involve large treasury outlays, whereas import taxes contribute to government revenue. Whether promoting rural industrialization to provide more part-time, off-farm work for farm households would be more efficient than agricultural protection is a moot point discussed in the final section of this chapter. The other key reason why Koreans have tolerated high food prices has to do with their perceived military threat from communist North Korea. Perhaps food self-sufficiency provides the community with a greater sense of security, but in addition the government may feel it needs to "buy" the support of farmers to maintain political stability and thereby reduce the likelihood of infiltration from the North.

Some Effects of Protection

Food Production, Consumption, and Trade[6]

Tyers and Anderson (1986) represent the world food economy as a system of interrelated supply and demand equations for the seven commodity groups shown in table 7 in thirty countries or groups of countries spanning the world. For each country and commodity, partial-adjustment supply response equations and demand equations are included to capture the facts that production responses are spread over a number of years and that the production or consumption of each commodity depends on both its own and other commodities' prices. The base period is 1980–82, for which nominal protection rates have been estimated for each country and commodity. The model projects forward each year to 1995 according to values of parameters such as population and income growth rates, and price-independent production growth rates, as well as own- and cross-price elasticities of demand and supply (short as well as longer run), income elasticities of demand, and future protection rate assumptions. The key parameters for Korea are summarized in appendix tables B.1, B.2, and B.3.

Changes to any one or more of these assumed parameter values for any country and/or commodity will generate a different set of simulation outcomes for each year to 1995, which can be compared with the reference simulation that involves the authors' best judgments as to the magnitude of the various parameters. Thus the model is ideally suited to estimate the effects of any one country's food policies. For example, it can be used in

6. This and the next two sections draw heavily on recent research done jointly with Rod Tyers, whose collaboration is acknowledged with thanks.

static mode to estimate the impact of existing policies in Korea by first simulating the Korean (and the rest of the world's) food economy in 1987, assuming the 1980–82 levels of protection prevailed through to 1987 there and elsewhere. (In fact the 1987 protection rates were probably somewhat higher than those in 1980–82, according to the preliminary estimates for 1985 shown in tables 5 and A, so the results below err on the conservative side.) The results of this reference simulation are then compared with those of an alternative scenario in which Korea's protection in 1987 is zero and all other countries' protection rates remain unchanged. This alternative scenario is obtained using only long-run elasticities in this static version of the model, so that the estimated effects after full adjustment are captured.

The differences between these two scenarios in Korea's food economy are summarized in table 8. The first two rows simply show the extent of the price declines required to bring domestic prices down to international price levels (the latter being affected by less than 1 percent from such a liberalization, according to the model's results, because of Korea's relative unimportance in the world food economy). The third row shows that meat and milk production would be half its current level in a Korea without protection, while grain production would be only slightly less because of the much lower grain supply responsiveness to price changes (see appendix table B.3). Consumption of livestock products and sugar would be two or three times as great without protection, while rice consumption would be less than 20 percent greater and wheat and barley consumption would be reduced as consumers move toward their now cheaper preferred staple (rice). Corn consumption by the now reduced numbers of livestock also would be lower. Together these changes require larger imports of all but wheat and coarse grains. Rice self-sufficiency would be 75 instead of 90 percent, and self-sufficiency in other grains and livestock products would be below 20 percent, according to the model's results. This would inflate the food import bill to the extent of $5 billion (in 1985 U.S. dollars).

Economic Welfare

The model also estimates the welfare effects of policies by measuring the differences between the reference scenario and the no-protection scenario in producer surplus, the Hicksian equivalent variation in income of consumers, and the net change in government revenue as a result of removing production, consumption, and trade taxes or subsidies.[7]

Table 9 summarizes the transfers and net costs associated with agricul-

7. On the appropriateness of these measures of welfare changes, see, for example, Just, Hueth, and Schmitz (1982). Details of this and other aspects including qualifications of the model and its assumed parameters are provided in the main text and in appendix C of Tyers and Anderson (1986).

TABLE 8.   Estimated effects of liberalizing all grain, livestock product, and sugar markets in Korea, 1987

	Rice	Wheat	Coarse grain	Ruminant meat	Nonruminant meat	Dairy products	Sugar
Producer price (% change)	−63	−62	−57	−73	−60	−67	0
Consumer price (% change)	−62	−31	−24	−73	−60	−67	−66
Production level (% change)	−11	−13	0	−44	−48	−57	0
Consumption level (% change)	18	−8	−28	150	175	140	135
Net import volume (kt change)	1,670	−190	−1,760	340	1,370	1,500	710
Self-sufficiency (%)							
Actual 1980–83	90	4	19	70	100	98	0
After lib., 1987	74	3	23	12	14	15	0

SOURCE: Revision of Tyers and Anderson (1986).

TABLE 9.   The annual domestic costs of food price distortions to consumers and taxpayers and the transfer to producers, Korea, Japan, and Western Europe, 1987 (1985 U.S. $ billion)

	Consumer cost (1)	Taxpayer cost[a] (2)	Gross cost (3) = (1) + (2)	Producer benefit (4)	Total (5)	Net cost[b] per capita (1980 $) (6)	As a % of GNP (7)	Transfer ratio[c] (8) = (3)/(4)
Korea	14.6	−3.0	11.6	6.6	5.1	120	5.6	1.8
Japan	49.0	−7.2	41.8	21.6	20.1	170	1.2	1.9
EC-12[d]	61.8	5.3	67.1	54.1	13.1	40	0.3	1.2
EFTA-5[e]	12.7	2.1	14.8	12.1	2.9	90	0.5	1.2

SOURCE: Revision of Tyers and Anderson (1986).

[a]Government tariff and other import levy revenue from food imports exceeded payouts to producers to raise producer price support levels above consumer prices in Korea and Japan, whereas in Western Europe export subsidy and other payouts exceeded import levy revenues.

[b]Column (5) is column (3) minus column (4) minus stock profits. That is, it does not include the costs of raising and dispersing government tax revenue and of lobbying by farm groups, nor does it include the costs to the rest of the world.

[c]Ratio of gross costs to producer benefits, that is, the average cost in dollars to consumers and taxpayers per dollar transferred to producers.

[d]EC-12 refers to the twelve member countries of the European Economic Community.

[e]EFTA-5 refers to the five member countries of the European Free Trade Arrangement.

tural protection in Korea compared with Japan and Western Europe. Although the net cost in terms of dollars is not as large as in Japan or the Economic Community (EC), it exceeds the *combined* net cost for the member countries of the European Free Trade Association (EFTA—Austria, Finland, Norway, Sweden, and Switzerland; see column 5). Moreover, in per capita terms the net economic welfare effect of protection is larger in Korea than in Western Europe, and as a percentage of GNP it is much greater even than in Japan.

Income and Wealth Distribution

The net effect on economic welfare hides the fact that these food policies involve much larger transfers from domestic consumers to farmers. In Korea's case the results in table 9 suggest over $11 billion (in 1985 U.S. dollars) is transferred each year from consumers and taxpayers, or about $1,700 per nonfarm household (one-fifth of their total income). Producers, however, receive little more than one of every two dollars transferred from consumers-cum-taxpayers, the other dollar being a deadweight welfare loss. According to column 8, this degree of deadweight loss also occurs in Japan, but it is much greater than in Western Europe. These results underscore the wastefulness of present policies as instruments for transferring income to producers in Korea.

The effects of protection on income and wealth distribution *within* groups are far from equitable. Poorer consumers spend the largest proportion of their income on food, so they are the subgroup affected most adversely by high consumer prices. Within agriculture, too, direct benefits from high producer prices are received in proportion to the volume of marketed output, so the largest producers receive the most.

Moreover, the benefits to producers tend to be incorporated into land and other capital values, which then boosts wealth in proportion to the size of a person's agricultural capital. Some evidence of the effect of the protection increases on farm land prices is provided in table 10 and figure 2. Arable land prices rose steeply in nominal won terms throughout the period shown, but fell somewhat in the early 1980s in U.S. dollar terms when there was a coincidence of a further increase in petroleum import prices from 1979; a one-third shortfall in the 1980 rice crop necessitating rice imports; and political uncertainty following President Park's assassination, which discouraged capital inflows. These three events together resulted in a slowdown in the economy generally and in agricultural investment in particular, as well as a steady depreciation relative to the U.S. dollar. However, as the economy recovered and the government continued its policy of high protection for agriculture, so paddy land prices began rising again in 1983. Paddy land prices in Korea are currently as much as twenty times those of similarly productive irrigated land in Australia.

The main reason for protecting livestock production has not been to increase food security (which it cannot do when livestock production is so heavily dependent on imported feedgrains). Rather, it has been to boost the supplementary incomes of rice farmers. Meat and dairy protection has undoubtedly had that effect, since most farmers own at least one draft animal. But it is worth noting that during the past decade there has been a marked increase in the proportion of livestock raised on large, specialized livestock farms. Between 1975 and 1984 there was a drop from 92 to 45

TABLE 10.   Farm land prices, Korea, 1973–84
(current U.S. dollars per hectare)

	Paddy land	Arable upland	Mountainous grazing land
1973	7,320	5,160	n.a.
1974	10,390	6,600	n.a.
1975	11,920	6,940	1,140
1976	15,760	9,750	2,480
1977	19,980	12,830	3,040
1978	21,570	14,030	4,170
1979	23,620	15,450	5,120
1980	19,080	12,910	3,800
1981	19,080	13,080	3,350
1982	19,670	13,310	3,800
1983	23,890	13,530	2,270
1984	25,650	14,480	2,170

SOURCE: World Bank (1984), table A.11, based on survey data from Korea's National Agricultural Cooperatives Federation (1983 and 1984 added from NACF data).

FIGURE 2. Producer price of rice and price of paddy land, Korea, 1973–84 (current U.S. dollars)

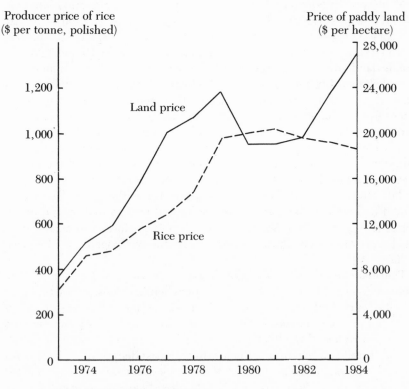

SOURCE: See table 10 and appendix table A.

TABLE 11.   Distribution of livestock numbers by
herd/flock size, Korea, 1975–84 (percent)

	1975	1978	1982	1984
Beef and native cattle				
1–2	92	84	66	45
3–9	6	13	26	43
10+	2	3	8	12
Dairy cattle				
1–4	13	14	9	12
5–19	44	47	49	52
20+	43	39	42	36
Pigs				
1–9	65	57	32	19
10–99	15	23	32	32
100+	20	20	36	49
Chickens				
1–999	34	18	7	4
1,000–9,999	43	56	57	37
10,000+	23	26	36	59

SOURCES: National Livestock Cooperatives Federation (1982 and 1985)
and Ministry of Agriculture and Fisheries (unpublished data).

percent in the proportion of beef and native cattle in herds of less than 3,
from 65 to 19 percent in the proportion of pigs in piggeries with less than
10 sows, and from 34 to 4 percent in the proportion of chickens in chicken
farms with fewer than 1,000 birds (table 11). This follows a similar trend in
Japan as large-scale, imported-feed intensive enterprises in these industries gradually replace livestock production by rice farmers. Thus over
time the benefits of livestock protection will tend to go increasingly to the
specialized producers rather than as side income to rice farmers—even
though, as indicated earlier, those large producers may be generating
negative value-added when output and inputs are measured at border
prices.

Projected Effects to 1995

The above estimates of the effects of removing protection are presented
simply to give some indication of the effects of recent policies. Complete
liberalization of Korea's food market is unlikely to be politically feasible,
however, not least because of the reduction in the value of farm capital
assets that would result, but also because of the substantially increased
dependence on food imports that would be required. There is value,
therefore, in using also the dynamic version of the model of world food
markets to simulate the effects of more realistic changes in policy.

Two of the more obvious scenarios to consider are (1) that Korea's
agricultural protection rates continue to grow, or (2) that they decline

somewhat. The protection growth scenario presented in this section assumes that agricultural protection rates continue to grow during the projection period 1983–95, but only half as fast as in the period 1971–73 to 1981–83. The partial liberalization scenario, on the other hand, assumes protection rates are gradually reduced by a total of one-quarter during the 1987–90 period and remain 25 percent below the 1980–82 rates thereafter. Because real international prices in both scenarios change little over the projection period, these scenarios represent increasing and decreasing domestic prices, respectively. The two sets of projected domestic market conditions are summarized in table 12.

The first point to note, from column 3 of table 12, is that if protection continues to grow, Korea is likely to have surpluses of rice and milk, which, as in Japan in the case of rice and Western Europe in the case of milk and other products, will have to be disposed of with the help of government subsidies.[8] (Indeed, milk was already in surplus in Korea by the mid-1980s. To reduce the surplus, milk is being distributed at a small fraction of its purchase price to cattle producers for feed use and to elementary schools for lunches.) On the other hand, if protection rates from 1990 were only three-quarters of those in the early 1980s, rice self-sufficiency would still be greater then than now, even if slightly below 100 percent.

The second point to note is that wheat imports are much the same in the two scenarios, while coarse grain imports are less in the partial liberalization scenario because livestock production and hence feed demand is lower. Meat self-sufficiency is around 50 percent by the mid-1990s in the partial liberalization scenario.

The difference in national economic welfare in these two scenarios is very substantial. By 1990 it amounts to $3.2 billion and by 1995 to $5.8 billion per year (in 1985 U.S. dollars) or 3 percent of GNP. If the difference each year from 1987 is discounted at 5 percent per year to obtain a real net value in 1987 of all future benefits (assuming the benefit in 1995 continues each year thereafter), it accumulates to over $100 billion or $2,400 per capita. And of course the difference in the transfers from consumers to producers keeps growing over time as well.

Domestic Price Stability

How successful have Korea's food policies been in reducing instability of domestic food prices around trend? One way to gauge this for year-to-year fluctuations is to deflate the price series, estimate regression trend lines, and then measure the coefficients of variation of deflated domestic and border prices around those trend lines. The results that emerge for Korea's grain and livestock products for the two periods 1961–71 and 1972–83 are

---

8. On the social costs of surplus rice production in Japan, see Otsuka and Hayami (1985).

summarized in table 13. Two points are worth noting from these numbers. First, the instability of domestic grain prices has been less in the 1970s than in the 1960s, while the opposite is true of border prices. Second, the instability of domestic prices of meat and milk has been greater in the 1970s than in the 1960s, but the instability of international meat prices has increased much more. These data suggest that Korea's food policy in the 1970s has contributed substantially to the year-to-year stability of domestic grain and beef prices, the coefficients of variation for which are only 25–40 percent those of border prices, but it has done little to stabilize pork and milk prices and appears to have destabilized chicken prices (column 8). On the other hand, it appears that Korea's food policy in the 1960s generated greater instability in domestic grain and meat prices than would have prevailed in the absence of intervention (column 7). [9]

Agricultural Productivity

No attempt has been made to quantify the effects of Korea's food policy per se on agricultural productivity. However, a recent study by Ban (1981), which has quantified the rates of agricultural productivity growth in Korea since 1918, is illuminating. During the interwar years, output grew at 1.6 percent per year, but so too did inputs, so there was no measured productivity growth during this period of exploitation by the Japanese (table 14). Agriculture went into decline during the Pacific War and took until after the Korean War to recover. Thereafter, productivity growth accelerated: it increased at 1.4 percent during the 1954–65 period in which food prices domestically were below international levels; it grew at 2.0 percent in the latter 1960s as domestic prices began to rise above international prices; and it averaged 4.7 percent during the 1970s period of high and rising agricultural protection (column 3). Farm labor productivity accelerated even more rapidly than total factor productivity as workers were attracted

9. It is probably also true that Korea's food policies have reduced the intrayear instability of domestic prices through government stockpiling at harvest time and the release of stocks later in the year. To some extent this government activity has simply crowded out private stockholding. The author is unaware of any analysis that has quantified either the extent of any additional stability over and above what private stockholding would have provided, or the social cost of achieving that stability.

It might also be argued that even though Korea's high degree of food self-sufficiency is superficial only because production depends on imports for the essential inputs of fertilizer and feedstuffs, there is nonetheless some benefit from protecting rice and livestock production in the form of more food security, because their product prices internationally are more volatile than fertilizer and feedgrain prices. The evidence in column 6 of table 13 for the 1972–83 period provides only weak support for this view. Rice and beef price volatility has been greater than that for corn (and soybean and fertilizer, not shown); but the variability of prices for pork, chicken, and dairy products has been lower than that for corn. Thus any nonpecuniary benefit attached to being reliant on international markets for fertilizer and feedstuffs rather than rice and livestock products is likely to be very small relative to the costs of Korea's protection policy.

TABLE 12. Domestic effects of protection growth versus partial liberalization, Korea, 1980–83, 1990, and 1995[a] (Kt per year and per cent)

	Nominal rate of protection (%)[b] (1)	Production (2)	Net imports (3)	Availability (4)	Consumption per capita (kg/yr) (5)	Self-sufficiency (%) (6)	Domestic price difference (%)[c] (7)
Rice							
Actual 1980–83	150 (140)	4,910	730	5,510	141	89	
Protection growth							
1990	175 (170)	6,220	−220	6,000	137	104	
1995	190 (190)	6,950	−550	6,400	137	109	
Partial liberalization							
1990	110 (105)	6,010	360	6,370	146	94	−27 (−30)
1995	110 (105)	6,640	300	6,940	148	96	−34 (−38)
Wheat							
Actual 1980–83	145 (45)	80	1,920	1,990	51	4	
Protection growth							
1990	190 (50)	80	2,780	2,860	65	3	
1995	225 (50)	90	3,220	3,310	71	3	
Partial liberalization							
1990	110 (35)	70	2,670	2,740	63	3	−35 (−12)
1995	110 (35)	70	3,030	3,100	66	3	−45 (−15)
Coarse grain							
Actual 1980–83	130 (30)	940	3,910	4,950	127	20	
Protection growth							
1990	150 (35)	1,100	6,030	7,130	163	15	
1995	165 (40)	1,220	7,510	8,730	186	14	
Partial liberalization							
1990	100 (20)	1,100	5,470	6,570	150	17	−26 (−19)
1995	100 (20)	1,210	6,660	7,870	168	15	−32 (−26)
Ruminant meat							
Actual 1980–83	275	90	50	130	3	67	
Protection growth							
1990	370	120	100	220	5	55	
1995	450	160	130	290	6	55	

Partial liberalization							
1990	210	110	160	270	6	41	−27
1995	210	140	230	370	8	38	−31
Nonruminant meat							
Actual 1980–83	150	390	0	390	10	100	
Protection growth							
1990	160	600	100	700	16	86	
1995	170	800	240	1,040	22	77	
Partial liberalization							
1990	110	530	310	840	19	63	−21
1995	110	700	580	1,280	27	55	−24
Dairy products							
Actual 1980–83	195	540	10	550	14	98	
Protection growth							
1990	230	880	−60	820	19	107	
1995	260	1,160	−140	1,020	22	114	
Partial liberalization							
1990	145	680	410	1,090	25	62	−30
1995	145	830	650	1,480	32	56	−37
Sugar							
Actual 1980–83	0 (190)	0	410	410	10	0	
Protection growth							
1990	0 (240)	0	520	520	12	0	
1995	0 (270)	0	610	610	13	0	
Partial liberalization							
1990	0 (140)	0	720	720	16	0	0 (−33)
1995	0 (140)	0	930	930	20	0	0 (−42)

SOURCE: Based on unpublished simulation runs prepared by Rod Tyers, whose collaboration is acknowledged with thanks.

a. Actual protection rates shown are for 1980–82 as in the model and in table 7, rather than for 1980–83. The protection growth scenario assumes Korea's agricultural protection rates continue to grow during the projection period 1983–95 but only half as fast as in the previous two decades; the partial liberalization scenario assumes protection rates are gradually reduced by a total of one-quarter during the 1986–90 period and remain 25 percent below the 1980–82 rates thereafter.

b. The distortion to consumer prices is shown in parentheses when it differs from the producer price distortion.

c. The percentage by which the domestic producer (consumer) price is lower in the partial liberalization scenario relative to that price in the protection growth scenario.

136   KYM ANDERSON

TABLE 13. Coefficients of variation of deflated Korean domestic and border prices for grain and livestock products around trend, 1961–83

	Producer price		Consumer price		Border price			
	1961–71 (1)	1972–83 (2)	1961–71 (3)	1972–83 (4)	1961–71 (5)	1972–83 (6)	(1)/(5) (7)	(2)/(6) (8)
Rice	.20	.09	.20	.11	.17	.32	1.18	.26
Wheat	.29	.10	.19	.15	.06	.25	4.83	.40
Barley	.28	.08	.26	.09	.12	.25	2.33	.32
Corn	.28	.08			.07	.23	4.00	.35
Beef	.10	.15	.10	.12	.06	.39	1.67	.38
Pork	.20	.19	.11	.14	.09	.20	2.22	.95
Chicken	.18	.19	.18	.20	.04	.10	4.50	1.90
Milk	.08	.09			.12	.11	.67	.82

SOURCE: Revision of Tyers and Anderson (1986).

to part-time or full-time work off the farm and farmers adopted more capital-intensive technologies (column 4). The substitution of machinery for labor (see table 2) has been in response to marked changes in the ratio of farm wages to farm implement prices: this ratio increased by 100 percent between 1964 and 1977, and by a further 63 percent between 1977 and 1979 (Anderson and Joo, 1984, p. 111).

Factor Rewards and Other Sectors' Production and Exports

The empirical model used above to estimate the effects of Korea's food price policies on production, consumption, trade, and welfare is partial equilibrium in nature and does not include factor markets. To estimate the effects of price distortions on factor markets, it would be possible to again use a partial equilibrium model, for example, of the type developed by Floyd (1965). But for developing economies such as Korea, where agriculture employs a large proportion of the country's labor and other productive resources, a general equilibrium approach is more suitable.

The simplest general equilibrium model for capturing the effects of food price and trade policies is one with three sectors and three factors of production. The three sectors in Korea's case are those producing food, tradable manufactures and services, and nontradable products. The three factors are land, which is specific to the food sector, unskilled labor, and skilled labor. Both types of labor are assumed typically to be intersectorally mobile but internationally immobile. Capital is also required for production in each sector, but since Korea is so open to international capital flows and is a small country incapable of influencing the international price of capital, this factor can be treated like all other intermediate inputs that can be assumed to be traded at given prices.

In such a model the effects of agricultural protection on the various factor and product markets depend not simply on factor intensities in the three sectors, as in the standard Heckscher-Ohlin model involving only

TABLE 14. Growth of agricultural output, inputs, and factor productivity, Korea, 1918–78 (percent per year)[a]

| | Output (1) | Inputs (2) | Productivity | | |
			All factors (3)	Labor (4)	Land (5)
1920–39	1.6	1.6	−0.0	1.1	1.5
1939–45	−3.5	−1.9	−1.6	−2.5	−2.7
1945–54	3.5	2.1	1.4	3.6	3.6
1954–65	4.0	2.5	1.4	0.7	2.6
1965–70	3.1	1.1	2.0	5.6	2.4
1970–77	5.5	0.7	4.7	9.1	5.9

SOURCE: Ban (1981), appendix table 3.
  [a]Based on five-year moving averages from 1920 to 1945 and on three-year moving averages thereafter.

traded goods sectors. They depend also on the demand and supply characteristics of the market for nontradables, since these characteristics determine the endogenous response of the price of nontradables to a change in food policy.

According to a recent study by Anderson and Warr (1987), which uses a general equilibrium model of this type, the parameter values for Korea are such that agricultural protection benefits both unskilled laborers and landowners at the expense of skilled labor. This is because it raises the demand for unskilled labor and land by more than enough to offset the negative effect of higher food prices on these groups' spending power. In addition it has the effect of discouraging manufacturing and services production and exports as well as encouraging agricultural production and self-sufficiency in Korea. It also is likely to encourage more skill-intensive activities within these sectors relative to a free-trade situation because of the reduction in wage differentials between skilled and unskilled work. Korea's greater orientation toward skill-intensive heavy manufacturing rather than light, unskilled labor-intensive manufacturing, relative to other newly industrializing countries at similar stages of development, may be partly due to the reduction in wage differentials caused by agricultural protection. Reduced wage differentials would also have helped bring about a relatively more equal income distribution in urban Korea than otherwise would have been obtained. Offsetting this of course is the fact that landholders benefit in direct proportion to their landholdings and hence their wealth, so protection would have exacerbated rural inequality.

A reduction in wage differentials for different skills may seem a desirable by-product of agricultural protection from a comparative static equity perspective. From an economic growth perspective, however, the squeezing of differentials may well be considered undesirable, because in addition to lowering national income in a comparative static sense, protection also weakens the incentive for workers to invest in their own human capital, thereby potentially lowering the rate of economic growth.

Summary and Conclusions

Summary of Findings

The extremely rapid growth and structural transformation of the resource-poor Korean economy since the late 1950s has been accompanied by equally dramatic changes in the country's food price policy. The heavy taxation of agriculture relative to manufacturing in the 1950s gave way to a more neutral policy regime in the mid-1960s, but from the late 1960s government incentive policies have increasingly favored farmers relative to industrialists. By the early 1980s, agricultural support levels in Korea rivaled those of the most protectionist of the advanced industrial countries, including Japan.

During the period of Japanese occupation (1910–45), Korean rice production was boosted by investments in research, irrigation, and related infrastructure, and by access to the protected Japanese market. While these colonial policies led to increased rice exports to Japan, agricultural productivity growth was sluggish and the Korean people, few of whom were landowners, suffered declines in food consumption and in their living standards generally in that interwar period.

Korea's food production suffered a 30 percent decline during the Pacific War, picked up in the late 1940s, and then declined again during the Korean War. Thus food production in 1953 was still no greater than in 1939. From this very low base, it grew somewhat in the remaining years of the Rhee Government but was hampered by distortions to incentives that favored import-competing manufacturing at the expense of agriculture. During this period food prices were low by international standards (when valued using the shadow exchange rate).

The steady increases in domestic food prices and the large reductions in assistance to the manufacturing sector during the 1960s and 1970s certainly boosted agricultural production and productivity relative to what otherwise would have occurred, but at increasing cost to consumers and the economy generally. By the mid-1980s, when Korea's food prices were three times those in international markets, the average nonfarm household was implicitly taxed $1,700 per year (in 1985 U.S. dollars), or one-fifth of its total household income, to maintain that support level.

One of the key objectives of Korea's food price policy in recent years has been to ensure that farm household incomes caught up with and then grew at the same pace as incomes of urban wage and salary earners. The available evidence suggests that this objective has been achieved, in part because food price and trade policies implicitly have transferred large amounts to farmers from consumers. But these policies have been very inefficient in bringing about that transfer: only half of the implicit $1,700 tax on nonfarm households reached farmers, the other half being a deadweight loss in economic welfare. The extent of the inefficiency is clearest for the livestock sector, in which value-added at world prices is negative, that is, the economy would be better off if livestock production ceased and the government paid these farmers their current income out of consolidated revenue.

The other key objective of Korea's food price policy has been to maintain an "adequate" degree of food security. Generally this has been interpreted to mean a low dependence on imports for feeding the nation. That objective has been difficult to achieve because of Korea's relative scarcity of agricultural land and its rapidly strengthening comparative advantage in industrial production (and hence comparative disadvantage in agricultural production). While it is true that self-sufficiency is high in the traditional grain staples, rice and barley, and in intensive livestock products (but low in wheat and declining in beef), this product self-sufficiency is heavily dependent on imports of the raw materials for the crucial inputs of fertilizer and animal feedstuffs. Thus it is probably fair to say that the present policy maintains only a veneer of food security.

This evaluation of the extent to which Korea's food price policy has achieved its objectives would be incomplete without considering also the extent to which other factors contributed to these goals, and the cost of chosen policies as compared with alternative policies. At least three other factors were also important causes of the rise in farm incomes and food self-sufficiency in Korea in the 1970s. The first was the very rapid response of farmers to increases in the manufacturing sector in real wages (6 percent a year in the first half of the 1970s and 16 percent in the second half) that attracted farm workers to part-time and full-time jobs outside agriculture. It has been estimated that the percentage of the farm labor force leaving agriculture rose from less than 3 percent a year in the late 1960s to around 5 percent in the mid-1970s and then to more than 7 percent in the late 1970s (Y. S. Kim et al., 1980). The second important factor was on-farm adjustment. The rise in wages relative to the cost of farm machinery services induced a substantial and increasing degree of capital-labor substitution on farms (table 2). As a result, farm labor productivity grew at 9 percent a year during the 1970s, compared with 5.6 percent in the late 1960s and only 0.7 percent in the decade before that (table 14). The third factor was the development and dissemination of new farm technologies. High-yielding, fertilizer-responsive rice varieties boosted land productivity in the 1970s by almost 6 percent a year compared with about 2.5 percent in the late 1950s and the 1960s (table 14). This not only raised farm incomes, but also boosted food self-sufficiency and forestalled some decline in the sector's competitiveness.

Thus society's needs have been met in large part by the ability of farmers to adjust efficiently to changing economic circumstances: their adoption of profitable new technologies as they became available; their substitution of machinery for labor and draft power as relative factor prices changed; and, most important, their ability to allow some members of their families to leave agriculture and obtain employment in nonfarm sectors.

Policy Alternatives

In view of the high and rapidly rising cost of Korea's current food price policy, and in view of the likelihood that Korea's comparative disadvantage in agriculture will continue to increase, it is appropriate to ask also whether there are less costly ways to achieve Korea's policy objectives because the instruments currently used can achieve them only at ever greater cost to consumers, taxpayers, and the economy generally.

One possibility is to look for ways to lower the cost of producing food in Korea. There appears to be limited scope for doing this profitably for grains through further investments in crop land and irrigation development, since virtually all of the cultivable land in Korea is used intensively already. Prospects for Korea ever becoming an internationally efficient producer of beef and dairy products are even bleaker. Cattle require more roughage than nonruminant animals, and dairy cows especially require some green pasture feed. Korea's climate, soils, and topography offer virtually no scope for providing such feed at anything close to internationally competitive prices, and the cost of importing hay, lucerne pellets, and the like is prohibitively expensive. Very little pasture establishment has occurred over the past fifteen years (an average of less than five thousand hectares per year), despite the fact that the government has been prepared to pay as much as 70 percent or more of pasture development costs. Moreover, as the area of pasture has expanded, the cost per hectare of further development has risen rapidly, from around $200 in the early 1970s to around $1,400 in 1982 (table 15). In 1982 the cost of further pasture development in Korea (excluding the purchase price of land) was more than five times the cost of purchasing fully developed grazing pasture land of similar carrying capacity in land-extensive countries like Australia. And, in addition to further pasture development being unprofitable economically, it is also undesirable on ecological grounds because of the erosion that is likely to result from clearing the steep slopes that are under consideration for development.

More scope may exist for investing profitably in producing new and adapting imported technologies. During the 1970s Korea spent only two-thirds as much on agricultural research per dollar of agricultural output (valued at constant 1961–65 prices) as other middle-income countries, and less than one-third as much in the 1960s (Boyce, Judd, and Evenson, 1982). It is true that research expenditure has continued to expand in recent years, but an increasing proportion of total expenditure on research

TABLE 15.   Investment in pasture establishment, Korea, 1967–82

	Area per year ('000 hectares)	Cost per hectare (current U.S. dollars)	Share of development cost paid by farmers (%)
1967–70	10	174	17
1971–74	5	348	25
1975–78	4	707	36
1979–82	3	1,286	22

SOURCE: Ministry of Agriculture and Fisheries (1982).

and extension is being devoted to extension (column 5 of table 16). Yet even in the 1970s Korea was spending more on extension relative to the value of output than other middle-income countries (Boyce and Evenson, 1975), and available evidence suggests that while there tends to be underinvestment in agricultural research in developing countries, this is not so for extension (Huffman, 1978; Ruttan, 1983). Thus it would appear that Korea may benefit from diverting more of its agricultural research and extension budget to research, particularly if it is devoted to nonrice research (given Korea's already very high rice yields per hectare). Indeed, a stronger emphasis on nonrice research has now begun. To further this, *ex ante* evaluations of expected returns from further public research expenditure on the relatively neglected fruit and vegetable crops might be undertaken.[10]

Another possible reform is to consider alternative ways of ensuring food security other than by boosting food self-sufficiency—which itself is dependent on imported raw materials for the crucial inputs of fertilizer and feedstuffs. Probably the most efficient means is simply to depend on import supplies and, if necessary, to borrow to finance the import bill in years when world prices are high or domestic production low (Siamwalla and Valdes, 1980). Domestic stockpiles, futures markets, and long-term contracts with exporting countries can be used to decrease the insecurity of relying heavily on food imports. Presumably, however, such measures are not adopted because food security is more an excuse for intervention than a real reason for it.

With respect to the equity objective of ensuring that farm household incomes keep pace with urban incomes, there exist several alternatives to the present approach of ever-increasing domestic prices of foods. These relate to facilitating the mobility of farm labor. One alternative is to examine the efficacy of more rural industrialization. It is true that one-third of farm household income has come from off-farm sources in recent

10. In 1982, only 16 percent of product-specific agricultural research expenditure in Korea was on fruit and vegetables, yet these products accounted for 23 percent of the value of farm production (at domestic prices) that year.

TABLE 16. Rural research and extension manpower and expenditure, Korea, 1970–82 (man-years and current U.S. million dollars)

| | Manpower | | Annual expenditure | | | Expenditure as a % of value of agricultural output at: | | | |
| | | | | | | Domestic prices | | Border prices[a] | |
	Research (1)	Extension (2)	Research (3)	Extension (4)	Extension as a % of total (5)	Research (6)	Extension (7)	Research (8)	Extension (9)
1970–74	709	6,127	4.6	13.0	74	.15	.40	.24	.63
1975–79	811	6,534	10.0	36.8	79	.11	.38	.26	.89
1980–82	901	7,792	16.7	67.2	80	.13	.54	.35	1.45

SOURCE: Office of Rural Development, Suweon (unpublished data).
a Inflated using the weighted average nominal agricultural protection coefficients from table 5.

years, up from one-fifth in the mid-1960s (table 2). But this share is still low compared with Taiwan and Japan, the 1980 shares for which were 74 and 80 percent, respectively. Moreover, while in the latter cases three-quarters of the off-farm income is from wages of farm household members, in Korea less than half is from wages (Anderson, Hayami, and others, 1986, table 1.4). That is, the majority of Korean farm households' off-farm income is simply gifts repatriated from family members living in the city. Clearly, there may be considerable scope for the provision of more part-time, nonfarm jobs in rural areas of Korea.[11] What is needed is an evaluation of the net social returns of diversifying geographically the industrial base away from the coastal cities somewhat. Even if those returns are negative, they may involve less social cost than the present system of agricultural protection.

Another way to improve the adaptability of farm workers is through more investments in education in rural areas. All the available evidence suggests that education enhances farmers' abilities to adjust to changing circumstances, especially if the changes require them to leave farming (Schultz, 1975; Jamison and Lau, 1981). I am unaware of studies specifically addressing social rates of return from expenditure on education in Korea's rural areas in particular. However, the results reported in Jeong (1977) and Psacharopoulos (1980) for the country as a whole suggest that returns from increased investment in primary and secondary schooling are likely to be considerably higher than the returns from further tertiary education expenditure; and since it is in rural areas that school leavers have the least education, returns from further pretertiary education are likely to be highest in these areas. Thus from an efficiency point of view alone, more expenditure on rural education may well be warranted. Furthermore, because rural people who migrate to the city take their skills with them and subsequently contribute to industrial growth, an equity case exists for compensating the farm sector for this loss by subsidizing both formal schooling and job retraining for farmers wishing to leave agriculture (Schultz, 1961).

Finally, it is probable that, even without reducing the extent of producer price support, welfare gains can be made simply by using more efficient policy instruments. For example, for beef, and perhaps dairy products, it may be possible to reduce the cost of protection to consumers by replacing import quotas with less restrictive tariffs and using the tariff revenue to subsidize the producer price up to its present quota-protected level (Anderson, Hayami, and others, 1986, chapter 7).

11. That Korean farmers are not averse to seeing their children leave the farm sector is suggested by the results of a recent opinion survey, which shows that 70 percent of rural residents would like their children to attend a tertiary college, and only 4 percent would like to see their children become farmers (D. I. Kim, 1980).

Prospects for Reform and Lessons for Less-Developed Countries

What are the prospects for reform of Korea's food price policy? More specifically, what is the likelihood of a slowdown or reversal of agricultural protection growth in the future? Unfortunately neither empirical evidence from other industrial countries nor the economic theory of politics offers much hope for major reform. Agricultural protection has been growing in most developed countries since the 1950s, although to a lesser extent in food-surplus North America and Australasia. In Western Europe the average nominal rate of agricultural protection is estimated to have risen from 38 percent in 1956–57 to 47 percent in 1963–64 and 62 percent in 1968–69 (Gulbrandsen and Lindbeck, 1973). It has risen further since then, reaching about 75 percent in the European Community and 120 percent in the European Free Trade Association by the late 1970s before dropping slightly in the early 1980s because of a temporary rise in international food prices (Tyers and Anderson, 1986). In Japan the increase has been even more dramatic, from 45 percent in the latter 1950s to 140 percent in the early 1980s (Anderson, 1983a). These estimates alone should be sobering to anyone hoping that as the farm sector declines in importance in growing economies, so too will the political power of those seeking agricultural protection.[12]

One reason the farm lobby becomes relatively stronger as incomes in a country grow is that food becomes progressively less important in urban household budgets. As a result, urban consumers have increasingly less incentive to oppose food price increases. So, too, do nonfarm employers, as food prices and the demand for labor on farms become less important in determining industrial wage levels. On the other hand, as the number of people in the farm sector declines, so too does the free rider problem of collective action (Olson, 1965), and for those farmers remaining there is an increasing incentive to lobby for assistance. Assistance is more likely to be forthcoming if it can be provided without government budgetary outlay, such as by tariff or levy protection against import competition. Hence one would expect and indeed observe higher rates of assistance to import-competing, as compared with exporting, sectors. But even assistance via export subsidies becomes possible politically once an industry is a sufficiently small part of the total economy. In addition, the political cost of providing farm assistance is lower in countries such as Korea, where there is widespread belief that such assistance is necessary to ensure an "adequate" degree of food security and to maintain farm incomes at a level close to rising urban incomes.[13]

12. For an explanation of why agriculture declines in relative size in growing economies, see Anderson (1987).

13. For an elaboration of the politico-economic reasons for protection growth in industrializing countries, see Anderson, Hayami, and others (1986), especially chapter 1.

Thus it is conceivable that agricultural protection in Korea will continue to increase. If Korea's protection grows half as fast in the next decade as in the 1960s and 1970s, then the only budgetary outlay that would be required by 1995 is that needed to finance export subsidies for rice and dairy, according to the modeling results presented in this chapter; and these outlays could be avoided simply by ensuring that domestic prices rise somewhat less rapidly than assumed in that scenario.

Making available more information both on the rising costs of such a policy trend, and on the availability of alternative, less costly, policies for achieving society's objectives, is one way to reduce the likelihood of continued protection growth. This is part of the justification for the analysis presented here.

Another reason for the analysis, however, is to draw out some implications for less-developed economies. Perhaps the most obvious one is that newly industrializing (or otherwise booming) economies should be aware of the huge cost of embarking on protectionism, as compared with more efficient strategies for solving the problems of rural/urban income disparity and perceived food insecurity. Secondly, such countries should be aware that if their agricultural comparative advantage continues to decline, protection can achieve its objectives only if it is increased continually over time. And perhaps most important, they need to be aware of the extreme political difficulty associated with trying to reverse a protectionist policy once it has been introduced. This is because the value of protection becomes incorporated into the capital value of sector-specific assets such as land, cattle, farm buildings, and the specific skills of farm workers. Because the owners of these assets would lose from the removal of protection, they have a strong incentive to form a group to lobby for the retention of that policy. This is now probably the single most important obstacle to reform of food policy in Korea.

Appendix A: Details of Agricultural Protection Estimates, 1955–85

The domestic-to-border price comparison data for 1955 to 1979 in appendix table A first appeared in Anderson (1981) and were reproduced in appendix 1 of Anderson, Hayami, and others (1986), except for milk. The 1980–85 estimates are revisions and extensions of the 1980–82 estimates in Anderson, Hayami, and others, while the estimates for milk first appeared in Tyers and Anderson (1986).

Estimating the nominal rates of agricultural protection involves comparing for each commodity the domestic price with the price at the country's border. The assumption is made throughout that Korea on its own is unable to influence international prices. (Even in the case of rice, Korea's protection lowers the world price by only 1 percent, according to the modeling results discussed in this chapter.) Care is needed in comparing domestic and border prices, however, even for relatively homogeneous farm products. In particular, adjustments need to be made for differences in quality between the domestic product and the internationally traded product to which the available price data refer, including adjustments to capture the various points that products have reached in their progress along the marketing chain. With this consideration in mind, wholesale rather than retail prices are used to compare consumer prices with border prices, since wholesale prices represent payments for approximately the same marketing services as are embodied in import prices. However, wholesale prices are not always good indicators of domestic producer grain prices (plus the costs of marketing to the wholesale level) because of various subsidies to producer prices. Data on grain marketing costs suggest that it cost about 20 percent of the border price to get grains to the wholesale level in the 1970s and 10 percent in the 1960s. Thus the nominal protection coefficient for grains and soybeans is defined as the producer-to-border price ratio plus 0.1 prior to 1970 and plus 0.2 thereafter. Marketing margins for meat are more difficult to obtain, so wholesale-to-border price ratios are used as proxies for nominal protection coefficients.

To arrive at border prices, the unit c.i.f. value of imports is used for those years in which a country imported substantial quantities of a product. In cases where the quantity traded by a country was small or unrepresentative of the average quality of the product consumed domestically, proxy border prices were obtained from the trade data of countries trading comparable products, as detailed below.

Domestic and border prices are expressed in U.S. dollars per tonne, converted at official exchange rates from 1964. (Before 1964, shadow exchange rates based on purchasing-power parity from Frank, Kim, and Westphal, 1975, pp. 70–73, are used because the official rates were highly overvalued.) These exchange rates are reported in the first column of appendix table A.

Rice (native), wheat, barley, corn, and soybean producer prices refer to grade B prices received by farmers, expressed in polished form in the case of rice and barley. Sugar is not produced in Korea, so no producer price appears. Wholesale prices for grains refer to average grades, for wheat flour to 80 percent extraction, for sugar to 99.5 percent white purity. Domestic prices are from the National Agricultural Cooperatives Federation, *Agricultural Cooperatives Yearbook* (Seoul, various issues) and Bank of Korea, *Price Statistics Summary* (Seoul, various issues).

Border prices for rice and barley are converted to a polished basis by dividing by 0.93 and 0.67, respectively. As a rule, Korea's unit c.i.f. import value is used as the border price. The exceptions are rice before 1968,

APPENDIX TABLE A.   Agricultural prices and nominal protection coefficients (NPC), Korea, 1955–85 (U.S. $ per tonne)

	Exchange rate (won/$ U.S.) (1)	Rice (polished)					Wheat			Wheat flour		
		Producer price (2)	Wholesale price (3)	Border price (4)	NPC (5)	3/4 (6)	Producer price (7)	Border price (8)	NPC (9)	Wholesale price (10)	Border price (11)	10/11 (12)
1955	114	88	96	158	0.66	0.61	45	73	0.72	80	100	0.80
1956	130	132	135	153	0.96	0.88	58	73	0.89	91	96	0.95
1957	116	173	171	147	1.28	1.16	72	73	1.09	108	88	1.23
1958	121	133	135	146	1.00	0.92	57	72	0.89	92	94	0.98
1959	120	114	121	144	0.88	0.83	53	75	0.82	84	106	0.79
1960	135	121	127	144	0.94	0.88	58	67	0.97	82	106	0.77
1961	245	83	86	144	0.68	0.60	38	72	0.63	62	103	0.60
1962	227	95	97	149	0.76	0.67	51	70	0.87	70	99	0.70
1963	189	182	185	157	1.32	1.24	92	74	1.34	82	104	0.79
1964	214	200	203	159	1.37	1.29	119	96	1.34	121	105	1.15
1965	266	151	157	167	1.05	0.99	82	76	1.18	121	105	1.15
1966	270	157	158	173	1.04	0.95	85	91	1.03	120	102	1.17
1967	268	174	172	175	1.11	0.99	91	75	1.31	116	102	1.14
1968	276	199	194	191	1.24	1.11	91	77	1.28	115	93	1.24
1969	288	236	223	189	1.34	1.17	85	69	1.33	112	90	1.24
1970	310	245	233	149	1.50	1.23	77	67	1.35	104	90	1.15
1971	350	274	255	137	2.04	1.71	84	69	1.42	103	93	1.10
1972	394	309	312	251	2.46	2.28	97	98	1.19	104	98	1.07
1973	399	320	305	426	1.47	1.21	105	99	1.26	129	151	0.85
1974	406	454	363	404	1.27	0.85	157	227	0.87	198	277	0.72
1975	484	482	474	263	1.39	1.17	170	193	1.08	207	251	0.83
1976	484	580	574	219	2.41	2.18	187	154	1.41	222	236	0.94
1977	484	642	625	328	3.13	2.85	222	137	1.82	219	196	1.12
1978	484	752	728	309	2.49	2.20	258	144	1.99	217	176	1.23
1979	484	976	970	448	3.36	3.14	266	176	1.71	225	194	1.16
1980	608	1,005	981	451	2.44	2.19	425	196	2.37	259	227	1.14
1981	681	1,020	1,090	410	2.46	2.42	431	207	2.28	305	245	1.24
1982	731	983	1,038	288	2.60	2.53	457	180	2.74	280	215	1.30
1983	776	960	985	280	3.53	3.42	433	180	2.61	248	201	1.23
1984	806	936	953	280	3.54	3.40	360	184	2.16	237	207	1.15
1985	872	949	931	270	3.71	3.45	316	169	2.07	248	190	1.31

APPENDIX TABLE A. (Continued)

	Barley (polished)					Corn			Soybean				
	Producer price (13)	Wholesale price (14)	Border price (15)	NPC (16)	14/15 (17)	Producer price (18)	Border price (19)	NPC (20)	Producer price (21)	Wholesale price (22)	Border price (23)	NPC (24)	22/23 (25)
1955	45	61	103	0.54	0.59	n.a.	76	n.a.	70	73	122	0.67	0.60
1956	81	92	100	0.91	0.92	n.a.	74	n.a.	73	76	118	0.72	0.64
1957	114	126	99	1.26	1.27	n.a.	71	n.a.	99	103	116	0.95	0.89
1958	87	94	81	1.17	1.16	n.a.	55	n.a.	88	91	111	0.89	0.82
1959	69	73	85	0.91	0.86	50	64	0.88	101	105	99	1.12	1.06
1960	78	83	85	1.02	0.97	49	61	0.90	111	116	93	1.29	1.25
1961	59	63	79	0.85	0.80	41	64	0.74	62	64	109	0.67	0.59
1962	71	77	106	0.77	0.73	48	70	0.79	72	74	108	0.77	0.69
1963	149	147	100	1.59	1.47	90	69	1.40	143	147	109	1.61	1.35
1964	173	170	112	1.64	1.52	131	66	2.08	194	198	129	1.60	1.53
1965	105	108	125	0.94	0.87	73	66	1.21	164	168	122	1.44	1.37
1966	98	106	137	0.82	0.78	87	90	1.07	181	187	125	1.55	1.50
1967	114	119	145	0.89	0.82	93	78	1.29	242	247	125	2.04	1.97
1968	121	120	113	1.17	1.06	99	77	1.39	164	159	128	1.38	1.24
1969	135	121	104	1.40	1.17	91	66	1.48	172	180	120	1.53	1.50
1970	137	137	131	1.24	1.05	91	71	1.48	247	257	117	2.31	2.20
1971	168	169	101	1.86	1.67	95	73	1.50	226	239	145	1.76	1.65
1972	191	163	100	2.11	1.63	106	61	1.94	251	262	138	2.02	1.90
1973	193	157	166	1.36	0.95	122	72	1.89	291	284	228	1.48	1.25
1974	240	181	257	1.13	0.70	172	152	1.33	352	333	286	1.43	1.16
1975	282	214	297	1.15	0.72	173	161	1.27	362	360	261	1.59	1.38
1976	287	229	307	1.13	0.74	191	132	1.65	491	492	261	2.08	1.89
1977	389	248	181	2.35	1.37	217	119	2.02	641	605	323	2.18	1.87
1978	443	262	186	2.58	1.41	245	123	2.19	691	668	272	2.74	2.46
1979	512	273	210	2.64	1.30	269	134	2.21	732	681	316	2.52	2.16
1980	523	244	256	2.24	0.95	318	160	2.19	862	844	309	2.99	2.73
1981	541	345	294	2.04	1.17	313	143	2.39	1,123	1,170	338	3.52	3.46
1982	571	396	227	2.72	1.74	288	135	2.33	995	1,080	269	3.90	4.01
1983	554	476	211	2.83	2.26	301	147	2.25	1,039	1,103	279	3.92	3.95
1984	550	505	227	2.62	2.22	342	146	2.54	990	990	317	3.32	3.12
1985	540	484	180	3.20	2.69	323	121	2.87	888	880	250	3.75	3.52

APPENDIX TABLE A. (Continued)

	Beef (boneless)			Pork (boneless)			Chicken			Milk (fresh)			Sugar (refined)		
	Wholesale price (26)	Border price (27)	NPC 26/27 (28)	Wholesale price (29)	Border price (30)	NPC 29/30 (31)	Wholesale price (32)	Border price (33)	NPC 32/33 (34)	Producer price (35)	Border price (36)	NPC 35/36 (37)	Wholesale price (38)	Border price (39)	38/39 (40)
1955	570	792	0.71	350	580	0.61	510	n.a.	n.a.	n.a.	n.a.	n.a.	135	114	1.19
1956	540	768	0.70	360	510	0.70	510	n.a.	n.a.	n.a.	n.a.	n.a.	170	119	1.43
1957	730	672	1.10	540	520	1.03	670	n.a.	n.a.	n.a.	n.a.	n.a.	267	82	3.25
1958	720	744	0.98	530	470	1.13	710	n.a.	n.a.	n.a.	n.a.	n.a.	198	67	2.95
1959	750	948	0.80	520	530	0.99	760	820	0.93	n.a.	n.a.	n.a.	206	104	1.99
1960	850	948	0.90	500	510	0.98	660	620	1.06	n.a.	n.a.	n.a.	229	114	2.00
1961	550	900	0.62	310	520	0.59	390	580	0.67	n.a.	n.a.	n.a.	153	110	1.39
1962	640	840	0.77	400	490	0.81	480	550	0.87	n.a.	n.a.	n.a.	193	89	2.17
1963	810	852	0.96	520	440	1.18	630	560	1.13	n.a.	n.a.	n.a.	332	122	2.72
1964	830	864	0.98	630	540	1.17	790	490	1.61	n.a.	n.a.	n.a.	821	158	5.20
1965	890	888	1.00	690	470	1.47	920	510	1.80	n.a.	n.a.	n.a.	379	85	4.45
1966	990	1,032	0.96	720	480	1.50	960	530	1.81	n.a.	n.a.	n.a.	321	67	4.79
1967	1,290	1,080	1.19	860	500	1.72	1,200	510	2.35	155	76	2.05	320	66	4.84
1968	1,820	1,116	1.63	1,170	500	2.34	1,430	470	3.04	180	58	3.10	337	70	4.81
1969	2,060	1,236	1.67	1,170	570	2.05	1,350	520	2.60	165	54	3.05	332	83	4.00
1970	2,110	1,320	1.60	1,130	530	2.13	1,320	520	2.54	172	54	3.16	328	101	3.24
1971	2,420	1,404	1.73	1,410	530	2.66	1,230	490	2.51	152	65	2.33	319	127	2.51
1972	2,540	1,512	1.68	1,260	560	2.25	980	550	1.78	136	96	1.41	386	189	2.04
1973	2,730	2,040	1.34	1,410	690	2.04	1,160	760	1.53	168	105	1.60	400	254	1.57
1974	3,210	2,172	1.48	1,710	1,150	1.49	1,630	910	1.79	231	119	1.94	766	606	1.26
1975	3,020	1,320	2.29	1,960	1,100	1.78	2,070	900	2.30	238	102	2.33	905	589	1.54
1976	4,470	1,560	2.87	2,780	1,370	2.03	2,390	1,050	2.28	269	94	2.87	902	408	2.21
1977	5,820	1,512	3.85	2,900	1,540	1.88	2,650	980	2.70	286	99	2.89	839	289	2.90
1978	6,980	1,836	3.80	4,080	1,570	2.60	2,960	1,020	2.90	321	117	2.75	827	246	3.36
1979	8,540	2,796	3.06	3,900	1,650	2.36	2,580	1,050	2.46	432	120	3.61	827	276	3.00
1980	7,940	2,916	2.73	3,390	1,620	2.09	3,000	1,220	2.46	438	136	3.23	1,088	587	1.85
1981	9,470	2,628	3.60	5,020	1,860	2.70	3,370	1,080	3.12	451	154	2.94	1,311	418	3.14
1982	11,780	2,388	4.93	4,800	2,000	2.40	2,820	1,050	2.69	427	159	2.69	1,058	277	3.84
1983	13,900	2,472	5.63	4,680	1,950	2.40	2,520	970	2.60	403	159	2.53	901	250	3.60
1984	12,700	2,388	5.32	3,770	1,810	2.08	2,770	1,100	2.52	388	149	2.60	804	267	3.01
1985	7,135	2,262	3.16	4,327	1,490	2.90	2,710	1,040	2.61	364	160	2.28	610	208	2.93

APPENDIX B.　Essential Parameters for Korea Used in the Simulation Model of World Food Markets

APPENDIX TABLE B1.　Price ratios, production growth, and income elasticities

	Producer (consumer)-to-border price ratio, 1980–82	Price-independent production growth rate, 1983–95 (percent per annum)	Income elasticity of demand
Rice	2.50 (2.40)	2.0	0.05
Wheat	2.45 (1.45)	0.0	0.10
Coarse grain	2.30 (1.30)	2.0	0.00
Ruminant meat	3.75 (3.75)	4.5	0.80
Nonruminant meat	2.50 (2.50)	6.0	0.80
Dairy products	2.95 (2.95)	4.0	0.70
Sugar	1.00 (2.90)	0.0	0.60

SOURCE: Tyers and Anderson (forthcoming).

APPENDIX TABLE B2.　Demand elasticities

	Elasticity of demand with respect to the price of:						
	Rice	Wheat	Coarse grain	Ruminant meat	Nonruminant meat	Dairy products	Sugar
Rice	−0.18	0.02	0.01				
Wheat	0.20	−0.36	0.08				
Coarse grain	0.10	0.10	−0.22	0.02	0.20	0.04	
Ruminant meat				−1.00	0.45		
Nonruminant meat				0.26	−1.50		
Dairy products						−0.80	
Sugar	0.01						−0.80

SOURCE: Tyers and Anderson (forthcoming).

APPENDIX TABLE B3.　Supply elasticities

	Elasticity of supply with respect to the price of:					
	Rice	Wheat	Coarse grain	Ruminant meat	Nonruminant meat	Dairy products
Rice	0.14		−0.03			
Wheat	−0.01	0.55	−0.45			
Coarse grain	−0.20	−0.04	0.28			
Ruminant meat			−0.11	0.50	−0.10	0.04
Nonruminant meat			−0.23	−0.04	0.85	
Dairy products			−0.11	−0.06		0.80

SOURCE: Tyers and Anderson (forthcoming).

when Korea would have been a rice exporter in the absence of distortionary policies (instead, the f.o.b. unit export value for Taiwan is used), and in occasional years since 1970 when Korea imported no rice (c.i.f. unit import value for Japan), wheat flour, pork, chicken (c.i.f. unit import value for Hong Kong), beef (c.i.f. unit import value for the United States plus 20 percent to adjust for quality differences), milk (the producer price in New Zealand, plus an allowance of one-third to cover the cost of drying, transportation, and reconstitution in Korea), and refined sugar (c.i.f. unit import value for Hong Kong). These trade data are from the Food and Agriculture Organization's *Trade Yearbook* (Rome, various issues).

Note that 1985 prices are preliminary and so are subject to revision.

References

Aghevli, B. B., and J. Marquez-Ruarte. 1985. *A Case of Successful Adjustment: Korea's Experience During 1980–84.* Occasional Paper no. 39. Washington, D.C.: International Monetary Fund.

Ahn, I. C. 1982. *Changing Comparative Advantage in Korean Agriculture: A Domestic Resource Cost Study.* Master's Thesis, Australian National University, Canberra.

Anderson, K. 1981. *Northeast Asian Agricultural Protection in Historical and Comparative Perspective: The Case of South Korea.* Research Report no. 82. Canberra: Australia-Japan Research Centre.

——. 1983a. "Growth of Agricultural Protection in East Asia." *Food Policy* 8(4): 327–36.

——. 1983b. "Economic Growth, Comparative Advantage and Agricultural Trade of Pacific Rim Countries." *Review of Marketing and Agricultural Economics* 51(3): 231–48.

——. 1983c. "Fertilizer Policy in Korea." *Journal of Rural Development* 6(1): 43–57.

——. 1987. "On Why Agriculture Declines with Economic Growth." *Agricultural Economics* 1(3): 195–207.

——, Y. Hayami, and others. 1986. *The Political Economy of Agricultural Protection: East Asia in International Perspective.* Sydney: Allen & Unwin.

——, and Y. J. Joo. 1984. "South Korea's Rapid Industrialization and Its Implications for Agricultural Trade." In M. Adams, ed., *Economic Development and Change in East and Southeast Asia,* 107–130. Canberra: Australian Government Publishing Service for the Bureau of Agricultural Economics.

——, and P. G. Warr. 1987. "General Equilibrium Effects of Agricultural Price Distortions: A Simple Model for Korea." *Food Research Institute Studies* 20(3): 245–64.

Balassa, B. 1965. "Trade, Liberalization and 'Revealed' Comparative Advantage." *Manchester School for Economic and Social Studies* 33(2): 99–124.

Ban, S. H. 1981. "The Growth of Agricultural Output and Productivity in Korea, 1918 to 1978." *Journal of Rural Development* 4(1): 1–18.

——, P. Y. Moon, and D. H. Perkins. 1980. *Rural Development.* Studies in the Modernization of the Republic of Korea: 1945–1975. Harvard East Asian Monograph no. 89. Cambridge: Harvard University Press.

Boyce, J. K., and R. E. Evenson. 1975. *National and International Agricultural Research and Extension Programs.* New York: Agricultural Development Council.

——, M. A. Judd, and R. E. Evenson. 1982. "Inter-country and Inter-regional Comparisons of the Allocation of Resources to Agricultural Research and Extension." Mimeo, Yale University.

Economic Planning Board. 1985a and earlier. *Korean Statistical Yearbook*. Seoul: Economic Planning Board.

——. 1985b and earlier. *Major Statistics of Korean Economy*. Seoul: Economic Planning Board.

Floyd, J. E. 1965. "The Effects of Farm Price Supports on the Returns to Land and Labor in Agriculture." *Journal of Political Economy* 73(2): 148–58.

Food and Agriculture Organization. 1984 and earlier. *Production Yearbook*. Rome: Food and Agriculture Organization.

Frank, C. R., K. S. Kim, and L. Westphal. 1975. *Foreign Trade Regimes and Economic Development: South Korea*. New York: Columbia University Press for the National Bureau of Economic Research.

Gulbandsen, O., and A. Lindbeck. 1973. *The Economics of the Agricultural Sector*. Stockholm: Almqvist & Wicksell.

Hayami, Y., and V. W. Ruttan. 1985. *Agricultural Development: An International Perspective*. Rev. ed. Baltimore: Johns Hopkins University Press.

Huffman, W. E. 1978. "Assessing Returns to Agricultural Extension." *American Journal of Agricultural Economics* 60(5): 969–75.

Jamison, D. T., and L. J. Lau. 1981. *Farmer Education and Farm Efficiency*. Baltimore: Johns Hopkins University Press.

Jeong, C. Y. 1977. "Rates of Return on Investment in Education." In C. K. Kim, ed., *Industrial and Social Development Issues*. Seoul: Korea Development Institute Press.

Johnston, B. F. 1953. *Japanese Food Management in World War II*. Stanford: Stanford University Press.

Just, R. E., D. L. Hueth, and A. Schmitz. 1982. *Applied Welfare Economics and Public Policy*. Englewood Cliffs, N.J.: Prentice Hall.

Kim, D. I. 1980. "A Profile of Korean Rural Villages, Farmers and Their Changing Quality of Life." *Journal of Rural Development* 3(2): 193–212.

Kim, K. S., and M. Roemer. 1980. *Growth and Structural Transformation*. Studies in the Modernization of the Republic of Korea, 1945–1975. Harvard East Asian Monograph no. 86. Cambridge: Harvard University Press.

Kim, Y. S., et al. 1980. *Decreasing Farm Labor Force and Farm Mechanization* (in Korean). Seoul: Korea Rural Economics Institute.

Krueger, A. O. 1979. *The Developmental Role of the Foreign Trade Sector and Aid*. Studies in the Modernization of the Republic of Korea: 1945–1975. Harvard East Asian Monograph no. 87. Cambridge: Harvard University Press.

Ministry of Agriculture and Fisheries. 1982. *Dairy Situation*. Seoul: Ministry of Agriculture and Fisheries.

——. 1985 and earlier. *Yearbook of Agriculture and Forestry Statistics*. Seoul: Ministry of Agriculture and Fisheries.

Moon, P. Y. 1975. "The Evolution of Rice Policy in Korea." *Food Research Institute Studies* 14(4): 381–402.

Nam, C. H. 1981. "Trade and Industrial Policies and the Structure of Protection in Korea." In W. Wong and L. Krause, eds., *Trade and Growth of the Advanced Developing Countries in the Pacific Basin*. Seoul: Korea Development Institute Press.

National Agricultural Cooperatives Federation. 1985. *Agricultural Cooperatives Yearbook*. Seoul: National Agricultural Cooperatives Federation.

National Livestock Cooperatives Federation. 1982. *Quarterly Review*. Seoul: National Livestock Cooperatives Federation.

——. 1985. *Livestock Marketing Handbook*. Seoul: National Livestock Cooperatives Federation.

Olson, M. 1965. *The Logic of Collective Action*. Cambridge: Harvard University Press.

Otsuka, K., and Y. Hayami. 1985. "Goals and Consequences of Rice Policy in Japan, 1965–80." *American Journal of Agricultural Economics* 67(3): 529–38.

Psacharopoulos, G. 1980. "Returns to Education: An Updated International Comparison." In T. King, ed., *Education and Income*. World Bank Staff Working Paper no. 402. Washington, D.C.: World Bank.

Ruttan, V. W. 1983. *Agricultural Research Policy*. Minneapolis: University of Minnesota Press.

Schultz, T. W. 1961. "A Policy to Redistribute the Losses from Economic Progress." *Journal of Farm Economics* 43(3): 554–65.

———. 1975. "The Value of the Ability to Deal with Disequilibria." *Journal of Economic Literature* 13(3): 827–46.

Siamwalla, A., and A. Valdes. 1980. "Food Insecurity in Developing Countries." *Food Policy* 5(4): 258–72.

Suh, S. C. 1978. *Growth and Structural Changes in the Korean Economy, 1910–1940*. Cambridge: Harvard University Press for the Council on East Asian Studies.

Tyers, R., and K. Anderson. 1986. "Distortions in World Food Markets: A Quantitative Assessment." Mimeo, background paper prepared for the World Bank *World Development Report 1986*. Washington, D.C.: World Bank.

———. Forthcoming. *Disarray in World Food Markets*. Cambridge: Cambridge University Press.

The World Bank. 1984. *Republic of Korea Agriculture Sector Survey*. Report no. 4709–KO. Washington, D.C.

Young, S., et al. 1982. *Basic Objective of Industrial Policy and Reform Proposals for Industrial Incentives* (in Korean). Seoul: Korea Development Institute.

5. Philippines: Price Policy in Transition

Cristina C. David

The Philippine economy is currently suffering from its deepest economic crisis. The annual growth rate of gross domestic product (GDP) averaged only 3 percent from 1980 to 1983. The GDP growth became negative in 1984 and 1985 due to the political uncertainty following the Aquino assassination and the severe contractionary policies accompanying the peso devaluation. Per capita income has declined to 1975 levels. Unemployment is widespread as wages in real terms dropped to half the levels in 1960. Nearly 40 percent of export receipts are required to service foreign debts.

The level of Philippine economic development, which was second only to Japan at the start of the postwar period, now ranks near the bottom among the Association of Southeast Asian Nations (ASEAN) and East Asian countries. Philippine GDP increased at an annual average of 5 percent between 1955 and 1982 compared to 7–8 percent in Thailand, Malaysia, and Indonesia and 10 percent or more in the East Asian countries. The difference in per capita GDP growth rate is even more striking as population grew faster in the Philippines. Moreover, the structural transformation typically accompanying economic growth has been essentially absent. Agriculture's share in gross domestic product changed only from 29 to 26 percent and the manufacturing sector from 24 to 25 percent. The share of agriculture in total employment fell from about 60 percent during the 1960s to 54 percent by 1970 and has changed only slightly since then.

What is more disturbing is the worsening of income distribution and the rate at which rural incomes have fallen behind. Average family income in the rural sector is now only 40 percent of the urban income, down from almost 60 percent in 1970 and 75 percent in 1975. Over 40 percent of rural families live below the poverty threshold as compared to only 20 percent in the urban areas. The rural sector accounts for about 80 percent of the poorest 30 percent of total households, with the corn and coconut farmers together with landless agricultural workers and fishermen being the most disadvantaged.

There are many other qualitative dimensions of the country's crisis—the degradation of the environment, the level of graft and corruption, the inefficiency of government administration. All these eventually led to the people power revolution that toppled the twenty-year rule of the Marcos administration and the installation of the new Cory Aquino government.

The new government is faced with a formidable challenge as well as a unique opportunity to reverse the economic retrogression by economic, social, and institutional reforms necessary to achieve sustained and equitable economic development. The economic and institutional framework that will evolve and the possibility of success in implementing the reforms depends on political, social, and economic factors within and outside the Philippines. Correct analysis of the underlying causes of the crisis, however, is crucial in being able to develop the appropriate framework and structural reforms.

The Philippine postwar economic history has been marked by a series of economic crises manifested through balance of payments problems. These had led to the decontrol policy in the early 1960s and the floating of the exchange rate in 1970. While crony capitalism, excessive corruption, and more pervasive government interventions in the 1970s undoubtedly exacerbated the present economic crisis, one underlying cause of the earlier crises, that is, a prolonged import substitution industrialization strategy (Bautista, Power, and associates, 1979), is a no less compelling factor. The policy response to the earlier crises did not translate the rhetoric of shifting to an export-led strategy and balanced agro-industrial growth into reality as import controls in the 1950s were replaced only by an equally protective tariff and tax structure.

Industrialization via import substitution had continued to be the central thrust of the Philippine development strategy throughout the postwar period. Agricultural policies pursued were primarily in support of the industrial promotion thrust, as the agricultural sector was simply viewed as supplying foreign exchange, cheap food and raw materials, and capital resources for this effort. Industrial promotion policies encouraged industries that were relatively inefficient, capital-intensive, located mostly near large urban areas, and serving primarily the domestic market (ILO, 1977). Chronic balance of payments difficulties, periodic food crises, slow growth of employment, and uneven distribution of income are problems associated with this development strategy.

Promoting industrialization by artificially depressing food and raw material prices, and raising the prices of manufactured goods that the agricultural sector buys, limits growth in several ways. The lower profitability of agricultural production reduces the agricultural surplus needed to sustain the high import and capital requirements of industrialization. It discourages public and private sector investments in research, extension, irrigation, and other means of increasing productivity that could have efficiently produced cheaper food and raw materials. When technical progress is slow and land becomes increasingly scarce, the cost of producing food and foreign exchange to support further industrialization efforts increases. Higher food prices raise the cost of labor for industry and increased food imports further tighten the foreign exchange constraint.

The efficiency and equity costs of a prolonged bias of economic policies against agriculture are high. The continuing importance and trade surplus position of Philippine agriculture clearly indicates a measure of comparative advantage in agricultural production. Recent studies do show that the agricultural sector is, on the whole, a more efficient earner and saver of foreign exchange than the industrial sector (David, 1983a). It has also been frequently overlooked that rapid increases in agricultural incomes have strong growth linkage effects (i.e., income and employment multipliers) in the whole economy as consumption of the rural population is heavily oriented to food and relatively labor-intensive industrial consumer goods and services (Hazell and Roell, 1983).

This chapter is an examination of the present economic crisis from the perspective of food policy. Food and agriculture are treated together in this chapter because the issue of reconciling consumers' (or users of raw material) and producers' interests is central to both food and raw material policies. A macroeconomic perspective is emphasized because of the broad implications to the whole economy of the performance and policies of the agricultural sector; macroeconomic policies, on the other hand, have important and pervasive, but usually unrecognized, effects on the sector. While the focus of the analysis here is on price intervention policies (both commodity specific and macroeconomic), the role of credit and public expenditure policies shall also be briefly discussed.

The objectives of this chapter are, first, to analyze the structure, changes, causes, and consequences of Philippine agricultural policies, and second, to draw implications for policy reforms and briefly discuss the new government's progress and constraints in instituting reforms during this exceedingly difficult transition period. The first section deals with sector-specific policies, their objectives, instruments, and impact on prices. This is followed by an analysis of macroeconomic policies relating to foreign exchange, credit, and public expenditures. The third section assesses the consequences of the policy structure. The final section describes briefly the new government's progress and constraints in implementing policy reforms.

Sector-Specific Policies
Policy Goals

The stated goals of Philippine agricultural policy are clear and consistent throughout the postwar period. They are cheap food and raw material prices, high farm income, food security through food self-sufficiency, and stable prices to both consumers and producers. From the viewpoint of price policies, these goals often conflict with each other. Low food and raw material prices reduce farm income and incentives to increase production, ultimately threatening the objective of food self-sufficiency or promotion of industry. High prices, on the other hand, hurt nutritional welfare of the poor and raise cost of production to industry. In the short run, output price or input price subsidies can overcome this price policy dilemma. However, in the long run, public investments in research, extension, irrigation, and other infrastructure are more efficient instruments for lowering food prices without harming farm income. In both cases, budgetary outlays are required. Hence, while the political economy factors ultimately determine the policy decisions, the parameters for reconciling these objectives particularly in the short run depend on the budget constraint.

Policy Instruments

The policy instruments affecting agricultural prices generally differ from those in manufacturing, where tariffs and indirect sales tax are the main tools. Quantitative trade restrictions, price controls, operations of national marketing agencies, export taxes, and other forms of levies have been more important instruments affecting agricultural prices.

With the exception of rice, corn, and sugar, there were few commodity-specific policies in the 1950s and 1960s. Import controls in the 1950s and tariffs in the 1960s may have potentially provided protection to a limited number of minor import-competing agricultural products. There were few attempts to intervene in the production and trade of export crops except in the special case of sugar, and briefly, by restricting foreign currency conversion as a stabilization measure after the 1962 devaluation. Because of the need to administer the Philippine sugar quota to the highly protected United States market, a domestic quota system guided its distribution among the domestic producers. In the 1960s sugar exports were restricted to reduce the burden on domestic consumers of the higher export prices resulting from the 1962 devaluation and the greater United States quota allocation resulting from the Cuban crisis.

A greater variety of price and marketing interventions were instituted during the 1970s initially as a policy response to the floating of the exchange rate in 1970 and then to the unprecedented turbulence in the oil and commodity markets from 1973 to 1975. The policy instruments used to address this short-run problem of price instability, however, eventually led to the pervasive regulation of the agricultural sector and the government's direct involvement, frequently as a monopoly, in the marketing of virtually all major agricultural commodities.

The government has directly intervened in the marketing of rice and corn since the late 1930s. Its short-run impact on domestic price levels and defense of official floor and ceiling prices have been principally through the control of import/export of rice and corn and through domestic procurement and disbursement operations. Up to 1972 the Rice and Corn Administration (RCA) administered the government marketing operations, with their import policy and budget being determined by the legislature. The RCA was abolished and the National Grains Authority (NGA) was established as a corporation in order to have adequate funds, operational flexibility, and independence from immediate political pressures. When world prices of wheat tripled in 1974, the wheat millers requested the NGA to import the wheat grains and avail indirectly of the tax exemption privileges of a government corporation in order to comply with the official ceiling price of wheat flour. When world prices declined in 1975, monopoly rights were formally conferred to NGA, supposedly to stabilize supply and prices of wheat products in the domestic market. In 1981 the NGA was renamed the National Food Authority (NFA) and empowered to regulate the marketing of all foods. In addition to the major grains, the NFA directly determined domestic pricing of soybeans, soybean meal, and other feedstuff through its monopoly control on imports. Price margins on imports that are duty-free and subsidized credit rather than budgetary outlays have financed the expanded domestic marketing operations of NFA.

Taxation of agricultural exports began with the floating of the exchange rate in 1970 when export taxes from 4 to 6 percent were imposed as a stabilization measure. These have been continued, however, as a convenient means of taxing agriculture. A higher rate is levied on traditional exports of copra and sugar (6 percent) to promote new and greater processing of agricultural exports. Most of the other agricultural commodities are subject to a 4 percent export tax.[1] Between 1973 and 1975 additional export premium duties were temporarily levied to siphon off part of the gains from higher world prices.

The end of the United States sugar quota policy in 1973 initially motivated the nationalization of the domestic and international wholesale marketing of sugar, first under the Philippine Exchange (PHILEX) and later under the National Sugar Trading (NASUTRA). Under the system, producers are paid a composite price, which is derived as a weighted average of the export price, domestic wholesale price, and a domestic reserve price. These weights change depending on the export price and what the government decides to be the consumer price.

The problem of protecting domestic consumers from the sharp rise in world prices of coconut products initially motivated the imposition of a

---

1. These are coconut oil, dessicated coconut, molasses, abaca, bananas, pineapples, tobacco, shrimp and prawns, lumber, plywood, and veneer.

levy called the Coconut Consumers Stabilization Fund in 1973.[2] Using part of the levy receipts, almost 80 percent of the coconut oil milling industry was purchased and put under the monopoly control of United Coconut Mills (UNICOM). The establishment of UNICOM was an attempt to address the problem of overcapacity in the coconut oil milling industry induced mainly by investment incentives provided by the Board of Investments. The UNICOM, however, operated as a monopolist and therefore further lowered the farm price of copra (Clarete and Roumasset, 1983). As world prices of coconut oil dropped in 1982, the levy was lifted only to be replaced by a copra export ban to protect coconut oil mills, a common policy response that sacrifices the farm in favor of the industrial sector.

With respect to agricultural inputs, pricing of irrigation water and fertilizer has been directly regulated by the government whereas prices of agricultural machineries and chemicals have been affected by tariffs and differential sales taxes. All gravity irrigation systems, which comprise at least 90 percent of irrigated area, have been constructed with public funds, and farmers are charged irrigation fees that do not fully cover cost. Direct regulation of fertilizer prices was a policy initiated to protect domestic food production from the quadrupling of world prices of fertilizer following the oil crisis in 1973. A domestic price ceiling has been defended by tax-free importations of finished fertilizers and raw materials together with cash subsidies for losses incurred by the fertilizer manufacturers. The privilege to import tax free was given to the four domestic fertilizer manufacturers, and the profits derived from imports constituted part of their protection.

Impact on Prices

To evaluate the impact of commodity-specific policies on prices, actual domestic prices of agricultural outputs and inputs are compared in this section to those prices which would have prevailed without price intervention policies. Because most agricultural commodities are tradable and the Philippines can generally be considered a small country relative to the international market, this undistorted price can be approximated by the world or border price, that is, f.o.b. unit value for exportables and c.i.f. unit value for importables converted at the official exchange rate.

Three summary indicators have been used: nominal protection rates

2. About 20 percent of the revenues from the tax supported the direct subsidy on domestic consumption of coconut oil products. The remainder was supposed to finance development programs in the coconut industry such as replanting, vertical integration, and scholarships. Only a small segment of the coconut industry actually receives the benefits from these programs (David, 1977). On the other hand, the gains from the replanting program are uncertain. It is not known how well hybrid seeds will perform under diverse Philippine conditions. Furthermore, small coconut farmers with no alternative source of income have been hesitant to face the prospect of waiting for three years to harvest a first crop.

(NPR) and implicit tariff (IT) measure the percentage difference between domestic and border prices of agricultural output and inputs, respectively.[3] Care was taken to define these prices at a comparable point in the marketing chain to insure that the observed divergence in prices are caused by government market interventions and not by real marketing costs. The third indicator is the effective protection rate that provides a net measure of the impact of government interventions on both output and intermediate input prices by taking the percentage difference between value added at domestic and at border prices. All border prices are converted at the official exchange rates in these measures.

Three general patterns emerge from comparing the domestic and border prices of the major commodities (table 1). First, average nominal protection rates in agriculture are low. Legal tariff rates may be high, but since many of these commodities are either nontraded or exported, or are governed in international trade by national marketing agencies, these relatively high protection rates are not fully realized.

Second, export commodities, as expected, receive less protection than import-competing products. What is perhaps not well recognized is the extent by which major exports, especially copra and sugar, have been penalized by price intervention policies.

Finally, price protection has declined over time and indeed, for export commodities, has in effect been negative in the 1970s. This trend has not been entirely due to changes in price policy. In rice, productivity gains since the late 1960s have transformed the Philippines from being a net importer of 5 to 10 percent of its annual rice requirements to being a marginal rice exporter by the late 1970s. In relation to the world price, the domestic rice price declined without reducing profitability of rice at the farm level, and the government marketing agency's task changed from managing deficits to managing surpluses in rice supply after 1977. During the importing years, price policies tended to favor producers, as the level of imports kept domestic prices about 15 percent higher than border prices. During the exporting years, the government's failure to export more surplus stock has permitted the domestic price to fall slightly below world prices (Unnevehr and Balisacan, 1983).[4]

3.

$$\text{NPR} = \left[\frac{P_d^o}{P_b^o} - 1 \right] \times 100; \quad \text{IT} = \left[\frac{P_d^i}{P_b^i} - 1 \right] \times 100; \quad \text{where } P_b$$

is border price, P_d is domestic price, and the superscripts o and i refer to output and inputs, respectively. A distinction is made between the concept of nominal protection and implicit tariff because Philippine government policies often create a difference in the domestic price from the point of view of the producer and that of the user of the same product. This is, of course, not true for border price.

4. The government's pricing policy is frequently expressed in terms of defending official floor and ceiling prices and minimizing seasonal and geographical price spreads. Thus its

TABLE 1.   Trends in nominal protection rates (NPR)[a] in Philippine agriculture, 1960–82

	1960–1964	1965–1969	1970–1974	1975–1979	1980–1982
Rice	21	15	7	−5	−5
Corn	46	38	20	20	20
Sugar	32	174	36	−16	4
Copra	0	0	−12	−22	−30
Banana, pineapple, tobacco, abaca	0	0	−4	−4	−4
Beef	45	−4	−32	17	57
Pork	54	50	18	−3	6
Chicken	97	122	55	58	85
Eggs	60	48	18	11	37

[a]The percentage difference between domestic and border prices at official exchange rate.

Although price policy of corn was part of the RCA's mandate, there was no attempt to intervene directly in corn marketing until the early 1970s. The nominal protection of corn was about 40 percent before 1970 when imports were small and erratic. The rapid commercialization of livestock and poultry production accelerated the demand for corn as feed and led to the greater involvement of the government in importing corn in order to lower domestic prices. Given the ceiling prices imposed on meat products and the price elastic demand for meat, feedmillers and livestock producers strongly lobbied for higher corn imports. Tariffs for meat and other animals changed only from 15 to 10 percent. Poultry has been the most favored agricultural commodity.

The high protection enjoyed by sugar before 1973 was not due to domestic economic policies but to the United States policy of protecting its sugar industry. The nominal protection rate turned negative after the end of Philippine preferential access to the United States sugar market in 1973. The excess of export to producer prices of sugar was used to finance consumer subsidies in the Philippines, which were felt necessary especially when world prices of sugar peaked in 1974 (Nelson and Agcaoili, 1983).

The coconut farmers were the most heavily penalized by price interven-

---

effectiveness is evaluated in terms of the extent to which these objectives are achieved. Retail prices of rice were typically above the ceiling prices and farm prices below support prices during the importing years. Since 1977, because of the changing trade balance, ceiling prices have been maintained, but the degree to which market farm prices have fallen below support prices increased despite the wider official margins (covering milling and transport but not storage costs) during this period (Unnevehr, 1986). Seasonal and geographic price variations were substantially reduced as domestic procurement rates reached 8–10 percent compared to 3 percent in earlier periods. Subsidizing the very high cost of achieving stabilization was made possible by the fiscal "autonomy" of NFA, as profits from imports and credit subsidies became the principal sources of its financial support.

tion policies since the 1970s. The various policy instruments that were ostensibly to benefit the sector—the levy, UNICOM, copra export ban—only served to increase the implicit tax to 30 percent by the early 1980s.

Tariffs, the main source of protection for livestock products, have changed only after 1980. Before 1980 tariffs for eggs and chicken meat were 100 percent and 70 percent, respectively. Tariffs for meat of other animals changed from only 15 percent to 10 percent. The apparent decline in nominal protection rates indicates the growing efficiency of these enterprises. The shift to commercial type of production and the vertical integration of feedmilling and livestock production (such as contract farming in broiler production) generated economies of scale and facilitated international technology transfer (Cabanilla, 1983). Together with the more liberal import policy in corn during the 1970s, these lowered unit costs of production and hence domestic prices, making a significant part of the tariff protection redundant.

Implicit Tariffs on Agricultural Inputs

Government interventions in the agricultural input markets are often intended to offset the low output price objective of agricultural price policy. With the exception of gravity irrigation, which covers about 44 percent of rice area, government policies tended to tax farmers for use of agricultural inputs (table 2). Because of low collection rates, the effective subsidy rate on gravity irrigation is close to 90 percent as compared to the 60 percent implied by the official irrigation fee. Implicit tariffs on pumps for irrigation and hand tractors are higher than those for larger-scale machinery. This promotes domestic production of smaller machines but indirectly encourages use of more labor-displacing machines.[5]

Since imports of mixed feeds are insignificant, the weighted average implicit tariff of feed ingredients for various formulations are estimated. Based on legal tariff and tax rates, these were about 33 percent in 1974 (Medalla and Power, 1979). Because nontariff trade barriers are more common, the average implicit tariff based on price comparison was estimated, and these varied from 7 to 23 percent (Cabanilla, 1983).

Despite price controls, tax-free importations, and direct subsidies to fertilizer companies, farmers have paid a premium of approximately 10 percent over the border price between 1973 and 1981. This price difference varied across years depending on the world price fluctuation and the type of fertilizer (table 3). The price of mixed fertilizer has received a small subsidy, but urea has been priced at 16 percent above border prices,

5. If the impact of subsidized interest rate and overvaluation of domestic currency are included, there actually has been a net subsidy to user's cost of these items of capital equipment and, therefore, a tendency for government policy to promote farm mechanization (David, 1983b).

TABLE 2. Implicit tariff on agricultural inputs in the Philippines, 1970

Input	Implicit tariff
Irrigation[a]	
(gravity)	−86
(communal)	−92
Irrigation pumps	43
Hand tractors	43
Four-wheeled tractors	21
Animal feeds	
(hog grower mash)	7
(cattle feeds)	17
(layer mash)	20
(broiler mash)	23
Agricultural chemicals	23
Fertilizer	10

[a]Estimated by taking the percentage difference between the annual collection of irrigation fees and the annual cost of capital service of gravity irrigation.

TABLE 3. Implicit tariff of four grades of finished fertilizer, 1973–82, Philippines

	Fertilizer grade				Weighted average
	Urea	Ammosul	Mixed	Muriate of potash	
1973					
Food crops	−25	−9	−49	—	−5
Export crops	31	39	−2	119	—
1974					
Food crops	−11	−23	−33		7
Export crops	50	44	17	81	—
1975					
Food crops	−39	−43	−56	—	−30
Export crops	−5	−5	−31	86	—
1976	65	86	30	85	56
1977	55	59	13	105	41
1978	28	37	−5	96	19
1979	34	52	15	89	32
1980	7	43	−14	68	5
1981	8	45	−11	80	7
1973–81 (weighted average)	16	27	−4	86	10
1982	44	103	42	111	65

ammonium sulphate at 27 percent, and muriate of potash at 86 percent. In contrast, the fertilizer industry during the same period received a total subsidy equivalent of about 50 percent of border price per unit of domestically produced fertilizer. In 1982, implicit tariffs have risen even further to 65 percent as direct subsidies to fertilizer manufacturers were suspended.

Effective Protection Rate in Agriculture Relative to Manufacturing

The direction and rate of resource flows between agriculture and non-agriculture is influenced not only by the effective rate of protection (EPR) in agriculture but also by the nature of incentives in the nonagricultural sectors. The overall price effect of sector-specific price interventions, as indicated by the effective protection rates in table 4, has been to create an incentive structure that is significantly biased against agriculture compared to manufacturing. While value added in manufacturing has been artificially raised by an average of 44 percent (Tan, 1979), price intervention policies have reduced values of agricultural production during the last decade both through lower product prices and higher input prices. Traditional and even new agricultural exports have been heavily penalized by negative protection. Rice is essentially not protected. Subsidies in irrigation offset the implicit taxes paid by farms covered by the national irrigation system. Rainfed farms, however, comprising more than half of rice area continue to face a small negative protection.

The high EPR for desiccated coconut and coconut oil in the 1980s was achieved by depressing prices of the raw products at the expense of the farmers producing those products.[6] This pattern of protection commonly observed in agro-processing is in contrast to manufacturing industries where it is the domestic consumers who typically bear the burden of protection in terms of higher product prices.

Macroeconomic Policies

Overvaluation of the Peso

Over the past decade it has become increasingly clear that macroeconomic policies have pervasive and important effects on intersectoral incentives and thus allocation of resources. Indeed, distortions in the foreign exchange have been the most important source of bias against agricultural incentives. Overvaluation of the peso results from the industrial protection system and from the tendency to delay foreign exchange adjustments to correct the disequilibrium in the balance of payments. The structure of tariffs, indirect sales tax, and other trade restrictions to promote industry reduce import demand, artificially raising the value of the peso relative to other currencies. Disequilibrium in the balance of payments defended by

6. Another example of the government's tendency to discriminate against agriculture in favor of processing is in the case of cotton. Nominal protection on cotton lint (i.e., processed cotton, which is the tradable commodity) was close to 30 percent in the late 1970s. Production of raw cotton is penalized by a farm price that is below the border price of the raw cotton equivalent of cotton lint. Effective protection rate of cotton lint, therefore, would be higher than its nominal protection rate. The farm price of cotton is set by the Philippine Cotton Corporation, the government agency that has a monopoly on domestic cotton lint processing (Balisacan, 1982).

TABLE 4. Effective (EPR) and net effective (NEPR) protection rates for major agricultural commodities and for manufacturing in the Philippines

	Reference year	EPR	· NEPR
Agriculture			
Rice	1979	−0.4	−19
Rainfed	1979	−5	−21
Irrigated	1979	4	−14
Corn	1980	20	0
Copra	1973–79	−24	−37
(include UNICOM effect)	1980–81	−29	−41
Coconut oil	1973–79	−2	−19
(include UNICOM effect)	1980–81	42	18
Dessicated coconut	1973–79	−4	−20
	1980	18	−2
Sugar	1974–80	−23	−36
Cotton	1975–81	−12	−27
Pork	1980	−20 to 17	−34 to −3
Beef	1980	−16 to 8	−30 to −10
Chicken	1980	155 to 241	125 to 184
Eggs	1980	7 to 19	−11 to −1
Manufacturing[a]	1974	44	20

[a]Tan (1979).

drawing down international reserves prior to the 1962 and 1970 devaluations and by heavy foreign borrowing since the late 1970s also have periodically exacerbated the peso overvaluation.

The generally high level of protection received by manufacturing more than offsets the disincentive effect of an artificially low price of foreign exchange. Medalla's (1979) estimate of the rate of overvaluation due to the industrial protection system ranges from 20 percent to 30 percent depending on assumptions about optimal trade regimes. Assuming the lower value, the manufacturing sector still enjoys a 20 percent net effective protection rate (table 4).[7] In contrast, the agricultural sector had to bear most of the penalty imposed on exports and unprotected import substitutes, as net effective protection was generally negative, especially in copra and sugar. The only exception appears to be poultry, which remains significantly protected. The penalty imposed by the distortion of foreign exchange rate, therefore, is even more severe than many commodity-specific policies.

The ratio of the estimated equilibrium exchange rate to the actual exchange rate (Intal, 1987) indicates a higher degree of overvaluation than that caused by the protection structure (table 5). Assuming again a 20 percent overvaluation from the industrial protection system, there has been at least a 10 percent additional rate of distortion due to balance of

7. Net effective protection rate is the percentage difference between value added at market price and value added at border price converted at the shadow exchange rate.

TABLE 5.   Comparison of actual and equilibrium exchange rates in real terms, Philippines

Year	Real exchange rates (P/$)		2/1
	Actual (1)	Equilibrium (2)	
1960	3.26	3.95	1.21
1961	3.23	3.92	1.21
1962	5.77	6.74	1.17
1963	5.62	6.28	1.12
1964	5.22	6.18	1.18
1965	5.19	6.03	1.16
1966	5.08	5.81	1.14
1967	4.82	5.96	1.24
1968	4.81	6.05	1.26
1969	4.85	6.01	1.24
1970	6.67	7.85	1.18
1971	6.43	7.99	1.24
1972	6.25	7.98	1.28
1973	6.28	7.47	1.19
1974	5.86	7.77	1.33
1975	6.16	8.52	1.38
1976	6.29	8.37	1.33
1977	6.06	7.83	1.29
1978	5.77	7.52	1.30
1979	5.44	7.04	1.29
1980	5.43	7.11	1.31
1981	5.30	7.04	1.33
1982	5.36	7.34	1.37

SOURCE: Intal (1987).

payments disequilibrium. With the early 1980s came a worsening trend as world commodity prices dropped, entry of foreign loans and capital slowed down, and import controls tightened. Exchange rate policy has failed to make the necessary short-term adjustments to avoid prolonged overvaluation of the peso, further keeping agricultural prices relatively low over long periods of time.

Credit Policies

Credit policies—mainly in terms of concessionary interest rates—have not significantly altered the unfavorable economic incentives in agriculture caused by price intervention policies. Interest rate ceilings discourage lending to agriculture because of the higher risk and cost of administration. Special credit programs, preferential rediscounting, and credit quotas did not prevent the decline in real and relative loans granted to agriculture since the late 1960s (table 6). Most of the growth in agricultural lending in real terms took place in the 1960s. Agricultural loans as a percent of both net value added in agriculture, and total loans granted, declined from 22 percent and 20 percent in 1955–69 to 19 percent and 11 percent, respectively, in the 1970s. Moreover, 88 percent of the redis-

TABLE 6. Selected indicators of trends in loans granted for agricultural production by bank and nonbank financial institutions, 1951–79, Philippines

Year	Value of agricultural loans (P million in 1979 prices)	Agricultural loans as a % of	
		Agricultural value-added	Total loans granted
1951	376	13	40
1955	534	17	24
1960	2,757	14	20
1961	3,636	19	22
1962	4,022	21	20
1963	4,461	24	20
1964	4,503	25	19
1965	4,420	23	19
1966	4,582	24	19
1967	5,556	27	20
1968	5,665	25	16
1969	5,794	22	16
1970	4,557	22	15
1971	3,943	21	13
1972	3,424	20	12
1973	2,590	19	10
1974	1,725	22	12
1975	1,718	21	9
1976	982	13	—
1977	1,096	6	8
1978	2,534	13	—
1979	3,378	19	—

SOURCES: Unpublished reports by the Technical Board of Agricultural Credit, Central Bank of the Philippines, and the National Economic Development Authority.

counted loans in 1982 were allocated to the National Food Authority and to sugar and coconut sectors including NASUTRA and UNICOM. Rice and corn production loans accounted for merely 4 percent and only half of this went to the noncollateral credit programs. Not only did government marketing institutions received a disproportionate share of subsidized credit, interest rates paid were less than half the rates for the private sector on their share of subsidized credit for agriculture.

The declining trends are not surprising because technology and relative prices across sectors and commodities, and between inputs and outputs, are more important determinants of relative profitability and hence direction of resource allocation. The use of credit policies to compensate for the effects of policies that turn terms of trade against food and agriculture is futile. Preferential interest rates have little effect on relative profitability, and because credit is fungible, additional liquidity supplied by credit will be allocated to the most profitable enterprise or to consumption, whichever provides the greatest utility.

To compare the quantitative impact of credit policies to price policies, the effective subsidy rate (ESR) expressing the amount of interest rate subsidy as a percent of net value added in agriculture at border prices can be compared with estimates of net effective protection rates. Interest rate subsidy may be defined as the difference in the cost of borrowing between agricultural and nonagricultural loans multiplied by the value of agricultural loans granted. Alternatively, it may be defined as the difference in the cost of borrowing between the formal and informal credit market.

The difference in interest rates between agricultural and nonagricultural loans from the banking sector is relatively small, at most 2 percent in favor of agriculture. A cost-of-borrowing differential of 6 percent in favor of agriculture amounts to an ESR of only 1 percent. Assuming an interest rate differential of 30 percent, as would be the case in comparing cost of borrowing between formal and informal credit market, a 5 percent ESR would still not be sufficient to significantly alter the unfavorable incentive structure in agriculture vis-à-vis nonagriculture. On the other hand, the low interest rate policy seriously impairs the ability of rural financial markets to perform the financial intermediation process efficiently. It does not provide incentives for mobilizing financial savings. Its impact is generally regressive because it induces allocation of credit that is based on size of collateral, wealth, or political power, rather than on productivity of credit use.

Public Expenditure Policy

Public investments in research, extension, irrigation, and other infrastructure to increase productivity are long-term policy instruments to lower food prices without reducing farm income. Output prices themselves, however, affect the benefit-cost ratios of these investments. Although the public sector investments presumably consider social rates of return, the private sector base their decisions on private rates of return. Private sector's role in irrigation has been relatively minor, as more than 90 percent of irrigated areas is under gravity system; but in agricultural research, these have been relatively high in commercial crops and livestock (Pray and Ruttan, 1985). Negative rates of price protection, therefore, may retard technological progress.

Public expenditures for agriculture increased tenfold between 1955 and 1981 or an average annual rate of 12 percent in real terms (table 7). The share of agriculture to total government expenditures rose from about 6 percent to about 9 percent, and the ratio of public expenditure to gross value-added in agriculture increased from 2 percent to 6 percent between the late 1950s to the late 1970s. With the contractionary policies after 1980, however, the agricultural sector received the greatest cuts as public support for the sector was reduced to 40 percent of the peak level in 1978 and its share in total public expenditures was reduced from a high of 10

TABLE 7.   Selected indicators of trends and
relative importance of national government
expenditures on agriculture, Philippines

Year	Agriculture (P million) (1972 prices)	Agriculture expenditures as % of	
		Net value-added in agriculture[a]	Total govt. expenditures
1955	122	1.5	5.3
1956	176	2.1	6.9
1957	205	2.4	7.9
1958	167	1.9	6.8
1959	166	1.8	6.6
1960	179	1.9	6.3
1961	182	1.8	6.1
1962	206	2.0	6.4
1963	355	3.2	9.9
1964	306	2.8	8.4
1965	265	2.2	7.3
1966	264	2.2	7.1
1967	296	2.4	7.2
1968	416	3.1	8.8
1969	435	3.2	8.3
1970	361	2.6	7.1
1971	452	3.1	8.5
1972	567	3.8	8.9
1973	767	4.9	9.0
1974	1,354	8.5	13.0
1975	1,135	6.7	9.9
1976	1,018	5.4	7.8
1977	1,107	6.0	9.7
1978	1,323	6.8	10.0
1979	1,235	5.5	9.4
1980	1,241	5.2	9.6
1981[b]	1,339	5.4	7.7
1982[b]	1,149	4.5	6.5
1983[c]	1,013	4.1	7.5
1984[c]	522	2.1	4.8

SOURCE OF BASIC DATA: Philippines (Rep.), Budget Ministry.
[a]Gross Value Added (GVA) data was used for 1979–84.
[b]Data on expenditures were based on annual agency appropriations
as provided in the General Appropriations Act.
[c]Estimate.

percent in 1977 to 5 percent in 1985. Relative to gross value added in
agriculture and to the total government budget, public expenditures for
agriculture in 1984 were only at the same level as in 1955.

Table 8 presents the trends of public agricultural expenditures by policy
tools to infer the priorities pursued by the government. The rice sector was
the main beneficiary of the growth of public expenditures in agriculture
during the 1970s, especially in terms of irrigation.[8] The new rice technol-

8. It should be noted that the cost of price and marketing operations of government
monopolies is not reflected in the column on price and marketing, as most of them are
derived from marketing profits and subsidized credit from the Central Bank.

TABLE 8.   Distribution of national government expenditures on agriculture by type of policy instruments, 1955–84[a] (in P million, constant 1972 prices), Philippines

Year	Pricing & marketing	Irrigation	Research	Extension	Social development	Env'l mgmt. & conservation
1955	—	43	9	28	3	39
1956	—	86	10	33	5	42
1957	—	92	10	35	20	48
1958	15	50	10	38	21	48
1959	28	20	12	48	10	47
1960	24	24	13	52	15	51
1961	16	27	15	55	14	55
1962	97	36	17	63	13	60
1963	155	32	17	70	19	62
1964	106	19	17	76	29	60
1965	54	21	18	80	33	39
1966	34	25	17	77	50	61
1967	33	40	17	72	57	77
1968	37	35	21	73	146	104
1969	41	25	22	75	156	113
1970	28	39	19	66	116	93
1971	25	120	19	71	123	94
1972	30	187	24	104	114	108
1973	68	171	44	198	190	96
1974	83	684	55	202	231	99
1975	60	462	56	175	233	149
1976	46	382	64	167	187	172
1977	43	379	77	170	301	137
1978	34	558	100	244	217	170
1979	22	643	98	198	114	160
1980	21	634	134	157	128	167
1981	40	573	148	205	137	236
1982	39	380	158	197	130	242
1983	48	280	172	180	115	218
1984	25	150	62	97	63	242

SOURCE: Updated table from de Leon (1983), p. 27.

ogy, the growing land constraint, the trends in world rice price, and the easy availability of developmental loans induced the accelerated investment in irrigation. The role of the modern rice varieties in lowering the cost of irrigation per unit increase in output has been empirically demonstrated (Hayami et al., 1976). Hayami and Kikuchi (1978), on the other hand, found a strong correlation between shifts in investment and short-run changes in the world price of rice.

Although growth rate of public expenditure for agricultural research appears to be high, the level and growth rate of Philippine agricultural research expenditures are low by international and even by Asian standards (table 9). The ratio of Philippine expenditures in agricultural research to agricultural value-added is less than 0.2 percent compared to 0.4 in other Asian countries and 1–1.5 percent in developed countries. This is

TABLE 9. Government expenditures and manpower in agricultural research in selected Asian countries

	India	Indonesia	Philippines	Thailand	Pakistan	Bangladesh
Index of Real Research Expenditures, 1959 = 100						
1959	100	100	100	100	100	100
1962	119	400	131	273	114	117
1965	165	834	153	482	146	203
1968	184	1203	175	622	177	323
1971	266	1540	198	756	188	387
1974	269	1423	246	739	187	438
1977	418	7487	311	1517	191	660
1980	484	5887	343	1392	217	1546
Expenditures (constant 1980 U.S. $000)						
1980	120,167	33,200	9,533	21,600	29,899	27,613
Manpower (SMYs)*						
1980	2,345	1,473	640	1,264	1,212	1,320
Research Expenditure as a % of Agricultural GDP						
1980	0.29	0.44	0.16	0.26	0.41	0.48

SOURCE: Pray and Ruttan (1985).
*Scientific man years.

partly due to the reliance of the Philippines on the International Rice Research Institute for the rice research. Nevertheless, the difference in growth rates of public investments in agricultural research particularly with respect to Indonesia, Thailand, and Bangladesh is striking.

Impact of Price Intervention Policies
Impact on Agricultural Terms of Trade

Trends in agricultural terms of trade between agriculture and non-agriculture provide an overall summary measure of what is happening over time to economic incentives in agriculture vis-à-vis the other sectors in the economy. The contrast in the trends of agricultural terms of trade between the world and the Philippines illustrates the critical role that economic policies have played in determining agricultural incentives (figure 1). Engel's Law predicts a declining agricultural terms of trade over time. The fact that the declining pattern in world terms of trade coexisted with high growth rates of agricultural output reflects the important contribution of technical progress in world price trends. For an individual country, the secular decline in agricultural terms of trade predicted by Engel's Law need not be a logical necessity if land is scarce, the country trades internationally, or if government intervenes in the market.

FIGURE 1. Trends in terms of trade between agriculture and nonagriculture in the Philippines and the world and the Philippine exchange rate

Terms of trade (1980 = 100)

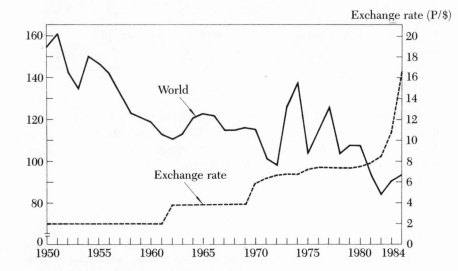

Domestic economic policies affect prices directly or indirectly through distortions in the macro price of foreign exchange and through public investments in productivity-enhancing activities. Despite the commodity boom resulting from the Korean War in the early 1950s, the Philippine agricultural terms of trade was generally declining during the 1950s. The dismantling of import and foreign exchange controls between 1958 and 1962 started to reverse this trend by the early 1960s, though the full impact of this policy change was observed only when the retention scheme for export receipts was lifted after 1965. The rising trend in the terms of trade was reinforced by the floating of the exchange rate in 1970 and the commodity boom of 1973–75.

The dramatic improvement of agricultural terms of trade between 1962 and 1975 was followed by a sharply deteriorating trend after 1975. Two oil price shocks and the subsequent prolonged recession in many of the Philippine trading partners severely dampened demand for the country's major agricultural export products. Moreover, the real price of paddy in particular, and also corn, declined significantly as the yields have increased (fig. 2).

Results of econometric analysis of the impact of exchange rate policies on the changes in the terms of trade based on data from 1950 to 1980 as shown below reveal the crucial role that devaluations have had in determining agricultural incentives.

(1) $\quad\quad$ $T^d = 132.52 - 0.26\ T^i,$ $\quad\quad\quad\quad$ $R^2 = 0.09$
$\quad\quad\quad\quad\quad$ (-1.662)
(2) $\quad\quad$ $T^d = 32.57 + 0.30\ T^i + 6.99\ FX,$ $\quad\quad$ $R^2 = 0.77$
$\quad\quad\quad\quad\quad$ $(3.098)\quad\ (9.59)$

International terms of trade (T^i) by itself is not significantly correlated to domestic terms of trade (T^d); and R^2 is almost zero. When both the international terms of trade and the official exchange rate (FX) are specified, more than three-fourths of the variation in domestic terms of trade is explained. International terms of trade becomes significant but the foreign exchange rate turns out to be a more important explanatory variable. Specifying variables to indicate increasing taxation of agriculture and the rapid technical progress in rice would further raise the correlation coefficient.

Failure to maintain an equilibrium exchange rate strongly discriminates against agriculture. Although devaluations favor prices of trade over nontraded goods and services, the agricultural sector will benefit relatively more than nonagriculture because a greater proportion of the sector produces tradables. Agricultural incentives are also likely to improve not only relative to the service sector but also relative to manufacturing because some manufacturing activities with very high protection have been virtually isolated from the international market, making them effectively nontraded (Medalla and Power, 1979). Additional protection afforded by the higher cost of foreign exchange will be redundant for these industries. Average domestic prices of manufactured products will increase at a lower rate than agricultural products, which are either exportable or receive very little protection. Manufacturing profits may, in fact, be generally squeezed as prices of intermediate inputs that typically receive low protection increase at a higher rate than product prices. Thus devaluations correct not

FIGURE 2. Trends in real farm price of paddy and corn, fertilizer-paddy and fertilizer-corn price ratio, Philippines

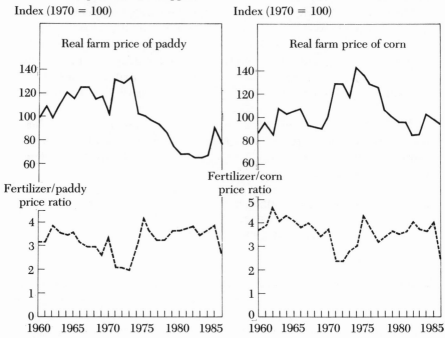

Index (1970 = 100)   Index (1970 = 100)

only distortions due to disequilibrium in the balance of payments but also part of the intersectoral distortions due to the protection system.

Effect on Intersectoral Capital Flows and Income Distribution

Although a secular decline in the share of the agricultural sector characterizes a growing economy (Chenery and Syrquin, 1977), accelerating this decline by domestic economic policies that discriminate against agriculture is more likely to hinder rather than reinforce this growth. Price intervention policies play a role in affecting this process of structural change because the trends in the agricultural terms of trade influence intersectoral capital flows. Based on a comparison of intersectoral rates of capital flows relative to labor flows, the analysis that follows also addresses the implications of these policies on income distribution.

Table 10 presents Paauw's (1968) and de Leon's (1982) estimates of trends in the rate of net capital outflow from agriculture from 1950 to 1978. From 1950 to 1965, as agricultural terms of trade was falling, net private capital outflow from agriculture was rising and averaged about 21 percent of agriculture's value-added. Between 1969 and 1974, when the terms of

TABLE 10. Trends in net private capital outflows
from agriculture and agricultural value-added
(GVA), in million pesos at 1972 prices, Philippines

	Agricultural GVA (1)	Net capital outflows (2)	(2)/(1)
Paauw[a]			
1950	5,838	1,290	.22
1951–55	7,215	1,560	.22
1956–60	9,410	1,974	.21
1961–65	11,121	2,373	.21
de Leon[b]			
1961	10,643	2,454	.23
1965	11,891	2,669	.22
1969	14,412	1,772	.12
1974	17,465	2,232	.13
1978	21,502	4,590	.21

[a]Estimates from Paauw (1968).
[b]Estimates from de Leon (1982).

trade improved substantially, net private capital outflows declined, and as a proportion of agricultural value-added, it was only half that of earlier years. After the mid-1970s, as agricultural terms of trade dropped sharply, the net private capital outflow accelerated and rose again to about 21 percent of agricultural value-added. This inverse relation between net private capital outflow and agricultural terms of trade suggests that prices have an important effect on intersectoral resource allocation.

Price intervention policies distort the terms of trade and so transfer capital from agriculture to nonagriculture by requiring agriculture to trade more in real goods and services for less in return. With respect to international trade, these penalties show up explicitly in tax revenues (export duties and customs duties). In the case of domestic trade, these are implicit taxes involving transfers through market price distortions. The proportion of net private capital outflow that could be directly attributed to price intervention policies provides a measure of this implicit tax.

Estimate of implicit tax on agriculture was considerably greater than that of explicit taxes. Based on Macaranas's (1975) estimate of the tax revenue contributed by agriculture to the total tax collections (7 percent) at the start of the 1970s and adding in export taxes, the explicit tax on agriculture was equal to 13 percent of total tax collections.[9] The explicit tax

9. This estimate would not have significantly changed during the 1970s. However, this excludes the implicit tax on exports of coconut, sugar, and logs due to the coconut levy, pricing of sugar, and log export ban where no revenues accrue to the government but are nevertheless paid by producers.

as a ratio of agricultural value-added was 7 percent, whereas the same ratio for nonagriculture was about 18 percent. The implicit tax from price intervention policies on domestic trade is conservatively estimated at 20 percent (de Leon, 1982), and hence total effective tax paid by agriculture is nearly 30 percent of agricultural value-added.

The implicit tax paid by agriculture is a direct resource transfer to consumers of agricultural products and producers of nonagricultural commodities purchased by the agricultural sector. It is, therefore, an implicit subsidy from the point of view of nonagriculture. The total effective tax (net of this implicit subsidy) as a ratio of value-added in nonagriculture is then on the average only about 8 percent, though this may be quite different across the various nonagricultural subsector. From this perspective then, and in view of the much lower per capita income in agriculture compared to nonagriculture, the agricultural sector is excessively taxed.

It is possible that the agricultural sector has received proportionately larger public expenditures. Assuming this was so, estimated value of implicit tax extracted from agriculture in 1974 still exceeds the highest value of capital inflow calculated without the implicit tax (de Leon, 1982). The procedure for deriving agriculture's share tended to overstate the benefits received by agriculture. General expenditure such as for defense, education, infrastructure was allocated simply based on the agriculture's share in employment and income. Even benefits considered to be directly received by agriculture such as irrigation, extension, and research may not fully accrue to farmers. By raising productivity in rice, for example, rice price in real terms significantly declined, primarily benefiting urban consumers (fig. 2).

De Leon estimated labor outflows from agriculture by comparing the actual number of agricultural workers with the natural level, that is, what the number would be without sectoral labor shifts. He found that the flow of surplus labor out of agriculture that should naturally accompany capital outflow has been limited. Even in the years when the net labor outflow was positive, the private capital outflow was far greater than the estimates of capital labor ratio in all manufacturing (ILO, 1977). Because of the excessively capital-intensive investments in the industrial sector that could not compete in the world market, the agriculture and the service sectors where self-employment is more common have had to employ nominally those that cannot be absorbed in the manufacturing sector. It is not surprising that real wages in both the urban and rural sector rapidly declined (fig. 3). Thus accelerating the industrialization process by artificially depressing agricultural incentives will increase the factor share of capital relative to labor in the total economy and hence worsen income distribution.

FIGURE 3. Trends in rural and urban wages in real terms, Philippines
Index (1964/66 = 100)

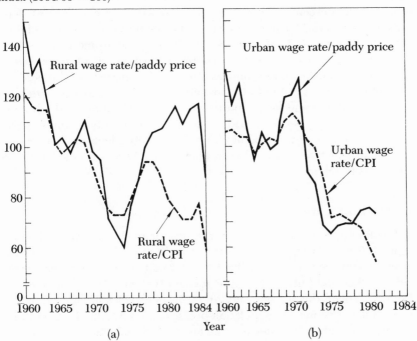

(a)   Year   (b)

Effects on Production, Consumption, and Trade

A rapid transfer of capital out of agriculture may be economically efficient if this direction is toward more socially profitable activities. However, recent studies have shown that agriculture is a more efficient earner
and saver of foreign exchange than the industrial sector (David, 1983a). It
has also been amply demonstrated in the literature that small farmers are
responsive to prices. The fact that economic policies—both macroeconomic and sector-specific—have tended on balance to penalize rather than
promote the sector indicate a suppression of the country's comparative
advantage in agriculture.

Bautista's (1986) recent econometric estimates of the impact of price
intervention policies on food consumption, production, and trade indicate
the potential economic growth foregone by the price intervention policies.
In general, Bautista found that reducing price distortions had a greater
positive effect on production, and therefore income, than any negative
effect on consumer prices on food consumption. A 15 percent devaluation
would have raised food production by 3.0 percent, and lower food con-

sumption and imports by 0.9 percent and 3.0 percent, respectively. Removing export taxes would have led to a 24.3 percent increase in food exports, a 2.1 percent rise in food production, a 0.5 percent decline in food consumption, and a 1.9 percent increase in food imports. Abolition of the 7 percent sales tax on food products would have led to increases in food production and consumption by 1.6 percent and 1.8 percent, respectively, and to reductions in exports and imports by 3.2 percent and 6.0 percent, respectively. Overall, the study showed a markedly high degree of responsiveness of Philippine food exports to trade liberalization, and a proportionally smaller response of food production, consumption, and imports. He concluded that trade liberalization through its effects on food exports will be an effective means of alleviating the country's chronic balance of payments problems.

Policy Implications

The Philippines is not unique in taxing agriculture. At low levels of per capita income, countries typically tax agriculture, and as per capita income grows, countries switch from effectively taxing to heavily subsidizing agriculture (Bale and Lutz, 1979; Anderson and Hayami, 1986). Anderson and Hayami explain this phenomenon in terms of changes in demand for and supply of protection. As population presses on limited land, agriculture's comparative advantage declines in favor of manufacturing. Farm producers demand agricultural protection to reduce the rural-urban income disparity and to minimize social costs shouldered by the rural population in the process of intersectoral resource adjustment. On the other hand, as per capita income increases and relative size of the agricultural sector declines, reducing the per capita burden of agricultural protection on the nonagricultural population, the political resistance against agricultural protection declines.

The increase in agricultural protection over time will occur at a later stage of development in countries where the per capita endowment of land and other natural resources is greater, the progress of the industrial sector is slower, and technical change in agriculture is faster relative to the rest of the world. The present Philippine land endowment per worker is still relatively higher than those in East Asian countries in the 1960s when they began protecting their agricultural sector. The increase in agricultural protection over time is, therefore, expected to occur later in the Philippines. In the Philippines, however, nominal protection rates for agriculture have declined rather than risen. This would imply a growing comparative advantage in agriculture versus industry.

Productivity has, in fact, grown more rapidly in agriculture than in manufacturing. Annual growth in total factor productivity in agriculture was about 3 percent in the 1970s, rising from 1.5 percent in the previous period (David, Barker, and Palacpac, 1984). In contrast, total factor productivity in manufacturing increased only by 0.3 percent from 1956 to 1980 and in fact declined by 1 percent annually after 1975 (Hooley, 1984). In the farm sector, much of the increase in productivity was concentrated in rice, and in the nontraditional export crops.

The floating of the exchange rate in 1970 and the substantial increase in world commodity prices of major exports in the mid-1970s increased international competitiveness and raised the domestic profitability of most traded agricultural commodities. The government's attempt to protect consumers and agro-processing industries from higher food and raw material prices and to reduce windfall profits motivated the new explicit and implicit taxes imposed on agricultural exports in the 1970s. The increase in taxation of agricultural exports, especially on sugar and copra, was severe, and it was prolonged beyond the boom period into the early 1980s when world commodity prices dropped sharply. This has limited the country's ability to benefit from the extraordinary growth of world trade during the 1970s. As a result, growth of agricultural exports in the Philippines was only 9 percent compared to 20 percent per year in the other ASEAN countries during the 1970s.

The switch from taxing to subsidizing agriculture has, in general, taken place in countries experiencing rapid economic growth and structural transformation. The Philippine economic performance has been relatively low, particularly in the manufacturing sector. In terms of both contributions to gross domestic product and employment, the Philippines show the lowest rate of sectoral shift among the large ASEAN countries. Real wages have been declining sharply. Political pressures, therefore, will favor a low agricultural price policy.

This analysis does not necessarily suggest that the country increase protection in agriculture, but that it reduce distortions created by economic policies. The new government seems committed to raising the welfare of the agricultural population and to developing a more open economy with a minimum of government intervention. It has taken significant steps in altering specific policies so as to reduce the sources of bias against agricultural incentives. Nearly all the unfavorable commodity-specific policies have been removed. Export taxes including the copra export ban have been abolished. Government monopolies in grain marketing, sugar, coconut, fertilizer, and others have been effectively dismantled. These policy reforms have met little resistance. Because of the depressed commodity prices, the main issue is how to raise farm income rather than reduce food prices to consumers. Moreover, the major beneficiaries of the monopolies, that is, the Marcos family and cronies, have lost political power.

Progress has been slow in macroeconomic policies, such as trade liberalization, to reduce exchange rate distortions and to lower prices of the inputs and manufactured goods that agriculture buys. The industrial sector has a strong political voice in the Aquino government, which was installed basically by the urban sector. Because of the depressed state of the economy and thus the pervasive low capacity utilization in manufacturing, even the efficient firms have joined in resisting greater foreign competition. Moreover, the logical constituent of trade liberalization, the farmer, does not sufficiently recognize the benefits to the sector.

It is unfortunate that, politically, these policy reforms could be instituted only during the period of low world commodity prices and generally depressed state of the economy. The boost in farm production expected from the policy reforms has not been strong, in part because it has been partial and has served merely to reduce adverse effects of falling world commodity prices. The increase in foreign exchange earnings and growth linkage effects of a rapidly growing agricultural sector, which could have reduced the adjustment costs by the industrial sector of trade liberalization, has not yet been realized. Moreover, the severe budgetary constraint and the inevitable dislocation in the bureaucracy during the period of political transition have limited efforts to make more effective the delivery of support services—agricultural research, extension, market infrastructure, irrigation, and others—that are needed to accelerate agricultural development in the context of a reformed policy framework.

References

Anderson, K., and Y. Hayami. 1986. *The Political Economy of Agricultural Protection*. Sydney: Allen & Unwin.

Bale, M., and E. Lutz. 1979. "Price Distortions in Agriculture and Their Effects: An International Comparison." World Bank Staff Working Paper no. 359. Washington, D.C.: World Bank.

Balisacan, A. 1982. "Economic Incentives and Comparative Advantage in Philippine Agriculture: The Case of the National Cotton Development Program." Thesis, University of the Philippines at Los Banos College, Laguna.

Bautista, R. M. 1986. *Effects of Price Intervention Policies on Aggregate Food Production, Consumption, and Trade in a Developing Country*. Washington, D.C.: International Food Policy Research Institute.

———, J. H. Power, and associates. 1979. *Industrial Promotion Policies in the Philippines*. Makati: Philippine Institute for Development Studies.

Cabanilla, L. S. 1983. "Economic Incentives and Comparative Advantage in the Livestock Industry." Philippine Institute for Development Studies Working Paper no. 83–07. Makati: Philippine Institute for Development Studies.

Chenery, H., and M. Syrquin. 1977. *Patterns of Development, 1950–1970*. New York: Oxford University Press.

Clarete, R. L., and J. A. Roumasset. 1983. "An Analysis of the Economic Policies Affecting the Philippine Coconut Industry." Philippine Institute for Development Studies Working Paper no. 83–08, Makati: Philippine Institute for Development Studies.

David, C. C. 1983a. "Economic Policies and Philippine Agriculture." Philippine Institute for Development Studies Working Paper no. 83–02. Makati: Philippine Institute for Development Studies.

———. 1983b. "Government Policies and Farm Mechanization in the Philippines." In Workshop Papers on *The Consequences of Small Rice Farm Mechanization in the Philippines*. Los Baños, Philippines: International Rice Research Institute (IRRI).

David, C. C., R. Barker, and A. Palacpac. 1987. "Agricultural Productivity Measurement and Analysis: Philippines." In *Productivity Measurement and Analysis: Asian Agriculture*, 409–438. Tokyo: Asia Productivity Organization.

David, V. 1977. "The Barrier in the Development of the Philippine Coconut Industry." Thesis, Ateneo de Manila University, Philippines.

De Leon, M. S. J. 1982. "Intersectoral Capital Flows and Price Intervention Policies in Philippine Agriculture." Dissertation, University of the Philippines at Los Baños, College, Laguna.

———. 1983. "Government Expenditures and Agricultural Policies in the Philippines, 1955–80." Philippine Institute for Development Studies Working Paper no. 83–06. Manila.

Foreign Trade Statistics. Philippine National Census and Statistics Office. Various issues.

Hayami, Y., C. C. David, P. Flores, and M. Kikuchi. 1976. "Agricultural Growth against a Land Resource Constraint: The Philippine Experience." *Australian Journal of Agricultural Economics* 20(3):144–159.

Hayami, Y., and M. Kikuchi. 1978. "Investment Inducements to Public Infrastructure: Irrigation in the Philippines." *Review of Economics and Statistics* 60:70–77.

Hazell, P. B., and A. Roell. 1983. *Rural Growth Linkages: Household Expenditure Patterns in Malaysia and Nigeria*. Research Report no. 41. Washington D.C.: International Food Policy Research Institute.

Hooley, R. 1984. "Productivity Growth in Philippine Manufacturing: Retrospect and Future Prospects." Staff Paper, July 25, Philippine Institute for Development Studies.

Intal, P. 1987. "Political Economy of Agricultural Pricing Policy: The Philippines." A World Bank Project Report.

International Labor Organization. 1977. *Sharing in Development: A Programme of Employment, Equity, and Growth for the Philippines*. Geneva.

Macaranas, F. M. 1975. "Development Issues Concerning the Impact and Incidence of Agricultural Taxation in the Philippines." Thesis, Purdue University.

Medalla, E. M. 1979. "Estimating the Shadow Exchange Rate Under Alternative Policy Assumption." In R. M. Bautista, and J. H. Power, eds., *Industrial Promotion Policies in the Philippines*, 79–125. Makati: Philippine Institute for Development Studies.

Medalla, E. M., and J. H. Power. 1979. "Estimating Implicit Tariffs and Nominal Rates of Protection." In R. M. Bautista, and J. H. Power, eds., *Industrial Promotion Policies in the Philippines*, 251–262. Makati: Philippine Institute for Development Studies.

Nelson, G., and M. Agcaoili. 1983. "Impact of Government Policies on Philippine Sugar Industry." PIDS Working Paper no. 83–04. Makati: Philippine Institute for Development Studies.

Paauw, D. S., and J. L. Tryon. 1968. "Agriculture-Industry Interrelationships in an Open Dualistic Economy: The Philippines, 1949–1964." *Philippine Economic Journal* 7(1):53–88.

Pray, C. E., and Vernon W. Ruttan. "1985 Completion Report of the Asian Agricultural Project." Economic Development Center Bulletin no. 85–2. St. Paul, Minn.: University of Minnesota.

Tan, N. 1979. "The Structure of Protection and Resource Flows in the Philippines." In R. H. Bautista and J. H. Power, eds., *Industrial Promotion Policies in the Philippines*, 127–171. Makati: Philippine Institute for Development Studies.

Unnevehr, L. J. 1986. "Changing Comparative Advantage in Philippine Rice Production: 1966 to 1982." *Food Research Institute Studies* 20(1):43–69.

Unnevehr, L. J., and A. Balisacan. 1983. "Changing Comparative Advantage in Philippine Rice Production." PIDS Working Paper no. 83–03. Makati: Philippine Institute for Development Studies.

6. Nepal: Food Pricing with an Open Border

Michael B. Wallace

Food price policy in Nepal is significantly influenced by economic, geographic, climatic, and political factors. Nepal is one of the poorest countries in the world and the prospects for significant economic development are dim; regional geographic and climatic differences lead to pronounced inequalities in per capita food production; the open border with India prevents independent policy implementation; and Nepal's poverty and landlocked position severely limit trade policy options.

For Nepal, obvious food policy goals include efficient growth of food production to feed the growing population, equitable distribution of food to improve the nutritional status of the population, and increased food security resulting from reduced variability in total food production. Such goals could be pursued through a combination of producer price policies designed to promote efficient use of inputs, increase output, and reduce output fluctuations, and consumer price policies designed to equitably distribute food and improve nutrition.

Among these objectives, Nepal has mostly emphasized increased production. Nepal has traditionally exported foodgrain, and past government policies have been formulated in this context. Nearly all the over two hundred projects currently being implemented by the Ministry of Agriculture are production-oriented projects designed to increase irrigated area, cropped area, and use of improved inputs. This focus has been based on low per capita food production in the hills and mountains, and on the lack of comparative advantage in producing other goods for export. Increasing emphasis has been placed on this objective as per capita food production has declined.

Regional equality has received attention through efforts to distribute

I thank Terry Sicular and Wally Falcon, Food Research Institute, Stanford University, for providing the encouragement and deadlines necessary to complete research papers; the Agricultural Development Council and Winrock International—particularly Ted Smith, David Nygaard, and John Cool—for viewing this work as consistent with my professional responsibilities; Steve Radelet, Harvard University, whose work on a related topic conveniently preceded this effort; Gerald Nelson, University of Illinois, who provided conceptual criticism and substantive advice while he was a consultant in Nepal for the Asian Development Bank; Robert Herdt, World Bank, for valuable comments on the first draft; Ram Chandra Bhattarai, for research assistance; and Simin Litkouhi and Pirooz Wallace, for their endless patience and good humor.

domestic production and food aid to disadvantaged citizens, and improved nutrition has been linked with food policy in the goal of meeting the population's basic needs. Food self-sufficiency has recently received attention as Nepal loses the race to feed its ever-growing population. Food security has been discussed mostly in terms of domestic procurement and distribution, not in terms of total production or trade possibilities. Thus all Nepal's food policy objectives have been linked with and based on the primary goal of increasing food production.

The major price policy instruments that have been used in Nepal to achieve food policy objectives include food subsidies to consumers, particularly in the Kathmandu Valley; product price interventions, mostly for rice and wheat; and input price interventions, primarily for fertilizer. Trade policies and macro price policies such as interest rate and exchange rate policies, while primarily intended to serve other purposes, have also affected the achievement of food policy objectives.

Food subsidies have been provided to consumers through government procurement and purchase of paddy and wheat in surplus areas for resale in deficit areas. Procurement has also been nominally used to support paddy and wheat producer prices. Fertilizer, once sold on a cost-plus basis, is now subsidized and sold at a uniform price throughout Nepal. Government corporations are solely responsible for foodgrain procurement and distribution, and for fertilizer import and sales.

Food Policy Context

Nepal is a roughly rectangular country about 800 km long and 175 km wide. Its population—nearly 90 percent dependent on agriculture—is now over 17 million, and growing by more than 2.6 percent each year. Per capita annual income is less than U.S. $200, and this meager amount is unevenly distributed: half the people earn less than $100 per year.[1] The 1985–86 national budget was about $450 million, of which over one-third was foreign grants and loans, and one-seventh internal loans (Ministry of Finance, 1987). Nepal's lack of resources and infrastructure—particularly transportation and communication in the hills and mountains—severely limits the possibilities for implementing any government policy designed to significantly improve the economic condition of its rural inhabitants.

Geographically, Nepal can be divided into the high mountains bordering China, the middle hills, the Kathmandu Valley, and the Tarai plains bordering India (fig. 1). Villagers in the dry, cold mountains subsist on livestock, potatoes, barley, and millet. Maize is the main food in the

1. In 1976–77, 50 percent of the population earned less than U.S. $60 (NPC, 1978). A more recent calculation indicates that 40 percent of the population earns less than U.S. $90 (NPC, 1986).

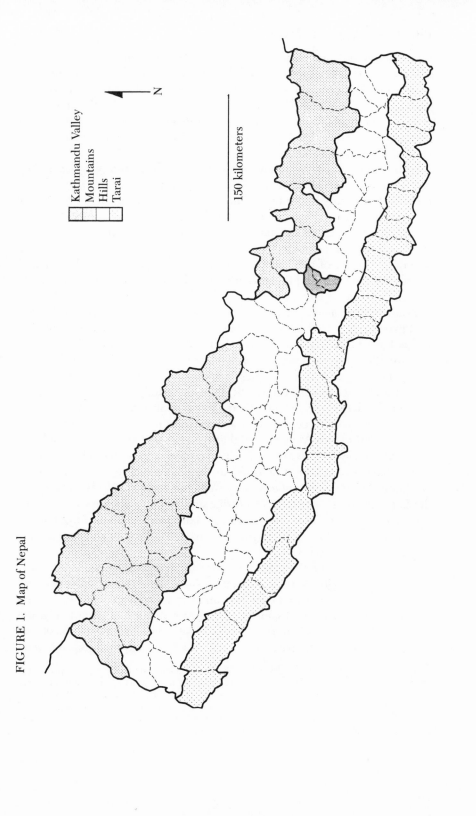

FIGURE 1. Map of Nepal

Kathmandu Valley
Mountains
Hills
Tarai

N

150 kilometers

temperate/semitropical middle hills. Rice is the main foodgrain in the tropical Tarai plains, but wheat has become increasingly popular since the Green Revolution in the mid-1960s. The Kathmandu Valley, still considered to be "Nepal" by villagers in many remote areas, is the traditional center of political power—its rich soil and its inhabitants' economic power provide residents with a varied diet that includes imported fruits and vegetables as well as foodgrains.

Although the hills and mountains have more total land per person than the Tarai, there are eight people for each cultivated hectare in the hills and mountains and only five in the Tarai. Despite land reform efforts beginning in 1964 that limited the amount of land a person can own, little land has been redistributed to poor farmers, and land ownership remains significantly skewed. The poorest half of the people, who own an average of barely one-tenth of a hectare per household, now cultivate less than 7 percent of the land, and their position has deteriorated in the last twenty-five years (tables 1 and 2).

Production of major food crops increased by less than 30 percent in the past two decades, primarily as a result of increases in cropped area, as crop yields have been stagnant.[2] (Average paddy yields are now 2.0–2.2 mt/hectare (ha), maize and wheat 1.2–1.5 mt/ha, millet and barley 0.9 mt/ha, and potatoes 6.2–6.4 mt/ha; these yields are among the lowest in Asia.) Wheat area has increased dramatically while paddy and maize area have remained relatively constant. Yield increases on irrigated land with improved seed have been offset by extensive cultivation on steep slopes. Yields in Kathmandu Valley are higher than in other regions, and yields in the Tarai are lower. This may reflect greater use of fertilizer in Kathmandu, and relative availability of land in the Tarai. Regionally, there is no marketed surplus in the mountains, hills, or Kathmandu Valley. The Tarai has a marketed surplus: some goes to India, and some to Kathmandu and the hills. Because per capita production is highest in the Tarai, food policies have been designed to redistribute food from the Tarai to Kathmandu and the hills and mountains.

Nepal is falling behind in its attempt to feed its growing population. From 1971 to 1986, Nepal's population increased by nearly 50 percent, from 11.6 million to over 17 million, an average increase of over 2.6 percent per year. During that same period, the production of major foodgrains increased by less than 25 percent, from about 3.5 million metric tons to 4.3 million metric tons, an average increase of less than 1.4 percent per year.

2. Production statistics are calculated by the Department of Food and Agricultural Marketing Services (DFAMS) by multiplying yield and area estimates. Tarai data are more accurate than hill data because sample surveys are used more in the Tarai and subjective estimates more in the hills. When Land Resources Mapping Project data—based on 1978–79 aerial photography—became available recently (see WEC, 1986), hill cultivated area (and production) estimates were revised upward substantially.

TABLE 1.   Land (000 hectare) and people (000) in Nepal

	Land	Population			Cultivated land		
		1961	1971	1981	1961	1971	1981
Mountains	4,676		1,139	1,303		83	123
Hills	6,188		5,452	6,397		345	890
Kathmandu	76		619	766		31	50
Tarai	3,270		4,346	6,557		1,167	1,401
Nepal	14,210	9,413	11,556	15,023	1,657	1,626	2,464

	Land per capita (hectare)			Cultivated land/cap (hectare)		
	1961	1971	1981	1961	1971	1981
Mountains		4.11	3.62		0.07	0.09
Hills		1.13	0.97		0.06	0.14
Kathmandu		0.12	0.10		0.05	0.07
Tarai		0.75	0.50		0.27	0.21
Nepal	1.51	1.23	0.95	0.18	0.14	0.16

SOURCE: CBS, *National Sample Census of Agriculture, 1961–62, 1971–72, 1981–82*. As a result of land reform beginning in 1964, the 1971–72 census may underestimate cultivated land. (Note unlikely *decrease* in total area from 1961–62 to 1971–72.) Land Resources Mapping Project (LRMP) data, based on 1978–79 aerial photos and reported in WEC (1986), indicates that total cultivated land was then 2.968 million hectares (more than reported in any agricultural census), and per capita cultivated land was fairly evenly distributed across geographic regions— about .21 hectares/capita in the mountains, hills, and Tarai.

In 1971 average foodgrain production was about 300 kg per person per year; by 1981 that had declined to about 260 kg; and soon it is likely to be less than 250 kg (table 3).

From 250 kg of gross foodgrain production per person per year, less than 180 kg is available in edible form. This is 500 g per day, which provides less than 1,650 calories and slightly more than 30 g of protein. Vegetables (including potatoes, an important source of food in the hills and mountains) and animal products may increase these totals by 20 percent, so the totals may be 2,000 calories and 36 g of protein per person per day. Estimates of the requirements for calories and protein in Nepal vary, but they are all above these figures. Nutrition is at a low level and is declining for most of the population.

These overall figures mask inequalities in the distribution of the food produced in Nepal. Some people are well fed, others suffer from extreme malnutrition. These inequalities are most obvious across districts, but there are also disparities within districts, within villages, and even within families (adult males receive preference). The combination of declining per capita food production and increasing inequality of land distribution implies that poorer groups in the population are becoming worse off than the averages imply.

More food is produced per capita in the Tarai than in the Kathmandu Valley and the hills, which are in turn better off than the mountains. In all areas, per capita food production has declined in the past fifteen years, and

TABLE 2. Area and distribution of landholdings, 1981–82

	Number households	Area wet (hectares)	Area dry (hectares)	Total area	Percent households	Percent of area	Average holding
Nonagri.	391,198	0	0	0	15.1	0.0	0.00
No land	8,224	0	0	0	0.3	0.0	0.00
0.0–0.5 hectares	1,099,677	57,892	104,107	161,999	42.5	6.6	0.15
0.5–1.0 hectares	355,420	115,716	149,214	264,930	13.7	10.8	0.75
1.0–2.0 hectares	379,051	223,029	267,384	490,413	14.7	19.9	1.29
Over 2 hectares	351,584	1,020,974	525,401	1,546,375	13.6	62.8	4.40
Total	2,585,154	1,417,611	1,046,106	2,463,717	100.0	100.0	0.95

NOTE: Gini coefficients for distribution of landholdings—1961–62: 0.690; 1971–72: 0.685; 1981–82: 0.700. These coefficients are calculated from more detailed data than shown. Inequality in landholding distribution is less pronounced within regions than nationally—gini coefficients for the mountains, hills, Kathmandu, and Tarai are lower than national coefficients.

"Nonagri." includes households having neither operational control of land nor livestock (excluded from Census of Agriculture). "No land" includes households with livestock (included in census) without operational control of land.

SOURCES: CBS, National Sample Census of Agriculture, 1961–62, 1971–72, 1981–82; and CBS, Population Census, 1961, 1971, 1981.

TABLE 3.   Food availability

| Year | Population (000) | Crop production (000 mt) | | | | | | TotCal (billion) | Cal (per capita per day) | Grain (per capita per year) (kg) | Edible grain (kg) |
		Paddy	Maize	Wheat	Millet	Barley	Potato				
Mountains											
1985–86	1,375	61	70	29	21	9	86	605	1,207	139	111
Hills											
1985–86	6,939	514	553	183	105	12	180	3,887	1,535	197	155
Kathmandu Valley											
1985–86	854	74	39	24	2	0	12	364	1,168	161	119
Tarai											
1985–86	8,059	2,155	212	362	10	3	79	6,437	2,188	340	226
Nepal											
1961–62	9,413	2,108	843	138	63	NA	NA	7,726	2,249	335	234
1965–66	10,430	2,207	856	147	120	28	277	8,509	2,235	322	226
1970–71	11,556	2,305	833	193	130	25	273	8,800	2,086	302	212
1975–76	13,176	2,605	748	387	143	25	314	9,821	2,042	297	208
1980–81	15,023	2,464	743	477	122	23	281	9,679	1,765	255	180
1981–82	15,422	2,560	752	526	122	23	329	10,101	1,794	258	183
1982–83	15,832	1,833	704	656	121	21	373	8,827	1,528	211	155
1983–84	16,253	2,757	761	671	115	22	363	10,990	1,853	266	189
1984–85	16,685	2,710	820	534	125	24	420	10,747	1,765	252	178
1985–86	17,129	2,804	874	598	138	23	357	11,293	1,806	259	184
Conversion		0.6	0.9	0.9	0.9	0.9	0.9				
Cal/100 gm		354	349	332	332	340	100				

SOURCES: DFAMS (1972, 1977, 1983, 1985b, unpublished data); CBS, *Population Census, 1961, 1971, 1981.*

it is below nutritional requirements by most standards in all areas except the Tarai. Of Nepal's seventy-five districts (fifty-five hill/mountain, twenty Tarai), in 1985 only fifteen were self-sufficient in foodgrain production, and ten of them were in the Tarai (Ministry of Supplies, 1986). This disparity in per capita food production has been documented for at least twenty years (HMG, 1967; Rana and Joshi, 1968).

Food Policy Objectives

Increased food availability can be achieved either by increasing food production or by increasing food imports. As Nepal's ability to earn foreign exchange is limited, increasing food imports is not a feasible alternative. Until a solid base for earning foreign exchange is established, Nepal must rely on its own production for nearly all of its food needs. Food aid supplied as grants from donor agencies is sometimes available, but the politics of food aid are variable and the bureaucratic procedures involved are slow. Even if Nepal were willing to become a perpetual recipient of food aid, this would not be an acceptable solution to hunger and malnutrition problems.

Food security—in the sense of reduced variation in availability or price—has not been an explicitly stated policy issue in Nepal. Food security objectives have been implicit in policies designed to reduce food prices in urban areas and increase food availability in rural areas. Most Nepalese citizens still have links with the land in the form of family ownership and can rely on these links in times of need. Thus food security has been less important in Nepal than in countries such as Bangladesh that have large landless populations.

Production objectives are influenced by low output in the hills and mountains, which cover most of Nepal, by the difficulty of transporting improved inputs to these areas, and by dependence on the monsoon for water. Objectives that might be achieved through trade are hindered by Nepal's landlocked position between China and India. Its northern border with the Tibetan region of China is defined by the Himalayan mountains—traversable by only a few mountain passes, and thus limiting overland trade. In contrast, its southern border with India is flat and open—unpatrolled paddy fields, where Nepalese and Indian citizens freely come and go. As a result, Nepal's economy is dominated by events in India, and Nepal's economic policies cannot deviate too much from those of her southern neighbor. Sometimes described as a yam between two boulders, Nepal is more like the flea on an elephant's back—no matter which way the flea turns, it will travel in the elephant's direction.

Official Food Policies

Nepal's official food policy dates back at least to the establishment of the Paddy Milling Sales Department in 1946 in response to a sudden rise in the rice price (APROSC, 1982b, p. 15). This department was charged with procurement and distribution of food to the army, police, and civilians in Kathmandu. Paddy was procured through a levy charged per unit of land and producers received an equivalent rebate in land taxes. While this was not an explicit price policy, its objective was clear: to provide food to favored groups of consumers at lower than open market prices.

After the overthrow of the Rana regime in 1951, the history of Nepal's public policies related to food can be traced through statements made in National Plans. The main objectives of the first four National Plans (1956–75) were to develop infrastructural and institutional foundations. Increased production was a stated goal not limited to agriculture, though the Third Plan explicitly mentioned increased foodgrain production. The Fifth Plan (1975–80) gave top priority to the agricultural sector and attempted to exploit the comparative advantages of the hills and the Tarai by concentrating on foodgrain and cash crops in the Tarai and on horticulture and livestock in the hills.

The Sixth Plan (1980–85) recognized that hill-Tarai transportation links were insufficient to justify continued reliance on the Tarai as a source of foodgrains for the hills, and it emphasized foodgrain production in the hills as well as in the Tarai. Food was identified as a basic need, and increased agricultural production was an explicit goal to meet that need, as well as to help balance international trade by increasing exports and providing raw materials for domestic agro-industries.

The Seventh Plan (1985–90) lists foodgrain as the first basic need of the people; its first development strategy is "to accord topmost priority to the agricultural sector"; and one of its policies is to make the mountain and hill regions self-sufficient in food within ten years:

> Food production has now reached a level where it cannot be deemed sufficient to meet the minimum nutritional needs of the people. In the hill areas food crisis is now so frequent that it has almost become an annual feature. The rising cost of food distribution has exerted increasing pressure on the budget year by year. The foodgrain savings of the Tarai region have started declining, and as an increasing amount of the decreasing savings is being dispatched to the hills, foodgrain export has plummeted, throwing the foreign trade off balance. (National Planning Commission, 1984, p. 18)

Although "top priority" has been given to agriculture since 1975, budget expenditures have not followed suit. Actual expenditures in agriculture (excluding irrigation) have never exceeded Rs 55 (U.S. $2.50) per capita per year, and have never been more than 10 percent of the total budget (Rs 863 million out of Rs 9.8 billion in 1985–86) (Ministry of Finance, 1987a).

Donor agencies' influence in Nepal's agricultural (and other) development policies should not be underestimated. In 1985–86, foreign aid (grants and loans) constituted over 37 percent (Rs 3.7 billion out of Rs 9.8 billion) of total government expenditure, and over 72 percent (Rs 626 million out of Rs 863 million) of agricultural expenditure (Ministry of Finance, 1987b).

The objectives of Nepal's food policies have almost always been stated in terms of increased production, by setting production targets. When production targets have been met, it has not been primarily the result of successful government programs. This is partly because the institutions through which technological improvements were to be implemented are inefficient, and mostly because the ability of the government to significantly affect crop output in an agricultural system constrained by rudimentary transportation, and dependent on an uncertain monsoon, is extremely limited. The Seventh Plan states: "Agricultural sector, the source of livelihood and employment of the bulk of the population, continues to lean heavily on the whims of the weather gods."[3]

Use of Major Price Policy Instruments and Their Effects

Nepal's stated food price policies include providing subsidized food to consumers in deficit areas, and production incentives to farmers through output support prices and subsidized input prices. Consumer subsidies have been provided for rice and wheat; producer paddy and wheat prices have been (nominally) supported; and fertilizer sales have been subsidized. Price policies for irrigation facilities, improved seeds, pesticides, and credit have played a minor role. The stated target populations for these policies have been poor people, but the actual beneficiaries have been politically important groups. Army and government officials, and economically influential Kathmandu residents, have been the main beneficiaries of food subsidies, while relatively richer farmers and traders have benefited from fertilizer subsidies.

These policies have achieved their goals only to a limited extent. Food production has been increasing, but this has been mostly the result of increases in cropped area. Higher yields resulting from increased use of fertilizer on irrigated fields have been offset by lower yields on rain-fed lands as hill farmers bring steeper slopes under cultivation. Increased fertilizer use has probably resulted more from farmers learning about this input than from the official price subsidy. Output price supports have not provided any incentive to increase production because they have not been (and cannot be) implemented. With a few exceptions in cases of crop

3. National Planning Commission (1984), p. 10. Monsoon rainfall data for the Kathmandu Valley (which has less weather variation than most of Nepal) for 1921–75 (DIHM, 1977) verify this statement.

failure or natural disasters, food subsidies have neither improved nutrition nor equalized income distribution.

All the price policies discussed in this chapter must be viewed against the background of Nepal's relationship to the Indian economy. The long, open border and the relative sizes of the Indian and Nepalese economies mean that prices in Nepal, particularly in the Tarai, are highly correlated with prices in India. Prices elsewhere in Nepal depend on transport costs from India and on local production. In general, Tarai prices are lowest, followed by those in Kathmandu, the hills, and the mountains. However, as a result of the uneven, minimal transportation facilities linking hill and mountain villages with each other and the Tarai, local production is often a dominant influence on hill and mountain prices.

Figures 2–4 and table 4 show that Indian and Tarai markets are closely linked, Kathmandu is moderately linked, and hill and mountain markets are somewhat independent of the others. The weaker correlation of Kathmandu, hill, and mountain prices with Indian and Tarai prices and with each other is one result of the higher transport costs involved in moving goods to, from, and among these markets.

Seasonal price variation is significant, with annual high points preceding and low points following harvests. This hurts poor farmers who must sell grain to repay loans at harvest time. Unfortunately, lack of adequate data prevents systematic analysis of this phenomenon.

Consumer Food Subsidies—Grain Procurement and Distribution

Food subsidies to consumers have been provided through a combination of government procurement and sales at below-market prices. While the explicit objective of the food subsidy policy has been to help eliminate food deficits and to stabilize market prices, its main effect has been to keep prices low for favored groups of consumers, especially Kathmandu residents and government officials in food-deficit areas.

Until the 1970s, public intervention in foodgrain markets consisted of paddy procured through a levy in the Tarai, which was sent to Kathmandu for distribution among the army, government officials, and urban residents. In 1974 the Nepal Food Corporation (NFC) was formed to procure and distribute foodgrain on a larger scale. The NFC's stated objectives are to collect, store, transport, and sell food at low prices to eliminate food deficits in remote areas, and to execute policy with respect to institutional rice export. The NFC's role thus includes providing fair prices to both producers and consumers.

Eight semigovernmental Rice Exporting Companies (RECs) were established by His Majesty's Government (HMG) in 1974 and 1975 to provide production incentive prices to farmers, facilitate trade in paddy and rice, and encourage internal trade of foodgrain to meet the requirements

FIGURE 2. Coarse paddy prices (Rs/kg)

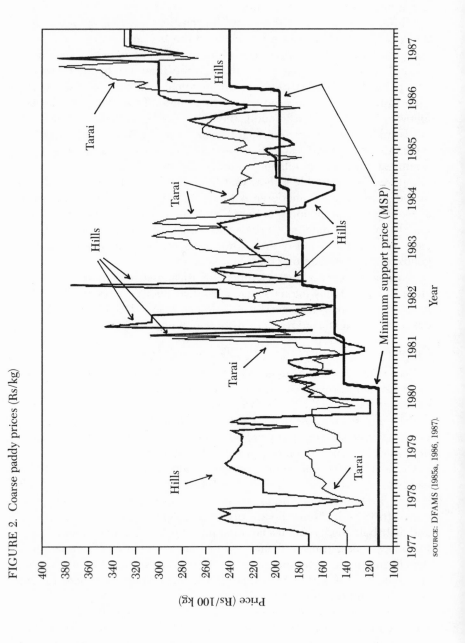

SOURCE: DFAMS (1985a, 1986, 1987).

FIGURE 3. Raw coarse rice prices (Rs/kg)

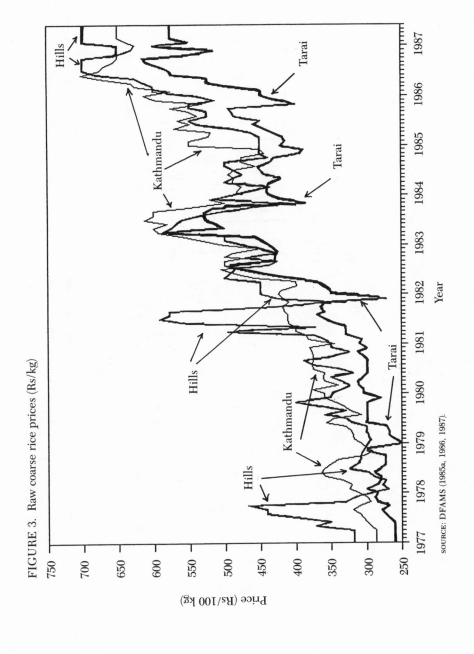

SOURCE: DFAMS (1985a, 1986, 1987).

FIGURE 4. Wheat prices (Rs/kg)

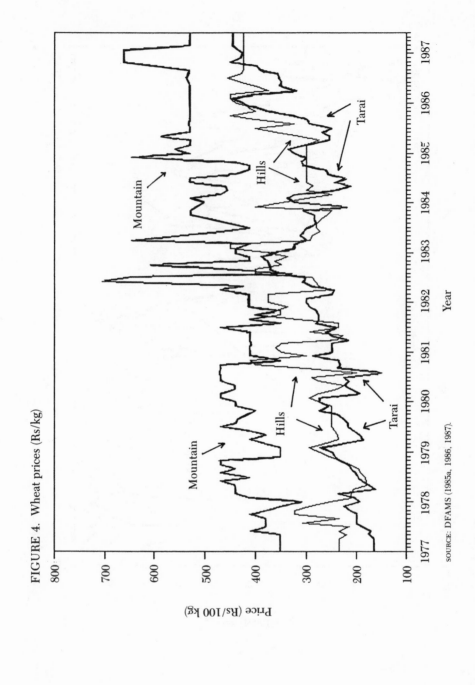

Price (Rs/100 kg)

Year

SOURCE: DFAMS (1985a, 1986, 1987).

TABLE 4. Monthly foodgrain price correlations between India and Nepal, 1975–84

	Paddy			Rice			Wheat	
	Uttar Pradesh	Bihar	West Bengal	Uttar Pradesh	Bihar	West Bengal	Uttar Pradesh	Bihar
Kathmandu	0.73	0.65	0.65	0.90	0.92	0.93	0.79	0.87
E. Tarai (Morang)	0.82	0.87	0.85	0.86	0.94	0.93	0.81	0.89
W. Tarai (Banke)	0.90	0.87	0.82	0.93	0.91	0.95	0.88	0.88

SOURCES: Ministry of Agriculture (1984); DFAMS (1985a).

of food-deficit areas. The RECs procured rice from millers and paddy directly from farmers through their own buying centers and government cooperatives, and sold rice primarily to India. Initially the RECs supplied the NFC with all the rice it needed for distribution by selling 20–30 percent of the amount exported to the NFC at a levy price of about half the market price (table 5). After two profitable years (the result of sales to southern India that took advantage of restrictions on interstate grain movements in India), the RECs incurred heavy losses (when trade restrictions were removed), and they were dissolved in 1980, when the government removed the ban on private exports, and rice exports were allowed under a quota scheme.

Grain procurement and distribution is now the NFC's responsibility. It began to procure grain on the open market in 1977 when the RECs levy on exports no longer fully supplied its needs. Initially, most grain was purchased from wholesalers or millers through sealed tenders or direct nego-

TABLE 5. Rice levy rates and prices

Date	Rate (percent)	On	Price (Rs/mt)	
2/75–5/75	25	Exports	1,393	This price was 30–50 percent lower than REC purchase price.
5/75–2/76	30	Exports	1,393	
2/76–11/76	25	Exports	1,393	
11/76–11/80	20	Exports	1,393	
11/80–3/83	10	Exports	2,000	
	(no levy on exports to India)			
1983–84	25	Mills with >25 hp		
Coarse/fine paddy			1,901/2,000	
Coarse/fine rice			3,410/3,500	
1984/85–1985/86	10	Mills with >25 hp		
Coarse/fine paddy			1,970/2,070	
Coarse/fine rice			3,530/3,620	
1986–87	All foodgrain exports banned; rice levy abolished.			

SOURCES: 1975–83 from Mudbhary (1983); 1983/84–present from NFC, unpublished data.

tiation. Only about 1 percent of NFC grain has been purchased directly from producers—there is no price incentive for farmers to sell to the NFC, and no mechanism for direct procurement from farmers. During 1983/84–1986/87, the NFC procured foodgrain through a levy on mills using larger than twenty-five horsepower engines. In 1986–87 this levy was abolished, and now the NFC obtains all of its grain from open market purchases. The NFC procurement has always been almost all from the Tarai.

The Nepal Food Corporation distributes grain through a network of government cooperatives, private traders, and its own field offices. The amount distributed to each district is determined at the central level by the NFC and the Department of Food and Agricultural Marketing Services (DFAMS) and must be approved by the Ministry of Agriculture. Calculations of food requirements based on crop production and population are overshadowed by political considerations. In particular, calculations of per capita annual foodgrain requirements have been based on food consumption surveys (Scherer, 1985):

Mountains	120 kg
Hills	144 kg
Kathmandu Valley	180 kg
Tarai	165 kg

Climates and the proportions of the labor force working in agriculture in the different regions indicate that the relative food needs of the people are exactly opposite of the above figures. This is one indication of the political influence of Kathmandu Valley residents.[4]

The NFC distribution targets were based on food balance calculations by the DFAMS until 1982. These balance sheets were based on population, calorie needs, and trade surveys measuring private sector food movements in Nepal. Since 1982 other factors have been included: previous years' food distribution, requirements estimated by the chief district officer, NFC field staff observations, and availability of HMG funds.

The NFC's distribution targets are set to meet 22 percent of calculated food deficits in the mountains and 15 percent in the hills, but there have been wide variations for specific areas. In 1983 the calculated deficit for Kathmandu was 35,706 mt, and the distribution target was 18,000 mt, over

---

4. One writer notes: "Probably the only justification for the continuation of the subsidy program in the Valley may be the low income wage earners, who have also benefitted by the program. However, in no case does the Valley deserve subsidized rice in quantities it has been receiving currently" (APROSC, 1984b, p. 16). Another states: "Following the policy of a just social development for all inhabitants of Nepal, the prevailing HMG price strategy providing foodgrains at subsidized prices to consumers in high income areas such as Kathmandu cannot be backed by supporting arguments. This situation aggravates even further when taking into account that e.g. the Kathmandu Valley population already benefits from the most advanced infrastructures which have been developed at the expense of the whole country" (Scherer, 1986, p. 4).

half of the deficit. For the rest of the Central Hills, the calculated deficit was 10,100 mt, and the distribution target was 2,700 mt, about one-fourth of the deficit. The Midwest Mountains had a deficit of 33,705 mt, while the distribution target was only 1,050 mt, less than 3 percent of the deficit (Scherer, 1985).

From 1974 to 1985, the NFC distributed over 400,000 metric tons of grain, of which 54 percent went to the Kathmandu Valley, 39 percent to the hills, and 7 percent to the mountains (table 6). This satisfied 34 percent of the food deficit in Kathmandu, 19 percent in the hills, and 7 percent in the mountains (unpublished NFC records; Scherer, 1985; DFAMS, 1983, 1985b). Although the Sixth Five-Year Plan (1980–85) stipulated that the NFC halt grain sales to Kathmandu by 1985, the percentage of grain distributed there has not decreased. There are financial and political reasons for concentrating distribution in Kathmandu. Distribution by the NFC has thus done little to alleviate food shortage problems anywhere in Nepal, especially outside Kathmandu.[5]

Subsidized food sales are a substantial portion of consumption in Kathmandu. In 1983–84, 22,483 mt of foodgrain was supplied to Kathmandu. If 180 kg per capita is the annual requirement, Kathmandu (1983–84 population 818,000) required 147,000 mt, so NFC supplied nearly one-sixth of the requirement. Although this is distributed at below-market prices, the depressing effect on foodgrain prices in Kathmandu is probably small because supplies at the margin come from Tarai farmers and traders, not from the NFC (and NFC supplies are originally from the Tarai).

Nepal Food Corporation distribution prices are determined by the Ministry of Supplies, and vary by district. In remote areas, prices are higher because of transportation costs. The HMG subsidizes transport costs, so remote districts have the largest subsidy per ton of grain distributed. Although transport costs to the mountains are often double the cost of the grain itself, procurement and distribution costs have always been highest in Kathmandu, which receives the most grain (APROSC, 1984b, pp. 27–28). There was little change in NFC prices from 1975 to 1981, although market prices rose considerably (figs. 5 and 6), and NFC losses for each ton of grain distributed rose from less than Rs 200 to over Rs 2,400. Since 1981, NFC prices have risen, more than doubling in some areas, and NFC losses temporarily declined (table 7). These losses, totaling over Rs 500 million, are financed by loans from Nepal's banks at the HMG's request. In mid-1985 the NFC had outstanding bank loans of nearly Rs 200 million (Nepal Rastra Bank, 1986a).

The NFC's price policy also provides an illustration of the political power of Kathmandu Valley residents. Food distribution prices are lower

5. See DFAMS (1984b) for detailed information on the Far Western Development Region.

TABLE 6.   Public foodgrain procurement and distribution (mt)

Year	Procurement			Distribution			
	Purchases*	Aid	Total	Mountain	Hills	Kathmandu	Total
1974–75	20,758	7,914	28,672	349	7,289	16,574	24,212
1975–76	42,197	1,493	43,690	711	9,835	15,742	26,288
1976–77	35,814	1,091	36,905	831	19,865	11,865	32,561
1977–78	38,959	4,658	43,617	1,297	15,011	18,292	34,600
1978–79	31,893	7,095	38,988	1,329	9,543	18,461	29,333
1979–80	51,500	29,287	80,787	2,692	19,132	24,985	46,809
1980–81	44,736	29,634	74,370	4,599	19,071	26,946	50,616
1981–82	35,362	8,813	44,175	4,031	14,730	18,206	36,967
1982–83	51,325	73,372	124,697	9,774	29,835	31,699	71,308
1983–84	35,885	13,928	49,813	7,422	20,418	22,483	50,323
1984–85	23,582	4,008	27,590	5,258	13,836**	20,592	39,686
1985–86	33,230	0	33,230	6,398	13,371	16,900	36,669

SOURCES: Food aid 1974/75–1980/81 from DFAMS (1984a); 1974–75 data from APROSC (1982c); 1975/76–1982/83 procurement from FAO (1984); distribution, food aid, and 1983–84 data from APROSC (1982b) and Scherer (1985); 1984/85–1985/86 data from unpublished NFC records.
*Except for 1984–85, rice has always constituted at least 75 percent of total purchases.
**Includes 944 kg to the Tarai.

here than in other areas of the country with similar marketing costs, despite residents' higher incomes and greater access to food supplies than their village counterparts. In March 1985 a price increase was approved to reduce NFC losses: while this increase is still in effect for the rest of the country, it lasted only eight days in Kathmandu.

Total actual food subsidies provided to consumers are now at least Rs 150 million (minimum Rs 1,000/mt price subsidy for 50,000 mt distributed, plus Rs 100 million transport subsidy) per year (calculated from Scherer, 1985, 1986). This subsidy would constitute over one-fifth of the annual allocation for agriculture if it were incorporated into the national budget.

Each district has a Food Management Committee to organize distribution of allotted grain. In times of shortage, one member of the committee, the chief district officer, issues coupons for specified amounts of grain. A 1982 study found that 24–33 percent of NFC grain is sold to government officials and the military, whereas most of what goes to the general public is sold to influential members of society. Very little reaches the poor. Furthermore, a large portion of the grain that is purchased by wealthier people is resold to poor people at higher prices, used to produce local liquor or to pay laborers, or transported across the Tibetan border for resale (APROSC, 1982a, annex 9). Scherer (1986) writes:

> In Nepal, foodgrain marketing activities involving government organizations are rooted in the historic tradition of paying tribute to the center of power. Thus, government marketing operations in the country's most recent history initially commenced [in 1946] with

FIGURE 5. Retail prices of NFC raw coarse rice (Rs/kg)

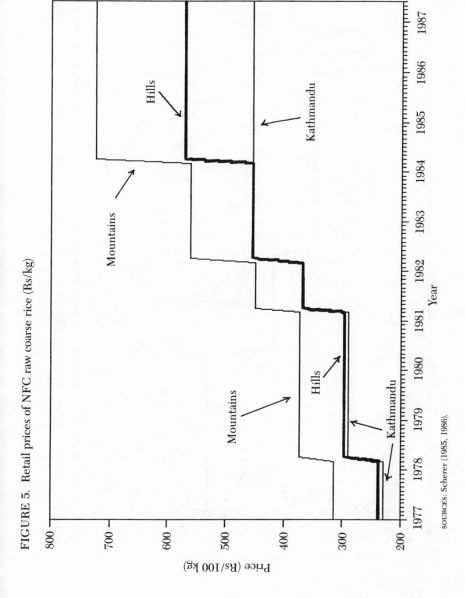

SOURCES: Scherer (1985, 1986).

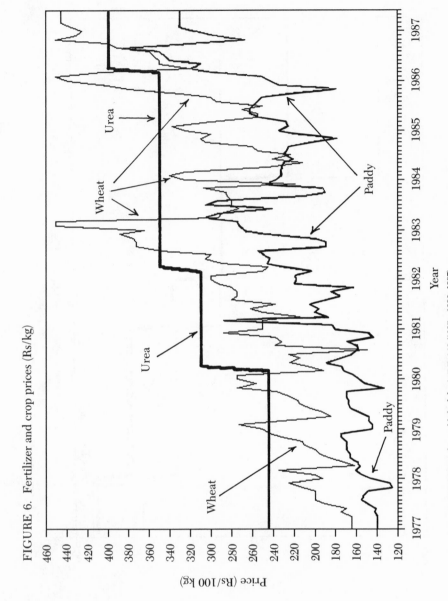

FIGURE 6. Fertilizer and crop prices (Rs/kg)

SOURCES: AIC (1983 and unpublished data); DFAMS (1985a, 1986, 1987).

TABLE 7. Food subsidies and Nepal Food Corporation finances (Rs million)

Fiscal year	74/5	75/6	76/7	77/8	78/9	79/0	80/1	81/2	82/3	83/4	84/5	85/6
Gross sales	42	73	155	199	110	147	143	101	213	159	154	257
Cost of sales	41	78	161	230	141	226	265	107	281	221	331	390
Net profit	1	-4	-6	-30	-31	-78	-122	-6	-68	-62	-177	-133
Fixed assets	6	7	16	19	20	21	23	25	29	32	37	39
Current assets	54	117	123	148	154	161	189	200	287	245	61	91
Current liability	55	101	108	145	171	243	386	374	534	556	555	598
Subsidy	0	0	0	0	8	2	0	69	80	32	44	44
Sales 000 mt	24	26	33	35	29	47	51	37	71	50	40	54
Loss per mt	32	-165	-190	-881	-1,073	-1,673	-2,414	-153	-954	-1,240	-4,372	-2,453

SOURCES: NFC, Ministry of Finance (unpublished data). Estimates for 1985–86.

the objective of securing foodgrain supplies from the Tarai belt for the Kathmandu Valley. Only in the beginning of the 1970s, HMG's foodgrain marketing involvements expanded to providing supplies to other districts and food deficit areas of the country as well. However, the mentality accepting that government servants and important persons have the right to claim the main share of such supplies remained. Until today, this attitude hampers in most areas the implementation of the objectives of the original governmental policy to reach the poor and needy groups of the population in times of local food shortages. In the case of the Kathmandu Valley, the tradition and habit of receiving through governmental entities foodgrains at advantageous prices has entrenched itself as a right taken for granted. Such developments are typical for situations where the government servants and policy-making groups belong to the beneficiaries and reap advantages for themselves, their families, servants or commercial enterprises. (pp. 1–2)

Most grain distributed by the NFC has been rice, perhaps because this is Nepal's main foodgrain. Although maize and wheat have higher calorie and protein values per rupee than rice, rice is a preferred food, desired by rich as well as poor people. Thus distributing more maize and wheat (and lower quality rice) would provide a self-targeting mechanism to insure that truly needy people received foodgrain (Scherer, 1986, p. 22).

Much food aid has been sent to Nepal in times of natural disasters such as earthquakes or extremely unfavorable weather. The amounts and timing of such aid have not been consistent, as they depend on external political and economic factors. Sometimes food aid, requested in response to low production or natural disasters, has arrived in time to depress prices for the following season. Food aid, important at times, cannot be considered a consistent source of food (table 6).[6]

Conceptually, the NFC maintains stocks for normal operations and for disaster relief. The Food and Agricultural Organization (FAO) has recommended that working stocks for normal operations should be 10,000–15,000 mt, and that 5,000 mt should be held for relief operations (FAO Food Security Review Mission, 1984). As NFC stocks since 1981–82 have always been above 20,000 mt, the level of stocks has not been a problem.

Product Price Interventions—Output Price Supports

The HMG first announced support prices for rice and wheat in 1976–77. Support prices are fixed by the Central Food Management Committee on the basis of production cost, the general foodgrain production situation, prices in Indian border markets, prices in main producing areas, transpor-

6. See Fletcher and Sahn (1984) for a detailed analysis of food aid.

tation costs, and Indian support prices (Mudbhary, 1983, pp. 35–36). Indian support prices have been—and must be—the most important factor; in some years Nepal has delayed announcing prices because Indian support prices have been announced late. Support prices have almost never been used to procure grain, and levy prices have been used to procure paddy and rice only.

The Indian Agricultural Prices Commission fixes the levels of three prices: minimum support prices, announced at sowing time, for major field crops, below which market prices are not allowed to fall; procurement prices, fixed at the start of the marketing season, for cereal grains to be procured by government agencies for release through the public distribution system (these are generally higher than support, but lower than free market, prices); and issue (subsidized) prices for grains when they are distributed to consumers (Sarma, 1984; Kahlon and Tyagi, 1983, pp. 7–15). India now has over 30 million mt of foodgrain in storage as a result of good harvests in recent years, and the real problem is poverty, not production— poor people do not have the purchasing power to obtain this surplus grain.

Support prices have been ineffective in influencing foodgrain market prices and production. The NFC has not procured enough grain to affect open market prices, largely because of budget limitations. Between 1980–81 and 1985–86, the NFC procured less than 225,000 mt of grain, which was less than 2 percent of the grain produced. Procurement has been almost entirely in the Tarai, providing no incentive to increase production in the hills and mountains, which have the greatest food deficits.

The amount of purchase necessary to affect open market prices varies with demand and supply elasticities, which are in turn influenced by buyers' and sellers' trading strategies. A secure market may be as important to sellers as a good price, and the NFC can provide psychological assurance to farmers simply by opening stores to defend the minimum price, even if only small amounts of grain are purchased.

Announced prices have consistently been lower than market prices. Support prices have thus provided no incentive for farmers to produce or market more foodgrain. Most grain has been procured as a levy on traders and millers, with the rest coming from open market purchases, also generally from traders and millers. Grain could be obtained from farmers as a way of collecting outstanding fertilizer loans (Lee, 1971), but no mechanism exists to purchase grain directly from farmers.

Prices have usually been announced well after harvests, which is too late to affect planting decisions or encourage the use of fertilizer and improved seed varieties. The HMG has pledged to announce support prices earlier in the season. Since 1984 support prices have often been announced before harvest, but never before planting.

Until the HMG can consistently announce remunerative prices in a timely fashion and back them up with sufficient purchases, Nepal's food-grain price support system will remain a policy on paper only. However, Nepal cannot have a support price policy that deviates from Indian border market prices by more than transport costs. If Nepal's support price is higher than the Indian price, grain will move from India to Nepal, and if Nepal's price is lower, Nepalese farmers will sell to India.

Some writers suggest that there are a few large Tarai grain millers who collude to control grain prices, and that a support price lower than the market price may enable millers to justify offering a lower price than they otherwise would (Johl, 1981; Mudbhary, 1983; APROSC, 1984a). Given the large size of the Indian market, it is more likely that Tarai grain millers cannot avoid responding to Indian prices. Good harvests in Nepal and India often coincide, so price movements in Nepal can be accentuated by similar changes in India. (Nepalese merchants' associations that fix commodity prices are not necessarily evidence of monopoly—these associations may simply be transferring market signals from India. Analyzing possible monopoly aspects of the Indian grain trade is beyond the scope of this chapter.)

Input Price Interventions—Fertilizer Price Policy

In Nepal, the fertilizer price is a major policy issue attracting public attention whenever it is changed. Fertilizer is the most important purchased input for most farmers, requiring them either to spend precious cash or to obtain loans from time-consuming formal or expensive informal sources. Although fertilizer may represent only about 10 percent of the total cost of production, it is often most or all of the cash cost. While the average farmer uses less than 50 kg of fertilizer per year, and this costs less than Rs 200 (U.S. $10), farmers know that the government fixes fertilizer prices, and they direct their complaints accordingly when the price rises. Farmers with sizable operations spend considerably more than the average and complain more loudly. A rise or fall in the fertilizer price thus has a politically visible effect on the welfare of farmers—a large, vocal, and sometimes politically powerful group of people.

Fertilizer price policy has both efficiency and equity objectives. The efficiency objective is to increase crop production by encouraging farmers to use more fertilizer. The equity objective is to ensure that fertilizer price policy does not disadvantage poor hill farmers.

Transport costs are lower for the Tarai and the Kathmandu Valley, so it is easier to increase fertilizer use in these areas than in the hills. However, the poorer half of Nepal's population lives in the hills where food deficits have become chronic, so there are equity reasons for subsidizing their fertilizer use. Transporting food to the hills is also more expensive than transporting fertilizer to grow food.

Fertilizer sales have been subsidized by the Nepalese government and by foreign donor agencies to encourage increased use by farmers and thereby increase crop production. Fertilizer sales have quadrupled in the last fifteen years, and some of the increase in crop production during that time can be attributed to fertilizer. However, the financial burden of the subsidy for both the Nepalese government and foreign donor agencies has also risen substantially along with fertilizer use.

Fertilizer Use. Fertilizer use officially began in Nepal in 1965–66 when 3,169 mt were received as aid from India and the USSR. Since then both foreign aid and imports have increased steadily, with aid accounting for between one-fifth and nine-tenths of the annual supply since 1975–76 (table 8a). Since 1981–82, Nepal has also received fertilizer through World Bank and Asian Development Bank loans, and in 1984–85 loans provided over half the fertilizer supply.

Fertilizer is imported and received as aid from a variety of countries, with one notable exception: no fertilizer is officially imported from India. India—both a fertilizer producer and (net) importer—has prohibited the export of this commodity since 1965–66 (APROSC, 1978, p. 14).

Annual fertilizer sales are now over 100,000 mt, often increasing by more than 15 percent per year, with urea and complex each accounting for about half the total. Fertilizer is used in more than sixty of Nepal's seventy-five districts. Average fertilizer use, as measured by sales, is still less than 20 nutrient-kg/ha, one of the lowest rates in the world.

Based on sales, more chemical fertilizer is used on summer crops (mostly rice and maize) than on winter crops (mostly wheat) (table 8b). However, more fertilizer is used per hectare on winter wheat than on summer rice and maize. This is probably because most wheat strains are recently introduced high-yielding fertilizer-responsive varieties, while most rice and maize strains are traditional varieties that have long been cultivated without chemical fertilizer.

Much more fertilizer is sold in Kathmandu and the Tarai than in the hills and mountains (table 8c). Kathmandu contains about 2 percent of Nepal's cultivated area, but farmers there purchase over one-seventh of all fertilizer. The Tarai has about half the cultivated land, and farmers there buy over three-fifths of all fertilizer. Hill farmers, who cultivate nearly half of Nepal's farmland, buy about one-fifth of the fertilizer. If fertilizer is used where it is sold, on a per-hectare basis Kathmandu farmers use over 95 nutrient-kg, while Tarai farmers use 19 kg, and those in the hills use 10 kg.

While this geographical distribution of fertilizer may be consistent with a policy of concentrating fertilizer in areas where irrigation facilities are available and therefore productive capacity is highest, it is more likely that this distribution pattern is the result of lower transportation costs and

TABLE 8a.   Sources and sales of fertilizer, 1975/76–1985/86 (mt)

Year	Foreign aid	Loan	Import	Total	Sales
1975–76	5,000	0	0	5,000	31,131
1976–77	20,069	0	17,000	37,069	37,835
1977–78	37,316	0	9,000	46,316	45,282
1978–79	42,218	0	5,000	47,218	45,591
1979–80	25,176	0	13,325	38,501	50,168
1980–81	31,359	0	22,825	54,184	54,000
1981–82	25,945	12,075	41,276	79,296	56,444
1982–83	31,300	20,100	48,400	99,800	73,715
1983–84	17,500	5,000	55,730	78,230	86,916
1984–85	25,600	59,700	30,000	115,300	100,120
1985–86	33,007	16,370	80,744	130,121	102,196

TABLE 8b.   Seasonal fertilizer sales

Year	Summer	Winter	Total	Summer	Winter	Total
	(total nutrient-mt)			(nutrient-kg/ha)*		
1975–76	4,994	7,273	12,267	2.9	22.1	6.0
1976–77	10,274	4,621	14,895	6.0	13.3	7.2
1977–78	11,723	5,744	17,467	6.9	15.7	8.4
1978–79	10,884	7,660	18,544	6.3	21.5	8.9
1979–80	12,645	8,320	20,964	7.5	22.7	10.2
1980–81	11,202	11,256	22,458	6.5	28.7	10.6
1981–82	12,943	10,880	23,823	7.3	27.2	11.0
1982–83	16,033	15,246	31,279	9.1	31.6	13.9
1983–84	20,967	16,330	37,297	12.1	34.6	16.9
1984–85	18,675	24,157	42,832	9.6	53.5	17.8
1985–86	28,616	14,792	43,408	14.3	30.6	17.4

*Per-hectare calculations assume all fertilizer is used on paddy, wheat, and maize, which covers 85 percent of Nepal's cropped area. Fertilizer is also used on vegetables and cash crops, so per hectare use may be slightly overestimated, but relative magnitudes should be correct.

TABLE 8c.   Fertilizer sales by region

Year	Mountain	Hills	Kathmandu	Tarai	Mountain	Hills	Kathmandu	Tarai
	(total nutrient-mt)				(nutrient-kg/ha)*			
1975–76	107	1,380	4,575	6,205	1.3	2.8	70.1	4.5
1976–77	179	1,823	5,165	7,727	2.2	3.6	81.7	5.5
1977–78	455	2,529	5,379	9,105	5.5	4.8	84.8	6.5
1978–79	434	2,588	6,096	9,427	5.3	4.8	93.7	6.8
1979–80	652	3,353	6,498	10,462	8.0	6.3	109.8	7.6
1980–81	878	3,150	7,261	11,170	10.6	5.6	121.5	7.9
1981–82	913	3,557	6,780	12,573	11.0	5.8	117.1	8.9
1982–83	1,232	4,531	7,498	18,017	15.5	6.8	125.5	12.5
1983–84	1,305	5,324	8,431	22,237	15.3	8.0	142.2	15.9
1984–85	1,284	8,280	6,555	26,711	12.7	10.3	111.9	18.5
1985–86	1,439	8,916	6,357	26,696	12.3	10.3	95.4	18.6

SOURCES: AIC (1983 and unpublished data); DFAMS (1983, 1985b, and unpublished data).
    *Per-hectare calculations assume all fertilizer is used on paddy, wheat, and maize, which cover 85 percent of Nepal's cropped area. Fertilizer is also used on vegetables and cash crops, so per-hectare use may be slightly overestimated, but relative magnitudes should be correct.

greater farmer purchasing (and political) power in Kathmandu and the Tarai. While more research is needed on the costs and benefits of fertilizer use on hill crops, this distribution probably does not maximize the social value of additional crop production.

Fertilizer sales are increasing in the hills and Tarai, but have been decreasing recently in Kathmandu. Per hectare, the absolute increase in fertilizer use from 1975/76–1985/86 was highest in Kathmandu (from 70 to 95 kg), followed by the Tarai (from 5 to 19 kg) and the hills (from 3 to 10 kg).

Fertilizer use and fertilizer demand may be quite different. Most fertilizer is officially imported and sold through the Agricultural Inputs Corporation (AIC), and the rest is unofficially imported from India. Farmers' demand has little direct impact on the fertilizer available each crop season—foreign aid grants and loans, and AIC's management capacity, are much more influential factors. Total fertilizer demand is thus probably much greater than sales and actual use.

Fertilizer demand is based on the expected impact of fertilizer use on crop production, and on the expected value of crop output, and thus is directly related to farmers' expectations about crop prices. Since 1971–72 fertilizer prices have generally not risen faster than crop prices, and in many periods crop prices have risen considerably more than fertilizer prices (see fig. 6).

Fertilizer use is also related to farmers' expectations about water, which complements fertilizer and is necessary to achieve high yields from modern seeds. Low fertilizer use is partly a reflection of the dependence on irregular monsoon rains and the lack of assured irrigation to supplement rainfall. However, given the low levels of fertilizer use, considerable production gains could probably be realized from increased fertilizer use even without more irrigation facilities.

Fertilizer Prices. The price of fertilizer in Nepal is determined by the HMG Cabinet of Ministers. The AIC general manager can propose a price change to the AIC Board of Directors, and if the Board approves, the suggestion is sent to the Ministry of Agriculture. If the Ministry approves, the proposal goes to the full cabinet for a final decision.

Before 1972 the fertilizer selling price was based on AIC's import costs plus internal transportation costs. While this was logical from a cost viewpoint, the price was higher in India (a result of Indian taxes) than in the Tarai, and higher prices discouraged fertilizer use in the hills (Lee, 1972). In 1972 the Agricultural Marketing Conference recommended that "the selling price of fertilizer be equalized with that of neighboring Indian states, and that the base price of fertilizer be the same in both the Tarai and Hilly areas. The savings made by the equalization program should be utilized to subsidize the transportation costs to the Hilly areas and to partially cover the storage costs of fertilizer in order to insure timely distribution" (EAPD/MFA, 1972, p. 5). The government established a uniform national price for fertilizer in 1972, and this policy is still in effect. This lowered fertilizer prices in the hills and raised them in the Tarai. Although fertilizer prices have been raised several times since 1972, mostly in response to changes in Indian prices, the AIC continues to suffer losses averaging over Rs 100 million annually (table 9). Sales prices do not cover the costs of importing and transporting fertilizer, even though considerable fertilizer is received as aid grants.

The subsidy provided by AIC, HMG, and donor agencies varies from year to year and from one kind of fertilizer to another. While it is difficult to determine who contributes what to the overall subsidy, it is estimated that the AIC and HMG have borne about half of the cost, and foreign donor agencies—including the World Bank and Asian Development Bank—have borne the other half (Hill, 1982). HMG pays the AIC to transport fertilizer to the hills, but this payment—now over Rs 20 million annually—does not cover transport costs. Other aspects of the subsidy are hidden because profits on grant-supplied fertilizer offset losses on purchased fertilizer. As a result of international loan and grant arrangements, the AIC has not had to borrow from commercial banks to cover operating losses.

While world fertilizer prices have fluctuated since Nepal began importing fertilizer twenty years ago, the fertilizer subsidy has usually been 30–50 percent of actual cost (table 9). Current world nitrogenous fertilizer prices are low, and as a result actual subsidies—at official domestic selling prices of RS 3.99 for both urea and complex—are now about 20 percent for urea and 40 percent for complex.[7] These are minimum estimates because Nepal receives some fertilizer under tied-source arrangements at higher than world market prices.

The subsidy from the Tarai farmers' viewpoint has always been less: prices in India are now Rs 3.78 per kg for urea and Rs 4.20 for complex (FAI, 1986; AIC unpublished data). There is thus no effective subsidy for urea for a farmer whose alternate source is India, and only Rs 0.21 per kg subsidy for complex. Indian prices have never been more than 25 percent over Nepalese prices.

The actual subsidy on fertilizer sold in Nepal varies tremendously. Fertilizer sold in the Tarai is subsidized the least, and that in the hills the most. Fertilizer that farmers buy from India and bring to Nepal on their backs or in bullock carts is not subsidized at all from Nepal's viewpoint, and fertilizer that Indians buy in Nepal is subsidized without any direct return to Nepal. Fertilizer subsidies have also often made it profitable to buy

7. Calculated from AIC data given in APROSC (1986), adjusted for current fertilizer prices.

TABLE 9. Fertilizer subsidies and Agricultural Inputs Corporation (AIC) finances (Rs 000)

Year	Sales	Cost	Profit	Transport subsidy	Fert. sales (mt)	Loss/mt (Rs)
1970–71	17,640	24,230	−6,590	n.a.	17,728	−372
1975–76	70,480	194,910	−124,430	2,900	31,131	−3,997
1980–81	159,700	196,000	−36,300	9,800	54,000	−672
1981–82	185,100	289,000	−103,900	11,250	56,444	−1,841
1982–83	235,800	295,700	−59,900	15,200	73,715	−813
1983–84	323,700	413,800	−90,100	15,200	86,916	−1,037
1984–85	402,100	667,000	−264,900	18,500	100,120	−2,646
1985–86	561,400	737,700	−176,300	20,000	102,196	−1,725

SOURCES: ADB (1982), vol. 2, appendices 4.24–4.25; Ministry of Finance (1987a); AIC (1983 and unpublished data). Asian Development Bank costs based on world prices, but cost to AIC of aid-financed fertilizer was less. As some fertilizer is obtained under tied-source arrangements at higher than world prices, these figures should be a reasonable estimate of total subsidies.

fertilizer in Nepal and take it to India for resale or use. Higher per-kg subsidies are provided to farmers living in the hills where transport costs are higher, but the main beneficiaries of the subsidy are Kathmandu farmers who use the most fertilizer per household, and traders who profit from price differences.

Agricultural Trade Policy

In the past, much of Nepal's foreign exchange earnings came from agricultural exports, particularly jute, and agricultural exports have sometimes been encouraged through a variety of direct and indirect subsidies. Nepal officially exported as much as 165,000 mt of rice worth Rs 518 million in 1981–82, but there was a net import of foodgrain in 1982–83 when the monsoon was unfavorable (table 10). Maize is the second major foodgrain export. Unofficial trade is hard to quantify, but much of the grain and fertilizer that moves both ways across the Nepal-India border is not recorded as official trade. Official trade probably accounts for less than one-fourth of all trade.

Current trade regulations include a ban on the export of all foodgrains as a result of the decline in food production resulting from the late monsoon in 1986. There are no import taxes levied on the import of foodgrain or fertilizer, and previous taxes on foodgrain imports have been minimal. Past trade policies have included periodic bans on the export of foodgrain following production declines. While these restrictions have undoubtedly reduced the amount of grain exported to India by raising the transactions cost, some grain has been exported every year.

There are also nonprice reasons for grain movements across the border. Restrictions on interstate movement of grain in India have been circumvented by moving grain from Uttar Pradesh into central Nepal, east along Nepal's roads, and back into Bihar. Lack of adequate roads and markets in

TABLE 10.   Foodgrain exports (mt) and value (Rs 000)

Year	Rice quantity	Value	Maize quantity	Value
1975–76	164,901	518,000	n.a.	n.a.
1980–81	45,453	141,700	17,749	24,500
1981–82	53,564	222,600	15,988	26,100
1982–83	2,509	11,300	214	300
1983–84	16,670	75,200	201	400
1984–85	52,586	236,300	7,718	10,700
1985–86	14,641	93,200	n.a.	n.a.

SOURCES: APROSC (1986), p. 63; 1985–86 from Ministry of Finance (1987b) and Rastra Bank unpublished data.

western Nepal can be overcome by moving grain from Nepal into India, along India's road and rail network, and back into central Nepal.

Nepal's most important policies affecting trade in agricultural commodities are related to the open border with India and the development of transportation links within Nepal. Despite political pressure to limit inmigration from India, Nepal also derives advantages from the open border, and restricting movement in either direction would be both politically and practically difficult. As the transportation network within Nepal is developed, the cost of carrying goods both within Nepal and to and from India will decline, and Nepalese in remote areas should benefit from increased access to markets for their labor and crops.

As "most price policies are implemented by interventions at the border—by taxing or subsidizing international trade,"[8] the open border and high transportation costs within Nepal mean that implementing any food price policy is difficult. International trade in foodgrains affects both consumers and producers in the Tarai (and sometimes Kathmandu), but government control over this trade is limited. For the mountains and hills, transportation costs for foodgrains are sufficiently high that international trade has little impact.

Macro Price Policy—Interest Rates and Exchange Rates

Interest Rates. The Agricultural Development Bank of Nepal (ADB/N) is the main institution providing subsidized credit for agriculture. Commercial banks have been instructed by the Nepal Rastra Bank to invest at

8. Timmer (1986), p. 26. The complete quotation is, "most price policies are implemented by interventions at the border—by taxing or subsidizing international trade in the commodity. It is quite difficult to implement a price policy in the absence of international trade in the commodity concerned; the mechanisms are much more complicated and require direct purchases and sales by a government-controlled marketing agent. Trade interventions, by contrast, can usually be implemented quite simply by the customs service, a government trading company, or both."

least 10 percent of their deposits in agricultural and rural development projects, but such lending has not exceeded 2 percent of ADB/N's disbursements (Nepal Rastra Bank, 1985, tables 58, 90). In 1985–86, ADB/N's outstanding loans totaled nearly Rs 1,500 million, with over Rs 300 million for crop production (ADB/N 1985, table 3; Ministry of Finance, 1987b). Crop production loans in 1985–86 totaled nearly Rs 200 million (table 11).

Current rates of interest charged by the ADB/N on loans to individual borrowers range from 10–17 percent. Nominal interest rates have not varied with inflation, and in some years the real interest rate (nominal rate less inflation) has been negative. Repayment has been uneven. The ratio of delinquent to outstanding loans has increased nearly every year, and now stands at about 40 percent (Nepal Rastra Bank, 1985, table 63).

Subsidized institutional credit for agriculture meets less than one-third of total demand. Three-fourths of borrowing families obtain credit from private sources, primarily friends, relatives, and village moneylenders (table 12). Farmers with large landholdings obtain most institutional credit, while poor villagers rely on private sources with higher interest rates (table 13). As with most subsidized, rationed commodities, credit has been allocated to influential people, not to people having the greatest need, or the greatest ability to use it most effectively.

Of the credit provided by the ADB/N, one-third has been for production. Until 1982 loans for labor costs of cultivation were limited to 20 percent of fertilizer and seed loans; since 1982 loans to cover labor costs can equal fertilizer and seed loans. Fertilizer and seed loans are provided in kind, while loans for labor costs are in cash.

One use for credit not sufficiently recognized by official policies is the flexibility it can give farmers to delay selling until prices rise from their postharvest low points. Informal moneylenders often require that loans be repaid at harvest time, forcing farmers to sell at low prices. Credit specifically for marketing could reduce interseasonal price variations and provide significant benefits to farmers.

Exchange Rates. Until 1945, when paper currency was first issued by the HMG, Indian currency was the only paper medium of exchange in Nepal. Fixed exchange rates were announced for the Indian rupee (IC) and U.S. dollar in April 1960. Since 1966, when IC was devalued and the Nepalese Rupee (NC) was exchanged almost at par with IC, NC has been devalued four times with respect to IC, and now the exchange rate is NC 168 = IC 100 (table 14). There has always been official convertibility of NC and IC, and IC circulates freely in the Tarai. However, NC has not been convertible into other currencies, and has generally been overvalued.

With respect to hard currencies, Nepal maintained a system of fixed

TABLE 11. Agricultural Development Bank annual disbursements (000 Rs)

Year	Production	Mechanization & irrigation	Livestock	Agro industry	Horticulture	Tea	Total
1975–76	42,011	22,453	9,636	34,166	1,804	4,245	114,315
1980–81	39,140	17,148	22,632	44,866	3,145	7,203	134,134
1981–82	59,589	27,178	37,830	121,384	3,611	6,826	256,418
1982–83	101,692	66,685	59,708	104,105	4,032	9,593	345,815
1983–84	133,146	70,543	88,674	175,469	7,391	1,024	476,247
1984–85	164,430	95,377	127,790	164,079	13,551	1,387	566,614
1985–86	193,400	117,900	172,500	161,100	14,600	4,300	663,800

SOURCES: ADB/N (1985); 1985–86 from Ministry of Finance (1987b).

TABLE 12. Families borrowing from various sources (percent)

	Small		Medium		Large		Total	
	1969–70	1976–77	1969–70	1976–77	1969–70	1976–77	1969–70	1976–77
Institutional	15	17	25	30	31	43	18	24
Private	85	83	75	70	69	57	82	76

NOTE: Small = 0–0.51 hectares (ha) in hills, 0–2.71 ha in Tarai; medium = 0.51–1.02 ha in hills, 2.71–5.42 ha in Tarai; large = above 1.02 ha in hills, above 5.42 ha in Tarai. Most Nepalese thus fall in the small category.
SOURCE: NRB (1980), vol. 1, p. 161.

exchange rates—with infrequent adjustments—until June 1983, when a floating exchange rate system using a basket of currencies was established. There is some evidence that there are only two currencies—the Indian rupee and the U.S. dollar—in this basket (Morris, 1984). In June 1986 the IC/NC rate was officially allowed to float, but the exchange rate has been steady. Despite a 17 percent devaluation in 1985, current black market exchange rates indicate that the Nepalese rupee is overvalued against the U.S. dollar by about 15 percent. Fluctuations in the black market rate indicate that it includes a premium for illegal activities and is not an equilibrium rate based on the currencies' relative buying power.

Nepal maintained a dual exchange rate for the U.S. dollar between March 1978 and September 1981. During this time exporters receiving dollars could exchange them for Nepalese currency at a premium (33 percent until February 1980, then 17 percent) over the normal exchange rate (Mudbhary, 1983, appendix 2). This system was used to provide incentives to all types of exporters. However, as most agricultural exports are to India, this system did not have a substantial impact on agricultural exports.

Most agricultural trade does not use official channels to obtain foreign exchange. Indian currency is readily available at Nepalese banks and is widely circulated in the Tarai where most of Nepal's agricultural surplus is produced. Overvaluation relative to hard foreign currencies probably has less direct effect on agricultural trade than overvaluation relative to Indian currency. Prices adjust quickly when the exchange rate with India changes. After the devaluation in November 1985, Tarai markets responded within hours by raising prices.

In general, exchange rate policies, combined with import and export license regulations, have made investments in the agricultural sector less remunerative than investments in small-scale industry and trade. As a result, considerable energy is devoted to obtaining scarce foreign exchange through trade in consumer goods, and little effort is devoted to improving the prospects for agricultural exports.

TABLE 13. Amounts borrowed from various sources (Rs/family)

	Small		Medium		Large		Interest rates	
	1969–70	1976–77	1969–70	1976–77	1969–70	1976–77	1969–70	1976–77
Institutional								
Cooperatives	18	76	44	117	143	476	9.5–10	11–14
Agricultural Development Bank/Nepal		78	2	183	356	1,000	10	8–14
Commercial banks	4	35	22	71	49	271	9.5–10	11–18
Total	22	189	68	371	548	1,747		
Private								
Moneylenders	108	275	142	261	292	556	10–50	15–100
Friends/relatives	93	340	176	333	168	175	10–50	15–100
Others	22	146	36	76	115	146	10–50	10–150
Total	223	761	354	670	575	877		
Total	245	950	422	1,041	1,123	2,624		

NOTE: Farm sizes same as in table 12.
SOURCE: NRB (1980), vol. 1, p. 168.

TABLE 14. Official exchange rates of U.S. dollar and Indian rupee

	U.S. dollar		Indian rupee	
Year	Buying rate	Date	Buying rate	Date
1966–67	7.60	4/13/60	1.01	6/06/66
1971–72	10.10	12/08/67	1.39	12/22/71
1976–77	12.45	10/09/75	1.39	
1981–82	13.10	9/19/81	1.45	
1982–83	14.20	12/17/82	1.45	
1983–84	14.40	6/01/83 floating	1.45	
1984–85	17.40	11/02/84 floating	1.45	
1985–86	20.40	11/30/85 floating	1.70	11/30/85
1986–87	21.90	12/01/86 floating	1.68	6/02/86 floating

SOURCES: Mudbhary (1983); NRB (1986b).

Tradeoffs in Price Policy

Nepal has faced few explicit dilemmas in its food price policies, partly because policies designed to achieve conflicting goals have never been fully implemented. The NFC has rarely purchased foodgrain at announced support prices, so the tradeoff between high producer and low consumer prices has not been faced. Most of the fertilizer that the AIC distributes is obtained through foreign aid grants or low-interest loans, so while some fertilizer subsidy costs have been implicitly borne by the HMG, these costs have not appeared in the HMG budget. Losses from the NFC's distribution of food at subsidized prices and the AIC's operating losses have been covered by government-guaranteed commercial bank loans, so the budgetary consequences of these policies have been delayed. Although government-guaranteed loans to the NFC and AIC have increased the money supply and may have weakened the financial position of the commercial banks, these consequences do not seem to have affected agricultural policy discussions.

The implicit costs of NFC and AIC operations are considerable. The opportunity costs of the food and fertilizer distributed by these agencies may be double the losses indicated in the agencies' financial statements. These costs include the actual costs of the food received as aid and the fertilizer received through long-term loans.

The long, open border with India has prevented Nepal from even trying to insulate its domestic markets from international price movements, at least as these price movements are reflected in Indian markets. It has not been—and will not be—possible to insulate Nepalese markets from price changes in India. The potential conflict between reaping the benefits of using international prices and suffering the consequences of unfavorable international price movements has thus not been an issue.

If Nepal succeeded in implementing policies that have heretofore only been announced—supporting output prices, distributing food at subsidized prices to meet food deficits, and providing enough fertilizer at subsidized prices to increase production in food-deficit areas—the dilemmas inherent in tradeoffs between conflicting objectives would have to be faced unless market input and output prices and consumer and producer responses made it easy to achieve policy objectives. For now, Nepal faces different problems in implementing its food price policies.

Nepal has tried to achieve its food policy objectives through rice and wheat price supports, fertilizer price subsidies, and consumer food subsidies. The first two attempt to increase production by raising the output/input price ratio; the third attempts to reduce food deficits and improve the nutritional status of disadvantaged citizens. Food subsidies have been used mostly to keep prices low for Kathmandu consumers, so this policy must be evaluated on political as well as economic grounds—its purposes go well beyond improving the nutritional status of people living in food-deficit areas. Economic analysis can be used more directly to evaluate output price supports and fertilizer subsidies.

Scherer (1985) provides a description and analysis of Nepal's foodgrain distribution policy from a management perspective. He recommends emphasizing local production rather than distribution investments; replacing subsidized distribution with intervention at cost price; procuring foodgrain at Tarai prices plus full transport costs, thus stimulating local production efforts; providing budget funds for disaster and relief operations; and providing food allowances, not entitlements, to HMG officials. These recommendations would improve the economic efficiency and equity of NFC operations. Increasing food production in deficit areas is cheaper than distributing food to those areas, particularly in remote mountain regions where air transport is used for foodgrain distribution. Buying local grain when the market price is less than the Tarai price plus transport costs, and selling it when the market price exceeds this import cost, would rationalize the NFC's finances and provide an incentive for local production. Including the NFC in the HMG budget would also help rationalize the NFC's financial situation, eliminate the need for borrowing, and provide a forum for making decisions about the NFC's disaster and relief operations. Providing rupees rather than rice to government officials should make NFC stocks available to poor people during food shortages, and help make explicit the actual cost of the NFC's distribution program.

Scope for Price Policies

The scope for using output price supports and fertilizer subsidies to influence food production in Nepal is limited as a result of the long, open border with India and the relative sizes of these markets. (Indian states

FIGURE 7. Foodgrain and fertilizer demand and supply

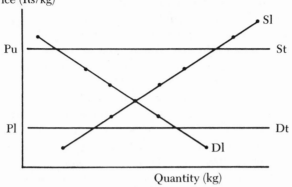

Fertilizer/foodgrain
  price (Rs/kg)

Quantity (kg)

Pu = Indian price plus transport/transaction costs; import price
Pl = Indian price minus transport/transaction costs; export price
Sl = Local supply (Nepal only); St = Total supply (Nepal plus India)
Dl = Local demand (Nepal only); Dt = Total demand (Nepal plus India)

bordering Nepal—West Bengal, Bihar, and Uttar Pradesh—produced over 46 million mt of cereal in 1984–85, whereas Nepal produced 4.2 million mt. In these states 2.4 million nutrient-mt of fertilizers were sold in 1985–86, compared to less than 0.05 million nutrient-mt in Nepal (FAI, 1986; Ministry of Finance, 1987b). Nepal can buy from or sell to India without affecting Indian prices.) These factors usually insure that the Nepalese price of any commodity is equal to the Indian border price plus or minus transportation and transaction costs, including taxes and trade regulations and bribes to border customs and inspection officials. As a result, Nepalese prices can be controlled with price policy instruments only within upper and lower bounds defined by transport and transaction costs.

Above price *Pu* (see fig. 7), Nepalese farmers are willing to supply foodgrain, but Indian farmers will supply more than enough for Nepal at price *Pu*, making the total supply curve *St* elastic. Below price *Pl*, total demand curve *Dt* becomes elastic because Indian consumers will buy all that Nepalese farmers can produce at price *Pl*. Similarly, above price *Pu*, fertilizer supply is elastic because villagers can bring as much as they want across the Indian border at price *Pu*. Below price *Pl*, demand is elastic because Indian farmers and traders will buy all of Nepal's fertilizer. This discussion of the relationship between the national Nepalese and Indian markets also applies to the relationship between mountain/hill/Kathmandu and Tarai regional markets—transport and transactions costs are the underlying feature, not national boundaries.

Prices Pu and Pl are not the same in all regions. Price Pu is highest in the hills and mountains, lowest in the Tarai, and in between in Kathmandu, whereas the opposite holds for Pl. Transport and transactions costs may not be symmetrical for imports and exports: anecdotal evidence indicates that the informal costs of transporting goods north across the border from India to Nepal are higher than costs in the other direction.

There are thus upper (Pu) and lower (Pl) bounds on Nepal's foodgrain and fertilizer prices. Below Pl demand from India swamps the market, and above Pu supply from India swamps the market. Only for prices between Pl and Pu, where goods are untraded and will not move north or south across the border, can Nepalese price policy be effective. The larger the range between Pl and Pu, the greater the scope for price policy. This price range varies by commodity and region. It is usually greater for cash crops than for food crops—sugarcane is bulky, and Indian tobacco and cotton markets are some distance from the border. It is virtually zero for the Tarai, moderate for Kathmandu, higher for the hills, and highest for the mountains. Tarai prices are often affected more by Indian prices than by Nepalese production.

Any attempt to use price policy instruments to move Nepalese commodity prices outside the range defined by Pl and Pu will lead to income transfers from the policy-implementing agencies to the individuals who receive the commodities. Individuals who receive subsidized commodities such as fertilizer can sell them at the Indian price and capture the difference as income. Supports for Nepalese crop prices will transfer income to individuals who buy at Indian prices and sell to the intervention agency. Even if beneficiaries of government policy do not actually buy or resell goods at Indian prices, their real incomes will increase.

This analysis applies to all traded commodities. The effect of the open border and different price policies in India and Nepal are best illustrated by the eastern Tarai, where many consumer goods are available primarily to satisfy Indian demand, and where a "carrier" system operates to transport goods both ways across the border, often at night.

One way to overcome the constraints arising from the long, open border is to concentrate agricultural policy efforts on nontradable goods. If investments are made that cannot be shifted from Nepal to India, the open border is not a problem. For example, investments in irrigation and transportation are nontradable. Unfortunately, the history of public sector irrigation efforts in the Tarai is not impressive, and little public sector work has been done to improve irrigation capacity in the hills. While all-weather roads are probably not economical for much of Nepal's rugged terrain, investments in suspension bridges, improved trails, and ropeways could have high payoffs.

Improving access to in-kind credit for fertilizer purchases is another way to concentrate on nontradable goods. While ultimately all credit is fungible, in-kind credit for fertilizer purchases by mountain and hill farmers is relatively difficult to trade. However, timely availability is the main constraint to fertilizer use, not credit.

The transferability of research is also limited, especially for Nepal's diverse variety of microclimatic regions. Technology appropriate for the Indian plains can be readily adopted to Tarai conditions, but this is not so for the hills and mountains, and little work has been done to improve the yields of "minor" rain-fed upland food crops—millet, barley, and potatoes. Investments in research for rain-fed hill and mountain crops could have high returns. However, as Yadav (1986) makes clear, funds would not entirely solve the problem of low productivity of existing research. Conceptual and institutional changes, which take time and effort, are also needed to improve the research environment.

Output Price Supports

The local effects of output price supports depend on the slope of the supply curve and on the possibilities for importing foodgrain. The more elastic the supply curve, the more impact price supports will have on local production. The lower the cost of importing foodgrain, the more impact price supports will have on local food supply through increased imports. In the mountains and hills, supply curves are relatively inelastic and import transport costs are high. In Kathmandu, supply is more elastic, and import costs are lower. Supply is most elastic in the Tarai, and import costs there are almost zero. Thus from a supply-side perspective, output price supports should be most effective in increasing local food production and supplies in the Tarai.

An examination of the demand side supports this conclusion. Households with more than 0.5 hectares of land usually produce something for market sale, and their production decisions are affected by output prices. Households with less than 0.5 hectares of land (over half the population) usually produce exclusively for home consumption, selling only enough output to purchase essential needs or to pay debts. Landless people include cash-income earners (civil servants and business people), and in-kind income earners (agricultural laborers). Subsistence farmers live in the mountains and hills; market-oriented farmers live in Kathmandu and in the Tarai; cash-income earners live in Kathmandu (and a few other towns); and in-kind income earners live mostly in the Tarai. Supply and demand relationships for these regions appear in figures 8a, b, and c.

In the mountains and hills, nearly all food is consumed by producing households themselves, and still there are foodgrain deficits. Many villagers migrate to India on a seasonal basis to augment their incomes, returning with cash or food, and to meet part of their consumption needs

FIGURE 8a. Foodgrain supply and demand—mountains and hills

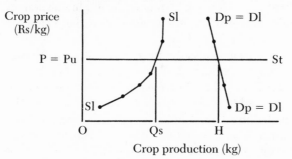

Crop production (kg)

FIGURE 8b. Foodgrain supply and demand—Kathmandu Valley

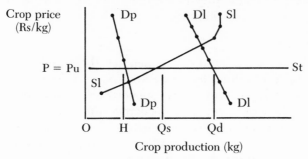

Crop production (kg)

FIGURE 8c. Foodgrain supply and demand—Tarai

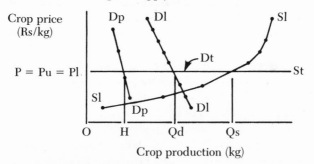

Crop production (kg)

Sl = Local supply
St = Total (local + Tarai/Indian) supply
Dp = Producer demand
Dl = Local (producer + other) demand
Dt = Total (Nepal + Indian) demand
Pu = Import price
Pl = Export price
OQs = Local foodgrain production
OH = Household foodgrain consumption by producers
QsH = Foodgrain deficit (met by imports or seasonal migration) (mountains and hills)
HQs = Foodgrain sold by producers (marketed surplus) (Kathmandu Valley and Tarai)
QsQd = Foodgrain deficit (Kathmandu Valley)
QdQs = Foodgrain surplus (Tarai)
At quantities greater than Qs, the total demand (Dt) and supply (St) curves coincide if Pu = Pl (Tarai).

from Indian food production. In Kathmandu, demand for home consumption by foodgrain producers is augmented by demand from cash-income earners, and as a result Kathmandu has a net food deficit. (Demand is like that in Kathmandu in a few other small urban areas.) In the Tarai, demand for home consumption by foodgrain producers (including demand by agricultural laborers) is less than the local supply. Surplus production is used to meet demand from the mountains and hills, Kathmandu, and India.

From a food security and national food balance viewpoint, Nepal would like to have the Tarai surplus ($QdQs$ in fig. 8c) exceed the total deficit in the mountains, hills, and Kathmandu (QsH in fig. 8a and $QsQd$ in fig. 8b). However, even if the Tarai surplus exceeds the sum of these deficits, there must be an effective mechanism for procuring surplus Tarai production, transporting it to deficit areas, and distributing it to poor people living there. Without such a mechanism, surplus production will be sold to Indian traders and consumers.

A crop price increase will increase production in the hills and mountains only marginally. There will be some production response in Kathmandu (by using more fertilizer and labor) and more response in the Tarai (by using more of all inputs, including land).

Even if there was a greater production response to prices in the hills, there are practical obstacles to implementing an output price support policy there. Hill markets are fragmented, with high transport costs from one small valley to another, so the government might have to open hundreds of shops to have a significant impact on food prices.[9]

Nepalese farmers—particularly Tarai farmers—do respond to market prices in making agricultural production decisions. This was dramatically illustrated in 1983–84, when wheat production was over 670,000 mt as a result of good weather in 1983–84 and good prices in 1982–83, a poor harvest year. Prices fell as low as Rs 1.65 per kg, nearly 50 percent below prices of the preceding year, primarily as a result of the good harvest in India, and because some food aid for the 1982–83 drought arrived late. Farmers complained loudly to the HMG, but the government did not respond, and farmers were forced to absorb losses. In 1984–85 wheat production declined by over 130,000 mt, mostly as a result of reduced area devoted to wheat cultivation in the Tarai. The AIC even had to auction unsold improved wheat seed because farmers' demand was so low. On the other hand, oilseed area and production increased in 1984–85, partly because oilseed prices had been high in 1983–84. Farmers respond to price movements, but these movements are determined by Indian markets: the HMG cannot influence agricultural prices in the Tarai.

Another approach to analyzing output support prices is to examine

9. Price policies are most effective when domestic markets are integrated. See Timmer (1986), pp. 39–41.

buyers and sellers in local foodgrain markets. In the mountains and hills, buyers and sellers are the same people—villagers producing grain and eating it. (Many villagers also buy food in Tarai or Indian markets on a seasonal basis.) In Kathmandu, buyers include cash-income earners who are not also food sellers. In the Tarai, buyers include traders (who sell food in Kathmandu or India) who do not produce food for sale.

When buyers and sellers of foodgrains are the same people, a price support can directly increase production only if a new buyer, such as the government, enters the market to purchase the price-supported grain and producers can buy another grain at a lower price. This is not the situation in Nepal's mountains and hills, so a price support cannot be expected to increase grain production there.[10] However, food price increases in Tarai and Indian markets may induce villagers to devote more resources to local food production as the cost of importing food rises. (While the NFC has recently made token attempts to procure foodgrain from hill producers, it is not practical both to support production and to subsidize consumption for the same foodgrain for the same villagers.)

On the other hand, when foodgrain buyers and sellers are different people—as in the Kathmandu Valley and the Tarai—a price support can increase production. As there is more scope for increasing production by increasing crop intensities and use of fertilizer in the Tarai, a price support would probably have more impact there than in Kathmandu.

However, this conclusion—supporting Tarai output prices—cannot be implemented for the reasons given above: price supports are constrained to operate within the band defined by transport and transactions costs from the Indian border, and are impossible to implement in the Tarai.

Thus output price supports are theoretically most effective precisely where they cannot practically be implemented. Reducing the cost of production by subsidizing fertilizer prices may theoretically offer more scope for encouraging increased production, but this policy also faces severe practical constraints, particularly in the Tarai.

Fertilizer Subsidies

The main objective of a fertilizer subsidy is to increase crop production by reducing the cost of an important input. A fertilizer subsidy is efficient if the real cost of the additional fertilizer used is less than the value of the increased output.

Total fertilizer sales are now over 100,000 mt per year, with urea and complex each accounting for about half the total. Current official urea and complex prices are both Rs 3.99 per kg, but actual costs are Rs 5.13 and Rs

---

10. On the other hand, most farmers believe that the distribution of subsidized foodgrain does not adversely affect incentives to increase production. See DFAMS (1984a), pp. 4, 37–40.

6.83. Thus the subsidy per kg is about one-third of actual cost, and total subsidy costs are nearly Rs 200 million per year—over U.S. $9 million at the official exchange rate. Although it is not in the national budget, this subsidy is more than one-fifth of the expenditure devoted to agriculture. Before the price increase in May 1986, the subsidy was estimated to cost Rs 330 million per year (*Rising Nepal*, 1986).

A subsidy is more effective the more elastic the demand for fertilizer, because a small subsidy will lead to a significant increase in fertilizer use and crop output. However, the price elasticity of demand for fertilizer in Nepal is probably low as a result of the currently low use rate and the limited supplies available at the official price.

Estimating price elasticity of demand from secondary data is not easy. Fertilizer prices and official import quantities are fixed by the government, so there is little variation in prices, and quantities sold probably lie below the true demand curve at the official price. Effects of year-to-year price changes on sales are difficult to distinguish from effects of increased knowledge about and experience with fertilizer use.

An informal survey of 264 farmers using fertilizer on the 1983–84 wheat crop indicated that fertilizer demand is relatively inelastic (table 15). Demand is more elastic in Kathmandu than in the Tarai and the hills, but the differences are not significant. Farmers with small farms are more responsive to price changes than those with larger farms (Wallace, 1986).

Farmers surveyed reported a variety of problems with obtaining and using fertilizer, but one stood out: fertilizer is not available on time.[11] Over a third of the farmers were unable to get fertilizer when they needed it. One-tenth reported that lack of water was a problem, and one-tenth reported both availability and water problems. One-fourth had no difficulties obtaining or using fertilizer. The price of fertilizer is not a constraint to increased use: fewer than one-sixteenth of the farmers interviewed said that cost was a problem. Availability is clearly a much greater problem than cost. Farmers would be willing to pay more for fertilizer if it were available on time. Demand is probably less elastic than the estimates shown in table 15.

Variations in fertilizer use can be partly explained by access to information about fertilizer use, by fertilizer/crop price ratios, by control of water, and by adoption of high-yielding varieties.

Access to Information about Fertilizer Use. Kathmandu farmers have more experience with fertilizer than Tarai and hill farmers. Kathmandu residents are more educated and have greater access to information than

11. This finding is confirmed by various reports of the Integrated Cereals Project (ICP). A problem for small farmers is lack of availability of small quantities of fertilizer: many dealers are unwilling to open bags and sell less than 50 kg at once.

TABLE 15. Price elasticity of fertilizer demand

| | Tarai | | | | Hills | Kathmandu Valley | | |
	Morang	Dhankuta	Chitwan	Rupandehi	Sallyan	Bhaktapur	Lalitpur	Kathmandu
Urea N	31	31	34	31	23	31	22	37
UPRE	-1.39	-1.97	-0.64	-1.30	-1.47	-2.03	-1.58	-1.37
	(1.57)	(2.67)	(1.66)	(1.94)	(1.28)	(1.91)	(1.63)	(1.48)
UPREW	-0.40	-1.01	-0.39	-0.52	-1.17	-1.72	-1.13	-1.34
UPREO	12	14	26	17	7	12	10	18
UPRQO	1	2	0	2	0	0	0	0
Complex N	27	30	0	1	22	11	6	2
CPRE	-0.54	-0.70	—	0.00	-0.90	-0.35	-0.88	-0.85
	(0.59)	(1.03)	—	(0.00)	(0.75)	(0.43)	(1.07)	(0.10)
CPREW	-0.25	-0.59	—	0.00	-0.79	-0.57	-0.86	-1.47
CPREO	10	16	—	1	4	6	3	0
CPRQO	1	2	—	0	0	0	1	0

SOURCE: Author's survey.
Urea N, Complex N = Number of farmers using urea or complex
UPRE, CPRE = Price rise elasticity of demand for urea (unweighted average across farmers)
UPREW, CPREW = Weighted price rise elasticity of demand for urea (weighted by fertilizer quantities)
UPREO, CPREO = Number of farmers for whom UPRE or CPRE = 0—whose fertilizer use will not change if the price rises
UPRQO, CPRQO = Number of farmers who will not buy any urea or complex if the price rises
Data means presented. Standard deviations of data in parentheses.

people living elsewhere in Nepal. Most government and foreign aid project offices are in Kathmandu, and Kathmandu is the main channel for
obtaining information. As the availability and use of new technology follow
information, fertilizer use has spread fastest in Kathmandu.

A price increase may thus not decrease fertilizer use at all—it may only
slow the rate of growth. Tarai and hill farmers are increasing fertilizer use
faster than Kathmandu farmers, and they may be simply catching up on
the learning curve. This rate of growth will slow more in the Kathmandu
Valley than in the Tarai and the hills, though fertilizer use is likely to
continue to increase in all areas.

Fertilizer/Crop Price Ratios. Kathmandu farmers receive higher prices
for their crops than Tarai farmers, while hill farmers often do not produce
enough to sell. Also, despite the uniform national fertilizer price, hill
farmers face higher fertilizer prices—in terms of greater transport and
waiting costs, and higher costs of obtaining credit from institutional or
informal sources—than other farmers.

Kathmandu farmers benefit more from fertilizer use than Tarai farmers
because crop prices are higher, and they benefit more than hill farmers
because fertilizer prices are lower. Kathmandu farmers thus face lower
fertilizer/crop price ratios than hill and Tarai farmers, they benefit more
from fertilizer use, and as a result, they use more fertilizer.

The effect of an increase in the national fertilizer price can be described
by an example. To illustrate, let the price elasticity of fertilizer demand be
−0.5 for all of Nepal. If the national price is doubled, Kathmandu farmers
will cut use by half, because their fertilizer/crop price ratio has been
doubled. Tarai farmers will reduce use by less than half unless the Indian
price is also doubled, because they can buy fertilizer from India by paying
the small extra transport cost, so doubling the Nepal price will not double
their fertilizer/crop price ratio. With a limited supply in Nepal, the Indian
price determines fertilizer use at the margin for Tarai farmers, so Nepalese
price changes will not influence Tarai fertilizer use. Hill farmers will
reduce use by less than half because their price is the sum of the national
price plus transport costs, and thus their fertilizer/crop price ratio is less
than doubled when the national price is doubled.

Moreover, a rise in the national fertilizer price will increase the availability of fertilizer, because farmers will have an added incentive to bring
fertilizer across the border from India. The AIC would also be able to
supply a much greater amount of fertilizer for the same budget if the
selling price of fertilizer were raised.

While lack of availability of fertilizer is conceptually the same as a high
price (the cost of obtaining fertilizer elsewhere plus transport costs), availability promotes learning about fertilizer both for farmers who do and

those who do not use it. There are thus benefits from availability that are not reflected in the direct costs and benefits of fertilizer use. As more is learned about fertilizer, more should be used where the value of increased output is greater than the additional cost. Availability and profitable use increase information and learning, which in turn increase demand and use, so lack of access is different than access at a high price. Lack of availability in the mountains and hills reinforces the conclusions of this analysis.

Control of Water. Hill and mountain farmers have less control over water than farmers in Kathmandu and the Tarai. Increases in crop production resulting from fertilizer use are more variable where water is less certain, so risk-averse hill and mountain farmers will purchase and use less fertilizer than their Kathmandu and Tarai counterparts.

Adoption of High-Yielding Varieties. Tarai and Kathmandu farmers have adopted high-yielding varieties (HYVs) of rice and wheat more than hill and mountain farmers. This is partly the result of information about and availability of HYVs, but the key factors are probably geography and climate: mountain and hill farmers grow less rice and wheat—and more maize, millet, and barley—than Kathmandu and Tarai farmers. There are HYVs for rice and wheat, but not for millet and barley.

The effects of access to information, fertilizer/crop price ratios, and control of water all lead to higher fertilizer consumption and greater response to fertilizer price changes (at current consumption levels) in Kathmandu than in the Tarai and the hills. While it is difficult to determine the relative importance of these effects, all contribute to significant differences in fertilizer use.

Farmers in the Tarai, hills, and Kathmandu will respond differently to a fertilizer price increase. Tarai farmers—who use little fertilizer, have some experience and easy access to information about fertilizer, and can buy fertilizer in India—are unlikely to decrease use if the price increases. Hill farmers—who use little fertilizer, have limited experience, lack ready access to information, and incur transport costs on top of the official price—will decrease use if the price is increased, particularly if more fertilizer is available as a result of the price rise. Kathmandu farmers—who use much fertilizer, and have both experience and access to information—will respond more like profit-maximizers and may decrease use if the price is raised.

An increase in the fertilizer price will least affect the Tarai, where the most productive cropland is; it will have some effect in the hills, where the poorest people live; and it will have most effect in Kathmandu, where the most political power is.

Economic Calculations. At the farm level, the economics of fertilizer use are relatively simple. Fertilizer now costs Rs 4.00 per kg. The most commonly used fertilizers, urea and complex, have 46 and 40 percent nutrient content, respectively. Yield-response ratios for improved varieties of paddy and wheat probably lie between 10 and 15. The value of these crops is Rs 2.00 or more per kilogram. Thus a farmer who spends Rs 4.00 on 1 kg of fertilizer can expect a return of at least $(.40) \times (10) \times (Rs\ 2) = Rs\ 8.00$, and often a return of as much as $(.46) \times (15) \times (Rs\ 3) = Rs\ 20.70$, with an average return of about Rs 14.00, a 3.5:1 benefit-cost ratio.[12] (However, this is not a risk-free investment—weather can change the yield-response ratio for better or worse, and crop values cannot be known with certainty before harvest. This calculation also omits transport costs, an important consideration in the hills where fertilizer is often sold only in district centers.)

This calculation, which has been verified many times on farmers' fields, indicates that even if the fertilizer price subsidy was eliminated and fertilizer sold for as much as Rs 7.00 per kilogram, farmers would still double their money on fertilizer investments. The subsidy is not needed to make fertilizer use profitable.[13] Subsidizing fertilizer may even encourage unwise use, because farmers may use it when the return is more than the subsidized price but less than real cost.

If the subsidy were eliminated, revenues and costs would be equal, and there would be a total annual savings of nearly Rs 200 million. This money could be used to ensure that sufficient fertilizer is available on time where farmers need it or to make other improvements in agriculture, such as supporting improved research or improving irrigation.

The economic gains of eliminating the fertilizer subsidy depend on the price elasticity of demand for fertilizer, the yield-response ratio, and crop values. The conceptual and empirical analyses presented here indicate that price elasticity is probably low, so eliminating the subsidy will not lead to a substantial reduction in fertilizer use. Fertilizer yield-response ratios and crop values are high enough to make it profitable for farmers to use fertilizer even if the subsidy is eliminated, so the overall gains of eliminating this subsidy should be significant.

Open Border. Another practical reason for eliminating the fertilizer subsidy is the open border. The possibility of moving agricultural com-

---

12. An almost identical calculation is given in Mathema, Van Der Veer, and Anjan (1981). See ARSAP (1977) and FADINAP (1984) for similar calculations. For a review of fertilizer response studies, see Kupferschmid (1983).

13. For similar observations and recommendations made during the past twenty years, see MEP/DOA (1966), Pant (1984), APROSC (1985).

modities both ways across the Indian border in response to price differences has already been discussed. An examination of relative prices in Nepal and India gives an indication of how frequently moving fertilizer one way or the other has been profitable (table 16). For urea, Nepalese prices have sometimes been higher and sometimes lower than in India. For complex, prices have usually been higher in India.

The amount of fertilizer that can move south to India when prices are higher there is strikingly illustrated by comparing AIC fertilizer-sales data and fertilizer-use data from the Central Bureau of Statistics (CBS) for 1981. The AIC records indicate that 54,000 mt of fertilizer were sold, but CBS records show that less than 15,000 mt of fertilizer were used on the five crops that dominate fertilizer use (table 17).

An examination of district-level data from CBS reveals that in all areas of the country that reported, use was less than recorded sales. The largest discrepancies are for the Kathmandu Valley, which indicates that considerable fertilizer is purchased there for use elsewhere.

There are several possible explanations for this substantial discrepancy between fertilizer sales and use: the CBS sample of households may have been unrepresentative; CBS respondents may have underestimated fertilizer use; farmers may purchase fertilizer and store it for later use; fertilizer may be used on crops not included in the CBS statistics; or fertilizer may have been purchased in Nepal and used in India.

The first three possible explanations are unlikely. First, CBS used two-stage stratified random sampling to select 83,000 households from a population of 2.6 million households, so substantial sampling bias in the results is extremely unlikely. Second, there is no reason for respondents to consistently underestimate fertilizer use by nearly three-fourths; there is no benefit for doing so, and fertilizer is a purchased input—for cash or credit—so farmers should have good memories of fertilizer use. Even if considerable memory bias is assumed, substantial differences remain between the CBS and AIC data.

Third, farmers are unlikely to buy more fertilizer than they need for the current crop season. Purchasing fertilizer diverts either cash or credit from other current consumption needs; and stored fertilizer can easily lose its nutrient value, particularly if it becomes wet.

Fertilizer is used on other crops besides paddy, maize, wheat, sugarcane, and potatoes. However, these five crops cover over 85 percent of Nepal's cropped area, and fertilizer use on vegetables, fruits, and cash crops such as jute and tobacco is unlikely to add substantially to the CBS statistics. The AIC estimates that over 75 percent of all fertilizer sold is used on paddy, wheat, and maize (AIC, undated).

This leaves the fifth explanation: fertilizer was purchased in Nepal and used in India. In the two years partially covered by the CBS survey, half

TABLE 16.   Nepal-India urea and complex fertilizer price ratios

Year	Exchange IC/NC	NC urea price	IC urea price	Urea* ratio	NC comp price	IC comp price	Comp* ratio
1967–68	1.35	1,313	840	1.16	913	n.a.	n.a.
1968–69	1.35	1,400	860	1.21	913	n.a.	n.a.
1969–70	1.35	1,400	943	1.10	1,064	n.a.	n.a.
1970–71	1.35	1,342	943	1.05	1,057	938	0.83
1971–72	1.35	1,535	923	1.23	1,557	1,035	1.11
1972–73	1.39	1,535	997	1.11	1,557	1,187	0.94
1973–74	1.39	2,193	1,842	0.86	2,214	1,400	1.14
1974–75	1.39	2,193	1,888	0.84	2,214	2,283	0.70
1975–76	1.39	2,440	1,750	1.00	2,270	2,571	0.64
1976–77	1.39	2,440	1,600	1.10	2,270	2,013	0.81
1977–78	1.39	2,440	1,550	1.13	2,270	n.a.	n.a.
1978–79	1.45	2,440	1,450	1.16	2,270	n.a.	n.a.
1979–80	1.45	2,440	1,908	0.88	2,270	1,500	1.04
1980–81	1.45	3,100	2,263	0.94	2,800	1,958	0.99
1981–82	1.45	3,100	2,350	0.91	2,800	2,313	0.83
1982–83	1.45	3,500	2,350	1.03	3,250	2,400	0.93
1983–84	1.45	3,500	2,350	1.03	3,250	2,250	1.00
1984–85	1.45	3,500	2,183	1.11	3,250	2,200	1.02
1985–86	1.70	3,500	2,250	0.92	3,250	2,500	0.76
1986–87	1.68	3,990	2,250	1.06	3,990	2,500	0.95

SOURCE: AIC (1983 and unpublished data) for Nepal prices; Fertilizer Association of India for Indian prices. Annual averages of Indian prices used for comparison.

*Nominal price ratio (Nepal price/Indian price) must be divided by exchange rate (IC/NC) to obtain real price ratio. A ratio greater than 1.0 means fertilizer is more expensive in Nepal than in India.

TABLE 17.   Fertilizer use 1981–82 (kg)

Crop	Holdings		Chemical fertilizer use		
	Number	Area (hectares)	Number	Area (hectares)	Quantity
Paddy	1,021,730	1,394,123	163,604	106,696	6,340,482
Maize	838,596	522,469	43,154	14,330	1,379,428
Wheat	649,510	389,172	174,445	64,781	5,377,063
Sugarcane	60,157	32,512	8,585	3,899	945,975
Potato	193,185	67,403	14,787	2,211	196,658
Total	2,763,178	2,405,679	404,575	191,917	14,239,606

NOTE: Fertilizer sales statistics (tables 8a,b,c) are compiled by the Agricultural Inputs Corporation (AIC) for Nepal's fiscal year (July 16 to July 15), while fertilizer-use statistics were recorded by the Central Bureau of Statistics (CBS) for the reference period of the National Sample Census of Agriculture 1981–82 (January 14, 1981, to January 13, 1982). Fertilizer use should be compared to sales for 1980–81 (winter crops) and 1981–82 (summer crops). Both sets of statistics report gross fertilizer weight, not net nutrient content.

SOURCE: CBS, *National Sample Census of Agriculture 1981–82.*

the fertilizer sold in Nepal was sold in the Tarai and half elsewhere (table 8c). However, even if fertilizer used on crops not included in the CBS survey and nonsampling errors triple total fertilizer use, half the fertilizer sold in the Tarai would have to have been used in India to reconcile the AIC and CBS statistics.

The reason for moving fertilizer from Nepal to India is evident from fertilizer prices (table 16). In early 1981 the Indian urea price was IC Rs 2,000 = NC Rs 2,900/mt, while the price in Nepal was NC Rs 3,100. In July the Indian urea price was raised to IC Rs 2,350 = NC Rs 3,408/mt, while the price in Nepal remained at NC Rs 3,100 until April 18, 1983. Similarly, in early 1981, the Indian complex price was IC Rs 2,050 = NC Rs 2,973, while the price in Nepal was NC Rs 2,800. In July the Indian price increased to IC Rs 2,400 = NC Rs 3,380, while the Nepalese price remained at NC Rs 2,800. Thus for almost two years nearly 10 percent profit could be made simply by moving urea across the border, and over 20 percent could be made on complex. This situation changed in April 1983 when fertilizer prices in Nepal were raised.

Nepal faced the same problem in late 1985. As a result of the devaluation of the Nepalese rupee in November 1985 from IC Rs 100 = NC Rs 145 to IC Rs 100 = NC Rs 170, the Indian urea price (IC Rs 2,250) increased from NC Rs 3,263 to NC Rs 3,825, while the price in Nepal was NC Rs 3,500. The Indian complex price also increased from NC Rs 3,625 to NC Rs 4,250, while the price in Nepal was NC Rs 3,250. This situation was remedied in May 1986 when both urea and complex prices in Nepal were raised to NC Rs 4,200 (reduced in July 1986 to Rs 3,990). Meanwhile, fertilizer dealers and traders reaped profits by buying in Nepal and selling in India. The policy implication is clear: fertilizer cannot be subsidized below the price of alternate (Indian) supplies. [14]

Output Price Support versus Fertilizer Subsidy

The above analysis indicates that output price support policies are likely to have little effect in the mountains and hills, simply because most farmers produce only enough for home consumption. Such policies may have an effect in the Kathmandu Valley, where there is still some scope for increasing production, but the likely outcome would be to encourage Tarai farmers to sell more of their output in Kathmandu. The greatest effect would be in the Tarai, where the potential for increasing production is the greatest. The problem with an output price support in the Tarai is that it is not possible to raise the price above the Indian market price without pulling grain north across the border.

Although a fertilizer price subsidy is not particularly effective in promoting crop production, it might be used on equity grounds to benefit mountain and hill farmers as well as those in Kathmandu and the Tarai. However, the effective subsidy for Nepalese farmers, measured against the opportunity cost of obtaining fertilizer from India, can never exceed inter-

14. Some Indian farmers prefer imported fertilizer from Nepal in synthetic bags instead of Indian-made fertilizer in jute bags, although chemically the two should be equivalent. As a result, Indian farmers may be willing to pay more than the official price for fertilizer from Nepal.

nal transport costs in Nepal. The political power of Kathmandu residents and Tarai farmers, combined with financial limits on the HMG's ability to subsidize internal transport costs, will insure that few benefits of the subsidy are obtained by hill and mountain farmers. This analysis is summarized as follows:

Analysis of price support and fertilizer subsidy by region

Region	Transport costs	Fertilizer subsidy	Price support
Mountains	highest	subsidy possible; lowest output response; equity objective	steepest supply curve; support possible but ineffective
Hills	high	subsidy possible; low output response; equity objective	steep supply curve; support possible but ineffective
Kathmandu	moderate	small subsidy possible; moderate output response; political objective	steep supply curve; small support possible, but little effect
Tarai	nearly zero	subsidy not possible below Indian price	support not possible above Indian price

Conclusion

Pricing Strategies: Intentions and Effects

Food Subsidies for Consumers. The HMG's policy objective in food-grain distribution is to benefit consumers living in deficit areas, but actual beneficiaries are Kathmandu residents, the army, and government officials. Kathmandu has had higher food distribution targets than the rest of the hills combined, and these targets have usually been exceeded. Political reasons for keeping Kathmandu prices low continue to weigh heavily in decision makers' calculations, so it is likely that the future rhetoric of food distribution will emphasize poor villagers in remote areas, and the reality will benefit politically favored groups.

High domestic transport costs make it difficult to move food to villagers living in remote areas. Until Nepal's transportation network is improved, financial constraints will complement political considerations to insure that the needs of poor rural villagers remain secondary to the demands of politically powerful urban residents.

Output Price Supports. Output price supports are supposed to benefit producers, but they have never been implemented—at most a support price has been used to obtain foodgrain for NFC distribution through levies on exporters and millers. Support prices have never provided an incentive for Nepalese farmers to increase production. The open border with India makes it impossible for Nepal to support grain prices above Indian prices to increase production in Nepal.

Politicians continue to call for price supports to provide incentives and adequate remuneration to farmers. However, financial constraints—whether on or off the official budget—complement geographical reality, and the government is unlikely to announce any support price policy more ambitious than the past token efforts.

Fertilizer Price Subsidies. Fertilizer subsidies are supposed to increase crop output by lowering production cost and benefit farmers in remote parts of the country. Primary beneficiaries have been Kathmandu farmers who received the most fertilizer and traders who profited when Indian prices have been higher. Lack of availability is a greater constraint to increased use than high prices. While crop production has increased since fertilizer was introduced in Nepal twenty years ago, the fertilizer subsidy has not been an important cause of this increase.

The open border makes it impossible for Nepal to reduce fertilizer prices below Indian prices to stimulate fertilizer use in Nepal. Financial constraints on fertilizer subsidies have been minimal, but donor agencies are pressing for market-oriented price policies.

Key Pricing Issues

Nepal's open border with India and the relative size of the two markets affect foodgrain and fertilizer price policies. No matter which way the Nepalese flea turns, it will travel in the Indian elephant's direction. The positive side of this analogy is that the flea can travel much faster on the elephant's back than it can hopping along by itself. While Nepal cannot maintain independent price policies, it can take advantage of Indian policies to achieve its own objectives.

Thus, to the extent that Indian policies shield Indian producers and consumers from the adverse impacts of international price changes (especially with respect to fertilizer prices), Nepal gains. On the other hand, when these policies prevent Nepal from taking advantage of favorable international (or Indian) price movements, Nepal loses.

Indian minimum support and procurement prices are the most important factors determining support prices fixed in Nepal. As these prices have never decreased from one year to the next, it is probably safe for Nepal to announce last year's Indian procurement price as a way of providing a psychological guarantee to Nepalese farmers.

Nepal should recognize that domestic foodgrain and fertilizer market activities are determined by Indian prices, and that price policies are possible only within the range defined by Indian prices, plus or minus transport costs. Any attempt to maintain prices outside this range will have adverse effects. When prices are low in Nepal, fertilizer and foodgrain will move south across the border, giving rise to shortages in Nepal. When prices are high in Nepal, these commodities will move north, and agencies responsible for maintaining high prices will transfer income to individuals able to sell at support prices.

Financial constraints on implementing agencies are another important pricing issue. The losses of both NFC and AIC have been kept out of the official government budget, but there is increasing pressure from major donor agencies to incorporate the budgets of these and other public enterprises into the national budget, and one effect of this may be to curtail significant expansion of these agencies' activities.

As population shifts from the hills to the Tarai, so does political power. While in 1961 two-thirds of Nepal's people lived in the hills, by 1981 nearly half were in the Tarai, and the next census is likely to show a majority in the Tarai. Complementing this population shift are communication and transportation networks, which are more developed in the Tarai than in the hills, and one result is likely to be a more vocal population with higher material and political expectations, and with direct access to India for ideas and commodities. Some implications for food pricing policy are obvious: Nepal will be forced to take more explicit account of Indian policies and the effects of the open border.

Foodgrain Policies

Food Subsidies for Consumers. The main issue with respect to food subsidies is the cost of maintaining low prices in Kathmandu. The population of Kathmandu is growing faster than that of any other food-deficit area (but slower than the Tarai), so the cost of maintaining low prices for this population will continue to increase. As overall production is increasing more slowly than population growth, it will become more difficult to procure foodgrains through levies on domestic traders, and more open market purchases will be necessary, entailing higher costs.

A related issue is the ever-growing NFC debt. Until now most of these losses have been financed by HMG-guaranteed loans from Nepalese commercial banks, so these losses have not appeared in government budget calculations. However, the consequences of this practice eventually must be faced. The NFC's outstanding debt is now nearly 8 percent of the (M1) money supply, and the effect on the banking system of the outstanding loans to all public enterprises is significant. The willingness of donor agencies to continue to provide funds to support the NFC's activities is declining, so there is likely to be external pressure to reorient its activities, perhaps by providing more disaster relief for rural villagers and less food subsidy for urban consumers.[15]

15. The 1984 Food and Agricultural Organization Food Security Review Mission recommended that the NFC enter the market as a purchaser only when private traders offer market prices below the minimum support price, and enter the Kathmandu market as a seller only

Current food subsidy policy implicitly includes both price and transport subsidies, with price subsidies being more important in Kathmandu and transport subsidies being more important in remote hill and mountain areas. If the government wanted to change its policy and target benefits more directly on poor villagers, a transport subsidy alone could be provided. Another way to help insure that needy people actually receive and consume subsidized food is to distribute only low-quality grain, rather than the selection now offered by the NFC, which includes several qualities of fine rice as well as parboiled rice.

Output Support Prices. Support prices for crops have never been implemented. The preceding analysis indicates that they would not be effective in increasing local production in any case. It is probably best for the Nepalese government either to refrain from announcing any support prices, and explicitly recognize that Indian market prices and transportation costs determine most market prices in Nepal, or simply to announce last year's Indian support price as a psychological measure.

The NFC may be able to provide benefits to farmers by opening small shops in major markets, and by offering prices slightly above market levels if prices are low. If this idea provides an alternative to whatever market power is now in the hands of traders and millers, and if it can be put into effect without pulling grain north across the border from India, it may be an easy way to benefit producers. If only a small amount of grain must be purchased from farmers to force traders to raise prices, the cost of such a plan would be low. This policy could be especially beneficial immediately following the harvest when prices are depressed.

Fertilizer Policies

Current fertilizer price policy is designed to address production efficiency and distribution equity goals. The import price subsidy provides an incentive for farmers to use more fertilizer and increase crop production. This is efficient if the real cost of the additional fertilizer used is less than the value of the increased output. The transport cost subsidy is an attempt to provide benefits to hill farmers who are relatively disadvantaged and is a recognition of the political power of Kathmandu farmers. This policy would be equitable if hill farmers actually received benefits comparable to farmers in other areas. However, people who buy fertilizer in Kathmandu are the main beneficiaries of the uniform national price policy as now implemented. Hill farmers benefit little because little fertilizer is transported to them.

---

when consumer prices rise too high. Scherer (1986) provides comprehensive suggestions for improving the overall operations of the NFC.

Any change from the current policy has efficiency and equity implications. Removing the transport cost subsidy would force hill farmers to take real transport costs into their decisions about fertilizer use. If this was combined with increased fertilizer availability, actual use might not decline. Maintaining the hill transport subsidy may have environmental benefits if it encourages intensive (and discourages extensive) cultivation. However, if the subsidy leads to increases in land under cultivation, it may entail environmental costs.

Reducing the fertilizer subsidy would save money for the AIC and HMG, and the AIC could import more fertilizer. Currently the more fertilizer the AIC sells, the more money it loses, so there is little incentive to increase imports. Lack of timely availability is a bigger problem than high price, so reducing the subsidy may not decrease fertilizer use, especially if this is accompanied by increased fertilizer availability. Chemical fertilizers are still new for most Nepalese farmers, and as more farmers learn about the economic advantages of using fertilizer even at nonsubsidized prices, demand will continue to increase.

For political reasons, it may be difficult to eliminate the transport subsidy. If this subsidy is retained, it should be recognized as an investment in transport services like building a road, and should be phased out as better transport becomes available. If this transport subsidy is maintained to benefit hill and mountain farmers, the HMG should allocate funds consistent with fertilizer demand in those areas.

The import price subsidy should gradually be reduced. The price of fertilizer in Nepal should be kept a little above the price in India. A policy that maintains the Nepal price at least 10 percent above the Indian price should discourage the informal export of fertilizer from the Tarai to the bordering states of India. A policy that allows for quick responses to changes in Indian prices is needed.

Politically, such a change in policy may be difficult to implement. The fertilizer price is a cabinet-level decision made after a recommendation by the AIC's general manager and approval by the AIC's Board of Directors and the Ministry of Agriculture. This can be a long, slow process, which has led to temporary suspension of sales in the Tarai following price changes in India. An improvement of this decision process is needed, but the suggested revision would explicitly acknowledge India's economic dominance, and this may be politically impossible.

The discussion thus far presumes that the AIC will continue to be the main source of fertilizer for Nepalese farmers. There are other possible sources: the private sector could be encouraged to import and distribute fertilizer, and the HMG's role could be substantially reduced, as in Bangladesh (IFDC, 1982). If the fertilizer subsidy were eliminated, the private sector should be eager to sell fertilizer in areas where profits can be made—in the Tarai (where transport costs are low) and Kathmandu (where demand is high). The private sector might not supply fertilizer to the hills where demand is low and transport costs are high. For equity reasons, the AIC could either continue to supply fertilizer to the hills, or pay the private sector to transport fertilizer there.

The arguments for a significantly decreased government role in fertilizer procurement and distribution are conceptually powerful, but political considerations indicate that the private sector's formal role will remain limited to dealerships for AIC-procured fertilizer. Thus it is likely that the government, through the AIC, will continue to be the main source of fertilizer supply for most of Nepal's farmers.

One useful role for the Nepalese government would be to negotiate with the Indian government to eliminate the ban on fertilizer exports from India to Nepal. Nepal could then take advantage of relative fluctuations in Indian and world fertilizer prices, importing from India when prices are lower there. Many problems associated with obtaining fertilizer from overseas sources and shipping it through Calcutta would also be eliminated if fertilizer were purchased directly from India.

A reduced fertilizer subsidy will benefit the HMG and AIC because their costs will be less. Farmers—for whom the value of increased output exceeds the cost of increased fertilizer use—will benefit if the AIC's decreased losses lead to timely fertilizer availability. Equity goals with respect to mountain and hill farmers can be achieved by maintaining the transport subsidy and by using the gains from eliminating the fertilizer subsidy for other purposes—for example, increased crop production research focusing on rain-fed areas could lead to improved technology choices for hill farmers, and improved transportation networks could both reduce the cost of fertilizer and increase access to markets.

Summing Up

Nepal has three explicit food price policies: food subsidies for consumers living in food-deficit areas; product price interventions for farmers producing rice and wheat; and input price interventions for farmers using fertilizer. None of these policies has achieved its officially stated objective. Food subsidies, officially intended for consumers living in remote areas, have primarily benefited Kathmandu residents; output support prices, formally designed to encourage increased foodgrain production, have been below market prices and thus have not provided any incentive to farmers; and subsidized fertilizer, intended to increase crop output, has been provided in such small quantities that there has been little overall impact on food production.

Moreover, these policies have been implemented more or less independently of each other. One HMG report concludes that the "NFC has still been mostly concerned in the crisis management year after year such that 'food policy' has been implemented on a piecemeal basis. As a result integration of food policy with 'price policy' and even 'agricultural policy' has lacked. Thus it has not been an instrument to the agricultural development of the country" (DFAMS, 1984a, p. 1). Coordination of policies related to subsidized food distribution, output price supports, input price subsidies, and overall foodgrain production strategy, while desirable, is likely to continue to prove difficult.

The scope for increasing the impact of any of these policies is limited. Financial constraints limit the ability of the government to move substantial quantities of food into the hills and mountains, and political considerations insure that Kathmandu Valley residents are well fed; even if financial constraints did not limit the government's ability to support output or subsidize input prices, the long, open border with India effectively prevents Nepal from implementing an independent price policy for either foodgrain or fertilizer.

In some respects "the Tarai is too open and the hills are too closed" for Nepal to implement effective price policies.[16] India's market dominates the Tarai, and transport costs dominate the hills and mountains. Thus perhaps "price" policy should focus on nontradable inputs: improving transportation and irrigation infrastructure in the hills and focusing research efforts on rain-fed upland crops could have high payoffs (see Timmer, 1986, p. 3). Improving local food productive capacity in the hills and mountains is a much better strategy than making investments in transportation and management related to food distribution.

The main issue facing the Nepalese government is thus to recognize the constraints on food price policies, and to avoid policies that cannot be implemented in the face of these constraints. Food subsidies are expensive in a country with high transport costs and cannot be maintained indefinitely even for Kathmandu residents. Output support prices and fertilizer subsidies can be maintained only within the range determined by market prices and transport costs from India. Political considerations may tempt government officials to ignore these constraints for short-term gains, but economic factors are almost certain to dominate in the long run.

16. Robert W. Herdt, Scientific Advisor, Consultative Group for International Agricultural Research (CGIAR), World Bank, provided this insight at a workshop at Stanford University in March 1986.

References

Agricultural Development Bank of Nepal (ADB/N). 1985. *Program and Budget, 1985–86.* Kathmandu.

Agriculture Inputs Corporation (AIC). 1983. *Basic Statistics of Agricultural Inputs in Nepal.* Kathmandu.

——. Undated. *AIC in Figures 1984–85*. Kathmandu.

Agricultural Projects Services Centre (APROSC). 1978. *Evaluation Study of Agricultural Inputs and Credit Services in Nepal*. Kathmandu.

——. 1982a. *Nepal: Foodgrain Marketing and Price Policy Study*. Final Report, vols. 1–3. Kathmandu.

——. 1982b. (Prakash Chandra Aryjal and Kamal Raj Paudyal). *Nepal Systems of Price Support and Procurement of Selected Agricultural Commodities*. Kathmandu.

——. 1982c. *Study on Primary Market Procurement of Food Grains by the Public Sector*. Kathmandu.

——. 1984a. *Study on Integration of Foodgrain Markets in the Tarai of Nepal and Those in Bordering States of India: Implications for Pricing Policies*. Kathmandu.

——. 1984b. *Study on Subsidized Foodgrain Distribution Programme in Nepal*. Kathmandu.

——. 1985. *Perspective Plan in Agriculture (1985–2000)*. Kathmandu.

——. 1986. *Import Substitution in Nepalese Agriculture: Nature, Structure and Impact*. Kathmandu.

Agricultural Requisites Scheme for Asia and the Pacific (ARSAP). 1977. *Marketing, Distribution and Use of Fertilizer in Nepal*. Bangkok.

Asian Development Bank (ADB). 1982. *Agricultural Sector Strategy Study*. Manila.

Central Bureau of Statistics (CBS). Undated. *National Sample Census of Agriculture 1961–62*. Kathmandu.

——. 1975. *Population Census 1971*. Kathmandu.

——. 1976. *National Sample Census of Agriculture 1971–72*. Kathmandu.

——. 1984. *Population Census 1981*. Kathmandu.

——. 1985. *National Sample Census of Agriculture 1981–82*. Kathmandu.

——. Undated. *Population Census 1961*. Kathmandu.

Department of Food and Agricultural Marketing Services (DFAMS). 1984a. *A Study on Impact of Subsidized Foodgrains Distribution on the Production of Main Agricultural Products in Nepal*. Kathmandu.

——. 1984b. *A Study on Long Term Foodgrains Supply Policy for the Food Deficit Districts of Nepal*. Vol. 1, *Far Western Development Region*. Kathmandu.

——. 1985a, 1986, 1987. *Agricultural Marketing Information Bulletin*. Special Issue. Kathmandu.

——. 1972, 1977, 1983, 1985b. *Agricultural Statistics of Nepal*. Kathmandu.

Department of Irrigation, Hydrology, and Meteorology (DIHM). 1977. *Climatological Records of Nepal*, vol. 2. Kathmandu.

Economic Analysis and Planning Division, Ministry of Food and Agriculture (EAPD/MFA). 1972. *Agricultural Marketing Conference Proceedings*, February 21–24. Kathmandu.

Fertiliser Association of India (FAI). 1986. *Fertiliser Statistics 1985–86*. New Delhi.

Fertilizer Advisory, Development and Information Network for Asia and the Pacific (FADINAP). 1984. *Marketing, Distribution and Use of Fertilizer in Nepal*. Bangkok.

Fletcher, Lehman B., and David E. Sahn. 1984. *An Assessment of Food Aid as a Development Resource in Nepal*. Report submitted to USAID/Nepal (Contract IQC–PDC–02620–I–10–3097–00).

Food and Agriculture Organization (FAO) Food Security Review Mission to Nepal.

1984. *FAO Food Security Assistance Scheme,* final report. Rome.

Hill, John M. 1982. *A Fertilizer Strategy for Nepal.* Kathmandu.

His Majesty's Government of Nepal (HMG). 1967. *The Food Problem in Nepal: Its Magnitude; Requirements for Solution.* Report of a Committee. Kathmandu.

International Fertilizer Development Center (IFDC). 1982. *Bangladesh Policy Options for the Development of the Fertilizer Sector.* Muscle Shoals.

Johl, S. S. 1981. *Marketing of Paddy in the Tarai of Nepal.* Kathmandu.

Kahlon, A. S., and D. S. Tyagi. 1983. *Agricultural Price Policy in India.* New Delhi: Allied Publishers.

Kupferschmid, Owen M. 1983. *Fertilizer Use in Nepal: Problems and Policy Responses.* Kathmandu.

Lee, C. Y. 1971. *Fertilizer-Food Exchange Programme.* Kathmandu: Food and Agriculture Organization.

———. 1972. *The Fertilizer Marketing System in Nepal.* Kathmandu: Food and Agriculture Organization Fertilizer Industry Advisory Committee.

Mathema, S. B., M. G. Van Der Veen, and G. Pradhan Anjan. 1981. "Notes on the Economics of the Use of Inorganic Fertilizer in Nepal." Paper presented at the Department of Agriculture Summer Crops Workshop, January, Rampur Agricultural Station.

Ministry of Agriculture, Government of India. 1984. *Bulletin on Food Statistics, 1982–84.* New Delhi: Directorate of Economics and Statistics.

Ministry of Economic Planning and Department of Agriculture (MEP/DOA). 1966. *The Distribution and Consumption of Fertilizer in Nepal.* Kathmandu.

Ministry of Finance. 1987a. *Budget in Nepal.*

———. 1987b. *Economic Survey 1986–87.*

Ministry of Supplies. 1986. *Comprehensive Master Plan for Improved Food Security in Nepal,* vols. 1–2. Lalitpur.

Morris, Paul D. 1984. *Nepal's Foreign Exchange Rate System.* Kathmandu: United States Agency for International Development (USAID).

Mudbhary, Purushottam K. 1983. *Impact of Rice Pricing Policy in Production, Consumption and Trade in Nepal.* Kathmandu: Agricultural Projects Services Centre.

National Planning Commission (NPC). 1978. *A Survey of Employment, Income Distribution and Consumption Patterns in Nepal.* Kathmandu.

———. 1984. *Basic Principles of the Seventh Plan (1985–1990).* Kathmandu.

———. 1986. *Preliminary Outline of Plan to Fulfill Basic Needs.* Task force report, Nepali. Kathmandu.

Nepal Rastra Bank (NRB). 1980. *Agricultural Credit Review Survey.* 5 vols. Kathmandu.

———. 1985. *Some Important Statistics in Agriculture, Nepal.* Kathmandu: Agricultural Credit Division.

———. 1986a. *Commercial Banking Statistics,* no. 20. Kathmandu.

———. 1986b. *Quarterly Economic Bulletin* 20(1, 2). Kathmandu.

Pant, Thakur N. 1984. "Fertilizer Price, Subsidy and Promotion Policies in Nepal." Paper presented at National Workshop on Fertilizer Use and Marketing in Nepal, March. Kathmandu.

Rana, Ratna S., and Tulsi R. Joshi. "Nepal's Food Grain Surplus and Deficit Regions." *National Geographic Journal of India* 14:165–175.

Rising Nepal. 1986. "Govt. Decides To Reduce Fertilizer Price By 5%." July 31. Kathmandu.

Sarma, J. S. 1984. "Principles and Procedures of Determination of Administered

Prices of Foodgrains in India." Paper presented at International Food Policy Research Institute Workshop on Food and Agricultural Price Policy, April 29–May 2. Washington, D.C.

Scherer, Alfred G. 1985. *Considerations about the Foodgrain Distribution Policy in Nepal*. Kathmandu: United Nations Development Program/Food and Agricultural Organization (UNDP/FAO).

———. 1986. *Market Intervention Programme for Controlling the Consumer Prices of Foodgrains by the Nepal Food Corporation at Accessible Consumer Centres in Nepal*. Kathmandu: UNDP/FAO.

Timmer, C. Peter. 1986. *Getting Prices Right: The Scope and Limits of Agricultural Price Policy*. Ithaca, N.Y.: Cornell University Press.

Wallace, Michael B. 1986. *Fertilizer Price Policy in Nepal*. Winrock Research and Planning Paper Series, no. 6. Kathmandu: Winrock International.

Water and Energy Commission (WEC), Ministry of Water Resources. 1986. *Land Use in Nepal: A Summary of the Land Resources Mapping Project Results (with Emphasis on Forest Land Use)*. Kathmandu.

Yadav, Ram P. 1986. "Resource Allocation, Structure and Incentives for Agricultural Research in Nepal." Revised draft. Washington, D.C.: International Food Policy Research Institute.

7. China: Food Pricing under Socialism

Terry Sicular

In China, as in other countries, food price policy is seen as an economic tool that can be used to promote national objectives. China's use of food price policy, however, has differed from that of other nations for several reasons. First, Chinese views about the desired nature of the overall economic system and the inherent superiority of socialism over capitalism have led to a different pricing context than in many other developing nations. Second, China's objectives and the priority assigned to various objectives have, in certain respects, been peculiarly its own.

Food pricing policy in China must be understood in the context of China's socialist economic system. One important feature of this system is the substantive role of government planning in resource allocation. At least until the mid-1980s, most agricultural prices were fixed administratively by the government. Food price policy, therefore, consisted primarily of adjustments in the level and relative values of state-planned prices, rather than state interventions in market price formation.

In addition, the government has had a relatively large number of policy tools at its disposal besides setting prices. Specifically, it has directly planned production, purchases from and sales to agriculture, and sales to industry and consumers in pursuit of food-related objectives. Food price policy has thus been only one of several policy instruments, and its effects must be understood in light of these other instruments.

Government planning has also applied to foreign trade. Until recently, the central government monopolized all international trade. Levels of imports and exports were determined by the central government, and trade was carried out through foreign trade corporations directly under the Ministry of Foreign Trade. The domestic economy was essentially separated from international markets, and domestic pricing divorced from international prices.

A second important feature of China's economic system has been the high degree of socialization, in the form of collective farming in agriculture and state-owned or quasi–state-owned enterprises in industry and commerce. As a consequence, the size of the private sector has been small. At times, especially in the 1950s, prices have been set so as to control the size of the private sector. The degree of socialization has influenced the economic effects of pricing: for example, collectivization in agriculture may have dampened the response of production to price signals.

Socialization of commerce and industry has created a close relationship between pricing policy, public finance, and inflation. Most commerce and industrial production has been carried out by enterprises whose profits and losses have, at least until recently, entered directly into the state budget. Pricing policy can be used to influence the profitability of industry and commerce, and thus state revenues and expenditures. Due to the close link between pricing and government finances, the government can, and has, used the relationship between output and input prices to tax agriculture implicitly. In addition, deviations of domestic from international prices enter the state budget as taxes or subsidies on imports and exports.

Because pricing is so intimately linked with the government budget, pricing policy influences the general price level through the national budget as well as directly. Pricing policies that increase government expenditures and reduce government revenues can lead to a budget deficit, and this in turn to inflation of the currency, thus affecting overall price stability. Food price policies, in fact, have probably contributed to increases in general prices and the cost of living during the past few years.

National Objectives and Food Pricing Policy

Food pricing policy in China has been greatly influenced by four interdependent national objectives: rapid economic development; distributional goals, including the distribution of wealth, provision of basic needs, and stabilization of living standards; national security; and progress toward socialist or communist social ideals.[1]

The desire for rapid economic development is certainly not unique to China, but Chinese views on the nature of growth have at times had a peculiarly Maoist flavor. From the early fifties on, China's communist regime has wanted to catch up with the developed world. In the eyes of Chinese policy-makers, industrialization was central to such growth. Growth involved structural change from a predominantly agrarian to a predominantly industrial economy. This focus led to pricing policies that have implicitly taxed agriculture so as to promote industrialization.

Ideas concerning how to achieve rapid development have shifted between two poles. Mao and certain other Chinese leaders viewed growth not as movement along an equilibrium path, but as a disequilibrium phenomenon, a process that moves in fits and starts. The emergence of

1. For examples of discussions by Chinese economists about the relationship between price policy and national objectives, see Xue (1969–70), Wang (1985b), and Commercial Prices Editorial Group (1980), pp. 115–16.

inefficiencies and bottlenecks was considered an integral part of the rapid growth process. An alternative view espoused by prominent policy makers like Chen Yun and Xue Muqiao emphasizes the importance of proportionate, balanced growth. They proposed that planners should anticipate bottlenecks, and economic policies should maintain a balance between supply and demand in various sectors.

Pricing policies varied depending on which of these two views was in ascendance. Under the Maoist view, prices were not key to the growth process, and they could diverge from values (both scarcity and labor values) for sustained periods. Those who emphasized the need for balance, however, tended to think that prices must reflect labor values and perhaps even scarcity values. Recent price policies have reflected these views.

Distributional objectives have received relatively high priority in China. Officially stated goals have fluctuated between distribution according to need and distribution according to contribution. Actual policies began in the fifties with a major redistribution of asset wealth accomplished by socialization of urban and industrial assets and redistribution of farmland. Since that time, distributional policies have reflected the objectives of providing basic needs and stabilizing real personal incomes. The widespread provision of public goods like health care and disaster assistance programs continues to promote these goals.[2]

Food supply and pricing policies have been among the tools used to promote distributional goals. Rationed supply at low, planned prices has equalized access to staple foodstuffs and other necessities in urban areas. Chinese leaders recognize the effect of agricultural pricing on farm incomes and have on occasion increased producer prices so as to raise rural incomes. Stable prices are considered essential to the stabilization of consumers' incomes, and food price policy has been used to maintain price stability and contain inflation.

Concern over national security has motivated China's desire for economic self-sufficiency. The priority placed on industrial development was to some extent prompted by a desire to reduce dependence on other nations for critical industrial products. Self-sufficiency in major food products has at times also been considered essential to national security. These two objectives call for somewhat contradictory food price policies, as the former would call for undervaluation of agricultural products to finance industrial investment, and the latter would call for maintaining food prices high enough to eliminate the need for imports by promoting output and reducing consumption. The government has attempted to resolve this contradiction by relying on nonprice policies such as production planning and rationing to reduce the need for food imports.

2. Vermeer (1982), pp. 18–19, discusses China's disaster and income relief programs in rural areas.

Since the seventies China has increasingly viewed trade as complementary to national development, and emphasis has shifted from maintaining strict self-sufficiency to maintaining balanced trade. Food, and especially grain, self-sufficiency, however, still remains an important goal: exports of raw or processed agricultural products are considered necessary to finance imports of important industrial and technological products.

Progress toward socialist or communist social ideals has been a fourth objective of China's leaders. These ideals are based on what the Chinese consider to be a good society, and at times economic objectives have been compromised for their sake. A good society is harmonious and without class struggle or exploitation: individuals work together, recognize what is in the public good, and place the public good above their private interests. Rewards in such a society are allocated according to need. If this is not possible in the short term, then rewards can be allocated according to work, but never according to capital assets or class position.

The use of price policy has been influenced by the importance Chinese leaders have placed on the need for material development to precede social development. Mao and his followers generally believed that social development must proceed even in an economically underdeveloped economy. According to this view, the use of prices to allocate resources was undesirable, as their effectiveness relied on material incentives and selfish behavior, though prices might still be used to influence income distribution and for accounting purposes. The alternative view has held that the good society was unattainable until the economy had reached a higher level of economic development. Because China is underdeveloped, one cannot expect the people to have a high level of political consciousness, and so the government must continue to rely on material incentives to guide resource allocation. Moreover, in its prevailing underdeveloped state, complete and accurate quantity planning has been impossible; therefore, the government must resort to price planning and even to limited market allocation to guide the economy. Change over time in the use of food price policy has reflected shifting views on these subjects.

Food Price Policy: A Historical Overview

Food price policy has passed through several stages since the early fifties. These stages can roughly be defined as follows: (1) First Five-Year Plan, 1953–57, (2) Great Leap Forward, 1958–60, (3) Readjustment Period, 1961–66, (4) Cultural Revolution, 1967–77, and (5) Post-Mao Reform Period, 1978 to the present.[3] During the First Five-Year Plan, Readjustment, and the post-Mao periods, pragmatic considerations to some extent

---

3. During the postwar recovery period, from 1949 to 1952, policy was primarily concerned with consolidating power and recovering from the long civil war.

prevailed over ideological objectives, and prices were used to influence resource allocation. During the Great Leap Forward and Cultural Revolution, such use of pricing policy was criticized, and the government employed other instruments to pursue its goals, with particular emphasis on quantity planning and ideological exhortation. The main functions of pricing during these periods were to stabilize incomes, promote certain distributional objectives, and serve as a means of taxation.

Changes in food pricing policy have, to some extent, reflected changes in the priorities assigned to the various national goals. As will be described in this section, shifts in the degree of emphasis on rapid growth, balanced growth, income distribution, national security, and progress toward socialist ideals have been translated into shifts in overall pricing strategy.

Agricultural Producer Prices

A full understanding of the history of farm pricing requires some knowledge of the agriculture pricing system and its evolution. Agricultural producers in China have faced a complex, multitiered price structure. From one to three different prices have applied to different categories of deliveries to the state; in addition, producers have also faced occasional quasi-price incentives, and, when private trade was permitted, market prices. Price differentials for quality, location, or season have further complicated the price structure, although spatial and seasonal price differentials in state prices were gradually reduced after 1953.

Different pricing systems and policies have applied to different agricultural products. Because grain has occupied over 80 percent of sown area and provides an equal proportion of the calories in the Chinese diet, grain production and marketing have been of central concern to Chinese policy makers.[4] The history of grain pricing thus reveals many of the tradeoffs and difficult choices faced by the Chinese leadership. For these reasons, and because more information is available for grains than for other farm products, the discussion below focuses on grain pricing policies.

Because pricing has been only one of several instruments used by the government to influence agriculture, producer price policy must also be understood in the broader policy context. The large size and powerful status of the government enabled it, at least within limits, to enforce production targets and commercial quotas. Quantity planning in the form of targets and quotas were used as a substitute for or in conjunction with prices to guide resource allocation. Nor has pricing been the sole method for taxing agriculture: the agricultural tax, essentially a land tax first instituted in the fifties, has also provided revenues. The importance of this

4. The Chinese statistical definition of grain includes not only cereals but also Irish and sweet potatoes, soybeans, and other pulses and tubers. Hereafter, the word *grain* will be used according to its Chinese definition.

direct taxation of agriculture has, however, declined considerably over time.

Various measures have also been available to influence the distribution of income. In the fifties the state resorted to forced redistribution, nationalization, and collectivization of physical wealth. Such drastic measures have been employed on a much more limited scale since then. Other methods have included direct income transfers, interventions in the urban wage system, regulation of the distribution of rural collective income, and controls on private income-generating activities. Producer pricing has occasionally assumed a prominent place among these various measures to redistribute income. In particular, it has been used to raise rural incomes and reduce rural-urban inequality.

With these considerations in mind, then, a history of agricultural producer pricing can be sketched. Since the subject has already been treated in some detail by Perkins (1966) and Lardy (1983a), this chapter will provide a general overview, going into depth only where the information or interpretation differs from that presented elsewhere.

First Five-Year-Plan

In 1953 China embarked on its First Five-Year Plan. The plan had a Stalinist flavor: high priority was placed on (1) achieving rapid rates of growth, with emphasis on industrial growth, especially in the heavy industries; (2) a high rate of savings and investment to sustain rapid growth; and (3) socialist transformation of the economy, including rapid enlargement of central planning, nationalization or collectivization in the nonagricultural sectors, and collectivization in agriculture (Eckstein, 1977, pp. 50–51).

Accordingly, the government began to expand the importance of planning, including planned pricing, and reduce the role of the market in resource allocation. Commercial planning in agriculture began in November 1953, with the introduction of the "unified purchase and unified sale" (*tonggou tongxiao*) system for grain and oil-bearing crops (Wang, 1985a, pp. 50–51). The "unified purchase and unified sale" system was initially prompted by grain shortages in urban areas following rapid urbanization occurring at this time. The aim of this program was to ensure adequate supplies of grain and oils to urban areas without a substantial increase in purchase prices, as low agricultural prices would make possible the high levels of saving and industrial investment anticipated under the First Five-Year Plan. Planned purchase and sale programs of slightly different design followed for cotton in 1954, hogs in 1955, and a wide variety of other farm products in 1956 and 1957 (Ministry of Commerce Institute of Commercial Economic Research, 1984, pp. 56–63).

Under "unified purchase and unified sale" the central government set grain purchase quotas that filtered down through the multiple levels of government until they reached the farm level. The quotas specified quantities of grain but were not differentiated by type of grain.[5] In theory, these quotas were to be set so as to allow farmers to retain enough grain to meet their own food, seed, and feed needs. After quotas were fulfilled, individuals could sell any remaining surplus either on a state-controlled grain market or informally to their neighbors. In practice, because state purchasing organs exercised little restraint and purchased as much grain as they could extract, farmers were left with little surplus (Perkins, 1966, chapter 3). Not surprisingly, state procurements of grain rose dramatically, from 23 percent of output in 1952 to 35 percent in 1954 (table 1). Growth in grain production, however, slowed. In part reflecting the farm response to excessively high quotas and the low state prices, growth in output declined from over 9 percent a year to less than 2 percent.[6]

An important component of the "unified purchase and unified sales" system was centrally planned pricing. Grain prices for quota purchases were initially set equal to the official price levels prevailing at the time the "unified purchase" directive was issued.[7] These prices had been 20 to 30 percent lower than prevailing market prices (Perkins, 1966, p. 50). State grain pricing at this time, then, served as a means to tax agriculture rather than promote output and sales.[8]

Although the new program had temporarily increased state grain purchases, by early 1955 its negative effects on production and ultimately on procurement as well threatened to slow national development. Raising the already high quota levels was no longer a viable means of promoting procurement and output. The alternative of increasing the planned price for grain was rejected because of the desire to channel available funds to industry. Instead, the state reduced the prices for certain manufactured inputs to agriculture by 30 to 40 percent. These price revisions began in 1955 and probably had some positive effect on production; however, since

5. Producers could in theory meet their quotas using any combination of wheat, rice, barley, soybeans, or other cereals, legumes or pulses (potatoes were counted at a rate of 5 to 1 before 1962, and 4 to 1 thereafter). In practice, local officials at times exercised control over the types of grain delivered by requiring that most of the quota be fulfilled right after the rice or wheat harvest, or by simply refusing to accept certain grains.

6. State Statistical Bureau (1984), p. 141, and table 1. The reduced rate of output growth could in part also have reflected the natural slowdown occurring after a period of rapid recovery from wartime destruction.

7. Perkins (1966), p. 49. Prior to this time state trading companies were already purchasing grain from farmers at officially set prices. These state trading companies, however, had coexisted with private trading companies and individual traders in a free market context. Prior to 1953, in other words, farm sales of grain to the state had been voluntary. See Perkins (1966), chapter 3.

8. Note that this "unified purchase and unified sales" system was superimposed on an extant agricultural tax. The agricultural tax was a fixed sum, in-kind tax. In many ways, then, it resembled the quota system, except that the price paid was zero and the amount of the tax was, at least from 1953 on, more or less constant. See Perkins (1966), chapter 3.

TABLE 1.   Grain production and state grain procurement (1,000s metric tons original grain)

Year	Grain production[a]	State procurement[b]	Percent procured
1952	163,915	37,361	22.8
1953	166,830	44,705	26.8
1954	169,515	60,012	35.4
1955	183,935	55,831	30.4
1956	192,745	47,133	24.5
1957	195,045	54,741	28.1
1958	200,000	62,446	31.2
1959	170,000	77,247	45.4
1960	143,500	56,066	39.1
1961	147,500	43,898	29.8
1962	160,000	38,771	24.2
1963	170,000	44,060	25.9
1964	187,500	48,054	25.6
1965	194,525	47,253	24.3
1966	214,000	49,898	23.3
1967	217,820	49,849	22.9
1968	209,055	48,681	23.3
1969	210,970	46,325	22.0
1970	239,955	56,012	23.3
1971	250,140	52,801	21.1
1972	240,480	46,428	19.3
1973	264,935	58,319	22.0
1974	275,270	56,494	20.5
1975	284,515	63,392	22.3
1976	286,305	59,211	20.7
1977	282,725	57,434	20.3
1978	304,765	61,114	20.1
1979	332,115	69,361	20.9
1980	320,555	68,759	21.4
1981	325,020	76,187	23.4
1982	354,500	86,849	24.5
1983	387,275	116,548	30.1
1984	407,305	129,494	31.8
1985	379,108	109,176	28.8

SOURCES: State Statistical Bureau (1984), p. 370; State Statistical Bureau (1986), pp. 542, 545; State Statistical Bureau, Department of Commerce and Price Statistics (1984), p. 156.

[a]Grain production is given in units original (unhusked) grain and is for the production year (April of year listed to March of the following year).

[b]State procurement (*guoying he gongxiao she shangye guonei chun goujin*) includes procurement by state commerce and by supply and marketing cooperatives, which have acted as state procurement agents. The sources do not specify if state procurement is for the production or calendar year, although it is likely the latter. State procurement is converted to original grain equivalents assuming a ratio of 0.83 units trade (husked) grain per unit original grain.

the level of modern input use was low, the supply response was undoubtedly smaller than that of raising output prices. The budgetary costs were also less.

Through the remainder of the First Five-Year Plan, the state persisted in avoiding increases in grain purchase prices. Relative price adjustments were employed fairly actively to influence the composition of agricultural output (Perkins, 1966, chapter 3), but grain prices were treated as a more or less fixed numeraire. Adjustments in the relative prices of nongrain crops thus occurred in relation to a fairly constant grain price (Ministry of Commerce Institute of Commercial Economic Research, 1984, pp. 67–68). Over the five years 1953 through 1957 the state price for grain rose only 3 percent, while the average price for economic crops rose 12 percent (table 2).[9]

During this period, efforts to stimulate grain production and marketing relied for the most part on nonprice instruments such as procurement planning and institutional reform. In mid-1955, the method for setting grain purchase quotas was changed, procurement reduced, procedures regularized, and greater incentives provided to producers. The new policy, called "three fix" (*san ding*), required that quotas be set with reference to the "normal" yield of the land, that is, the amount the land should produce in an ordinary year, and once set the quotas were not to be revised for three years. Not more than 40 percent of any increases in production during the next three years could be taken by the state; disposal of the other 60 percent was to be decided by the farmer (Perkins, 1966, pp. 50–52; Donnithorne, 1967, pp. 346–49).

Institutional reform in agriculture had occurred gradually prior to 1955 as the government encouraged the formation of mutual aid teams and producer cooperatives. By 1954 roughly 60 percent of all rural households had joined mutual aid teams, a rudimentary form of collective in which six or seven households pooled labor, and sometimes land and tools. Ownership remained vested in the households, which were compensated for resources used by the team as a whole. A small percentage of households had gone further, forming agricultural producer cooperatives (APCs) of thirty to fifty households.

In addition to being consistent with the state's ideological goals, collectivization was also seen as having certain economic advantages that would outweigh any possible negative effects on individual incentives. Specifically, the government hoped that collective farms would produce more efficiently and adopt new techniques more readily than household farms.

---

9. These percentage increases are calculated using the official "list" purchase prices (*shougou paijia*). Roughly the same increase occurred in grain's official list price and the weighted average grain price paid by the state (calculated by dividing total value of procurement by quantity of procurement) (*hunhe pingjun jiage*). Liu (1982), pp. 615, 630.

TABLE 2.   Indexes of state quota procurement prices for major products (1953 = 100)

| Year | Grain | Economic crops | Of which: | | | Meat animals |
			Oilseeds	Cotton	Sugar crops	
1950	72.9	88.6	82.5	93.4	110.7	86.4
1951	86.3	104.9	98.4	107.7	112.0	93.2
1952	88.5	100.1	89.3	105.8	96.6	88.8
1953	100.0	100.0	100.0	100.0	100.0	100.0
1954	100.0	105.7	101.6	101.7	100.4	107.0
1955	100.1	106.3	101.1	103.7	101.4	104.0
1956	102.0	108.6	104.1	103.7	111.8	108.5
1957	103.1	112.0	138.5	103.7	114.0	123.5
1958	105.8	113.3	141.8	103.7	115.2	127.5
1959	107.2	115.1	152.9	103.7	126.0	128.4
1960	110.6	118.5	171.7	103.8	127.2	132.1
1961	140.0	124.5	201.5	103.9	143.7	158.8
1962	140.3	128.4	203.5	103.9	142.5	161.9
1963	139.2	135.4	203.5	114.8	141.1	163.2
1964	138.0	135.2	203.5	114.8	149.8	167.0
1965	139.2	135.3	203.5	114.8	149.8	167.0
1966	161.1	135.3	203.5	114.8	149.8	167.0
1967	161.3	137.2	203.5	114.8	149.8	167.0
1968	161.3	137.2	203.5	114.8	149.8	167.0
1969	161.3	137.2	203.5	114.8	149.8	167.0
1970	161.3	137.2	203.5	114.8	149.8	167.0
1971	161.9	143.0	251.7	116.2	160.5	168.3
1972	162.1	145.4	254.0	118.5	167.6	169.2
1973	162.1	146.1	254.0	118.5	167.6	170.0
1974	162.2	146.2	254.0	118.5	167.6	172.0
1975	162.5	146.2	254.0	118.5	167.6	172.3
1976	162.5	146.2	254.0	118.5	167.6	172.3
1977	162.5	146.9	260.2	118.5	167.6	172.5
1978	163.7	154.1	265.1	129.6	167.8	173.0
1979	197.9	177.5	328.5	151.6	204.5	214.9

SOURCE: Liu (1982), pp. 615–17.

Furthermore, the government expected that collectivization would facilitate agricultural planning and increase the state's ability to extract grain. With these advantages in mind, in mid-1955 the state stepped up the pace and level of collectivization. By the end of 1956, only eighteen months later, almost 90 percent of households belonged to "higher-level" APCs. The higher-level APCs embraced two hundred to three hundred households, which now received compensation on the basis of their labor contribution and not on the basis of any land or tools brought with them. Moreover, not more than 5–10 percent of the land could be cultivated privately by households: the rest was to be cultivated collectively (Eckstein, 1977, pp. 69–71; Perkins, 1966, p. 74).

The effects of the 1955 policies were mixed. State purchases of grain fell by 7 percent in 1955 and another 16 percent in 1956 (table 1). Grain

TABLE 3.   Per capita grain
consumption (kilograms husked grain)

Year	National average	Urban	Rural
1952	198	241	192
1953	197	242	191
1954	196	236	190
1955	198	215	196
1956	204	201	205
1957	203	196	205
1958	198	186	201
1959	187	201	183
1960	164	193	156
1961	159	180	154
1962	165	184	161
1963	165	190	160
1964	182	200	179
1965	183	211	177
1966	190	206	187
1967	186	200	184
1968	174	189	171
1969	174	192	171
1970	187	202	185
1971	188	200	186
1972	173	206	166
1973	192	208	189
1974	188	205	185
1975	191	210	187
1976	190	212	186
1977	192	211	189
1978	195	206	194
1979	207	211	206
1980	214	214	214
1981	219	216	220
1982	225	218	228
1983	232	n.a.	n.a.
1984	252	n.a.	n.a.
1985	254	n.a.	n.a.

SOURCES: State Statistical Bureau (1984), p. 477; State
Statistical Bureau (1985), p. 551; State Statistical Bureau
(1986), p. 645; Ministry of Commerce, Institute of Commercial Economic Research (1984), p. 509.

production, on the other hand, grew 8.5 percent in 1955 and 4.8 percent in
1956. The new quota regulations apparently permitted cooperatives to
retain more grain, and rural direct grain consumption per capita rose from
190 kg in 1954 to a peak of 205 kg in 1956 (table 3).[10]

These rural gains were not without costs. First, the decline in state

10. Total calories consumed per capita (both rural and urban) in the form of grain rose from
1,677 kcal in 1954 to 1,825 kcal in 1956 (estimates from Piazza, 1983, pp. 9, 17). After 1956 per
capita rural grain consumption and calories provided by grain began to decline. Grain
consumption per capita in rural areas did not regain its 1956 level until twenty-three years
later, in 1979.

procurement contributed to a 15 percent fall in urban per capita grain consumption between 1954 and 1956 (table 3). Second, under the new cooperative system, production was decided by local political cadres who were inclined to place political objectives above the economic interests of the cooperative members. One consequence of this was a precipitous decline in certain subsidiary occupations like vegetable cultivation and hog and poultry raising, and in handicrafts such as production of sandals and small farm implements, items produced mostly by individual households. Such occupations were considered competitive with collective work, and political leaders asked (or compelled) cooperative members to devote less time to them (Perkins, 1966, pp. 72–73). In addition, the change in who made production decisions contributed to a general decline in the sensitivity of farm production to economic signals and an increase in its sensitivity to political currents (Perkins, 1966, pp. 62–68).

Despite the introduction of and reforms in commercial planning, and despite collectivization, as of 1957 grain shortages persisted in the cities, and agriculture remained a bottleneck to continued industrial expansion. Continued high priority on saving for industrial investment led the state once again to reject raising grain prices or otherwise increasing its financial commitment to agriculture. Instead, China turned to even more radical institutional change—communization—and mass mobilization campaigns in the countryside. This marked the beginning of the Great Leap Forward.

The Great Leap Forward

As the First Five-Year Plan period drew to a close, Chinese leaders began to reevaluate their development strategy. The state had attempted to accomplish major changes in the economy, and rates of growth for the economy as a whole had been high; but several serious problems had emerged. Measures to promote rapid growth and structural change had caused severe economic dislocations and disproportionalities like the decline in grain supplies going to the rapidly growing urban population. As the role of central planning grew, its ever increasing complexity magnified problems of coordination and enforcement.

In response to these and other factors, the government broke with the Stalinist model and called for further institutional transformation in agriculture. The APCs were organized into even larger collective units called communes that embraced twenty thousand to thirty thousand people. Ownership and management of land and capital were now vested in the communes. Private plots were eliminated.

Concurrent changes occurred in resource allocation. The role of the center in planning was reduced, and more responsibility was given to local governments and commune leaders. Greater emphasis was placed on the role of the Communist Party and ideology in guiding local level economic decisions. Material incentives were condemned, egalitarian distribution schemes instituted, and free markets abolished.

As before, these measures were expected to induce rapid increases in agricultural output without diverting resources from industry. Under party leadership, with the proper indoctrination and mass mobilization of the rural populace, and in the context of the new commune system, farm production and state procurement were expected to rise.

Although passed over as a tool for encouraging deliveries to the state, grain pricing was used to pursue certain distributional objectives, and perhaps also to smooth the transition to commune organization. In 1957 procurement prices were raised in peripheral areas and poor mountainous regions. Prices were raised again in 1958 and 1960 in seven or eight interior and southern provinces.[11] The stated reasons for these price adjustments were to improve the situation of peripheral counties that, due to the method of calculating transport costs, received low prices for their output, but paid high prices for manufactures; to reduce price differentials between the coast and the interior; and to raise grain prices where they were especially low, particularly in ethnic minority areas (Wang, 1985a, p. 50).

Although these price increases applied to only a subset of provinces, they raised the national average state purchase price for grain by 8 percent over the four-year period 1956–60 (table 2) (Liu, 1982, p. 615). Other factors, however, far overshadowed price policy in determining production and marketing trends. The agricultural and demographic disaster caused by overzealous implementation of Great Leap policies is well-known, and this paper will not treat it in detail.[12] Suffice it to say that economic considerations such as prices and costs were given low priority in resource allocation. Moreover, extensive overreporting of grain production led to severe overprocurement,[13] and rural areas were left with insufficient grain to meet their food, seed, and feed needs. Malnutrition and widespread slaughter of livestock resulted. Loss of draft power and manure, combined with a labor force weakened by food shortages, led to

11. Grain prices were raised in the Northeast, Inner Mongolia, Hunan, Hubei, Guizhou, Yunnan, Guangxi, and Jiangxi in 1958. In 1960, prices were raised in Hunan, Hubei, Guizhou, Guangxi, Jiangxi, Yunnan, and Sichuan.

12. For a description of the Great Leap and the resulting agricultural disaster, see Walker (1984), chapter 5.

13. The official figure for grain production (excluding soybeans) initially reported by the central government in 1958 was 375 million tons, double the amount produced in 1957. Acknowledging irregularities in statistical work, Mao considered 365 million tons a more realistic estimate. By mid-1959, Chou Enlai suggested a revised figure of 250 million tons. Actual output is now thought to have been 200 million tons, only slightly higher than output in 1957. See Walker (1984), pp. 129–55, for more details on grain misreporting and its disastrous consequences.

further reductions in agricultural output. For the first time since 1949, China became a net importer of cereals.

Readjustment Period

By 1961 the government realized the extent of the agricultural disaster, and during the next several years it responded with major policy initiatives. The new policies reflected more pragmatic views about the importance of economic considerations and acknowledged the need to devote more resources to agriculture. The government announced that it intended to follow an "agriculture first" development strategy.[14]

An important change was the retreat from high-level collectivization. Negative incentive effects and the complexity of agricultural production had made uneconomic the management of production and distribution at the commune level. The communes were not disbanded, but authority for decision making was shifted down from the commune to production teams made up of only fifty to sixty households. Within production teams, distribution became less egalitarian, and rewards were tied more closely to work done. Private plots were reinstated, and free markets permitted to reemerge (Perkins, 1966, pp. 90–95). In some localities production responsibilities were even contracted out to individual households, foreshadowing the current responsibility system reforms. Emergence of contracting to households was tolerated for a time in the early sixties, but later criticized and eliminated (Donnithorne, 1967, p. 54; Ma, 1982, p. 113).

Increased emphasis on economic considerations was accompanied by an announced shift to a balanced development strategy with primary emphasis on agriculture. Although some have argued convincingly that the government never actually treated agriculture as the priority sector,[15] measures implemented at that time certainly improved agriculture's relative status. These included increased direct state investment in agriculture and in industries producing modern inputs for agriculture, large reductions in the state grain tax and quotas,[16] and a substantial increase in farm prices.

With renewed emphasis on material incentives and a shift in sectoral priorities, it is not surprising that during this period various price and quasi-price measures were employed to encourage agricultural production and marketing. The government procurement price for grain was increased sharply in 1961 and 1966, and smaller adjustments were made between those two years. In 1961 the average price for six major grains

14. The official slogan put forth at that time—"agriculture is the foundation and industry the leading factor"—was actually a bit more ambiguous.

15. See, for example, Lardy (1983b), especially chapter 3.

16. In 1961 the grain base quota and tax was reduced 8.85 million tons, and in 1962 another 2.1 million tons. See Ministry of Commerce Institute of Commercial Economic Research (1984), p. 216.

(wheat, paddy, millet, sorghum, corn, and soybeans) was raised 25 percent, and in 1966 an additional 17 percent.[17] Minor adjustments, including in 1965 an increase of grain purchase prices in seven interior provinces in South-Central China, also took place, although their effect on the national average grain price was small.[18] These price revisions were intended to help correct the undervaluation of agricultural products relative to industrial products, to promote grain production and deliveries, and to reduce regional price differentials. Prices of certain other farm products were also raised between 1960 and 1966, but by less than that of grain (table 2).

Analyses of Chinese prices often look only at revisions in the basic state purchase prices for quota deliveries and ignore important price bonus and material incentive programs. In the early sixties the central and local governments began to employ such incentive programs to raise the effective price of grain. The two most important incentive programs were price bonuses for excess deliveries to the state and encouragement sales programs.

Both the 1961 and 1966 grain price revisions were preceded by price bonus programs for increased deliveries to the state. In 1960 the state began to give a 10 percent price bonus to production teams for deliveries to the state in excess of a certain fixed amount per team member.[19] This price bonus was carried through 1961 and eliminated in 1962. A 12 percent bonus was reinstated in 1965 but superseded by a new program in 1966 when grain prices were raised a second time. At that time it was decided that base purchase quotas were to be fixed and unchanged for three-year periods (*yi ding san nian*), and that half of grain deliveries above quota would receive a 30–50 percent price bonus, while the other half would receive encouragement sales awards (below). The exact percentage of the bonus was decided by provincial-level governments (Ministry of Commerce Institute of Commercial Economic Research, 1984, p. 386; Xiao, 1983, p. 33; and Xu et al, 1982, p. 121). (See table 4.)

Price bonuses were used in combination with various material incentive programs that, for the most part, awarded farmers the right to buy goods in short supply in return for deliveries of agricultural products to the state. By tying sales of otherwise unavailable commodities to deliveries, the state effectively raised the returns for grain delivered to the state. These programs, referred to as encouragement sales (*jiangshou*) or barter purchase

17. Wang (1985a), p. 51; Liu (1982), pp. 475–76. Also see table 2.

18. Prices were raised in Hunan, Hubei, Guizhou, Guangxi, Jiangxi, Yunnan, and Sichuan in 1965 (Wang, 1985a, p. 50). The national average list purchase price fluctuated by less than 1 percent a year between 1961 and 1966 (Liu, 1982, p. 615). See table 2.

19. In 1960–62 the fixed amount ranged from 50 to 150 kg per team member, depending on the region. In 1965–66 the fixed amount was a uniform 50 kg nationwide. Deliveries of grain in fulfillment of the agricultural tax could not be counted toward these amounts. See Xiao (1983), p. 33, and Liu (1982), pp. 475–76.

TABLE 4. Quota and above-quota grain
procurement price indexes (1953 = 100)

Year	Quota price index	Percentage bonus	Above-quota price index
1950	72.9		72.9
1951	86.3		86.3
1952	88.5		88.5
1953	100.0		100.0
1954	100.0		100.0
1955	100.1		100.1
1956	102.0		102.0
1957	103.1		103.1
1958	105.8		105.8
1959	107.2		107.2
1960	110.6	10%	121.7
1961	140.0		140.0
1962	140.3		140.3
1963	139.2		139.2
1964	138.0		138.0
1965	139.2	12%	156.0
1966	161.1	½ × (30%–50%)	185–201
1967	161.3	½ × (30%–50%)	185–202
1968	161.3	½ × (30%–50%)	185–202
1969	161.3	½ × (30%–50%)	185–202
1970	161.3	½ × (30%–50%)	185–202
1971	161.9	30%	210.5
1972	162.1	30%	210.7
1973	162.1	30%	210.7
1974	162.2	30%	210.9
1975	162.5	30%	211.3
1976	162.5	30%	211.3
1977	162.5	30%	211.3
1978	163.7	30%	212.8
1979	197.9	50%	296.8
1980	n.a.	50%	n.a.
1981	n.a.	50%	n.a.
1982	n.a.	50%	n.a.
1983	n.a.	50%	n.a.
1984	n.a.	50%	n.a.

SOURCES: Table 2 and text.

aThe above-quota price bonus is zero unless shown to be a positive percentage.

bFrom 1966 to 1970 the bonus applied to half the above-quota deliveries, and ranged from 30% to 50%, depending on the province.

cIn 1960 and 1965 the bonus applied to deliveries exceeding a certain quantity per team member. Thereafter, they apply to above-quota deliveries.

(huangou) programs, were first used widely at the end of the Great Leap Forward to stabilize the area sown to commercial crops, increase state procurement, and help increase the supply of manufactures to rural areas. The incentives in some cases applied to all deliveries (except for tax payments in kind), and in some cases applied only to above-quota deliveries; moreover, the design of the incentives appears to have varied by product, region, and year. For a time such material incentive programs were quite extensive. At their peak in 1962–63, they applied to 169 agricultural products, and goods used as material incentives included grain (for commercial crop farmers), cotton cloth, chemical fertilizer, sugar, cigarettes, knitted goods, kerosene, rubber galoshes, tea, and soap (Ministry of Commerce Institute of Commercial Economic Research, 1984, p. 219).

Material incentive programs for grain began in 1961, when the central government announced that for each 50 kg of grain sold to the state above the quota, the state would award the right to buy 10 *chi* cotton cloth[20] and a pair of rubber galoshes. Local governments were apparently allowed some flexibility in implementation of the incentives. In Hubei, for example, production teams were awarded ration coupons for certain amounts of cloth, knitwear, cigarettes, sugar, and galoshes for each 750 kg of grain delivered (exclusive of the agricultural tax). Teams that sold more than 5,000 kg to the state—a rare accomplishment—received the right to purchase a diesel engine.[21] The effect of these encouragement sales programs on the relative returns to grain is difficult to evaluate, as comprehensive information on the prices charged for encouragement sales items and the sorts of encouragement sales awards for other crops is unavailable.

By the mid-sixties the government began to reduce the scope of national material incentive programs, although they continued on a more limited scale through the Cultural Revolution and post-Mao periods. By 1965 only 144 products were eligible, and awards were limited to grain, cotton cloth, and chemical fertilizer. The effectiveness of these programs had, anyway, declined as the availability of grain and manufactures in rural areas had improved. At least temporarily, however, the overall magnitude of these programs had been substantial: over the five years 1961–65 the state had supplied 7.75 million tons of grain, 250 million meters of cloth, and 6.16 million tons of chemical fertilizer to rural areas through such tied sales (Ministry of Commerce Institute of Commercial Economic Research, 1984, pp. 219–20).

The grain price increases that occurred during this time were, then, large: by 1966 the state base grain price was 46 percent higher than in 1960. To the extent that material incentive programs continued, the effective price increase was even higher. Thus grain price increases in the early and mid-sixties exceeded considerably those during the fifties; moreover, the sixties' grain price increases applied nationwide, while those during the fifties had to a greater extent applied only to certain regions.

Trends in production and deliveries during this period were, on the

20. A *chi* is a Chinese unit of measurement. Three *chi* equal one meter.
21. Author interviews in Mianyang County, Hubei Province.

whole, encouraging. Output of grain and other crops grew rapidly in the early sixties, in most cases reaching or surpassing past peak output levels by the mid-sixties (table 5). This growth was due to several factors, including recovery, institutional reforms, and increased fertilizer supplies, as well as price and planning policies. Grain deliveries declined in 1961 and 1962, during which years the state quota and tax were reduced. Thereafter deliveries began to rise, although more slowly than production; indeed, the absolute level of state grain procurement remained below 50 million tons and the percentage of total output procured fell to 23 percent in the mid-sixties (table 1). The slow increase in state grain procurement was in part the result of the new "three-year fix" quota policies.

Per capita consumption of grain in both rural and urban areas rose, although rural consumption levels remained lower than they had been in the fifties. Continued imports of grain helped maintain urban supplies.

Cultural Revolution

The Great Proletarian Cultural Revolution began in 1966. Unlike the Great Leap Forward, the Cultural Revolution was not a response to economic difficulties but a program for social and political reform. The new policies nevertheless had certain economic implications. With the drive to combat elitism and fossilization of bureaucratic hierarchies, emphasis on localism and local self-reliance increased. In addition to causing general political disruption, these policies ultimately contributed to a decline in interregional agricultural trade and loss of gains from regional specialization. Efforts were also made to limit economic institutions and practices that promoted capitalist attitudes. A strict egalitarian approach to income distribution, downplay of consumerism and material desires, reduced use of material incentives to guide resource allocation, and repression of private economic activities such as private plots and free markets ensued. In general, both with regard to policies and personnel, emphasis was placed on ideology and political attitude rather than economic considerations.

Not surprisingly, the Cultural Revolution is seen as a period when the government relied on quantity planning and ideological exhortation rather than pricing to guide resource allocation. Such an interpretation is, for the most part, accurate: from 1967 through 1970 and again from 1973 through 1976, state prices for agricultural products remained virtually frozen (tables 2 and 4). At least within certain political circles, however, the need for price adjustments was recognized, and during a brief two-year period (1971–72) the government carried out limited revisions.

The need for price adjustments was initially raised in the mid-sixties, at which time a five-year program (1966–70) to correct the price structure was developed (Xue, 1985, p. 48). This program was laid aside in August 1967, when the central government issued a communique stating that

TABLE 5.   Production of major crops

Year	Production (1,000s mt)			Index of production (1970 = 100)		
	Grain	Cotton	Oilseeds	Grain	Cotton	Oilseeds
1952	163,920	1,304	4,193	68	57	111
1953	166,830	1,175	3,856	70	52	102
1954	169,520	1,065	4,305	71	47	114
1955	183,940	1,518	4,827	77	67	128
1956	192,750	1,445	5,086	80	63	135
1957	195,050	1,640	4,196	81	72	111
1958	200,000	1,969	4,770	83	86	126
1959	170,000	1,709	4,104	71	75	109
1960	143,500	1,063	1,941	60	47	51
1961	147,500	800	1,814	61	35	48
1962	160,000	750	2,003	67	33	53
1963	170,000	1,200	2,458	71	53	65
1964	187,500	1,663	3,368	78	73	89
1965	194,530	2,098	3,625	81	92	96
1966	214,000	2,337	n.a.	89	103	n.a.
1967	217,820	2,354	n.a.	91	103	n.a.
1968	209,060	2,354	n.a.	87	103	n.a.
1969	210,970	2,079	n.a.	88	91	n.a.
1970	239,960	2,277	3,772	100	100	100
1971	250,140	2,105	4,113	104	92	109
1972	240,480	1,958	4,118	100	86	109
1973	264,940	2,562	4,186	110	113	111
1974	275,270	2,461	4,414	115	108	117
1975	284,520	2,381	4,521	119	105	120
1976	286,310	2,055	4,008	119	90	106
1977	282,730	2,049	4,017	118	90	106
1978	304,770	2,167	5,218	127	95	138
1979	332,120	2,207	6,435	138	97	171
1980	320,560	2,707	7,691	134	119	204
1981	325,020	2,968	10,205	135	130	271
1982	354,500	3,598	11,817	148	158	313
1983	387,280	4,637	10,550	161	204	280
1984	407,310	6,258	11,910	170	275	316
1985	379,110	4,147	15,784	158	182	418

SOURCES: State Statistical Bureau (1984), pp. 141–42; State Statistical Bureau (1986), p. 180.

even though certain aspects of the price structure were irrational, prices were not to be adjusted until the end of the Cultural Revolution period. The communique was in part a measure to maintain control over pricing during a period when the government bureaucracy was undergoing a thorough shake-up (Commercial Prices Editorial Group, 1980, pp. 211–12).

In the early seventies certain pricing issues were revived, in particular, the need to correct irrationalities in agricultural pricing. The most important price adjustments at this time (1971–72) were for sugar crops, whose quota prices were raised 12 percent, and oilseeds, whose quota prices were raised 25 percent. These changes were intended to moderate a perceived underpricing of sugar and oilseeds relative to grain. The purchase price for cotton was also increased 3 percent, but cotton quality standards were concurrently modified so that after adjusting for the change in standards, the cotton price actually declined (Sicular, 1986, p. 413). Except for soybeans and certain pulses, the quota prices of grains remained unchanged (table 2).[22]

Aside from adjustments in quota prices, during these two years the prices farmers received were further affected by changes in above-quota pricing policies and in quota levels. In 1971 the government instituted a nationwide 30 percent price bonus for above-quota deliveries of grain and of vegetable oil or oilseeds (Liu, 1982, p. 476; Xu et al., 1982, p. 121). These price bonuses replaced existing, regionally diverse bonus programs that had been implemented beginning in 1966 (table 4).

In 1971 the government also increased the basic grain quota and tax and altered the "three-year fix" (*yi ding san nian*) policy to a "five-year fix" (*yi ding wu nian*) policy (Liu, 1982, p. 476; Xu et al., 1982, p. 121), which lengthened the period for which quotas were fixed to five years. The grain quota and tax was initially raised 5.6 percent, and in 1972 readjusted downwards to a level 4 percent higher than the 1970 quota (table 6) (Ministry of Commerce Institute of Commercial Economic Research, 1984, pp. 386–87). Under the multitiered price structure, such an adjustment effectively lowered the average price paid for grain deliveries without reducing the marginal price paid for above-quota deliveries. Because the change in the quota level was small in percentage terms, its effect on average prices was not large. The adjustment reduced annual budgetary outlays for grain procurement by roughly 100 million yuan.[23]

In 1973 a national meeting was held to discuss an overall price investigation and rectification. The resulting agenda for price work was soon accused of promoting the resurgence of capitalism, and price reform was once again interrupted by political factors (Commercial Prices Editorial Group, 1980, pp. 211–12). Thereafter, no significant changes were made in either quota or above-quota prices until 1977.

Little information is available about encouragement sales programs during the Cultural Revolution. Such programs had been reduced in the mid-sixties but were apparently maintained in some form during the

22. The upward movement in 1971–72 in the average grain quota price index in table 2 reflects the adjustments for soybeans and certain pulses (Xiao [1983], p. 33, and author interviews in China, 1980–81).

23. The average quota price for the six major grains in 1971 was 217.60 yuan per ton (Agricultural Technical Economics Handbook Editorial Group, 1984, p. 712), so that the price bonus per ton above-quota grain was approximately 65 yuan. This is multiplied by the 1.5 million ton increase in the quota between 1971 and 1973 to estimate total budgetary savings. Note that this was equivalent to roughly one-tenth of 1 percent of total government expenditures, which at this time ranged between 73 and 81 billion yuan (table 9).

TABLE 6. Various components of state grain procurement

| Year | Quota and tax (mmt) | Degree of quota fulfillment | Shares of total deliveries procured at: | |
			Quota price (including tax grain)	Above-quota or negotiated prices
1955	40.00			
1965	36.25			
1966	36.25			
1967	36.25			
1968	36.25			
1969	36.25			
1970	36.25			
1971	38.25			
1972	37.75			
1973	37.75			
1974	37.75			
1975	37.75			
1976	37.75			
1977	37.75			
1978	37.75		68.5%	31.5%
1979	35.00	94.6%	49.5%	50.5%
1980	34.33	82.4%	46.5%	53.5%
1981	30.38	80.0%	40%	60%
1982	30.32		30%	70%
1983	n.a.		27.6%	72.4%

NOTE: Quota and tax grain is in trade (husked) grain equivalents.
SOURCES: Walker (1984), p. 62; Ministry of Commerce Institute of Commercial Economic Research (1984), pp. 386–87; Wang and Wang (1984), p. 30; Xu et al. (1982), p. 217; Wu (1982), p. 5; Wang (1985a), p. 52; and Nicholas R. Lardy, personal communication.

Cultural Revolution. Additional research would be required to ascertain if they were expanded or reduced.

During this ten-year period, then, pricing policy's primary objective was to maintain price stability, and only for a brief period was pricing used to influence resource allocation. In order to promote the priority agricultural objectives of grain production (take grain as the key link—*yi liang wei gang*) and self-sufficiency (*zi li geng sheng*), the government relied heavily on other policy instruments, principally production and commercial planning. Increased grain production was promoted by enforcing mandatory sown area targets for grain, and self-sufficiency by purchasing but not selling grain and oils in rural areas. Such measures were supplemented by ideological work.

Grain production did, in fact, grow over this period, but at substantial cost. Inattention to profitability led to a secular rise in unit costs of production, which, in combination with the lack of upward revisions in the prices of many important agricultural products, led to stagnation in rural living standards. Per capita grain consumption in rural areas had reached 187 kg in 1966 but never surpassed 190 kg until 1978 (table 3). In some areas, especially areas better suited to commercial crop production, living standards declined substantially (Lardy, 1983b, chapters 2 and 4). In addition, the production of crops that competed with grain for land suffered (table 5), and the proportion of grain output delivered to the state declined somewhat (table 1).

Post-Mao Period

The change in leadership following Mao's death has brought with it a revaluation of economic objectives and policies. Although long-term growth remains a primary objective, the new leaders recognize that in the past growth was imbalanced, and that the high levels of savings required to sustain such growth prevented improvement in living standards. Recent policies have been designed to raise living standards and promote intensive rather than extensive growth, with emphasis on economic efficiency rather than high levels of investment. Sectoral priorities have, at least nominally, shifted away from heavy industry toward light industry and agriculture.

Accompanying the restructuring of priorities has come a change in the methods used to achieve national objectives. Current leaders have called for increased reliance on "economic levers" to guide the economy. Direct planning of production and commerce are being phased out, whereas indirect planning instruments like prices, taxes, and monetary and fiscal policy have become more important. Institutional changes both in industry and agriculture that increase the responsiveness of producers to economic forces have also been a part of the reform program. The "responsibility system" reforms in agriculture have replaced collective with household farming in furtherance of this objective. Private trade and sideline household enterprises have been allowed, if not encouraged.

Price policy has played an important part in the recent reform program. Agricultural purchase price policy has gone through two stages since 1977. Between 1977 and 1982 the state actively used prices to increase rural incomes and to influence the level and composition of agricultural output. Pricing during these years for the most part consisted of adjustments in planned prices, bonuses, and quotas rather than major changes in the state pricing or procurement system. In 1978 the quota prices of selected products were revised. In 1979 the quota prices of most important farm products were raised substantially. Over the two years 1978 and 1979, prices for quota deliveries of grain rose 22 percent, oils 26 percent, live hogs 26 percent, sugar crops 22 percent, and cotton 28 percent (table 2) (Liu, 1982, pp. 615–16; He, 1981, p. 382). Further adjustments in quota prices continued through 1982 for products whose relative prices appeared to be low.

Quota price revisions were reinforced by higher above-quota price bonuses, reduced quota levels, and the selective use of encouragement sales. The percentage price bonus for grain and oils was increased from 30 percent to 50 percent in 1979 (table 4), and above-quota bonuses were instituted for cotton, tobacco, and certain other economic crops. The expansion of price bonuses was accompanied by gradual reductions in quota levels. The national grain quota and tax was reduced 20 percent between 1978 and 1982 (table 6) (Ministry of Commerce Institute of Commercial Economic Research, 1984, pp. 386–87). These quota and tax reductions were to some extent regionally targeted to benefit disadvantaged areas.

Encouragement sales were instituted to promote cotton and sugar production. Cotton and sugar farmers were permitted to purchase grain and chemical fertilizer, sometimes at preferential prices, in return for above-quota deliveries to the state (Ministry of Commerce Institute of Commercial Economic Research, 1984, pp. 390–91; Sicular, 1986, pp. 414–16).

The objectives of price, quota, and encouragement sales revisions between 1977 and 1982 were multiple. One important objective was to raise rural incomes, another was to stimulate agricultural production and encourage deliveries of farm products to the state. Planners also hoped to influence the composition of agricultural output through adjustments in relative prices and profitabilities.

The policies implemented in the late seventies led to rapid increases in production, marketing, and consumption. Grain output grew at an average annual rate of 4.6 percent between 1977 and 1982, and cotton and oilseeds at average rates of 11.9 percent and 24.1 percent, respectively (table 5). Grain deliveries to the state increased as a percentage of output, growing from 20 percent of output in 1977 to 25 percent in 1982 (table 1). Both urban and rural real incomes also grew rapidly, as did per capita grain consumption (table 3), with more rapid improvement in rural areas. Pricing, however, was only one of several policy initiatives responsible for these gains: the responsibility system and other planning reforms undoubtedly also played a role.

Despite these successes, certain problems with the overall structure of planned pricing and procurement began to emerge by 1982. The higher price and wider scope of bonuses for above-quota deliveries encouraged quota evasion, and the government's ability to enforce its quotas was weakened by decollectivization. Producers found various ways to sell at the above-quota price. One was to switch from crops with relatively high quotas to those with low or no quotas at all. Fields subject to grain quotas were converted to cotton or other economic crops, and vice versa. Another evasion tactic was to save output for one or two years and then deliver it all at once, or for several families to transfer their output to one family for delivery to the state. Finally, local officials, under pressure from their neighbors, on occasion carried out unauthorized reductions in quota levels. Such behavior resulted in underfulfillment of quotas while deliveries at the above-quota price increased (table 6) (Guo and Gu, 1983, p. 34; Xue, 1985, p. 42; and Xu et al., 1982, pp. 121–24, 216–17). Although total deliveries of grain to the state grew more than 10 percent a year,[24] quota fulfillment declined from 94.6 percent in 1979 to 82.4 percent in 1980 to 80 percent in 1981.[25] Farmers obviously benefited from these changes, but the state paid higher average prices for farm products than it had planned.

Another problem was that a procurement system designed to operate in a shortage economy was ill suited to handle emerging agricultural surpluses. Under the existing quota system the government was obliged to buy as much output as farmers wished to sell. As surpluses grew, the government found itself committed to buy ever-increasing quantities of products at high above-quota prices. This problem became especially severe in the early eighties when domestic free market prices for grain began to dip below state above-quota prices. The design of the procurement system, combined with the fact that state retail sales prices had not been raised to match the increases in purchase prices, led to ever-growing state losses on the trade of agricultural products. Such expenditures were unwelcome since, for various reasons (many of them independent of agricultural policies) the government found itself facing persistent budget deficits in the late seventies and early eighties.

An additional and related problem also arose in the new surplus environment. In the shortage economy that had existed for most of the previous two decades, matching supply to demand had never been a major concern because people would buy whatever was offered for sale. In the early eighties with growth in incomes leading to changes in consumption patterns and with the general improved availability of foodstuffs, this was no longer true. The state was now holding surplus stocks of undesirable commodities while unable to meet consumer demand for a variety of higher-quality nonstaple items. The procurement system's inability to pass on demand signals to producers became increasingly evident with time.

Finally, the procurement system was inequitable. Quota levels varied among regions, and so the accrual of above-quota price awards was unequal. Regions with low quotas were able to sell more at above-quota prices and so received higher average prices, while those with higher quotas received lower average prices. For example, cotton farmers in the north, especially the Yellow River basin, faced low cotton quotas and were receiving average prices of 200 yuan per ton or more. In the southern provinces, such as Hubei, quotas were higher, and average prices were less than 140 yuan (Guo and Gu, 1983, p. 34).

24. With the exception of 1980, when grain output fell 3 percent and deliveries to the state declined by less than 1 percent. See table 1.
25. See table 5. Note that the degree of underfulfillment increased despite the fact that the quota levels were being reduced.

These various problems contributed to a decision to carry out major modifications in the state procurement system and also to reduce the overall scope of planned commerce for agricultural products. Reform of the state procurement system began in 1983 when the government eliminated the price bonus for above-quota deliveries of oilseeds and began to pay a single price for both quota and above-quota deliveries. Although there was some variation by region and variety, in general the new oilseed price was a weighted average of 40 percent of the old quota price plus 60 percent of the old above-quota price (Wang, 1985a, p. 52). Similar reforms occurred for cotton in 1984,[26] and then for grain in 1985. For grain, the new price was set equal to 30 percent of the quota price, plus 70 percent of the above-quota price ("Jiage Wenjian Zhaibian," 1985, 4:51). This change to a single price system not only eliminated some of the structural problems with the above-quota bonus method, but also effectively lowered the prices the state paid for above-quota deliveries. Whether the average prices paid by the state increased or decreased varied from region to region, but from a national perspective the relative weights on quota and above-quota prices were close to the proportions of quota and above-quota (including negotiated) purchases (table 6).

In conjunction with these procurement price reforms, the government began to reduce the scope of state-planned commerce and allow the market to play a greater role in price determination and resource allocation. Actually, the government had begun to move in the direction of market allocation as early as 1978. At that time, even though the state-planned commercial system remained more or less in place, free markets for most agricultural products were encouraged to revive and play a more important role.

The state had also taken steps to make planned prices somewhat more responsive to market forces. The first step in this direction was to enlarge the role of "negotiated" prices in state commerce. Negotiated purchase prices were to be agreed upon jointly by the producer and local state commercial agents, and they were to apply to voluntary above-quota deliveries to the state. These prices, moreover, were to be decided on the basis of regional, yearly, seasonal, varietal, and quality considerations, and basically were to follow supply and demand trends; however, they were in general not to exceed local market prices (Wang, 1985a, p. 53). The revival

26. Almanac of China's Economy Editorial Group (1984), pp. IV–50, IX–132, and "Jiage Wenjian Zhaibian" (1985) 2:47. The new cotton pricing system was first experimented with in Hubei and Shandong in 1983, and then extended nationwide in 1984. In the north the new price was equal to .8 times the above-quota price plus .2 times the quota price. In the south, the new price was equal to .4 times the above-quota price plus .6 times the quota price. In 1985 the price weights in the north were changed to .7 times the above-quota price and .3 times the quota price. Under this new pricing system, prices were higher in the north than in the south, although this had already been true because the proportion of above-quota sales in the north had been considerably higher than in the south.

of negotiated price procurement gave the state commercial system more flexibility in responding to market conditions, and, together with negotiated price sales, provided a lever for influencing prices in the free market. Moreover, in areas where earnings from new sideline and nonagricultural work opportunities threatened to divert labor from agriculture, local officials could use the higher negotiated purchase prices to make agriculture competitive and maintain government procurement.[27] The importance of negotiated price procurement grew quite rapidly. For grain, negotiated price procurement rose from less than 3 percent of net state purchases in 1978 to roughly 17 percent by 1983 (State Statistical Bureau Department of Commercial and Price Statistics, 1984, pp. 156, 329).

In 1985 the state implemented a new set of reforms with the intent of reducing radically the scope of planned commerce and further enlarging the role of market allocation. On January 1, 1985, the government announced that, except for a few products, it would no longer send down procurement quotas to farmers. For grain and cotton, mandatory quotas were to be eliminated altogether and replaced by a program of contract and market purchases. Commercial departments were to negotiate purchase contracts with farmers before the sowing season and when necessary carry out supplemental procurement on the free market. The prices of these contracts was fixed at the new, weighted prices mentioned above, and farmers could choose freely whether or not they entered into contracts. Products not under contract could be retained, sold on the market, or sold to the state at a low, guaranteed price (equal to the old quota price) at harvest time. The state no longer promised to buy as much as farmers wished to sell at the higher above-quota or contract prices.

Planned procurement of agricultural products other than grain and cotton was to be gradually eliminated and replaced by free market allocation. State commercial departments would increasingly buy and sell on the market. Through market participation state commercial departments could not only make supplementary purchases to meet the need for exports and continued planned supply to urban areas, but also exert influence on free market trends ("Jiage Wenjian Zhaibian," 1985, 4:51).

The full effects of the second stage of commercial reforms are still unclear. Recent reports suggest that in practice the grain contracts are not always voluntary but more closely resemble the old procurement quotas, except that state procurements are limited (Oi, 1986, pp. 284–90, and author interviews in China). Production data indicate that reductions in the prices paid for additional deliveries have dampened producer incentives, and farm incomes have apparently fallen in some areas.[28] State

27. Huang (1983), pp. 36–37, discusses use of negotiated pricing for this purpose in Guangdong Province.
28. Oilseed production fell in 1983 after the switch to the weighted pricing scheme, although it recovered in 1984. Both grain and cotton production fell in 1985, the former by 6

procurements declined in 1985—for grain by 16 percent (table 1). The program has therefore probably helped ease state storage and budgetary problems.

Retail Prices

Policies regarding retail prices for grain and other foodstuffs have, like state purchase price policies, varied over time. On the consumer side as well as on the producer side, moreover, the state has often relied on nonprice instruments to promote allocational and distributional objectives. Commercial planning in the form of rationing has played an important role in this regard. The state has also used wage policies and income supplements in conjunction with retail pricing to resolve contradictions between consumer and producer interests.

An important feature of China's retail policies has been the differentiation between policies applying to the urban and rural populations. Rural and urban residents have been treated differently both with regard to quantities supplied through the state commercial system and with regard to the retail sales prices they pay. The state has followed a policy of, in general, buying grain from, but not selling grain to, rural areas. Rural residents, with the exception of those living in areas designated as specialized economic crop-producing or grain-deficit areas, have not been included in the food rationing program. Instead, rural food demand has been met largely by self-sufficient production. When policies have permitted, self-supply has been supplemented by purchases on free markets and through encouragement sales programs.

The state unified sales program has, then, focused primarily on supplying food to the urban population and providing raw materials to industry. Food has been supplied to urban residents under a system of fixed rations, where each individual, depending on his or her age and type of work, is given the right to purchase a certain quantity of grain and other foodstuffs at state retail prices.

In the 1950s after the implementation of state-planned commerce, state retail prices of grain and other food products were set equal to their planned purchase prices plus reasonable transport and handling fees, processing costs (where relevant), taxes, and profits according to government regulations. The state commercial system made slight profits from its trade in grain and other food products (Wang, 1985a, p. 51; see also table 7); and retail grain prices were 5–15 percent higher than state purchase prices, with larger differentials for retail prices in large- and medium-sized cities than for those in rural towns and county seats (Wang, 1985b, p. 61; Xiao, 1983, p. 32; and Xu et al., 1982, p. 125).

---

percent and the latter by 30 percent. The 1985 declines in output have been attributed to bad weather, but the new policies have undoubtedly also been influential.

TABLE 7. Losses of state grain commercial enterprises[a] (millions of yuan, net profits in parentheses)

	1953	1957	1965	1970	1973	1975	1976	1977	1978	1979	1980	1981	1982
Total losses	(328)	(385)	2,302[b]	2,461	2,981	4,292	5,175	4,774	3,231	7,806	10,252[e]	12,788	14,137
Breakdown:[c]													
1. Expenditures on above-quota price bonuses	—	—	—	251	636	1,001	1,220	1,108	1,132	3,172	4,190	6,025	6,429
2. Expenditures on grain purchased at negotiated price but sold at list price	—	—	294	—	—	—	—	—	—	68	367	574	961
3. Subsidies for recent quota price increases	—	—	—	—	—	—	—	—	65	2,450	3,561	4,068	4,591
4. Subsidies on grain purchased at quota price and sold at list price	(321)	(324)	1,738	2,328	2,704	3,644	4,261	4,074	2,647	2,849	3,241	3,626	4,095
5. Earnings on negotiated trade	—	—	(107)	(118)	(359)	(353)	(306)	(408)	(613)	(90)	(399)	(694)	(921)
6. Other earnings[d]	(7)	(61)	(317)	—	—	—	—	—	—	(643)	(708)	(810)	(1,018)

SOURCE: Ministry of Commerce Institute of Commercial Economic Research (1984), p. 521.
[a]The original table states that these are losses for "grain commercial enterprises," which I assume refers to state and parastatal commercial enterprises that engage in grain commerce.
[b]This includes 694 million yuan losses on grain imports (which do not appear in the breakdown). Other years do not include losses or profits on grain imports and exports.
[c]The way in which total losses are broken down reflects accounting and reporting practices of the grain commercial system.
[d]Includes earnings on industrial (probably processing) and transport activities, as well as other activities.
[e]Includes 45 million yuan in state storage subsidies.

Starting in the late fifties, the state began to raise purchase prices without carrying out commensurate increases in retail prices. Grain retail prices were not raised with the regional purchase price increases in 1958 and 1960. More important, in 1961 when farm prices for grain were raised 27 percent nationwide, retail prices for grain supplied under the rationing program remained unchanged (table 8).[29] This led to an inversion of the purchase and retail price (figure 1).[30] The government subsidized the resulting losses—estimated at roughly 0.04 yuan per kilogram (Xue, 1985, p. 45)—incurred by the state commercial system. (The price subsidies referred to in this section apply only to domestic trade, and do not include subsidies on imports, which are discussed below.)

Despite the fact that retail grain prices were gradually raised during the early and mid-sixties (table 8), the state still sustained losses on its grain commerce (table 7). Retail prices were not high enough to cover completely the costs of procuring grain at the list purchase price, let alone the additional costs of transportation and handling (Xu et al., 1982, pp. 125–26), and the state was paying even higher prices for grain purchased under the price bonus and material incentive programs.

Grain retail prices for urban residents have remained more or less unchanged since 1967.[31] State price subsidies for grain have meanwhile grown. Between 1965 and 1970, total grain price subsidies appear to have risen from about 1.6 to 2.5 billion yuan a year. By the mid-seventies they had reached 4 to 5 billion yuan a year. After the major price increase in 1979, state grain subsidies more than doubled, exceeding 10 billion yuan a year since 1980 (table 7). As a percentage of total government expenditures, grain price subsidies rose from roughly 5 percent in 1965 to over 10 percent in the 1980s (Ministry of Commerce Institute of Commercial Economic Research, 1984, p. 521; State Statistical Bureau, 1984, p. 417). The most important factors underlying this expansion have been growth in above-quota procurement and the 1979 hikes in grain purchase prices.

Reasons commonly given for maintaining grain price subsidies are that retail price increases for this important staple would reduce living standards and destabilize markets (Commercial Prices Editorial Group, 1980, p. 128; Wang, 1985a, p. 51; and Qiao, 1983, p. 18). Concern about the effects of price adjustments on urban living standards has been so strong, in fact, that similar policies have applied to other food products. For example, in 1971–72 when oilseed prices were raised 25 percent, retail

29. Higher prices were charged for beyond-ration purchases of certain foodstuffs. Commercial Prices Editorial Group (1980), pp. 213–14.

30. Xiao (1983), p. 32, states that the state grain purchase price was 19 percent higher than its retail sales price.

31. State retail grain prices for some categories of grain sold in rural areas have, however, been increased in the 1980s. In addition, state retail prices for a range of nongrain foods were raised in the late 1970s and early 1980s.

TABLE 8.   State quota procurement and retail grain price indexes (1965 = 100)

Year	Quota price index	Retail price index
1950	52.4	76.2
1951	62.0	78.9
1952	63.6	85.4
1953	71.8	92.1
1954	71.8	92.2
1955	71.9	92.2
1956	73.3	92.2
1957	74.1	91.8
1958	76.0	91.9
1959	77.0	92.1
1960	79.5	92.7
1961	100.5	93.2
1962	100.8	93.3
1963	100.0	94.4
1964	99.1	94.8
1965	100.0	100.0
1966	115.7	104.8
1967	115.8	110.4
1968	115.8	110.4
1969	115.8	110.4
1970	115.8	110.4
1971	116.3	110.4
1972	116.4	110.4
1973	116.4	110.5
1974	116.5	110.5
1975	116.7	110.5
1976	116.7	110.5
1977	116.7	110.5
1978	117.5	110.5
1979	142.1	112.2

NOTE: The year 1965 was chosen as a base year because in 1965 the retail price for grain was only slightly lower than the quota price. Comparison of these two indexes therefore gives a general idea of changes in the relationship between the quota and retail prices.
SOURCE: Liu (1982), pp. 613, 615.

sales prices for edible vegetable oils were not increased (Wang, 1985a, p. 52). Other products receiving price subsidies have included meat and poultry products, vegetables, cotton, and coal. Price subsidies of this type (i.e., due to inversion of purchase and sales prices) totaled 21 billion yuan in 1981, equal to 18 percent of total government expenditures.[32]

Further evidence of the government's concern about urban incomes is the fact that whenever the government has increased retail prices, it has almost always raised wages or implemented special wage supplements in urban areas. After the grain price increases in 1965–66, the state began to

32. Qiao (1983), p. 18, and State Statistical Bureau (1984), p. 417. This figure, like the other subsidy figures given in this section, does not include subsidies on imported foodstuffs.

FIGURE 1. State quota and retail price indexes

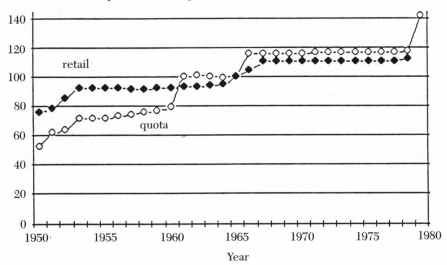

give urban workers and staff a "grain price wage supplement" (*liangjia butie*) (Wang, 1985a, p. 51). Similarly, after raising the prices of eight important nongrain foods (including pork and other red meats, vegetables, poultry products, aquatic products, and milk) in 1979, each urban worker began to receive a monthly wage supplement of 5 yuan, and 40 percent of all urban workers were promoted to higher wage grades (Wan, 1982, pp. 41–42). Such wage increases and supplements, which are not included in the figures for price subsidies given above, have placed an additional burden on the state budget.[33]

One measure used to control growing price subsidies and supplement the earnings of the state commercial system is charging higher, negotiated prices for beyond-ration purchases. In 1979 when the state reinstituted the negotiated purchase system, it also revived the negotiated sales program. Foodstuffs sold under this program have, in general, originally been purchased at negotiated prices. Their sales prices are supposed to equal the negotiated purchase price plus transport and handling fees and some small level of profit, and they are not supposed to exceed local free market prices (Wang, 1985a, p. 53). Although the volume of negotiated sales has grown, it appears that, on balance, negotiated commerce has not reduced state price subsidies. The reason for this is that negotiated sales have not kept up with negotiated purchases. For various reasons, including the fact that the ne-

33. Wan (1982), pp. 41–42, states that in one year the 5 yuan monthly wage supplements instituted in 1979 cost the state 5 billion yuan, exceeding the additional revenues earned by raising subsidiary foods' retail prices by 1 billion yuan.

gotiated procurement program has probably contributed to difficulties enforcing delivery quotas, the state has found itself selling products bought at
higher negotiated prices for the low retail list prices under its planned
supply program. Losses on these sales have offset the profits on grain sold
at negotiated prices (table 7).[34]

Tradeoffs in Price Policy

The history of China's food pricing reveals that Chinese policy makers
have faced (or in some cases, avoided) several key pricing issues. The most
important of these have been (1) the tradeoff between pricing for consumers versus pricing for producers, (2) the relationship between pricing
policy and government budgetary considerations, (3) the relationship between pricing policy and overall price stabilization, and (4) the relationship
between domestic pricing policy and international trade in foodstuffs.

Consumers versus Producers

Since the late fifties, food price policy in China has reflected attempts to
balance the interests of urban consumers and considerations of rural production and incomes. In order to protect urban incomes, the government
has tried to avoid raising retail prices. To some extent, concern about
urban food prices was a reaction against the hyperinflation of the 1940s.
More important, perhaps, has been the desire to prevent dissatisfaction in
the highly visible and powerful urban population, especially during periods when the state was simultaneously maintaining strict control over
urban wages.

Constancy of retail prices has made increases in producer prices undesirable, yet such increases stimulate production and marketing, and also
transfer income from the wealthier urban to the poorer rural population.[35]
Furthermore, upward adjustment in producer prices was necessary because the relative prices of agricultural products at the time when state
commercial planning was implemented were already low: in the early
fifties the prices of manufactured goods were high due to shortages during
the recovery from the civil war and due to diversion of resources during
the Korean War (Stone, 1988, p. 211).

For most of the past three decades, the government has tried to sidestep
this contradiction. One approach, used unsuccessfully during the First

34. For example, data given in Ministry of Commerce Institute of Commercial Economic
Research (1984), p. 521, show increasing subsidies for grain purchased at negotiated prices
but sold at regular list retail prices. For grain alone such subsidies amounted to 1 billion yuan
in 1982, exceeding profits on the negotiated price sale of grain.

35. Due to the numerous price subsidies received by urban residents, it is difficult to
estimate the differential between urban and rural incomes. Rough approximations suggest
that urban incomes have on average been two to three times those in rural areas.

Five-Year Plan period and Great Leap Forward, was to substitute institutional reorganization of agriculture for higher producer prices. Interestingly, institutional change has also been employed in the post-Mao period, although in conjunction with, rather than as a substitute for, producer price increases. A second approach was to use quantity planning as a substitute for price adjustments. The use of delivery quotas was important during both the fifties and the Cultural Revolution. Production planning, usually in the form of sown area targets, was also used during these two periods, although the government's ability to enforce such targets was limited during the fifties (Perkins, 1966, pp. 65–68).

Finally, when producer price increases seemed unavoidable, the state resorted to various distortions of the producer pricing system so as to raise prices without really raising prices. Above-quota price incentives and encouragement sales served this purpose. The former were used to increase prices but on only a portion of grain purchases, and so provide incentives to producers at less cost to the state. The latter were a form of disguised price increase, which, if not less costly than raising prices, at least shifted the costs from one level or branch of government to another.

At two times—in the early sixties and again in the late seventies—the state faced the issue head-on and raised producer prices by significant margins. In both instances the government decided to absorb the costs of the price increases rather than pass the costs on to urban consumers: retail prices were not raised commensurately.[36] Not surprisingly, these decisions occurred at points in time when concern about agriculture was great. Once agriculture had responded, the government took actions to reduce the burden of price subsidies on the budget. In the early and mid-sixties the government reduced the burden by raising retail grain prices, and in the mid-eighties both by raising retail prices and lowering producer prices.

State Budgetary Considerations

An issue closely related to the tradeoff between consumer and producer prices is the relationship between food price policy and the state budget. Until recently the profits of industrial and commercial enterprises have, for all practical purposes, entered directly into the state budget. Industrial and commercial profits, in fact, have generally provided between 40 percent and 60 percent of total government revenues.[37] Maintaining low prices for staples has allowed the state to keep wages low, which in turn has

---

36. In addition, the state raised oilseed purchase prices without raising edible vegetable oil sales prices in the early seventies.

37. State Statistical Bureau (1984), p. 419. These percentages are for direct enterprise income (*qiye shouru*) and do not include revenues from industrial and commercial taxes (*gongshang shuishou*).

enhanced the profitability of industrial enterprises and thus state revenues. For these reasons the low retail price strategy both benefited urban consumers and served as a means to transfer resources to the state sector and industry.

To maintain enterprise profits, the state not only had to keep wages and the prices of wage goods low, but also had to keep the prices of industrial products, especially those sold outside the industrial and urban sectors, high. The relationship between the state budget and pricing thus largely depended on the "price scissors," that is, the ratio between agricultural purchase prices and the prices charged for manufactured products sold in rural areas. The overvaluation of manufactures relative to agricultural products is to some extent a historical accident. At the time that the state began to fix prices, the early fifties, agricultural prices were low relative to industrial goods. In the following decades various factors should have caused improvement in agriculture's terms of trade: during the fifties rapid recovery of industry and the end of the Korean War should have reduced the relative prices of industrial products. In the longer run, rates of growth in industrial output far exceeding those for agriculture should also have induced improvement in agriculture's terms of trade.

The state did take steps to close the "price scissors" after the fifties; however, it is unlikely that prior to the post-Mao period these steps fully corrected the undervaluation of agricultural and overvaluation of industrial goods. Thus through the pricing mechanism the state has continued to invisibly transfer financial resources out of agriculture. Moreover, the extent of the transfer has grown considerably as purchases of manufactured producer and consumer goods in rural areas has risen.

Various evidence supports the conclusion that pricing has been used as a form of government finance. First, although the state made efforts to improve agriculture's terms of trade by raising procurement prices and gradually reducing the prices on certain modern inputs, it openly acknowledged that the invisible tax was an indispensable method for financing industrial capital accumulation. As late as 1979, the prominent economist Su Xing wrote

Can "scissors differential" be eliminated altogether? The key problem is whether agricultural production should be used to provide a portion of industrial accumulation. The main reason why the "scissors" cannot be eliminated now is that the state has to accumulate some of its industrial construction capital from the agricultural sector through the industrial and agricultural products price parity. . . . In our country, the agricultural taxation rate is not high . . . and could not have provided much for the industrial capital accumulation. The primary means of industrial accumulation from agricultural production is raised through the price parity between agricultural and industrial products . . . first by keeping the prices of certain farm products below their values [and] second by keeping the prices of certain industrial items above their values. (1974, p. 14)

Second, empirical studies by various non-Chinese economists including Lardy and Ishikawa (Lardy, 1983b, chapter 3; Ishikawa, 1967a and 1967b) have concluded that net transfers through the terms of trade have been from agriculture to industry. Third, cross-country comparisons of the ratios of agricultural product prices to modern input prices demonstrate that prior to 1979 China's ratios were low by international standards (Lardy, 1983a, pp. 55–66; Stone, 1988, p. 211; Sicular, 1980).

China is, of course, not the only developing or socialist country that has used pricing as a form of public finance. Such an approach to raising government revenues, however, has often been ineffective in the long run because in the long run producers respond to the low prices, and so the tax base is reduced. The effectiveness of the price tax, in other words, depends on the long-run supply elasticity of output with respect to price. Unfortunately, elasticity estimates are unavailable for China. Slow growth of grain production during periods when prices were not increased (or, as in 1985, decreased) and rapid growth under more favorable price regimes suggest that such a tradeoff may have existed.

As a consequence of the intimate relationship between pricing and the state budget, food pricing policy can influence the extent of government deficit and thus, indirectly, the overall price level. Since the early fifties, China has experienced two periods of major inflationary pressure: in the wake of the Great Leap in the early 1960s, and after 1979. Chinese economists blame inflation in both periods on the existence of a budget deficit that was financed by issuing money (table 9) (Xue, 1985, and Xu et al., 1982, pp. 199–222). Although many factors contributed to the existence of deficits at these times,[38] food pricing certainly was part of the problem, especially after 1979 when commercial price subsidies for food grew rapidly. By 1982 grain price subsidies alone exceeded 12 percent of total government expenditures (Ministry of Commerce Institute of Commercial Economic Research, 1984, p. 521, and State Statistical Bureau, 1984, p. 417).

Price Stabilization

China's leaders have revealed an almost obsessive concern with price stability. The extent of concern has been so great that they have used both fiscal and monetary policy and also direct administrative price control to

---

38. See Xu et al. (1982), pp. 199–222, for an interesting discussion of the factors underlying inflation during the post-Mao and earlier periods.

TABLE 9.   Government budgetary data,
1950–85 (in billion yuan)

Year	Revenues	Expenditures	Surplus or deficit	Government borrowing
1950	6.22	6.81	−.59	.30
1951	12.49	12.25	.24	.82
1952	17.39	17.60	−.21	.98
1953	21.33	22.01	−.68	.96
1954	24.52	24.63	−.11	1.72
1955	24.92	26.93	−2.01	2.28
1956	28.02	30.57	−2.55	.72
1957	30.32	30.42	−.10	.70
1958	37.96	40.94	−2.98	.80
1959	48.71	55.29	−6.58	0
1960	57.23	65.41	−8.18	0
1961	35.61	36.70	−1.09	0
1962	31.36	30.53	.83	0
1963	34.23	33.96	.27	0
1964	39.95	39.90	.05	0
1965	47.33	46.63	.70	0
1966	55.87	54.16	1.71	0
1967	41.94	44.19	−2.25	0
1968	36.13	35.98	.15	0
1969	52.68	52.59	.09	0
1970	66.29	64.94	1.35	0
1971	74.47	73.22	1.25	0
1972	76.66	76.64	.02	0
1973	80.97	80.93	.04	0
1974	78.31	79.08	−.77	0
1975	81.56	82.09	−.53	0
1976	77.66	80.62	−2.96	0
1977	87.45	84.35	3.10	0
1978	112.11	111.10	1.01	0
1979	106.80	127.39	−20.59	3.53
1980	104.22	121.27	−17.05	4.30
1981	101.64	111.50	−9.86	7.31
1982	104.01	115.33	−11.32	8.39
1983	116.96	129.25	−12.29	7.94
1984	142.46	154.64	−12.18	7.73
1985	177.65	184.48	−6.83	8.99

NOTE: Chinese government revenue data usually include government borrowing. In this table, borrowing has been taken out of revenues so that the revenue and surplus (or deficit) data are consistent with the western counterparts. Government borrowing includes domestic bond issues and borrowing from abroad.
SOURCES: State Statistical Bureau (1984), pp. 417–18; State Statistical Bureau (1986), pp. 595, 597.

ensure stability. The record of food price policy since 1953 reflects that for much of the past thirty years price stabilization has taken precedence over other considerations in price planning.

State pricing policy has reflected the concern with price stabilization in several ways. First, planned pricing has been used to control inflation by maintaining low state prices while enforcing quantity controls such as rationing and quotas. Price controls have been accompanied by appropriate macroeconomic measures. Indeed, for most of the sixties and seventies the government maintained budget surpluses and controlled growth in the money supply. Even in the early sixties and after 1979 when deficits emerged and money supply growth accelerated, the state quickly responded with strong measures. During these periods, however, direct price intervention was also employed to hold down inflation rates. Moreover, it is likely that direct price interventions have held the level of retail prices below its equilibrium during other periods.

Second, price planning has been used to maintain stable prices for basic foodstuffs in urban areas. Since wage levels were also controlled, such a pricing policy prevented fluctuations in real incomes and guaranteed that urban families could afford basic necessities. Even though urban residents were assured of price stability, however, some degree of uncertainty existed regarding availability. In particular, the availability of supplies for those who wanted to buy grain beyond their rations, and more important, the availability of high-quality grains and minor grain varieties, of meats, poultry, eggs, oils and fats, fruit, and vegetables, and of many other foods, was variable. Quantity rationing replaced price rationing, and uncertainty in quantities replaced price uncertainty.

Third, price stability was maintained on the producer side because planners postponed or minimized adjustments in agricultural producer prices despite long-term changes in demand and production costs. The lack of any producer price responses to changes in demand contributed to the uncertainty of supplies in urban areas. In addition, with major changes in technology and uneven technical change among different crops, the relationship between costs of production and prices became irrational, reducing economic efficiency and long-run growth in agriculture.

Finally, short-term annual and seasonal price fluctuations were eliminated or considerably reduced. The elimination of annual price fluctuations that resulted from year-to-year weather variation ensured more stable prices for producers, but eliminating the negative correlation between prices and yields may have made farm income more variable. Seasonal price differentials were gradually eliminated for almost all farm products, and as of 1979 remained only for products such as fruit and fresh vegetables, whose production was highly seasonal in nature and which were expensive to store. Seasonal price differentials of about 15 percent were revived for fresh eggs in 1979. Even for those products with seasonal pricing, the differentials were often too narrow (Zhou, 1985, pp. 54–55; Commercial Prices Editorial Group, 1980, p. 141).

In the absence of seasonal price variations, producers have had no incentive to increase off-season production of perishable farm products or to store less perishable output for sale in the off-season. The disincentives to storage were to some extent offset by state storage—the state commercial system has been responsible for much storage, and its storage costs are subsidized. Absence of seasonality in the prices for storable products, however, has translated into considerable seasonality in the timing of deliveries to the state and uneven utilization of state storage facilities. State procurement is concentrated in certain seasons, for example, the spring and fall harvest times for grain, because producers want to sell all their product to the state as soon as they can. The seasonal concentration of procurement causes poor capacity utilization of government warehouses. It has also contributed to situations in which local state procurement departments are unable to handle peak season deliveries, so that producers are unable to sell their grain to the state.[39]

Domestic Pricing and International Trade

Over the past thirty years China's domestic prices have been almost completely divorced from short- and long-term shifts in international prices, and the structure of domestic food and agricultural prices has diverged from that internationally. Although this has insulated domestic prices from short-term international price fluctuations, it has also promoted an economic structure that is not altogether consistent with China's international comparative advantage. Moreover, deviations between domestic and international prices have led to widely uneven levels of profit and loss across commodities for the state trading system.

In agriculture, inefficiencies have arisen because the relative prices among food products are out of line with those in international markets, and also because the relative prices of modern inputs are high. (See table 10.) For example, the domestic state prices of rice have been too low and of wheat too high relative to the prices of other crops. In international markets, although the rice/wheat price ratio declined to about 1.7 in the early eighties, in general milled rice prices have been at least twice the price of wheat. In China the two prices have been and continue to be about equal on both the procurement and retail sides.[40] Similarly, the cotton/rice procurement price ratio has been 50 percent to 100 percent higher and the cotton/wheat procurement price ratio 20 percent to 50 percent lower than that internationally.

These discrepancies imply that Chinese price ratios signaled producers (consumers) to overproduce (underconsume) wheat and underproduce (overconsume) rice, and that, at least on the margin, China could have benefited from exporting rice in exchange for imports of wheat. In addi-

---

39. See the articles by Li Feng (1985) and Feng Weimin (1984) for discussion of these problems. Both authors propose instituting seasonal grain price differentials as a solution.

40. Chinese procurement price ratios quoted in the text are calculated using above-quota prices.

TABLE 10. Chinese above-quota and international commodity price ratios

	1957	1962	1966	1971	1978	1979	1980	1981	1982	1983	1984
Rice/wheat											
China	0.95	0.99	1.00	1.00	0.97	0.96	1.01	1.01	1.01	1.01	1.01
Int'l	2.09	2.38	2.64	2.11	2.88	2.09	2.51	2.76	1.83	1.76	1.65
Wheat/corn											
China	1.60	1.52	1.48	1.48	1.55	1.54	1.47	1.47	1.47	1.47	1.47
Int'l	1.18	1.32	1.09	1.06	1.27	1.38	1.37	1.34	1.48	1.16	1.12
Cotton/rice											
China	10.12	7.52	6.85	5.35	6.72	7.27	8.00	8.10	8.10	8.10	n.a.
Int'l	6.68	4.85	3.51	4.69	3.45	4.09	4.13	3.29	4.51	5.45	5.96
Cotton/wheat											
China	9.59	7.41	6.86	5.35	6.51	6.98	8.05	8.15	8.15	8.15	n.a.
Int'l	13.94	11.52	9.26	9.89	9.93	8.55	10.38	9.08	8.26	9.59	9.85
Rice/soy											
China	1.03	0.90	0.91	0.82	0.66	0.69	0.69	0.69	0.69	0.85	0.85
Int'l	1.37	1.53	1.31	1.04	1.37	1.12	1.46	1.67	1.20	0.98	0.89
Wheat/soy											
China	1.09	0.91	0.91	0.82	0.68	0.71	0.68	0.68	0.68	0.84	0.84
Int'l	0.66	0.64	0.50	0.49	0.48	0.54	0.58	0.61	0.66	0.56	0.54

NOTE: Chinese paddy prices are converted to rice prices at a rate of 0.73.
SOURCES: International Monetary Fund, *International Financial Statistics Yearbook* (various issues). Appendix tables in this chapter.

tion, since wheat is generally grown in the north and rice in the south, these price relationships have encouraged overproduction in the south and underproduction in the north of cotton and other crops that competed with these major grains.

The divergence of the domestic from the international price structure has also caused widely uneven levels of profit and loss across traded commodities for the state foreign trade system. As mentioned above, food and agricultural products are undervalued relative to manufactures in China. In addition, retail prices for food products have been kept low. Consequently, state trading corporations tend to lose money on imports of agricultural products and earn money on their exportation. (The opposite tends to hold for trade in manufactures.)

China's exchange rate policies have to some extent mitigated the effects of the domestic price structure on the profitability of trade in food products. Overvaluation of the yuan relative to other currencies for many years made imports more profitable and exports less so. The official exchange rate declined after 1970 to 1.5 (yuan per U.S. dollar) in the late seventies. Since 1980 the state has gradually devalued the yuan, so that the exchange rate reached 2.32 in 1984 (table 11) and as of late 1985 was about 3.70. At least prior to 1984, these exchange rates probably overvalued the yuan: the domestic resource cost of obtaining one U.S. dollar has been estimated at between 2.3 and 2.6 yuan in the early eighties, somewhat higher than the exchange rate (World Bank, 1983, p. 449; Lardy, 1983a, p. 38).

Overvaluation reduced the earnings of state trading companies on food exports and increased their earnings on food imports, thus having the opposite effect of the domestic price structure. For manufactures, overvaluation has reinforced the effects of the domestic price structure. In general, China's exchange rate policies made foreign commodities seem inexpensive by domestic standards and so have encouraged trade deficits. This tendency has partly been corrected with devaluations since 1984.

Although exchange rate policies have to some degree offset the effects of the domestic price structure on China's food trade, state trading companies still lose money on food imports. As of 1982, the state was subsidizing imports of grains, cotton, and sugar (Qiao, 1983, pp. 17–18). Devaluation of the exchange rate after that date probably only magnified the size of food import subsidies. Of course, these subsidies are accounting losses and not necessarily social losses. Moreover, because a large proportion of China's trade is carried out by the state, government policy contains the response of the trading system to these economic signals, and within the state trading system, losses on food imports are offset by positive earnings on other imports and exports. Nevertheless, the government is concerned about losses on food imports because they contribute to the overall budget deficit. Also, as institutional reform and decentralization have taken place

TABLE 11.   The official exchange rate, 1957–70
(yuan per U.S. dollar)

Year	Exchange rate	Year	Exchange rate
1957	2.4618	1971	2.4618
1958	2.4618	1972	2.2451
1959	2.4618	1973	1.9894
1960	2.4618	1974	1.9612
1961	2.4618	1975	1.8598
1962	2.4618	1976	1.9414
1963	2.4618	1977	1.8578
1964	2.4618	1978	1.6836
1965	2.4618	1979	1.5550
1966	2.4618	1980	1.4984
1967	2.4618	1981	1.7045
1968	2.4618	1982	1.8925
1969	2.4618	1983	1.9757
1970	2.4618	1984	2.3200

SOURCE: International Monetary Fund (1985).

in foreign trade, the potential for trading agents to respond to incorrect price signals has increased.[41]

Although pricing policies have caused inefficiencies in China's foreign trade structure, China's large size makes such considerations somewhat less critical than for smaller nations. Furthermore, China has to some extent consciously forgone gains from trade in order to pursue national security objectives: by minimizing the need for imports of important commodities, China has reduced its dependence on other, potentially hostile, nations. Finally, the barriers between the domestic economy and international markets were, to a large extent, set up by other nations. Prior to the early seventies when the U.S. and China began to normalize their diplomatic relations, the U.S. had led many other western nations in a general embargo on trade with China.

Conclusion

Over the past three decades Chinese leaders have tried to design national policies to promote the objectives of rapid economic growth, equitable income distribution, national security, and a "good" society. More often than not, food pricing policy has promoted only a subset of these goals while detracting from one or more of the others. In such instances policy makers either have relied on nonprice instruments to promote the other objectives, or else have temporarily assigned those other objectives lower priority.

Food pricing policy has been related to the first objective, rapid eco-

41. Davie (1986), especially pp. 318–20, discusses many of these issues.

nomic growth, in several ways. On the one hand, undervaluation of agricultural products has been used as a mode of taxation to mobilize resources for industrial investment. On the other hand, this undervaluation has contributed to slow growth in agricultural output. Quantity planning and institutional reforms have been used to counteract the negative effects of low agricultural prices, but with only partial success. In recognition of these problems, in the early sixties and again in the post-Mao period, China has chosen to raise agricultural prices. Both these price revisions, however, contributed to government financial difficulties, and so reduced the state's ability to mobilize resources for industrial investment.

With respect to distributional objectives, in the late fifties and early sixties producer pricing measures were used to improve the regional distribution of income in rural areas. Since the early sixties, retail price policies have protected urban consumers and have helped maintain an equitable distribution of basic foods within urban areas. With the assistance of food pricing policy, China has attained a remarkable degree of intraurban equality. Improvement in the urban-rural and intrarural income distributions has, however, proven elusive. It is unlikely that pricing was the cause of or could have been a cure for the intrarural distribution problem—other sorts of policies would probably be more effective in this regard. Pricing has, however, contributed to urban-rural inequality. When facing the tradeoff between pricing for urban consumers or rural producers, the government has generally chosen the former, thus exacerbating existing differentials in living standards. Even when producer prices have been increased, urban consumers have been shielded either by price subsidies or by wage increases and supplements.

National security considerations have prompted Chinese leaders to try to achieve independent industrial and military capabilities. China has been quite successful in these endeavors, and at least in the short run, pricing has assisted by keeping wage costs low and otherwise mobilizing resources for industrial development. Industrial and military self-sufficiency have, however, been achieved at the expense of agricultural self-sufficiency. As the result of a combination of pricing and other policies, China changed from a nation that had traditionally exported agricultural products to a net importer not only of grain, but also of agricultural raw materials required by industry. Policies and price revisions since 1978 enabled China to reemerge, at least temporarily, as an exporter of agricultural products.

Finally, Chinese leaders have often considered the use of prices to guide resource allocation as being in direct conflict with certain social goals. In order for pricing to guide resources effectively, individuals have to be responsive to material incentives and interested in personal gain. Material incentives and personal gain can be used very effectively to promote economic growth, but they can also encourage undesirable social behavior.

China's current leaders have chosen a strategy that relies heavily on prices to guide resources. Their strategy is based on the belief that economic development is a precondition for a good society. In the short term, anticorruption, antipollution, and other ideological campaigns have been used to educate the populace about larger social goals and to explain when personal gain and collective gain are consistent or contradictory. Whether current price and other reforms ultimately contribute to or detract from social objectives remains to be seen.

APPENDIX TABLE A.   State quota procurement prices (yuan/metric ton)

Year	Wheat	Paddy	Corn	Soybeans	Sugarcane	Sugar beet	Cotton
1952	163.00	113.40	94.40	131.40	21.00	33.00	1,735.60
1957	178.60	123.60	111.60	164.00	22.60	40.00	1,713.40
1962	229.40	165.00	150.60	251.20	28.00	54.20	1,700.40
1966	268.60	196.20	181.80	296.60	30.00	54.60	1,842.20
1971	268.60	196.20	181.80	326.00	34.60	54.20	1,869.40
1978	272.20	192.60	176.00	401.20	34.60	60.00	2,304.80
1979	329.60	231.00	214.40	461.40	42.40	75.00	2,655.20
1980	314.40	231.00	214.40	461.40	42.40	75.00	2,921.60
1981	314.40	231.00	214.40	692.10	42.40	75.00	2,956.00
1982	314.40	231.00	214.40	692.10	42.40	75.00	2,956.00
1983	314.40	231.00	214.40	560.00	42.40	75.00	2,956.00
1984	314.40	231.00	214.40	560.00	42.40	75.00	n.a.

SOURCE: Agricultural Technical Economics Handbook Editorial Group (1984).

APPENDIX TABLE B.   State above-quota procurement prices (yuan/metric ton)

Year	Wheat	Paddy	Corn	Soybeans	Sugarcane	Sugar beet	Cotton
1952	163.00	113.40	94.40	131.40	21.00	33.00	1,735.60
1957	178.60	123.60	111.60	164.00	22.60	40.00	1,713.40
1962	229.40	165.00	150.60	251.20	28.00	54.20	1,700.40
1966	322.32	235.44	218.16	355.92	30.00	54.60	1,842.20
1971	349.18	255.06	236.34	423.80	34.60	54.20	1,869.40
1978	353.86	255.06	228.80	521.56	34.60	60.00	2,304.80
1979	494.40	346.50	321.60	692.10	42.40	75.00	3,451.76
1980	471.60	346.50	321.60	692.10	42.40	75.00	3,798.08
1981	471.60	346.50	321.60	692.10	42.40	75.00	3,842.80
1982	471.60	346.50	321.60	692.10	42.40	75.00	3,842.80
1983	471.60	346.50	321.60	560.00	42.40	75.00	3,842.80
1984	471.60	346.50	321.60	560.00	42.40	75.00	n.a.

NOTE: Grain and soybean prices for 1966 equal the quota prices plus a bonus of ½ × (40%), or 20%.
SOURCES: Table 4 and appendix table A.

References

Agricultural Technical Economics Handbook Editorial Group. 1984. *Nongye Jishu Jingji Shouce* (Agricultural technical economics handbook). Beijing: Nongye Chubanshe.

Almanac of China's Economy Editorial Group. 1984. *Zhongguo Jingji Nianjian 1984* (Almanac of China's economy). Beijing: Jingji Guanli Chubanshe.

Commercial Prices Editorial Group. 1980. *Shangye Wujia* (Commercial prices). Beijing: Zhongguo Caizheng Jingji Chubanshe.

Davie, John L. 1986. "China's International Trade and Finance." In Joint Economic Committee of the U.S. Congress, ed., *China's Economy Looks toward the Year 2000*, vol. 2, 311–34. Washington, D.C.: U.S. Government Printing Office.

Donnithorne, Audrey. 1967. *China's Economic System*. New York: Praeger.

Eckstein, Alexander. 1977. *China's Economic Revolution*. New York: Cambridge University Press.

Feng, Weimin. 1984. "Jianyi Liangshi Shougou Shixing Jijie Chajia" (A suggestion to implement seasonal price differentials for grain procurement). *Jiage Lilun yu Shijian* (Price theory and practice) 1: 38.

Guo, Zhiqiang, and Jianshi Gu. 1983. "Mianhua Chaogou Jiajia Cujinle Shengchan, Dan Yeyou Bibing" (Above-quota price bonuses for cotton have promoted production, but also have drawbacks). *Jiage Lilun yu Shijian* (Price theory and practice) 5: 34–35.

He, Jian, ed. 1981. *Zhongguo Nongye Nianjian 1980* (China agricultural yearbook). Beijing: Nongye Chubanshe.

Huang, Liwu. 1983. "Gongfuye Fazhan Dui Nongchanpin Jiagede Yinxiang" (Development of industry and sidelines influences agricultural product prices). *Jiage Lilun yu Shijian* (Price theory and practice) 6: 36–37.

International Monetary Fund. 1985. *International Financial Statistics Yearbook*. Washington, D.C.

Ishikawa, Shigeru. 1967a. *Economic Development in Asian Perspective*. Tokyo: Kinokuniya.

——. 1967b. "The Resource Flow Between Agriculture and Industry: The Chinese Experience." *The Developing Economies* 5(1): 3–49.

"Jiage Wenjian Zhaibian" (Excerpts of selected price documents). 1985. *Jiage Lilun yu Shijian* (Price theory and practice) 2: 47–49; 4: 51–54.

Lardy, Nicholas R. 1983a. *Agricultural Prices in China*. World Bank Staff Working Paper, no. 606. Washington, D.C.: World Bank.

——. 1983b. *Agriculture in China's Modern Economic Development*. New York: Cambridge University Press.

Li, Feng. 1985. "Liangshi Shougou Shixing Jijie Chajiade Haochu" (The benefits of implementing seasonal price differentials for grain procurement). *Jiage Lilun yu Shijian* (Price theory and practice) 1: 31.

Liu, Zhuofu. 1982. *Wujia Shouce* (Price handbook). Beijing: Zhongguo Caizheng Jingji Chubanshe.

Ma, Hong. 1982. *Xiandai Zhongguo Jingji Shidian* (A dictionary of economic matters in modern China). Beijing: Zhongguo Shehui Kexue Chubanshe.

Ministry of Commerce Institute of Commercial Economic Research. 1984. *Xin Zhongguo Shangye Shigao* (A short history of commerce in new China). Beijing: Zhongguo Caizheng Jingji Chubanshe.

Oi, Jean C. 1986. "Peasant Grain Marketing and State Procurement: China's Grain Contracting System." *China Quarterly* 106: 272–90.

Perkins, Dwight H. 1966. *Market Control and Planning in Communist China*. Harvard Economic Studies, vol. 78. Cambridge: Harvard University Press.

Piazza, Alan. 1983. *Trends in Food and Nutrient Availability in China, 1950–81*. World Bank Staff Working Paper, no. 607. Washington, D.C.: World Bank.

Qiao, Rongzhang. 1983. "Jiage Butiede Yange, Xianzhuang, Jiqi Zuoyong" (The evolution, current status, and purpose of price subsidies). *Jiage Lilun yu Shijian* (Price theory and practice) 1: 17–19.

Sicular, Terry. 1980. "Agricultural Pricing Policy in the People's Republic of China." Paper presented at the SSRC Joint Committee on Contemporary China Workshop on the Chinese Economy, February 15–16, Columbia University.

———. 1986. "Recent Agricultural Price Policies and Their Effects: The Case of Shandong." Joint Economic Committee of the U.S. Congress, ed., *China's Economy Looks toward the Year 2000*, vol. 1, 407–430. Washington, D.C.: U.S. Government Printing Office.

State Statistical Bureau. 1984. *Zhongguo Tongji Nianjian 1984* (China statistical yearbook). Hong Kong: Xianggang Jingji Daobaoshe.

———. 1985. *Zhongguo Tongji Zhaiyao 1985* (China statistical abstract). Beijing: Zhongguo Tongji Chubanshe.

———. 1986. *Zhongguo Tongji Nianjian 1986* (China statistical yearbook). Beijing: Zhongguo Tongji Chubanshe.

State Statistical Bureau Department of Commercial and Price Statistics. 1984. *Zhongguo Maoyi Wujia Tongji Ziliao 1952–1983* (China commerce and price statistical data 1952–1983). Beijing: Zhongguo Tongji Chubanshe.

Stone, Bruce. 1988. "Relative Foodgrain Prices in the People's Republic of China: Rural Taxation Through Public Monopsony." In John W. Mellor and Raisuddin Ahmed, eds., *Agricultural Price Policy for Developing Countries*. Baltimore: Johns Hopkins University Press.

Su, Xing. 1979. "The Question of Prices of Agricultural Products." *Shehui Kexue Zhanxian* 2: 101–8. Translated in Joint Publication Research Service 74496 *China Report: Agriculture* 58: 12–21.

Tian, Jiyun. 1986. "On The Present Economic Situation and Restructuring the Economy." *Beijing Review* 29 (February 10): I–XV.

Vermeer, E. B. 1982. "Income Differentials in Rural China." *China Quarterly* 89 (March): 1–33.

Walker, Kenneth R. 1984. *Food Grain Procurement and Consumption in China*. New York: Cambridge University Press.

Wan, Dianwu. 1982. *Zhongguode Shangye: 1977–1980* (China's commerce: 1977–1980). Zhongguo Shehui Zhuyi Xiandai Hua Jianshe 6. Beijing: Renmin Chubanshe.

Wang, Dahuai. 1985a. "Nongchanpin Jiage Zhishi Jiangzuo: Liangshi He Youliao Jiage (Shang)" (A course of lectures on agricultural prices: grain and oilseeds prices [first half]). *Jiage Lilun yu Shijian* (Price theory and practice) 2: 50–53.

———. 1985b. "Nongchanpin Jiage Zhishi Jiangzuo: Liangshi He Youliao Jiage (Xia)" (A course of lectures on agricultural prices: grain and oilseeds prices [second half]). *Jiage Lilun yu Shijian* (Price theory and practice) 3: 61–64, 43.

Wang, Zhenzhi, and Yongzhi Wang. 1984. "Woguo Jinnianlai Nongchanpin Jiage Wenti Taolun Qingkuang Pingjie" (A review of the state of discussion on recent agricultural price problems in our country). *Jiage Lilun yu Shijian* (Price theory and practice) 2: 28–30.

World Bank. 1983. *China: Socialist Economic Development*, vol. 2. Washington, D.C.

Wu, Zhenkun. 1982. "Several Issues in the Continued Reliance of Agriculture on Economic Planning." *Renmin Ribao* (People's daily), May 27, 5.

Xiao, Shuping. 1983. "Xin Zhongguo Chengli Yilaide Liangshi Jiage Jiqi Guanli" (Grain prices and their management since the founding of new China). *Jiage Lilun yu Shijian* (Price theory and practice) 5: 32–33.

Xu, Yi, Baosen Chen, and Wuxia Liang. 1982. *Shehui Zhuyi Jiage Wenti* (Price questions under socialism). Beijing: Zhongguo Caizheng Jingji Chubanshe.

Xue, Muqiao (Hsueh Mu-ch'iao). 1969–70. "The Law of Value and Our Price Policy." *Chinese Economic Studies* 3(2): 99–118. Translated from *Hongqi* (Red flag), 1963, nos. 7–8: 1–9.

———. 1985. "1979 Nian Yilai Wending He Tiaozheng Wujia Wenti" (Problems of stabilizing and adjusting prices since 1979). *Jingji Yanjiu* (Economic research) 6: 39–53.

Zhou, Jiaxiang. 1985. "Nongchanpin Jiage Zhishi Jiangzuo" (A lecture on agricultural prices). *Jiage Lilun yu Shijian* (Price theory and practice) 1: 50–55.

8. Conclusion: Structure and Motifs in the Food Price Policy Story

Terry Sicular

The chapters in this book tell the stories of food price policy in six countries. Policies and outcomes differ substantially. Yet the component parts of the stories are similar: each contains a context, main protagonists, and central conflicts. Within the context or setting, the protagonists react to these conflicts, and a policy plot develops. And each story has an outcome, or denouement, although not always that outcome intended by the actors. A common structure thus transcends the individual cases. The five components of this structure are the context, protagonists, conflicts, development, and denouement.

The Context

A country's natural resources, geographical features, size, and level of development constitute the context in which food policy operates. Institutions such as land tenure systems, market imperfections such as local monopoly power, fragmented credit markets, and erosion or salinization externalities, and external conditions—the state of international markets for farm products—are also important aspects of the policy context.

These background factors affect the motives of different actors and shape the conflicts that arise. Indeed, they may largely determine who the key actors are. In a poor country with few or no extractable resources and a small nonagricultural sector, conflicts may center on the allocation of scarce budgetary resources. Such conditions can affect the role of the Ministry of Finance and its representatives and can also enhance the ability of external donors to influence domestic policy. In Nepal, for example, where foreign aid constitutes 40 percent of government expenditures, the influence of external donors is substantial.

The context or setting also determines the feasibility of various solutions to conflicts. In a country with rich deposits of extractable resources such as Indonesia, policy makers may have some degree of choice in setting food prices. The pressure to tax agriculture through pricing is less, and the ability to subsidize the farmgate/retail price spread is greater. In countries with considerable yield variation and low demand elasticities, food prices can fluctuate widely from year to year. Such circumstances make the defense of floor and ceiling prices difficult unless trade policy is used to stabilize domestic supplies. Improved water control and the diffusion of stable-yielding varieties may, in such circumstances, be necessary first steps toward successful implementation of food price ceilings and floors.

Finally, the context influences the consequences of policy measures. The effects of a food price increase on marketed surplus, for example, are likely to be larger in an agricultural setting characterized by large-scale, specialized farms than in one characterized by small-scale, subsistence farms. Such examples illustrate that the formulation of food price policy should pay close attention to the setting in which that policy operates.

The Protagonists and Their Motives

The protagonists in the food policy story are numerous. Most visible are the leaders and government representatives directly engaged in making policy. Interest groups put pressure on these policy makers, and so play a role. The institutions and individuals that implement policy can determine the success of policy measures and thus are also important actors in the policy process. External actors can include international organizations such as the World Bank or International Monetary Fund, or countries that are major trade partners or unilateral donors. Who the main actors are, and the forces that drive them, are key elements in the policy story.

The country cases in this volume highlight the importance of two groups in food price policy. In all the countries urban interest groups have been highly influential. Despite rhetoric to the contrary, food pricing policy often benefits urban consumers and industry rather than farmers and agriculture. Urban groups benefit not only from direct price measures keeping food retail prices low, but also from industrial policies, which can indirectly alter the food price structure. The most obvious example of measures that change food prices in the interest of industrial objectives is the use of pricing to tax agriculture invisibly so as to finance industrial growth. China pursued such a policy for decades. Trade policies designed to protect domestic industry such as those adopted in the Philippines and Thailand have the same effect, biasing the terms of trade against agriculture. Awareness of the extent to which policies aimed at urban groups and industry drive food pricing would contribute to sounder policy.

A second group important to price policy is those agencies and individuals responsible for implementing policy. Effective price policy requires the existence of agencies that are able and willing to carry out policy measures. The defense of floor and ceiling prices requires a well-organized marketing agency like BULOG in Indonesia or the state commercial system in China. A country that wishes to implement such policies must establish the supporting institutions and provide them with incentives to carry out policy initiatives. Furthermore, since desirable policies and thus the tasks required of these institutions change with time, policy makers should encourage evolution of institutions and provide incentives for change. Institutional change is never instantaneous, and price policy may suffer during the transition. Because institutions change more slowly than policy objectives, policy analysts must allow for necessary lag and lead times.

In addition to knowing who the actors are, it is useful to understand their motives or objectives. The national food policy objectives outlined earlier in this volume include efficient growth in the food sector, improved income distribution, and security from fluctuations in food supply and prices. Yet national objectives may not be the sole concern of those involved in the policy process. The actors can be motivated by personal gain or by concern for the welfare of particular interest groups, rather than by a broader interest in national welfare.

The studies in this volume for the most part infer motives from observed policy. One important concern revealed by observed food price policy in these six countries has been a concern for stability. Stability has both political and economic facets. Political stability can require paying sufficient attention to the welfare of key political groups when setting food policy, sometimes at the expense of efficiency and equity. Economic stability has many aspects, one of which is simply price stability. Indeed, price variability is frequently of greater concern to policy actors than price levels. China provides a striking example of the overriding emphasis placed on stabilizing prices. Similar efforts to reduce food price variability are clearly evident in the other country cases.

Yet price stabilization can be expensive: maintaining buffer stocks to defend price floors and ceilings is costly. Furthermore, price variation can benefit some segments of the population. If, for example, crop prices vary inversely with yields, then price fluctuations help stabilize farm profits. In this case, pricing measures that dampen year-to-year food price variability, although attractive to consumers on fixed incomes, can have the adverse consequence of widening farm profit fluctuations. Policy concerned about profit, not just price, variability might favor a technological approach to stabilization: the adoption of stable-yielding varieties reduces price variability without exacerbating profit fluctuations.

Price stability is, of course, intimately tied to food security, that is, providing stable and adequate supplies of staple foodstuffs. In pursuit of food security, countries make choices about how heavily to rely on food imports and to what degree domestic prices should be linked to international prices. In the presence of international price variability, policy makers need to think carefully about how to interact with international markets. On the one hand, narrow-minded pursuit of food self-sufficiency can incur substantial costs in terms of gains from trade. On the other hand, opening the economy can destabilize prices internally, at times with negative economic and political consequences. Some countries try to resolve these problems by importing food while concurrently protecting domestic prices from the influence of international prices. Without careful planning, such an approach can create instability in the budgets of those agencies that maintain the buffer between domestic and international prices. Fearing the vagaries of international markets, countries such as Indonesia and Korea have shown reluctance to rely too heavily on imports of staple grains and have taken measures to delink domestic from international prices.

Food price policy is often only a secondary subplot to a larger policy story. Motives that have little to do with food-related objectives thus often drive food price policy. Exchange rate, trade, industrial, and macroeconomic policies can have as much, if not greater, impact on the food sector than direct food pricing interventions. Overvaluation of the exchange rate, as in the Philippines and Nepal, depresses the relative prices of agricultural products and so can counteract direct measures intended to encourage food production. State budgetary considerations can also motivate food pricing. When the government faces a tight budget, as it has recently in China and Indonesia, agricultural policy may be made by the Minister of Finance, who will have different objectives than the Ministers of Agriculture and Natural Resources. Industrial policies, mentioned above, can also affect food prices.

The Conflicts

The potential for conflicts centering on food pricing is great. Conflicts arise because food price policy requires making tradeoffs among different objectives and different beneficiaries. Which conflicts emerge as critical depends on the context and on the actors who dominate the plot. One important area of conflict in all the countries examined here is the level of farmgate versus retail prices for food. Higher farmgate prices benefit farmers, promote food production, and can reduce reliance on food imports. Against these benefits must be balanced the negative consequences of higher retail prices, which increase the cost of living for the nonagricultural population and the costs of production for industries that use food products as inputs. Government subsidies of marketing margins can resolve the farmgate/retail price contradiction, but such subsidies add a third set of interests to the conflict, government budgetary interests.

Government subsidies of chemical fertilizers and other inputs are sometimes used to offset artificially low farmgate prices or to correct for market failures. The studies here suggest that farmers respond to fertilizer prices: low fertilizer/paddy price ratios are associated with higher fertilizer applications and yields. Under the right circumstances, for example those existing in Indonesia during the late 1970s and early 1980s, fertilizer subsidies have promoted fertilizer use in a socially profitable manner. Input price subsidies have thus been used to offset imperfect information and lack of access to credit that hinder input use.

Input subsidies, however, also give rise to conflicts of interest. The costs of fertilizer subsidies are usually borne by the government, marketing agencies, or industry. In response to such subsidy programs, suppliers may reduce the supplies of fertilizer at the low prices. Such has been the case in Nepal and Thailand, where farmers cannot buy desired amounts of fertilizers at the subsidized prices. Conflict of interests between suppliers and users, then, can interfere with the implementation and thus the effectiveness of input subsidy programs.

The Development

Within the country context and in light of their multiple motives, actors in the food policy story react to conflicts among objectives and interests. These reactions lead to policy measures, which, especially when effective, give rise to a new context, new key actors and motives, and new conflicts. The actors once again react to the conflicts, new policies emerge, and the process repeats itself. This interactive process among context, actors, and conflicts constitutes the development of the policy story.

The case studies in this volume highlight the importance of change over time in food pricing, that is, in an ongoing development of the policy story. Economic and political settings are never constant, and so prices that are at one time "too low" may at another time be "too high." If, for example, a country shifts from being a food importer to a food exporter, as has been the case for Indonesia, appropriate price measures will change. Or if land resources become scarce, as in Thailand, revision of price policies may be necessary. Trends in international markets can also motivate food price policy reform: the shift from a high international price environment for primary goods in the 1970s to a lower price environment in the mid-1980s has led to the revaluation of many domestic food price regimes.

Changes in the key actors and their interests can also underlie the emergence of new policies. During economic development as the urban/industrial sectors expand and the relative size of the rural population shrinks, the political influence of the rural interests grows. Concurrently, as incomes rise, the importance of food in the household budget falls, so that higher food prices have less of an impact on real incomes. Over time, therefore, policies often shift from low to high food price regimes. Korea's experience, where undervaluation of food products has been supplanted by substantial overvaluation, illustrates this tendency.

Change in food price policy is rarely smooth and never instantaneous. Once in place, price policy instruments can be difficult to remove. Measures such as the rice premium in Thailand, fertilizer subsidies in Indonesia, price supports in Korea, and rationed grain supply in China create strong vested interests. The removal of or changes in such policies can thus incur political dissatisfaction. So as to reduce political opposition, rather than remove old policies, governments often simply add new ones. Alternatively, old instruments are rehabilitated to promote new objectives, as is the case for the rice premium in Thailand. Such reluctance to sweep the closet clean is one reason why governments rarely employ the most efficient methods to pursue their goals.

Whether efficiently or inefficiently, national food price policies should and usually do change over time. The more successful the policies, in fact, the greater will be the need for change. The inevitability of change can be anticipated by establishing flexible supporting institutions and by taking into account not just the short-term benefits, but also the long-term costs of choosing price measures that create strong vested interests.

The Denouement

What is the denouement—the result, outcome or resolution—of the food price policy story? Historical country experiences and cross-country comparisons discussed in earlier chapters reveal that the results of price policy are difficult to predict. High food prices are not clearly correlated with higher rates of agricultural or GNP growth. Dynamic growth can occur under a wide range of food price regimes, as can stagnation. The lack of predictable outcomes suggests that there is no general blueprint for a successful food price policy.

This conclusion raises questions about indiscriminate use of border prices as a guide for domestic pricing. Many economists consider border prices good indicators of economic scarcity and so favor national policies that bring domestic food prices in line with their international counterparts. Donor agencies often lean on recipient countries to implement policies consistent with the border price view. Such advice, however, can be too simplistic. Having domestic food prices that reflect border prices is neither a necessary nor sufficient condition for economic growth.

In addition, as the preceding chapters point out, certain practical problems exist in implementing a border-price based policy. Identifying internationally traded commodities comparable in quality and character to domestic commodities can be difficult. Even if such commodities can be identified, it is frequently unclear which exchange rate should be used to convert between international and domestic currency units, and what adjustments should be made for local transfer costs between the farmgate and border. Furthermore, international price levels for certain food commodities, for example rice, can be quite volatile. International price variability makes identifying the international price trends on which to base forward-looking domestic price measures problematic. Finally, for relatively large countries like Thailand, China, and Indonesia, and for products such as rice for which the volume of world trade is low, the small-country assumption is inappropriate. In such cases, the country's trade position can influence the level of international prices. These sorts of considerations can cause lack of consensus on domestic pricing even if agreement exists on the use of border prices as a guide.

Nevertheless, overvaluation or undervaluation of food products relative to world prices can be costly. Food price policies that cause substantial discrepancies between domestic and international prices can create domestic allocative and dynamic efficiency costs, reduced gains from trade, and deadweight welfare losses. Budgetary costs for state trading organs and smuggling are further consequences of ignoring border prices. For these reasons border prices remain an important reference. Policy makers may therefore wish to follow long-term trends in border prices, while paying less attention to their precise levels and short-term fluctuations.

Despite the absence of straightforward policy answers, careful examination of country experiences yields some general lessons for policy makers. In particular, it points to reasons for the lack of correlation between prices and outcomes. One fundamental reason is that profitability, not just prices, is what drives production. Factors other than pricing can affect profitability. Differences in the context—natural resource endowments, the state of productive and marketing infrastructures, rural institutions, and rates of technological change—create variation in the underlying profitability of food production, and so can explain why similar pricing measures have dissimilar consequences. Differences in the willingness of the actors to implement and respond to pricing measures can also play a role. Thus pricing policy must be designed with careful attention to the setting in which it will operate and the actors involved.

Unlike most novels, the resolution of the food price policy plot is rarely neat and never final. The stories told here, then, compose only one work in a multivolume set. They cannot definitively predict the future course of events. They can provide historical background. More importantly, they permit a better understanding of the key structural components and motifs in food price policy.

Index

DATE DUE

11/5/05³²			